INFORMATION FLOW

Cambridge Tracts in Theoretical Computer Science

Editorial Board

S. Abramsky, Department of Computing Science, Edinburgh University
P. H. Aczel, Department of Computer Science, University of Manchester
J. W. de Bakker, Centrum voor Wiskunde en Informatica, Amsterdam
J. A. Goguen, Programming Research Group, University of Oxford
Y. Gurevich, Department of Electrical Engineering and Computer Science, University of Michigan
J. V. Tucker, Department of Mathematics and Computer Science, University College of Swansea

Titles in the series

1. G. Chaitin *Algorithmic Information Theory*
2. L. C. Paulson *Logic and Computation*
3. M. Spivey *Understanding Z*
4. G. Revesz *Lambda Calculus, Combinators and Functional Programming*
5. A. Ramsay *Formal Methods in Artificial Intelligence*
6. S. Vickers *Topology via Logic*
7. J.-Y. Girard, Y. Lafont & P. Taylor *Proofs and Types*
8. J. Clifford *Formal Semantics & Pragmatics for Natural Language Processing*
9. M. Winslett *Updating Logical Database*
10. K. McEvoy & J. V. Tucker (eds) *Theoretical Foundations of VLSI Design*
11. T. H. Tse *A Unifying Framework for Stuctured Analysis and Design Models*
12. G. Brewka *Nonmonotonic Reasoning*
14. S. G. Hoggar *Mathematics for Computer Graphics*
15. S. Dasgupta *Design Theory and Computer Science*
17. J. C. M. Baeten (ed) *Applications of Process Algebra*
18. J. C. M. Baeten & W. P. Weijland *Process Algebra*
21. D. A. Wolfram *The Clausal Theory of Types*
23. E.-R. Olderog *Nets, Terms and Formulas*
26. P. D. Mosses *Action Semantics*
27. W. H. Hesselink *Programs, Recursion and Unbounded Choice*
28. P. Padawitz *Deductive and Declarative Programming*
29. P. Gärdenfors (ed) *Belief Revision*
30. M. Anthony & N. Biggs *Computational Learning Theory*
31. T. F. Melham *Higher Order Logic and Hardware Verification*
32. R. L. Carpenter *The Logic of Typed Feature Structures*
33. E. G. Manes *Predicate Transformer Semantics*
34. F. Nielson & H. R Nielson *Two Level Functional Languages*
35. L. Feijs & H. Jonkers *Formal Specification and Design*
36. S. Mauw & G. J. Veltink (eds) *Algebraic Specification of Communication Protocols*
37. V. Stavridou *Formal Methods in Circuit Design*
38. N. Shankar *Metamathematics, Machines and Gödel's Proof*
39. J. B. Pairs *The Uncertain Reasoner's Companion*
40. J. Desel & J. Esparza *Free Choice Petri Nets*
41. J.-J. Ch. Meyer & W. van der Hoek *Epistemic Logic for AI and Computer Science*

INFORMATION FLOW

The Logic of Distributed Systems

Jon Barwise
Indiana University

Jerry Seligman
National Chung-Cheng University, Taiwan

CAMBRIDGE
UNIVERSITY PRESS

CAMBRIDGE UNIVERSITY PRESS
Cambridge, New York, Melbourne, Madrid, Cape Town, Singapore, São Paulo

Cambridge University Press
The Edinburgh Building, Cambridge CB2 8RU, UK

Published in the United States of America by Cambridge University Press, New York

www.cambridge.org
Information on this title: www.cambridge.org/9780521583862

First published 1997
This digitally printed version 2008

A catalogue record for this publication is available from the British Library

Library of Congress Cataloguing in Publication data

Barwise, Jon.
Information flow: the logic of distributed systems / Jon Barwise,
Jerry Seligman.
p.   cm. – (Cambridge tracts in theoretical computer science:
44)
Includes bibliographical references and index.
ISBN 0-521-58386-1
1. Electronic data processing – Distributed processing.
I. Seligman, Jarry, 1964–   , II. Title.   III. Series.
QA76.9.D5B363   1997
003´.54–dc20   96-46111
                                                                  CIP

ISBN 978-0-521-58386-2 hardback
ISBN 978-0-521-07099-7 paperback

In the same way, the world is not the sum of all the things that are in it. It is the infinitely complex network of connections among them. As in the meanings of words, things take on meaning only in relationship to each other.

The Invention of Solitude   Paul Auster

Contents

Preface *page* xi

Part I: Introduction 1

1   Information Flow: A Review 3
1.1   The Worldly Commerce of Information 3
1.2   Regularity in Distributed Systems 7
1.3   Information and Knowledge 10
1.4   The Grammar of Information Flow 12
1.5   Approaches to Information 14
1.6   Summary 24

2   Information Channels: An Overview 26
2.1   Classifications and Infomorphisms 26
2.2   Information Channels 34
2.3   Local Logics 37
2.4   Exceptions 42
2.5   State Spaces 46

3   A Simple Distributed System 50
3.1   The Static Case 54
3.2   The Dynamic Case 62

Part II: Channel Theory 67

4   Classifications and Infomorphisms 69
4.1   Classifications 69

4.2 Infomorphisms 72

4.3 Information Channels Defined 75

4.4 Type-Token Duality 78

5 Operations on Classifications   **81**

5.1 Sums of Classifications 81

5.2 Invariants and Quotients 84

6 Distributed Systems   **89**

6.1 The Xerox Principle 89

6.2 Distributed Systems to Channels 91

7 Boolean Operations and Classifications   **98**

7.1 Boolean Operations on Classifications 98

7.2 Boolean Operations in Classifications 100

7.3 Boolean Classifications 100

8 State Spaces   **103**

8.1 State Spaces and Projections 103

8.2 Projections and Products 105

8.3 Subspaces 107

8.4 Event Classifications 108

8.5 State Spaces from Classifications 110

8.6 Back to Boole 111

8.7 State-Space Systems 114

9 Regular Theories   **117**

9.1 Theories 117

9.2 Finite Cut and Global Cut 125

9.3 The Theory of a State Space 126

9.4 Theory Interpretations 128

9.5 Representing Regular Theories 129

10 Operations on Theories   **132**

10.1 Sums of Theories 132

10.2 A Partial Order on Theories 133

10.3 Quotients of Theories 134

10.4 Moving Theories 135

10.5 Families of Theories 136

11 Boolean Operations and Theories **138**
   11.1 Boolean Operations on Theories 138
   11.2 Boolean Operations in Theories 141
   11.3 Boolean Inference in State Spaces 147

12 Local Logics **149**
   12.1 Local Logics Defined 149
   12.2 Soundness and Completeness 152
   12.3 Logic Infomorphisms 154
   12.4 Operations on Logics 156
   12.5 Boolean Operations and Logics 162

13 Reasoning at a Distance **165**
   13.1 Moving Logics 165
   13.2 Images of Logics 166
   13.3 Inverse Images of Logics 167
   13.4 More About Moving Logics 171

14 Representing Local Logics **174**
   14.1 Idealization 174
   14.2 Channel Infomorphisms 178

15 Distributed Logics **182**
   15.1 Information Systems 182
   15.2 File Copying: An Example 184
   15.3 The Distributed Logic of a Distributed System 189
   15.4 Distributing a Logic Along a Channel 190
   15.5 The Distributed Logic of a State-Space System 191

16 Logics and State Spaces **195**
   16.1 Subspaces of State Spaces 195
   16.2 From Local Logics to State Spaces 198

Part III: Explorations **201**

17 Speech Acts **203**
   17.1 Truth-Conditional Semantics and Speech Acts 203
   17.2 Austin's Model 204
   17.3 Austin's Four Speech Acts 205

18 Vagueness **211**
18.1 Height Classifications 212
18.2 Information Flow 215
18.3 An Intensional Logic 216
18.4 The Sorites Paradox 217

19 Commonsense Reasoning **221**
19.1 The Dimension of a State Space 223
19.2 Nonmonotonicity 225
19.3 The Frame Problem 233
19.4 Conclusions 233

20 Representation **235**
20.1 Modeling Representational Systems 235
20.2 Imperfect Representations 237
20.3 Shimojima's Thesis 238

21 Quantum Logic **243**
21.1 The Theory of a Manual 244
21.2 A Comparison with Quantum Logic 248

Answers to Selected Exercises **256**

Bibliography **268**

Glossary of Notation **270**

Index of Definitions **272**

Index of Names **274**

Preface

Information and talk of information is everywhere nowadays. Computers are thought of as information technology. Each living thing has a structure determined by information encoded in its DNA. Governments and companies spend vast fortunes to acquire information. People go to prison for the illicit use of information. In spite of all this, there is no accepted science of information. What *is* information? How is it possible for one thing to carry information about another? This book proposes answers to these questions.

But why does information matter, why is it so important? An obvious answer motivates the direction our theory takes. Living creatures rely on the regularity of their environment for almost everything they do. Successful perception, locomotion, reasoning, and planning all depend on the existence of a stable relationship between the agents and the world around them, near and far. The importance of regularity underlies the view of agents as information processors. The ability to gather information about parts of the world, often remote in time and space, and to use that information to plan and act successfully, depends on the existence of regularities. If the world were a completely chaotic, unpredictable affair, there would be no information to process.

Still, the place of information in the natural world of biological and physical systems is far from clear. A major problem is the lack of a general theory of regularity. In determining which aspects of the behavior of a system are regular, we typically defer to the scientific discipline suited to the task. For regularities in the movements of birds across large distances, we consult experts in ornithology; but if the movements are of bright lights in the night sky, we'd be better off with an astronomer. Each specialist provides an explanation using a theory or model suited to the specialty.

To whom can we turn for questions about information itself? Can there be a science of information? We think so and propose to lay its foundations in this book. Out of the wide variety of models, theories, and less formal modes of explanation used by specialists, we aim to extract what is essential to understanding the flow of information.

How to Read This Book

This book has several intended audiences, some interested in the big picture but not too concerned about the mathematical details, the other of the opposite sort. Here is a brief outline of the book, followed by indications of which parts various readers will want to read, and in what order.

Introduction to the Theory. The book has three parts. Part I contains a discussion of the motivations for a model of this kind and surveys some related work on information. An overview of our information-channel model is presented, and a simple but detailed example is worked out.

Development of the Theory. The heart of the book is in Part II and consists of a detailed elaboration of the mathematical model described in Part I. Although the basic picture presented in Part I is reasonably simple, there is a lot of mathematical spadework to be done to fill in the details. The mathematical part of the book culminates in a theory of inference and error using "local logics" in Lectures 12–16.

Applications of the Theory. The lectures in Part III explore some ideas for an assortment of applications, namely, applications to speech acts, vagueness, commonsense reasoning (focusing on monoticity and on the frame problem), representation, and quantum logic. Although there is some truth to the old saw that to a person with a hammer, everything looks like a nail, a wise person with a new tool tests it to see what its strengths and weaknesses are. It is in this spirit that we offer the "explorations" of Part III. We are interested in pounding nails but are equally interested in exploring our new hammer.

We have written the book so that philosophers and others less patient with mathematical detail can read Part I and then have a look through Part III for topics of interest. Mathematicians, logicians, and computer scientists less patient with philosophical issues might prefer to start with Lecture 2, and then turn to Part II, followed perhaps by poking around in Part III. Researchers in artificial intelligence would probably also want to start with Lecture 2 and some of the chapters in Part III, followed by a perusal of Parts I and II.

An index of definitions used in Part II, and a glossary of special notation used in Part II, can be found at the end of the book.

Mathematical Prerequisites. Although some familiarity with modern logic would be helpful in understanding the motivations for some of the topics we cover, the book really only requires familiarity with basic set theory of the sort used in most undergraduate mathematics courses. We review here some more or less standard notational conventions we follow.

If $a = \langle x, y \rangle$ is an ordered pair, then we write $1^{st}(a) = x$ and $2^{nd}(a) = y$. Given a function $f: X \to Y$, we write $f[X_0] = \{f(x) \mid x \in X_0\}$ (for $X_0 \subseteq X$) and $f^{-1}[Y_0] = \{x \in X \mid f(x) \in Y_0\}$ (for $Y_0 \subseteq Y$). By the range of f we mean $f[X]$. Given functions $f: X \to Y$ and $g: Y \to Z$, gf is the function that results from composing them to get the function $gf: X \to Z$ defined by $gf(x) = g(f(x))$. For any set A, pow A is its power set, that is, the set of all its subsets. If $\mathcal{X}$ is a set of subsets of A, then

$$\bigcup \mathcal{X} = \{x \in A \mid x \in X \text{ for some } X \in \mathcal{X}\}$$

and

$$\bigcap \mathcal{X} = \{x \in A \mid x \in X \text{ for all } X \in \mathcal{X}\}.$$

If $\mathcal{X}$ is empty, then so is $\bigcup \mathcal{X}$ but $\bigcap \mathcal{X} = A$.

The appearance of many diagrams may suggest that the book uses category theory. This suggestion is both correct and misleading. Category theory arose from the realization that the same kinds of diagrams appear in many branches of mathematics, so it is not surprising that some of these diagrams appear here. We must confess that we have found the basic perspective of category theory to be quite helpful as a guide in developing the theory. And, as it turned out, some of the category-theoretic notions (coproducts and, more generally, colimits) have an important information-theoretic interpretation. In writing this book we have tried to make clear the debt we owe to ideas from category theory, but, at the same time, not presuppose any familiarity with category theory, except in those exercises marked by a (†).

In mathematics it is typical practice to call the hard results "theorems" and the easier results "propositions." Because none of our results are very hard, we use "theorem" to designate the results that are most important to the overall theory we are developing. As a result, some of our theorems are simpler than some of our propositions.

World Wide Web Site. We have set up a home page for this book, to facilitate the distribution of developments based on the ideas presented here, as well as for any corrections that may need to be made. Its URL is

```
http : //www.phil.indiana.edu/~barwise/ifpage.html.
```

You can also send us e-mail from this page.

Acknowledgments

This book has been in the making for well over a decade. Barwise's attempts at trying to understand information flow date back at least to his book written with John Perry, *Situations and Attitudes*, which appeared in 1983, and include the following papers: Barwise (1986), Barwise (1983), Barwise (1989), Barwise (1991), Barwise and Etchemendy (1990), Barwise, Gabbay, and Hartonas (1996), Barwise (1993), and Barwise and Seligman (1994). Seligman has been working on the same topic since starting his dissertation, which was completed in 1991; see Seligman (1990), Seligman (1991b), Seligman (1991a), and Barwise and Seligman (1994). The theory developed in this book is the product of an intense collaboration between the authors over the past four years. We started working together on the topic during 1992–93, when Seligman was at Indiana University on a postdoctoral fellowship. Two drafts of Parts I and II were written during the academic year 1994–95, when Seligman returned to Indiana University for a year's visit. The explorations in Part III were undertaken by Barwise in 1995–96. During that year, Parts I and II were revised by the two of us, exploiting regularities of the internet to facilitate massive amounts of information flow.

Both authors have previously contributed to the development of situation theory, a programmatic theory of information whose roots go back to *Situations and Attitudes*, discussed at length in Barwise (1989) and further developed in Devlin (1991). Though not presupposing familiarity with situation theory, the present book can be seen as a contribution to that subject by considering those tokens that are situations or events, classified using "infons" as types. Indeed, we consider the notion of a constraint to be the most important notion of situation theory and have tried, in this book, to make this notion less problematic. The task of reconciling the development of the ideas presented here with other details of situation theory remains to be undertaken.

We express our gratitude to Robin Cooper for providing the initial connection between the two of us, to Faber and Faber for permission to use the quotation from Paul Auster's *The Invention of Solitude*, to Indiana University (I.U.) for support of many kinds, to the I.U. Computer Science and Philosophy class that worked through an earlier and much more opaque version during the fall of 1994, to the Situation Theory and Situation Semantics seminar at the Center for the Study of Language and Information (CSLI) for their interest in these topics over the years, to Imperial College for hospitality and support while Barwise wrote a draft of the first two lectures during July of 1995, to the members of the I.U. Program in Pure and Applied Logic for their support over the years, to Michael Dickson and Kenneth Kunen for helpful comments on the quantum logic chapter, to various readers, including Gerry Allwein, Kata Bimbo, Tony Chemero, Diarmuid Crowley, Steve Crowley, Albert Chapman-Leyland, Keith Devlin, Yuko Murakami, and an anonymous referee for helpful comments that have helped us improve the book, to Mary Jane Wilcox for assistance with proofreading, to Lauren Cowles of Cambridge University Press for her help of many kinds, to our families for putting up with us as we wrestled with the ideas that led to the theory, and to the members of the audiences at many talks we have given on this material over the past few years for their interest and questions. Finally, we thank you, the reader, for your attention to our book.

JON BARWISE
August 1996   JERRY SELIGMAN

Part I

Introduction

Lecture 1

Information Flow: A Review

The three lectures in the first part of the book present an informal overview of a theory whose technical details will be developed and applied later in the book. In this lecture we draw the reader's attention to the problems that motivated the development of the theory. In Lecture 2 we outline our proposed solution. A detailed example is worked out in Lecture 3.

In the course of the first two lectures we draw attention to four principles of information flow. These are the cornerstones of our theory. We do not attempt to present a philosophical argument for them. Rather, we illustrate and provide circumstantial evidence for the principles and then proceed to erect a theory on them. When the theory is erected, we shall be in a better position to judge them. Until that job is done, we present the principles as a means of understanding the mathematical model to be presented – not as an analysis of all and sundry present day intuitions about information and information flow.

1.1 The Worldly Commerce of Information

In recent years, information has become all the rage. The utopian vision of an information society has moved from the pages of science fiction novels to political manifestos. As the millennium approaches fast on the information highway, the ever-increasing speed and scope of communication networks are predicted to bring sweeping changes in the structure of the global economy. Individuals and companies are discovering that many transactions that used to require the movement of people and goods, often at great expense, may now be accomplished by the click of a mouse. Information can travel at the speed of light; people and goods cannot.[1] The result is no less than a reshaping of

---

[1] If information about the future is possible, as it seems to be, then information travels *faster* than the speed of light.

our shrinking planet as cultural and commercial boundaries are transformed, for better or worse, by the increasing volume of information flow.

No doubt such future-mongering should be taken with more than a pinch of salt, but there can be little doubt that the prospect of life in "cyberspace" has caught the imagination of our age. Even in the most sober of society's circles, there is a mixture of heady excitement and alarm, a sense of revolution of an almost metaphysical sort.

Once one reflects on the idea of information flowing, it can be seen to flow everywhere – not just in computers and along telephone wires but in every human gesture and fluctuation of the natural world. Information flow is necessary for life. It guides every action, molds every thought, and sustains the many complex interactions that make up any natural system or social organization. Clouds carry information about forthcoming storms; a scent on the breeze carries information to the predator about the location of prey; the rings of a tree carry information about its age; a line outside the gas station carries information about measures in the national budget; images on a television screen in Taiwan can carry information about simultaneous events in Britain; the light from a star carries information about the chemical composition of gases on the other side of the universe; and the resigned shrug of a loved one may carry information about a mental state that could not be conveyed in words.

With this perspective, the current revolution appears to be primarily technological, with people discovering new and more efficient ways to transform and transmit information. Information is and always was all around us, saturating the universe; now there are new ways of mining the raw material, generating new products, and shipping them to increasingly hungry markets.

This book, however, is not concerned with technology. Our primary interest is not so much in the ways information is processed but in the very possibility of one thing carrying information about another. The metaphor of information flow is a slippery one, suggesting the movement of a substance when what occurs does not necessarily involve either motion or a substance. The value of the metaphor lies largely in the question it raises: How *do* remote objects, situations, and events carry information about one another without any substance moving between them?

The question is not a new one. A variety of answers have been proposed by philosophers, mathematicians, and computer scientists. Our starting point was the work of Dretske, which will be discussed below. However, before going into details it is worth asking what such an answer is meant to achieve.

Consider the following story:

Judith, a keen but inexperienced mountaineer, embarked on an ascent of Mt. Ateb. She took with her a compass, a flashlight, a topographic map, and a bar of Lindt bittersweet chocolate. The map was made ten years previously, but she judged that the mountain would not have changed too much. Reaching the peak shortly after 2 P.M. she paused to eat two squares of chocolate and reflect on the majesty of her surroundings.

At 2:10 P.M. she set about the descent. Encouraged by the ease of the day's climb, she decided to take a different route down. It was clearly indicated on the map and clearly marked on the upper slopes, but as she descended the helpful little piles of stones left by previous hikers petered out. Before long she found herself struggling to make sense of compass bearings taken from ambiguously positioned rocky outcrops and the haphazard tree line below. By 4 P.M. Judith was hopelessly lost.

Scrambling down a scree slope, motivated only by the thought that down was a better bet than up, the loose stones betrayed her, and she tumbled a hundred feet before breaking her fall against a hardy uplands thorn. Clinging to the bush and wincing at the pain in her left leg, she took stock. It would soon be dark. Above her lay the treacherous scree, below her were perils as yet unknown. She ate the rest of the chocolate.

Suddenly, she remembered the flashlight. It was still working. She began to flash out into the twilight. By a miracle, her signal was seen by another day hiker, who was already near the foot of the mountain. Miranda quickly recognized the dots and dashes of the SOS and hurried on to her car where she phoned Mountain Rescue. Only twenty minutes later the searchlight from a helicopter scanned the precipitous east face of Mt. Ateb, illuminating the frightened Judith, still clinging to the thorn bush but now waving joyously at the aircraft.

Two previously unacquainted people, Judith and the helicopter pilot, met on the side of a mountain for the first time. How did this happen? What is the connection between the helicopter flight and Judith's fall, such that the one is guided by the location of the other?

Naturally, common sense provides answers – in broad outline, at least. We explain that the helicopter was flying over that part of the mountain because the pilot believed that there was someone in danger there. The location had been given to the pilot at the Mountain Rescue Center shortly after the telephone operator had turned Miranda's description into a range of coordinates. Miranda also conveyed the description by telephone, but her information was gained from the flashes of light coming from Judith's flashlight, which was responding to the desperate movements of Judith's right thumb as she clung to the mountainside.

This establishes a physical connection between the two events, but a lot is left unsaid. Most events are connected in one way or another. How is this particular connection capable of conveying the vital piece of information about Judith's location? Consider the nature of the connection. It is made up of a precarious thread of thoughts, actions, light, sound, and electricity. What is it about each of these parts and the way they are connected that allows the information to pass?

A full explanation would have to account for all the transitions. Some of them may be explained using existing scientific knowledge. The way in which the switch on Judith's flashlight controlled the flashes, the passage of light from the flashlight to Miranda's eyes, and the transformation of spoken words into electrical signals in telephone wires and radio waves may all be explained using models derived ultimately from our understanding of physics. The motion of Judith's thumb muscles and the firing of Miranda's retinal cells, as well as the many other critical processes making up the human actions in this story, require physiological explanation. A knowledge of the conventions of mapmakers and English speakers are needed to explain the link between the combinations of words, map coordinates, and the actual location on the mountain. And, finally, the psychology of the various people in the story must be understood to bridge the considerable gap between perception and action: between Judith's fall and her moving the switch, between the light falling on Miranda's retina and her mouthing sounds into a cellular phone, between the sounds coming from the telephone, the scribbled calculations on a message pad, and the pilot's hurried exit from the building.

A full explanation would have to include all these steps and more. It is no wonder that we speak of information, knowledge, and communication; life is too short to do without them. Yet it is not just the complexity of the explanation that makes the prospect of doing without information-based vocabulary so daunting. Stepping below the casual uniformity of talk about information, we see a great disunity of theoretical principles and modes of explanation. Psychology, physiology, physics, linguistics, and telephone engineering are very different disciplines. They use different mathematical models (if any), and it is far from clear how the separate models may be linked to account for the whole story. Moreover, at each stage, we must ask why the information that someone is in danger on the east face of Mt. Ateb is carried by the particular event being modeled. This question is not easily stated in terms appropriate to the various models. To explain why the pattern and frequency of firings in Miranda's retinas carry this information, for instance, we need more than a model of the inside of her eye; the question cannot even be stated in purely physiological terms.

What are the prospects for a rigorous understanding of the principles of information flow? It is relatively uncontroversial that the flow of information is ultimately determined by events in the natural world and that the best way of understanding those events is by means of the sciences. But explanations based on the transfer of information are not *obviously* reducible to scientific explanations, and even if they are, the hodgepodge of models and theoretical principles required would quickly obscure the regularities on which the information-based explanations depend. The possibility exists that a rigorous model of information flow can be given in its own terms; that such phenomena as the chaining together of information channels, the relationship between error and gaps in the chain, and the difference between a reliable information source and accidental correlations can be explained in a precise way, not by reducing the problem to physics or any other science, but by appealing to laws of information flow. This book aims to provide such a model.

1.2 Regularity in Distributed Systems

In determining the information carried by Judith's flashlight signal, a spectrograph is of little use. Whatever information is carried depends not on intrinsic properties of the light but on its relationship to Judith and other objects and events.

It is all too easy to forget this obvious point if one focuses on information conveyed by means of spoken or written language. The information in a newspaper article appears to depend little on the particular copy of the newspaper one reads or on the complex mechanism by which the article was researched, written, printed, and distributed. The words, we say, speak for themselves. The naïviety of this remark is quickly dispelled by a glance at a newspaper written in an unfamiliar language, such as Chinese. There is nothing in the intricate form of Chinese characters inscribed on a page that conveys anything to the foreigner illiterate in Chinese.

Logical and linguistic investigations into the topic of information give the impression that one should be concerned with properties of sentences. Even when it is acknowledged that information is not a syntactic property of sentences and that some system of interpretation is required to determine the information content of a sentence, the role of this system is typically kept firmly in the background. In Tarskian model theory, for example, and in the approaches to natural language semantics based on it, an interpretation of a language consists of an abstract relation between words and sets of entities. No attempt is made to model what it is about human language-using communities that makes this relation hold.[2]

By contrast, when one looks at nonlinguistic forms of communication, and the many other phenomena that we have listed as examples of information flow, the spatial and temporal relationships between parts of the system cannot be ignored. The very term "information flow" presupposes, albeit metaphorically, a spatial and temporal separation between the source and the receiver of the information.

---

[2] The criticism is not that the topic has been ignored, as philosophers of language have had much to say about it, but that their proposals have not been incorporated into logico-linguistic theories. The relation between a name and its bearer, for example, is taken to be a primitive relation of semantic theory; the contingent facts of language use that establish the relation are ignored on the grounds that the only semantically relevant feature of a name is its bearer.

We draw attention to the importance of examining information flow in the context of a system in our first Principle.

The First Principle of Information Flow: Information flow results from regularities in a distributed system.

Two features of this principle require immediate comment: that the systems in which information flows are *distributed* and that the flow results from *regularities* in the system. By describing a system in which information flows as "distributed," we mean that there is some way in which it is divided into parts, so that the flow of information is from one part (or parts) to another. For example, we may consider Judith's flashlight to be a system in which information flows: the lit bulb carries the information that the switch is on and the battery is charged and so forth. The flashlight may be divided into the following parts:

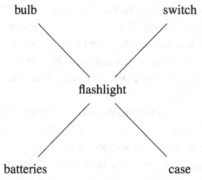

We do not intend to suggest that this division into parts is unique or comprehensive. Each of the components of the flashlight has parts that are not represented (but could be) and there are a host of different ways of decomposing the system that would not list any of the parts depicted above. (Indeed, the relativity of this decomposition is crucial to the story we will tell.)

The parts of an information system are often spatial or temporal parts but they do not need to be. The conception of information flow we develop is very broad, encompassing abstract systems such as mathematical proofs and taxonomic hierarchies as well as concrete ones like the above. In abstract systems the relation of whole to part is also abstract, and the metaphor of "flow" has to be interpreted even more loosely. We place no restriction on what kind of thing may count as a part, only that the choice of parts determines the way in which we understand what it is for information to flow from one part to another.

The first principle of information flow also states that information flow results from *regularities in the system*. It is the presence of regularities that links the parts of a system together in a way that permits the flow of information. The fact that the components of Judith's flashlight are more or less adjacent in space and have overlapping temporal extents is not sufficient to explain the information carried by the lit bulb about the position of the switch or the state of the batteries. It is of the greatest importance that the components of the flashlight are connected together in such a way that the whole flashlight behaves in a more or less predictable manner. In this case, the regularities that ensure the uniform behavior of the system are mostly electrical and mechanical in nature. The contacts in the switch, the design of the case, and many other details of the construction of the flashlight go to ensure that the flashing of the bulb is systematically related to the position of the switch.

The behavior of the system need not be entirely predictable for information to flow. Properties of components of the flashlight, such as the discoloring of the plastic case due to exposure to sunlight, are not at all predictable from properties of the other components; yet this indeterminacy does not interfere with the regular behavior of the system in the informationally relevant respects. More complex systems may even be highly nondeterministic while still allowing information flow. Yet, as a general rule, the more random the system the less information will flow.

The range of examples in the story of Judith on Mt. Ateb show that information flows may be due to a wide range of factors. Some of them are "nomic" regularities, of the kind studied in the sciences; others, such as those relating a map to the mapped terrain, are conventional; and others are of a purely abstract or logical character. Sometimes the regularity involved is very difficult to pin down. Parents can often tell when their children are getting ill just from the look of their eyes. The relationship between the appearance of the eyes and the condition permits this inference reliably, but even an ophthalmologist would hesitate to say on what exactly the inference depends.

Despite the wide range of regularities that permit information flow, it is important to distinguish genuine regularities from merely accidental, or "statistical" regularities. Accidents are not sufficient for information flow. To give an example, suppose that on the occasion of Judith's fall, Miranda caught sight of the light of the moon reflected from a small waterfall on the mountainside. By chance, we suppose, the waterfall reflected the moonlight in a sequence of flashes very similar to the Morse code SOS. In such circumstances, Miranda might have formed the belief that there was someone in trouble on the mountain in the approximate location of Judith's fall. Her belief would be true but she would not have the information. Information does not flow from A to B just because someone at B happens to have been misled into believing something correct about what is going on at A.

Now suppose that over the course of several months, a large number of climbers are saved from the treacherous slopes of Mt. Ateb by Mountain Rescue, alerted by reports of SOS signals flashed from the mountain. In fact, the flashes were all caused by reflected moonlight and a spate of visiting climbers, rather overzealous in their desire to report potential accidents. It is important that we assume that there really is no more to it that this, that is, no mysterious link between troubled climbers and water spirits. The result would be that a statistical regularity is established between flashes from the mountainside and climbers in distress. It should be clear that this spurious regularity is no more able to establish information flow than the one-time coincidence considered previously.[3]

1.3 Information and Knowledge

There is a close connection between information and knowledge. Puzzles similar to those discussed in the previous section are used by philosophers to test different theories of knowledge. Indeed, the origin of the work presented here was an attempt to elaborate and improve on a theory of knowledge presented by Fred Dretske (1981) in his book *Knowledge and the Flow of Information.* The informational role of regularities in distributed systems will be better appreciated if seen in the light of Dretske's theory.

Since Gettier's famous paper of 1963, philosophers have been looking for the missing link between true belief and knowledge. The "traditional" account is that knowledge is *justified* true belief. Miranda knows that someone is in trouble on the mountain because her belief is justified by her knowledge of Morse code and other relevant considerations. But consider the case in which the flashes were produced by reflected moonlight. Miranda's belief and its justification would remain the same, but she would not *know* that someone is in trouble. This is Gettier's argument and there have been many responses to it.[4]

Recently, the topic has largely been put aside, not because an agreed upon solution has been found but because many have been proposed and no clear victor has emerged. Dretske's solution was one of the first. He proposed that information is the missing link. Very roughly, Dretske claims that a person knows that p if she believes that p and her believing that p (or the events in her head responsible for this belief) carries the information that p. To the extent

---

[3] An interesting question, which tests the best of intuitions, is whether information is carried by Judith's flashlight signals against a background of fortuitously correct accident reports of the kind considered in our example.

[4] For a survey, see Shope (1983).

that our beliefs carry information about the world, they play an invaluable role in guiding our actions and in communicating with others.

We take Dretske's account of the relationship between information and knowledge to be an important insight.[5] As a bridge between two subjects, we can use it both as a means of applying our theory to epistemology and also as a way of incorporating epistemological considerations into the theory of information.

For example, the first principle of information flow is illuminated by considering some related epistemological puzzles. A perennial problem in the philosophy of knowledge is that of accounting for a person's knowledge of remote facts. Miranda's knowledge of the world must stem from her experience of it, and yet a great deal of her knowledge concerns things that are not and never were part of our immediate physical environment. She may never have climbed Mt. Ateb herself, and she is certainly not able to see what happened on the scree slope in the dark. How is she able to know about parts of the world that are beyond her experience?

A rough answer is as follows: Things outside Miranda's experience are connected in lawlike ways to things within her experience. If the world beyond her senses bore no relationship to her experience, then she would not be able to know about it. It is the regularity of the relationship that makes knowledge possible. This answer places the philosophical problem squarely within the scope of our current investigations. Miranda and the remote objects of her knowledge form a distributed system governed by regularities. The fact that the system is distributed gives rise to the problem; the regularity of the system provides the only hope of a solution.

Dretske's approach to the theory of knowledge is not dissimilar to those who claim that it is the *reliability* of the belief-producing process that constitutes the difference between knowledge and mere true belief (Goldman, 1979, 1986; Nozick, 1981; Swain, 1981). Indeed, there is a close connection between information flow and reliability. For a signal to carry information about a remote state of affairs, it must have been produced by a reliable process. An unreliable process will not permit information to flow.

Reliability, however, is clearly a matter of degree. Some processes are more reliable than others, and what counts as sufficiently reliable may vary with circumstances. Consider Judith's flashlight. The information that the bulb is lit carries the information that the switch is on, because they are linked by a

---

[5] We do not accept Dretske's account of information based on probability theory, and motivation for the design of our theory can be traced back to inadequacies in his proposals. Dretske's proposals will be discussed in more detail in Section 1.5 of the present chapter.

reliable mechanism. But the mechanism can become less reliable. If the battery is dead, the switch could be on but the bulb not lit. If there is a short circuit, the switch might be off but the bulb lit. Considerations of this kind make one wonder whether the bulb being lit really carries the information that the switch is on even when the flashlight is "working properly." Much depends on the standards of reliability being used.

Consider also Judith's map of Mt. Ateb. Such a map is full of information, vital to the mountain navigator. But it also contains a number of inaccurate details – details that misled Judith into taking the wrong path and resulted in her perilous descent of the scree slope. The map is reliable in some respects but fallible in others; it carries both information and misinformation. Judith's use of the map is partly responsible both for her knowledge of the mountainous terrain around her and for her mistakes.

Whenever one talks of information, the issue of reliability is close at hand. A goal of this book is to present a theory of information that is compatible with the facts about reliability, especially the treatment of partially reliable information sources and the ubiquitous possibility of error.

1.4 The Grammar of Information Flow

There are no completely safe ways of talking about information. The metaphor of information flowing is often misleading when applied to specific items of information, even if the general picture is usefully evocative of movement in space and time. The metaphor of information content is even worse, suggesting as it does that the information is somehow intrinsically contained in the source and so is equally informative to everyone and in every context.

Perhaps the least dangerous is the metaphor of carrying information. One can at least make sense of one thing carrying different items of information on different occasions and for different people, and the suggestion of movement and exchange adds a little color. What's more, there is a pleasant variety of words that may be used as alternatives to "carry": "bear," "bring," and "convey" can all be used in the appropriate context.

We therefore adopt the form "x carries/bears/conveys the information that y" as our primary means of making claims about the conveyance of information. Some comment about the values of x and y is in order.

The position occupied by y may be filled by any expression used in the attribution of propositional attitudes: the values for y in "She knows/believes/doubts/thinks/hopes that y." Company is comforting, but in this case especially, the sense of security may well be false. The problem of determining the semantic role of such expressions is notoriously difficult and we do not wish to suggest that anything we say about information involves a commitment to any alleged solution.

The position occupied by x may be filled by a variety of noun phrases:

The e-mail message bore the information that Albert would be late for dinner.

The rifle shot carried the information that the king was dead to the whole city.

Jane's being taller than Mary carries the information that Mary will fit under the arch.

The greyness of the sky carries the information that a storm is approaching.

The beating of drums conveyed the information that the enemy had been sighted.

Mary's kissing John carried the information that she had forgiven him.

It appears difficult to summarize this list. Events, such as Mary's kissing John, can carry information, so can objects, such as the e-mail message, and properties, such as the greyness of the sky. Perhaps more accurately, it is an object's being a certain way (e.g., the e-mail message's containing certain words in a certain order) and a property's being instantiated (e.g., the greyness of the sky) that really carries the information.

While recognizing these complications, we need some way of talking about the general case. Following Dretske, we choose to focus on claims of the form "a's being F carries the information that b is G." The main advantage of this form is that one can go on to ask what information is carried by b's being G, without committing too many grammatical offenses. A bonus is that the information carried by the Fness of a is likely to be the same as that carried by a's being F.

At first sight, Dretske's way of talking about information conveyance seems ill-suited to describing the information carried by events. There is no easy way of describing Mary's kissing John using an expression of the form "a's being F." We solve this problem by recognizing the distinction between a particular event (an event *token*) and a type of event. The occasion e of Mary kissing John on a particular day in a particular place and in a particular way is a token of the type E of kissings in which Mary is the kisser and John is the person she kissed. Thus we can talk of the information carried by e's being of type E and remain within Dretske's scheme. As will become apparent, the making of type-token distinctions is very important to our project, and the reasons for making the grammatical distinction here are not as superficial as they might at first appear.

1.5 Approaches to Information

In this section we survey a number of approaches to information flow, starting with Dretske's. In doing so, we have two motivations. One is to make clear some of the difficulties involved in answering our basic question, especially those having to do with exceptions and errors. The other is because our own proposal draws on aspects of each of these approaches. Our purpose here, then, is not to knock down straw men, but rather to pay our dues to important ideas that, although inadequate on their own, are in fact closely related to our own proposal.

Information, Probability, and Causation

The meteorologist who tells us that it will be warm and dry today in the Sahara desert is not being very informative. If she tells us that there will be three inches of rain, and she is right, then we will be properly awed.

The example suggests an inverse relationship between information and probability, namely, the less likely the message, the more informative it is. The connection is thoroughly exploited in communication theory, the quantitative theory of information used for the analysis of the efficiency of channels in communication networks.[6] Communication theorists consider a network to be composed of distinct, nondeterministic, interdependent processes, the behavior of which conforms to a probability distribution. A *channel* is a part of the network responsible for the probabilistic dependence between two of the component processes, called the *source* and the *receiver*. Quantities measuring the flow of information from source to receiver, the noise in the channel, channel capacity, and so on, can be computed from the probability distribution. The basic idea is that the amount of information associated with an event is determined by how unlikely it is to have occurred and so by the reciprocal of the probability of it occurring. Logarithms (to base 2) are taken in order to make the measure additive.

Communication theory is an established branch of engineering that has proved very useful to designers of communication devices. But its theoretical impact is far wider. Any physical system whose behavior is modeled in probabilistic terms can be regarded as an information system in which information flows according to the equations of the theory.

Impressed by the universality of the approach, a number of philosophers have tried to use the theory to elucidate our ordinary concept of information. Attractive as this appears, there are a number of obstacles. Firstly, communication

---

[6] The classical theory is presented in Shannon (1948). Dretske gives a summary of the relevant parts of the theory in Dretske (1981).

theory is concerned with "amounts of information ... not with the information that comes in those amounts" (Dretske, 1981, p. 3). The engineer is only interested in how much information is transmitted in a network or lost to noise, not in the details of the communication itself, which are consequently omitted from the mathematical model. Nonetheless, it may be hoped that the quantitative theory places constraints on solutions to the more philosophically interesting problem of determining what information is conveyed. Dretske adopts this view and proposes a number of such constraints.

The second obstacle is that communication theorists are interested only in averages. It is the average amount of noise, equivocation, and information transmitted that matters to the engineer, not the amount of information transmitted on a particular occasion. This is not such a serious problem, and Dretske shows that the mathematics of communication theory can be adapted to give a measure of the amounts of information involved in a particular communication between a source and a receiver. He defines the information $I(E)$ generated by an event E at the source and the amount of information $I_s(r)$ about the source process carried by the receiver process as a function of the state r of the receiver and the state s of the source.[7]

These quantities do not determine what information is carried by the signal, but they do constrain the search. If the receiver carries the information that the event E occurred at the source, then the amount of information about the source carried by the receiver must be *at least as much as* the amount of information generated by the occurrence of E at the source. Furthermore, E must have occurred, otherwise the information carried by the receiver is not information but *mis*information. Finally, Dretske claims that the information measured by $I_s(r)$ must "contain" the information measured by $I(E)$. Although lacking a precise sense for "containment" between quantities of information, he maintains that these conditions are sufficient to establish the following definition as the only viable contender:

Dretske's Information Content: To a person with prior knowledge k, r being F carries the information that s is G if and only if the conditional probability of s being G given that r is F is 1 (and less than 1 given k alone).

The role of a person's prior knowledge in determining whether information is carried is important for Dretske's epistemology. It allows him to distinguish

---

[7] Suppose that the source is in one of the mutually exclusive states $s_1, \ldots, s_n$ with probability $p(s_i)$. The probability $p(E)$ of E occurring at the source is given by the sum of the $p(s_i)$ for those s_i compatible with E's occurrence. Then $I(E) = \log(1/p(E)) = -\log p(E)$. Moreover, if $p(s_i \mid r)$ is the conditional probability of the source being in state s_i given that the receiver is in state r, then $I_s(r) = \sum_i p(s_i \mid r)(\log p(s_i \mid r) - \log p(s \mid r))$.

between an "internal" and an "external" contribution to assessing if something is known. The relativity of information to a person's prior knowledge is set against a background of probabilities, fixed by more or less objective features of the world.

Dretske's requirement that the conditional probability must be 1, not just very close to 1, in order for information to flow is supported by the following argument. Consider any repeatable method of sending messages. If the conditional probability that s is G given the receipt of a message is less than one, by however small a margin one cares to consider, then in principle one could resend the message using the same process so many times that the conditional probability that s is G given the final receipt of the message is close to zero. Dretske claims that if the process is good enough to transmit the information on one occasion, then no amount of duplication can prevent the information from flowing. This is captured by the following principle:

Dretske's Xerox Principle: If r being F carries the information that s is G, and s being G carries the information that t is H, then r being F carries the information that t is H.

The main objection to maximal conditional probability is that it sets too high a standard. In perception, for example, the possibility of perceptual mistakes suggests that the conditional probability of the scene being as one perceives it to be is seldom if ever as high as 1. Widespread skepticism would seem to be inevitable.[8]

Dretske has an interesting, and for our theory important, response. He points out that the relation between the probability of an event and its occurrence presupposes that certain conditions are met. The probability of a tossed coin landing heads may be $1/2$, but it will definitely not land heads if it is snatched from the air in midtoss. In assessing the probability to be $1/2$ we assume that such breaches of fair play do not occur – but that is not to say that they are impossible. Applying this strategy to perception, we can say that the assessment of probability for everyday perception presupposes that "normal" conditions obtain. When the stakes are higher, as they are in a murder trial for example, we may change the assessment of probability by considering a range of abnormal circumstances that may affect the veridicality of a witness's perception.

The strategy is a subtle one. When determining whether a signal carries some information, it is important for Dretske that there is a distinction between the "internal" contribution of a person's prior knowledge and the "external"

---

[8] On some versions of probability theory, events with zero or infinitesimally small probability may be regarded as possible. Koons (1996) has an ingenious proposal along these lines.

contribution of objective probabilities. But now it turns out that these probabilities, although objective, are relative, not absolute. In effect, Dretske admits a further parameter into the account: whether information flows depends not only on prior knowledge but also on the probability measure used. Different standards of relevant possibility and precision give different probability measures and so give different conclusions about information flow and knowledge. This relativism is downplayed in Dretske's book, but it is an unavoidable consequence of his treatment of skepticism.

Another objection, acknowledged by Dretske, is that his account makes no room for *a priori* knowledge. Consider, for example, Euclid's theorem that there are infinitely many prime numbers. If it makes any sense to talk of the probability of mathematical statements, then the probability of Euclid's theorem must be 1. Given any prior knowledge k, the conditional probability of Euclid's theorem given k is also 1 and so no signal can carry it as information. This is a serious defect that threatens any probabilistic theory of information flow.[9]

The use of probability to give an account of information is closely related to the similar use of probability to account for causation. A proposed solution to one problem often suggests a candidate for the other. Nonetheless, one must be careful to distinguish the two. Causal relations often underpin informational relations, but they are not the same. One important difference is that the direction of information flow is not necessarily aligned with the direction of causation. Present events can carry information about conditions in the remote past and about their future consequences, but there are strong arguments against the possibility of a present event causing a past event.

Moreover, a causal connection between two events, in whatever direction, is neither necessary nor sufficient for information flow. Suppose that Judith's flashlight may be switched on by either of two switches: a slider on the side of the case and a push button at the end. On a given occasion, Judith flashes the light with the push button. The occurrence of the flash was caused by the pushing of the button, but it does not carry the information that the button was pushed because the same effect could have been achieved using the slider. What about the other direction? Does the pushing of the button carry the information that the flashing occurs? Perhaps it does, in this case, but not in general. If there is a loose connection, for example, or the battery is running low, then the pushing of the button may happen to cause the light to flash without carrying the information that the light is flashing.

---

[9] It does no good to loosen the definition to allow unit conditional probability given the signal to be sufficient for information flow, irrespective of the conditional probability without the signal, for then *any* signal would be deemed to carry the information that there are infinitely many primes.

The above discussion shows that a causal connection, in either direction, is not sufficient for information to flow. That it is also not necessary can be seen by considering cases in which two causally unrelated events have a common cause. Suppose, for example, that two divers set their stopwatches for a thirty-minute dive. One watch going to zero carries the information that the other watch does the same, but neither event causes the other.

Information and the Elimination of Possibilities

A familiar idea in the philosophy of language is that the semantic value of a statement is given by the set of "possible worlds" in which it is true. This can be used to give an account of information content:

Possible-Worlds Information Content: To a person with prior knowledge k, r being F carries the information that s is G if in all the possible worlds compatible with k and in which r is F, s is G (and there is at least one possible world compatible with k in which s is not G).

Applying this account to epistemology, we see that it gives us a counterfactual account: whether one knows that p depends not only on the facts of this world but also on what goes on in other possible worlds.

As it stands, the account is open to the same skeptical charge leveled against Dretske in the previous section. The skeptic proposes that there is some possible world in which our perceptions are radically mistaken. The mere possibility of one such world is enough to ensure, on this definition of possible-worlds information content, that none of our perceptual beliefs carry the information they should.

Philosophers have addressed this problem by using a more sophisticated account of the semantics of counterfactual conditionals (Lewis, 1973; Stalnaker, 1984; Nozick, 1981; Dretske, 1970, 1971). The basic idea is to restrict the range of quantification from all possible worlds to all "near" or "normal" worlds, where what counts as "near" or "normal" may depend on the conditional being evaluated. Taking a cue from Dretske, we may interpret this move in terms of standards of evaluation. The statement that information flows presupposes that these standards are met. In Dretske's probabilistic account, the standards of evaluation are modeled by a probability measure. It is only in the context of an evaluation of probability that information is said to flow or not, and assessment of probability always presupposes that certain conditions are held fixed. In the theories of conditionals of Stalnaker and Lewis, we can think of what counts as a "near" possible world as modeling these standards.

Information and State Spaces

Within applied mathematics and experimental science, similar normality assumptions are made. The evaluation of some experimental data as confirming or conflicting with theory presupposes that "experimental conditions" were met. It is instructive, therefore, to examine the use of mathematical models in science, looking for the role played by this presupposition.

The most common kind of model used for studying regularities in physical systems is a "state space." A state space consists of a set Ω with some sort of mathematical structure defined on it, together with an assignment of elements of Ω to the system at different times in its evolution. The elements of Ω are called "states" because the characteristic feature of the model is that the system is deemed to be in only one state at a time.

Newtonian physics, for example, studies systems consisting of a finite number of particles in space. The complete state of the system is assumed to be determined by information about position (relative to some coordinate scheme) and velocity of each particle in the system. Because both position and velocity are determined by three magnitudes, the state of a system of n bodies can be modeled by a vector of $6n$ real numbers; that is, we can take Ω to be the vector space $\mathbb{R}^{6n}$, where $\mathbb{R}$ is the field of real numbers. The basic assumption of classical mechanics is that everything about such a system is a function of this state. The object of the enterprise is to figure out ways of writing down theories, usually in the form of some sort of equation that specifies the relationships between states of the system at different times.

State spaces are also used in computer science where computing machines are assumed to have a finite number of possible states, and that computation proceeds by means of transitions from state to state. These states are not assumed to have any *internal* structure; instead they are related by the possible transitions between them. Thus, in both examples, there is some additional mathematical structure on the set of states: a vector space in one case and a transition function in the other.

The term state *space* encourages one to regard such models using a spatial metaphor. The states of the space are thought of as locations in a landscape whose geography is molded by physical laws (as expressed by the equations). The evolution of the system is interpreted as motion in this abstract landscape, usually according to some principle of following the path of least resistance.

The construction of state spaces often proceeds by isolating certain measurable attributes, the so-called "observables" of the system, and a range of values for each observable. For example, in an experiment to investigate the behavior of gases, a scientist might decide that the pressure, volume, and temperature are the relevant observables, and that in his laboratory, these observables will take values within the ranges 1–20 bar, 0.001–2 liters, and 0–100 degrees Celsius, respectively. From these observables one can specify an initial set of states, namely, one for each assignment of values to the three attributes. The gas in the laboratory is in exactly one of these states at a time. Which state it is in can be determined by measurement.

The set of possible states is pared down by further investigation. Boyle's law tells us that only those states in which the product of the pressure and the volume is some specific multiple of the temperature are possible. This gives us a way of understanding information flow. For example, knowing that the gas is contained in a 1-liter bottle, the behavior of the thermometer carries information not just about the temperature but also about the pressure of the gas. We can define a notion of information content in a way that is parallel to the possible-worlds definition.

State-space Information Content: To a person with prior knowledge k, r being F carries the information that s is G if in every state compatible with k in which r is F, s is G (and there is at least one state compatible with k in which s is not G).

Despite formal similarities, there are several important differences from the possible-worlds version. Firstly, the definition clearly presupposes a notion of possible state, and therefore a notion of state space, according to our earlier analysis of the concept. Typically, the notion of state will be applicable to only a small part of the world for a limited duration of time. The gas experiment, for example, occurs inside a laboratory and only lasts for a few hours, at most. This is in contrast to the notion of a possible world, which is typically taken to be all-encompassing.[10]

Secondly, in the case of scientific experiments, certain "experimental conditions" must be maintained throughout the limited domain of application. For state-space models constructed by selecting observables and ranges of values, the experimental conditions are often taken to be that (i) the values of the selected observables should not exceed those in the specified ranges and (ii) all other observables (the parameters) should remain fixed throughout. The satisfaction of these conditions is a presupposition of the laws governing the system.

If during the gas experiment, the bottle containing the gas developed a slight fracture, allowing the gas to escape slowly into the surrounding room, then

[10] This is not true of Stalnaker's (1984) work. Indeed, one way of interpreting talk of possible worlds, close to Stalnaker's interpretation, is to identify possible worlds with possible states of this world.

the regularities expressed by Boyle's law would cease to be observed, and the behavior of the thermometer would no longer carry information about the pressure of the gas.

A failure of this kind is not considered a counterexample to Boyle's law; it is merely a case in which the law's presuppositions were not satisfied. For this reason, the possibility of a leak does not count against the claim that information flows when there is no leak.

We can now return to the question of how to make our definition of information content respect varying standards of evaluation. The basic idea is to apply something similar to the meeting of "experimental conditions" whenever the notion of a state space is used. For example, in describing a coin toss as having the outcomes heads and tails, we presuppose that the coin will be tossed in a "normal" manner, with no interference from participants and certainly no coin snatching in midtoss.

The example also illustrates the relationship between Dretske's definition information content and the state-space version. The rational assignment of probabilities to events presupposes a probability measure on a set of possible outcomes. If we take the set of outcomes to be our set of possible states, then we will have a state-space system within which the state-space definition of information content will be equivalent to Dretske's.

The state-space conditions of a state space constructed in this way are just those presupposed by assigning probabilities. As such, they reflect our standards of evaluation that may depend on many factors, but once fixed the resulting system of regularities determines an objective conception of information flow.

In practice, of course, it is next to impossible to pin down these conditions precisely. Often we can tell if a condition is violated; lacking any evidence that they are violated we will have reasonable confidence that they are obeyed. But the epistemologically important point is that the definition of information content (and hence of knowledge) only depends on the conditions being met, not on our knowing that they are met.[11]

In summary, recall that the First Principle of Information Flow is that information flow results from a distributed system of regularities. The question of whether information flows or not therefore presupposes a system of regularities against which it can be evaluated. In this section we have considered a model of systems of regularities using the notion of a state space. A definition of information content follows. It is formally similar to the possible-worlds definition

---

[11] The skeptic's hypothetical scenario shows that we *could* fail to detect that the conditions are not met, but this does not affect the issue of whether information actually flows, assuming that the conditions are in fact met.

but differs both in having a clearly limited domain of application and in clearly presupposing that certain conditions are met within that domain. It is similar to Dretske's definition but differs in not requiring a probability measure on sets of states.

Inference and Information

Inference has something crucial to do with information. On the one hand, inference is often characterized as the extraction of implicit information from explicit information. This seems reasonable, because it is clearly possible to obtain information by deduction from premises. In carrying out these inferences in real life, we take as premises some background theory of how the world works. On the other hand, getting information typically requires inference. Judith, for example, had to infer something about the mountain from her map, and Miranda had to infer something about Judith from the distress signal.

Some philosophers would go farther and maintain that the distinction between knowledge and true belief can be analyzed in terms of inferential relations alone. This "internalism" differs from the "externalist" position adopted here, according to which the world must participate in some way. On an internalist account, explanations of the sort used in discussing Judith's rescue would not be required to explain the fact that the pilot knew where to look. Still, they would be required to explain why it was that Judith was there to be found.

The close relation between inference and information suggests a different, more internalist, take on information:

Inferential Information Content: To a person with prior knowledge k, r being F carries the information that s is G if the person could legitimately infer that s is G from r being F together with k (but could not from k alone).

This proposal is refreshingly different from the earlier ones and is promising in a number of regards. First, it relativizes information to a person's ability to infer, that is, to some kind of information-processing abilities, a feature notably lacking in the other approaches.

Consider Judith and Miranda. If Judith had no knowledge of maps, she would not have been able to infer anything about where she was from the map, so the map would have carried no information to her. Similarly, if Miranda had known nothing about Morse code the outcome of the story would most likely have been quite different. Under these conditions she would not have taken the light flashes to be a signal of distress. There would have been no information flow, seemingly because there would have been no inference.

Secondly, the background theory k of the agent comes much more actively into this account. It is not just there as a parameter for weeding out possibilities;

it becomes a first-class participant in the inference process. It makes Judith's, Miranda's, and the pilot's everyday knowledge of the world play key roles in the story, which it seems it should.

Finally, by relativizing information flow to human inference, this definition makes room for different standards in what sorts of inferences the person is able and willing to make. This seems like a promising line on the notorious "monotonicity problem."

In classical logic, the inference from "α entails γ" to "α and β entails γ" is valid and fundamental. This form of inference is sometimes called "Monotonicity" or "Weakening" and is symbolized as follows:

$$\frac{\alpha \vdash \gamma}{\alpha, \beta \vdash \gamma}.$$

(In this way of formulating logic, initiated by Gentzen, multiple items on the left of $\vdash$ are treated conjunctively, multiple items on the right are treated disjunctively.) After all, if α and β both hold, then α holds, so we have γ. But consider the following:

The switch being on entails that the bulb is lit.

This regularity is a commonplace bit of information about Judith's flashlight. On the earlier accounts, it would be seen as capturing some kind of regularity of the system. On the present account, it might be seen as an inference permitted by Judith's background theory k of the world.

However, this conditional has exceptions. The battery might be dead, for example. From the logical point of view, this looks like a problem because weakening seems to allow us to conclude the following from the above regularity:

The switch being on and the battery being dead entails that the bulb is lit.

The inference is clearly unwarranted and unwelcome.

The difficulty seems closely related to the problem of error in information flow. In the first three approaches, error is seen as involved with changing the probability space, changing what counts as a normal or near possible world, or changing the state space. The present proposal, it seems, might simply take the ability to recognize such shifts as a property of legitimate human inference.

Difficulties start to appear, however, when we probe more deeply into the role "legitimate" plays in this account. It is clearly crucial, because without it the person could infer anything from anything and it would count as information for that person. But if Miranda had inferred from the light flashes that they were caused by giant fireflies on the mountain, she would have been misinformed by the flashes, not informed. Similarly, had the helicopter pilot inferred from Miranda's message that she was deluded, he would have been wrong and so misinformed. Such considerations show that the inferences allowed by the definition must, at the very least, be sound inferences.

In a way, this is promising, because it suggests that this proposal has to be related to a more semantic account and so might be seen as a strengthening of one or more of the earlier proposals. But the question is, why not allow any sound inference? In particular, why not allow the sound rule of weakening?

Taking our cue from the earlier responses to problems involving exceptions, it seems that one might try to pin the problem on the relationship of the person's theory k of the world and the background conditions and standards of the person. In our above example, it seems that the premise that the battery is dead violates the background theory k used for the first inference and so causes one to change k. The account of information flow presented here relates inference and background theory with the kinds of background conditions built into the more semantic approaches.[12]

1.6 Summary

In describing the role of information in the modern world, an old word has been appropriated and its meaning gradually transformed. Yet the new uses of "information" only serve to highlight its function as a linking term in everyday explanations. Whenever a complete understanding of some series of events is unavailable or unnecessary for providing an explanation, we can make do with information talk. Whether or not these partial explanations are ultimately reducible to a single physical science, there is sufficient reason to investigate the conception of information flow on which they rest.

Information is closely tied to knowledge. Following Dretske, we think that epistemology should be based on a theory of information. The epistemic properties of an agent's mental processes should be analyzed in terms of their informational relationships to each other, to the agent's actions, and to the agent's environment.

But what is information and how does it flow? We stated the first principle of information flow: information flow results from regularities of distributed systems. The systems in which information flows are distributed because they are made up of parts related by regularities. The existence of such a system

---

[12] Of the theories available, the Lewis and Stalnaker theories of nearby possible worlds seem most like this sort of theory.

is presupposed by talk of the flow of information, and if we are to understand informational explanation in any more than a metaphorical way, we must find out which system is presupposed.

The central question, in a nutshell, is this: *How is it that information about some components of a system carries information about other components of the system?* We have looked for an answer in various places: in Dretske's probabilistic analysis, in the idea that information eliminates possible worlds, in the idea that information tracks possible movement in a state space, and in the connection between information and inference relative to a theory. In each case we offered a preliminary definition of information flow and a discussion of the presuppositions of the definition, especially concerning the possibility of error.

The existence of such different approaches to the study of information flow might make one wonder whether there is any unity to the subject. However, the perceived relationships between these accounts suggest they might all be seen as part of a general theory. In this book, we present what we hope is such a theory.

Lecture 2

Information Channels: An Overview

To understand the account presented here, it is useful to distinguish two questions about information flow in a given system. What information flows through the system? Why does it flow? This book characterizes the first question in terms of a "local logic" and answers the second with the related notion of an "information channel." Within the resulting framework one can understand the basic structure of information flow. The local logic of a system is a model of the regularities that support information flow within the system, as well as the exceptions to these regularities. The information channel is a model of the system of connections within the system that underwrite this information flow.

The model of information flow developed here draws on ideas from the approaches to information discussed in Lecture 1 and, in the end, can be seen as a theory that unifies these various apparently competing theories. The model also draws on ideas from classical logic and from recent work in computer science. The present lecture gives an informal overview of this framework.

2.1 Classifications and Infomorphisms

Fundamental to the notions of information channel and local logic are the notions of "classification" and "infomorphisms." These terms may be unfamiliar, but the notions have been around in the literature for a long time.

Paying Attention to Particulars

We begin by introducing one of the distinctive features of the present approach, namely its "two-tier" nature, paying attention to both types and particulars.

Suppose we are giving a state-space analysis of a system consisting of two dice that are being tossed. There are thirty-six possible states of this system, corresponding to fact that each die can come up with one of the numbers $1, \ldots, 6$ on top. Thus the set Ω of possible states of the system is taken to be the set $\{\langle n, m \rangle \mid 1 \leq n, m \leq 6\}$. Suppose Judith is interested in the situation where the system happens to come up with a total of seven. Thus Judith is interested in the outcome being in a state in the set

$$\alpha = \{\langle 1, 6 \rangle, \langle 2, 5 \rangle, \langle 3, 4 \rangle, \langle 4, 3 \rangle, \langle 5, 2 \rangle, \langle 6, 1 \rangle\}$$

In probability theory, this set α is said to be the "event" of getting a seven.

This talk of events can be a bit misleading since α is not an event at all, but rather a type of event, that is, a way of classifying any particular roll of the pair of dice, or indeed, of any roll of any pair of dice that comes out with a total of seven. Whereas there are only thirty-six states, and so 2^{36} events, there are potentially an infinite number of particulars. Intuitively, the rolls of the dice are token events, α is (or models) a type of event.

Probability theory, and applied mathematics in general, works at the level of types. One considers a system that has various instances s_t at time t. Each instance s_t is assumed to be in a unique state in Ω, written state$(s_t) \in \Omega$. Sets α of states are called events. Intuitively, if state$(s_t) \in \alpha$, then s_t is of type α. Once this framework of states and events is set up, the instances themselves are usually ignored.

For a theory of information, however, these particulars, or instances, cannot be ignored. It is particulars, things in the world, that carry information; the information they carry is in the form of types. It was a particular lighting event that carried the information about Judith. That it was an event of type S.O.S. carried the information that Judith was in distress. It was a particular map that carried information (and misinformation) about the mountain. The map's being of a certain type carried information that the mountain was of some other type. We codify this observation in our second principle.

Second Principle of Information Flow: Information flow crucially involves both types and their particulars.

Notice that Dretske's account of information flow does not really respect this principle. On his analysis, information flow is characterized entirely in terms of conditional probabilities of "events." But, as we have seen, the events of probability theory are really types of events, not particular events. In spite of appearances to the contrary, there are no particulars in Dretske's analysis.

In this book we use the term "token" for the instances or particulars that carry information. For readers coming out of philosophy, this terminology may bring with it baggage from the philosophy of language that we hasten to avoid.

In particular, any suggestion that tokens must have something like "syntax" is quite unwelcome. By a token, we mean only something that is classified; by type, we mean only something that is used to classify.

Classifications

In order to relate the diverse approaches to information surveyed in Lecture 1, where one classifies tokens by sets of states (i.e., "events") in one approach, by sentences in others, and by a host of other devices in still others, the theory presented here uses a very general framework, the notion of a classification. This notion is a very simple one, and one that has been used in various contexts prior to this book.[1]

Definition. A *classification* $A = \langle A, \Sigma_A, \vDash_A \rangle$ consists of a set A of objects to be classified, called *tokens* of A, a set Σ_A of objects used to classify the tokens, called the *types* of A, and a binary relation $\vDash_A$ between A and Σ_A that tells one which tokens are classified as being of which types.

A classification is depicted by means of a diagram as follows.

Example 2.1. We might classify flashlight bulbs at times, say b_t, by means of three types LIT, UNLIT, and LIVE. For example, $b_t \vDash$ LIT if the bulb instance b_t is lit, that is, if b is lit at time t.

Example 2.2. A familiar example of a classification is that of a first-order language. Here the tokens are particular mathematical structures M, and the types are sentences α of the language, and $M \vDash \alpha$ if and only if α is true in M.

Example 2.3. Another example would be that of classifying rolls of a pair of dice. Suppose we use the set $\Omega = \{\langle n, m \rangle \mid 1 \leq n, m \leq 6\}$ as our state space

---

[1] G. D. Birkhoff dubbed such structures "polarities" in Birkhoff (1940). They are used in Hartonis and Dunn (1993). The literature on formal concept analysis calls them "contexts"; see Hardegree (1982) and, for a discussion and historical references, Chapter 11 of Davey and Priestley (1990). More recently they have been called "Chu spaces" in theoretical computer science. A large literature has grown up around this topic, especially in the work of Vaughan Pratt and his colleagues. A complete list of these papers can be found on the World Wide Web at http://boole.stanford.edu/chuguide.html.

Ω for analyzing these tosses. Let us suppose that the dice are chosen from a set D of six-sided dice. These dice may be tossed repeatedly. We might model particular tosses by triples like $x = \langle d_1, d_2, t \rangle$, where $d_1, d_2 \in D$ are distinct and t is the time of a particular toss. These form the tokens of a classification. Each toss x has, we assume, some state $state(x) \in \{\langle n, m \rangle \mid 1 \leq n, m \leq 6\}$. For example, the state of $\langle d_1, d_2, t \rangle$ is $\langle 1, 5 \rangle$ if and only if d_1 lands at t with the numeral 1 showing and d_2 lands at t with the numeral 5 showing. The types of our classification are, then, the events over Ω, that is, subsets $\alpha \subseteq \Omega$, and $x \vDash \alpha$ if and only if the state of x is in α.

As these examples illustrate, we sometimes take the tokens of a classification to be structureless mathematical objects, while at other times we give them structure so as to relate them to other tokens of other classifications more effectively.

If a particular classification models some device (or class of devices), say Judith's whole flashlight or the World Wide Web, then the types of the classification represent all the properties of the device of relevance to our model. If the tokens of the classifications represent all the possible instances of the device deemed relevant to the problem at hand, then the classification gives rise to a "theory" of the device, namely, those relationships between types that hold for all the tokens. We want to define this theory.

In logic it is usual to take a theory to be a set of sentences, together with some kind of notion of entailment, $\Gamma \vdash \alpha$, between theories and sentences. Because we are working in a more general setting, we want to allow theories that have as premises not just sets of sentences but quite generally sets of types. Moreover, following Gentzen, we treat entailment not just as a relation between sets of sentences and single sentences, but we allow sets on both sides. In doing so, however, things work much more elegantly if one treats the set Γ on the left side of $\Gamma \vdash \Delta$ conjunctively and that on the right disjunctively. By a *sequent* we just mean a pair $\langle \Gamma, \Delta \rangle$ of sets of types. The reader not familiar with logic may want to restrict attention to the case where there is a singleton set on the right-hand side, for now.

Definition. Let A be a classification and let $\langle \Gamma, \Delta \rangle$ be a sequent of A. A token a of A *satisfies* $\langle \Gamma, \Delta \rangle$ provided that if a is of type α for every $\alpha \in \Gamma$ then a is of type α for some $\alpha \in \Delta$. We say that Γ *entails* Δ in A, written $\Gamma \vdash_A \Delta$, if every token a of A satisfies $\langle \Gamma, \Delta \rangle$. If $\Gamma \vdash_A \Delta$ then the pair $\langle \Gamma, \Delta \rangle$ is called a *constraint* supported by the classification A.

The set of all constraints supported by A is called the complete theory of A and is denoted by Th(A). The complete theory of A represents all the regularities supported by the system being modeled by A.

Example 2.4. In Example 2.1 we get constraints like LIT ⊢ LIVE, since every lit bulb is live, and LIT, UNLIT ⊢. (Strictly speaking, we should be writing these as {LIT} ⊢ {LIVE} and {LIT, UNLIT} ⊢, but we leave out the set brackets because no confusion is likely.) The latter constraint says that no bulb is both lit and unlit, because it says that any bulb of both types on the left is of at least one type on the right, but there are no types on the right. Similarly, we get ⊢ LIT, UNLIT because every bulb is either lit or unlit.

In Example 2.2, we have $\Gamma \vdash \Delta$ if and only if every structure M that is a model of every sentence in Γ is a model of some sentence in Δ. This is just the classical notion of logical entailment from first-order logic.

In Example 2.3, suppose that each state $\langle n, m \rangle$ in every event in Γ is in at least one event in Δ. Then for any toss x, if it satisfies every type in Γ, it must also satisfy some type in Δ, and so $\Gamma \vdash \Delta$. Whether or not the converse holds will depend on whether the set of tokens of the classification contains, for each state $\langle n, m \rangle$, a toss with $\langle n, m \rangle$ as its state. If so, then the converse holds. But if not, then intuitively the theory of our classifications will capture some accidental generalizations. This is a theme we will be coming back to.

Here are five special kinds of constraint to keep in mind.

Entailment: A constraint of the form $\alpha \vdash \beta$ (the left- and right-hand sides are both singletons) represents the claim that α entails β.

Necessity: A constraint of the form $\vdash \alpha$ (the left-hand side is empty, the right is a singleton) represents the claim that the type α is necessarily the case, without any preconditions.

Exhaustive cases: A constraint of the form $\vdash \alpha, \beta$ (the left-hand side is empty, the right is a doubleton) represents the claim that every token is of one of the two types α and β, again without any preconditions.

Incompatible types: A constraint of the form $\alpha, \beta \vdash$ (the right-hand side is empty, the left is a doubleton) represents the claim that no token is of both types α and β. (This is because no token could satisfy any type on the right, because there are none, and hence could not satisfy both types on the left.)

Incoherent types: A constraint of the form $\alpha \vdash$ (the right-hand side is empty, the left is a singleton) represents the claim that no token is of types α.

Infomorphisms Between Classifications

In modeling a distributed system, one uses a classification for each of the components and another for the system as a whole. Consequently, we need a way to model the relationship between the whole and its parts.

As an analogy to guide us, let us think about the example of number theory considered as a part of set theory. Applying Example 2.2, suppose that L_1 is the language of arithmetic, with numerals 0 and 1 and additional nonlogical symbols like $<, +, \times, =$, and so on. By the tokens of L_1 we mean any structure that satisfies the basic axioms PA of Peano arithmetic; the types are sentences formulated using the above symbols plus standard symbols from logic. Let L_2 be the language of set theory, with only $\in$ and $=$ as nonlogical symbols. By the tokens of L_2 we mean any structure that satisfies the usual axioms ZFC of Zermelo-Fraenkel set theory; again types are sentences formulated in terms of $\in$, $=$, and the basic symbols of logic.

One of the standard themes in any course on set theory is to show how to translate number theory into set theory using the finite von Neumann ordinals. Formally, what is going on is the development of an "interpretation." One shows how to translate any sentence α of number theory into a sentence α^I of set theory.

At the level of structures, though, things go the other way. A model of number theory does not determine a unique model of set theory. Indeed, some models of number theory are not parts of any model of set theory at all, because set theory is much stronger than number theory.[2] By contrast, any model V of set theory does determine a unique model $N = V_I$ of number theory. The reversal of directions is quite important.

This example is a special case of the notion of an interpretation (sometimes called a translation) of one language into another. There are two aspects to an interpretation, one having to do with tokens (structures), the other with types (sentences). An interpretation $I : L_1 \rightleftarrows L_2$ of language L_1 into language L_2 does two things. At the level of types, it associates with every sentence α of L_1 a sentence α^I of L_2, its "translation." At the level of tokens, it associates with every structure M for the logic L_2 a structure M_I for the logic L_1. This might be diagramed as follows:

$$
\begin{array}{ccc}
L_1\text{-sentences} & \xrightarrow{\ I\ } & L_2\text{-sentences} \\[2pt]
\Big\vert \models_{L_1} & & \Big\vert \models_{L_2} \\[4pt]
L_1\text{-structures} & \xleftarrow[\ I\ ]{} & L_2\text{-structures}
\end{array}
$$

---

[2] If the model of number theory is one where some theorem of set theory about numbers, like Gödel's formal encoding of the consistency of PA, is false, then it cannot have an associated model of set theory.

One needs to make sure that the translation α^I of α means the right thing, that is, that the translation α^I says about a structure M what α itself says about the corresponding structure M_I. Hence one requires that

$$M_I \vDash_{L_1} \alpha \quad \text{iff} \quad M \vDash_{L_2} \alpha^I$$

for all structures M for L_2 and all sentences α of L_1.

Thinking of number theory as a "part of" set theory suggests that this sort of picture might apply more generally to distributed systems. The notion of an infomorphism $f : A \rightleftarrows C$ gives a mathematical model of the *whole-part relationship* between instances of a whole, as modeled by a classification C, and that of a part, as modeled by a classification A. This is obtained by generalizing the notion of interpretation from logics to arbitrary classifications in the natural way.

Definition. If $A = \langle A, \Sigma_A, \vDash_A \rangle$ and $C = \langle C, \Sigma_C, \vDash_C \rangle$ are classifications then an *infomorphism* is a pair $f = \langle f^\wedge, f^\vee \rangle$ of functions

$$
\begin{array}{ccc}
\Sigma_A & \xrightarrow{\ f^\wedge\ } & \Sigma_C \\
\Big\downarrow {\scriptstyle \vDash_A} & & \Big\downarrow {\scriptstyle \vDash_C} \\
A & \xleftarrow[\ f^\vee\ ]{} & C
\end{array}
$$

satisfying the analogous biconditional:

$$f^\vee(c) \vDash_A \alpha \quad \text{iff} \quad c \vDash_C f^\wedge(\alpha)$$

for all tokens c of C and all types α of A.

Such infomorphism is viewed as a "morphism" *from A to C*. The displayed biconditional will be used many times throughout the book. It is called the *fundamental property of infomorphisms*.

Think of the classification C on the right as a scientific classification of the tokens (instances) of the whole system, say Judith's flashlight, and the classification A on the left as a classification of tokens on one of the components of the system, say the bulb. The latter might be a scientific classification of the sort used by an engineer in designing the bulb or a more common sense classification of the sort Judith would use. By an instance of the flashlight we simply mean the flashlight at a given instant, rather than the flashlight as a type or as an object that persists through time. The infomorphism f has two parts. The lower part $f^\vee$ (read "f-down") assigns to each instance c of the whole flashlight the instance $a = f^{\vee}(c)$ of the bulb at the same time. The upper part $f^{\wedge}$ (read "f-up") assigns to each type α of the component classification A some "translation" $f^{\wedge}(\alpha)$ in the "language" of the classification C. For example, the classification of the bulb might be very simple, with types {LIT, UNLIT, LIVE}, and the classification of the flashlight might be quite complex, in the language of electrical engineering or even basic atomic physics. The biconditional in the definition of infomorphism insures that the translation of a type α says about the whole system what α says about the component.

The use of "infomorphism" for this notion is new here, but infomorphisms are not new. In the case of logical languages, they are, as we have indicated, just the old notion of interpretation of languages. In more a general setting, these infomorphisms are known in computer science as Chu transformations. They have been studied extensively by Chu, Barr, Pratt, and others. The present authors rediscovered them in a roundabout way, trying to solve the problems of information flow discussed above. So one could look at this book as an application of Chu spaces and Chu transformations to a theory of information.[3]

A great deal is known about classifications and their infomorphisms. For our purposes, the most important fact is that they can be combined by what is known as a "(co)limit" construction.[4] A special case of this construction allows one to "add" classifications. Given two (or more) classifications A and B, these classifications can be combined into a single classification $A + B$ with important properties. The tokens of $A + B$ consist of pairs $\langle a, b \rangle$ of tokens from each. The types of $A + B$ consist of the types of both, except that if there are any types in common, then we make distinct copies, so as not to confuse them. For example, if A and B both had contained the type LIT, then $A + B$ would have two types, LIT_A and LIT_B. A pair $\langle a, b \rangle$ would be of type LIT_A in $A + B$ if and only if a was of type LIT in A. Thus the classification $A + B$ gives us a way to compare types that classify tokens from both classifications.

This construction works nicely with infomorphisms as well. First of all, there are natural infomorphisms $\sigma_A : A \rightleftarrows A + B$ and $\sigma_B : B \rightleftarrows A + B$ defined as follows:

1. $\sigma_A(\alpha) = \alpha_A$ (the A-copy of α) for each $\alpha \in \text{typ}(A)$,
2. $\sigma_B(\beta) = \beta_B$ for each $\beta \in \text{typ}(B)$, and
3. for each pair $\langle a, b \rangle \in \text{tok}(A + B)$, $\sigma_A(\langle a, b \rangle) = a$ and $\sigma_B(\langle a, b \rangle) = b$.

---

[3] A good deal of the mathematical content of Lectures 4–6 is already known to the people who study Chu spaces. In particular, the existence of colimits was established by Chu in his appendix to Barr (1979). We hope they will be interested in how this material fits into the general theory of information developed here.

[4] We will work through this construction in Lecture 6, where we will see that it is intimately tied up with Dretske's Xerox principle.

More importantly, given any classification C and infomorphisms $f : A \rightleftarrows C$ and $g : B \rightleftarrows C$, there is a unique infomorphism $h = f + g$ such that the following diagram commutes. (Saying that a diagram commutes means you can go either way around the triangles and get the same result.)

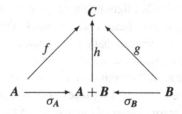

Each of the arrows represents an infomorphism and hence a pair of functions, one on types and another on tokens that goes in the opposite direction. The definition of h is obvious once you think about it. On tokens, $h(c) = \langle f(c), g(c) \rangle$. On types of the form α_A, h gives $f(\alpha)$. On types of the form α_B, use g.

2.2 Information Channels

One of the two central notions of the present approach, that of an information channel, can now be explained. Suppose there is a distributed system, modeled by means of a classification C, and several components, modeled by means of classifications A_i for i in some index set I. Because A_i is a part of C, there must be an infomorphism $f_i : A_i \rightleftarrows C$, one for each $i \in I$, reflecting the part-whole relationships between the system and its parts.

Definition. An *information channel* consists of an indexed family $C = \{ f_i : A_i \rightleftarrows C \}_{i \in I}$ of infomorphisms with a common codomain C, called the *core* of the channel.

An information channel for a distributed system with four components, like Judith's flashlight, can be diagrammed as follows:

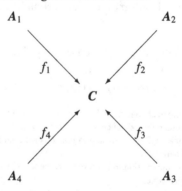

Again, each of the arrows represents an infomorphism, hence a pair of functions, one on types going in and another that goes in the opposite direction, taking each token c to its ith component $a_i = f_i(c)$.

The following simple observation is at the heart of the theory developed in this book. Think of the token c of the whole system as a "connection" between its various components, the various a_i. For example, a bulb at a time is connected by a switch at a time if they are connected by being parts of, say, a single flashlight. It is this connection that allows one to carry information about the other.

Third Principle of Information Flow: It is by virtue of regularities among connections that information about some components of a distributed system carries information about other components.

The classification C and its associated $\text{Th}(C)$ give us a way to model these regularities. Using the constraints of $\text{Th}(C)$ and the infomorphisms, we can capture the basic principles of information flow relating the components.

It is now clear why the first two principles are so important. The first focuses attention on distributed systems, the second on their tokens, which include connections. Without the tokens, we would not be able to track which things are connected to which others and so would have no idea how to tell what is carrying information about what.

This basic point can be illustrated with a simple example. If you flip a light switch, which light comes on depends on which light the switch is connected to. Similarly, suppose you have two photos, one each of two individuals. One photo carries information about one person, the other about the other person. But what determines which person a given photo carries information about is the connection between the person and his or her own photo, a connection rooted in the process of photography.

Given the notion of an information channel, we can now propose our analysis of information flow. In this introduction, we treat the simplest nontrivial case, that of two components, a and b, of a system.

Initial Proposal. Suppose that the token a is of type α. Then a's being of type α *carries the information that b is of type β*, relative to the channel C, if a and b are connected in C and if the translation α' of α entails the translation β' of β in the theory $\text{Th}(C)$, where C is the core of C.[5]

---

[5] If we compare this proposal to Dretske's probability proposal, we see one thing that Dretske has built in that we have ignored. Namely, in giving this definition one might want to exclude the case where β is a universal type, one that holds of all tokens.

Example 2.5. Here is a simple example using Judith's flashlight. Suppose $f : B \rightleftarrows F$ and $g : S \rightleftarrows F$ represent the part-whole relations between flashlights (tokens of F) classified scientifically, with bulbs (B) and switches (S) classified in commonsense ways. Let us suppose the classification F supports the constraint

$$g(\text{ON}) \vdash_F f(\text{LIT}),$$

where the antecedent ON is the type of S of switches that are on. In other words, we suppose that the flashlights that make up the tokens of F are all working normally. Then if switch s_t is connected to bulb b_t by some flashlight f_t in F, and b_t is on, this will carry the information that s_t is lit.

Let's examine a couple of the virtues of this proposal.

Veridicality

The proposal agrees with Dretske's in that it makes information veridical. That is, if a is of type α and this carries the information that b is of type β, then b is of type β. The reason is that the connection c between a and b must satisfy the constraint $\alpha' \vdash_c \beta'$ on the one hand, and it must be of type α' because a is of type α by the fundamental property of infomorphisms. Hence c must also be of type β'. But then b must be of type β, again by the fundamental property of infomorphisms.

The Xerox Principle

Dretske's Xerox principle also falls out of this proposal. If a being of type α carries the information that b is of type β, then it does so by virtue of some information channel C_1. Similarly, if b being of type β carries the information that d is of type δ, then it does so by virtue of a channel C_2. Let C be the limit of these channels. It turns out, as we will see, that this is exactly the channel we need to see that a being of type α carries the information that d is of type δ by virtue of the channel C. In other words, composing information channels amounts to taking their limit.

Shortcomings

By way of introducing the notion of a local logic, we point out a couple of shortcomings with our initial proposal, one aesthetic, one substantial. The aesthetic problem is that the proposal does not directly identify the regularities on the components of the system. Rather, it characterizes them indirectly in terms of constraints on the core and translations into this core. We would like to have the regularities among the components themselves as constraints.

More seriously, our initial proposal presupposes that we have complete information about the regularities on the core of our channel, that is, the complete theory Th(*C*) of *C*. The proposal gives a God's eye analysis of information flow. But in actual fact, we seldom (if ever) have complete information about the core of a real-world channel. Usually, we have at best some kind of commonsense theory of, or some scientific model of, the core of our channel; we use it to attribute information about one component to another component. We will have a more general theory of information if we relativize our proposal in a way that permits less than perfect information about the core.

2.3 Local Logics

In trying to model commonsense theories, artificial intelligence (AI) researchers have felt the need to introduce a variety of nonclassical logics to model the way people reason about these systems. Ordinary reasoning is not logically perfect; there are logical sins of commission (unsound inferences) and omission (inferences that are sound but not drawn). Modeling this, AI has had to cope with logics that are both unsound and incomplete. These are the sorts of logics we need in order to model our less than perfect information about the core of a channel.

We can see how unsound and incomplete logics arise in reasoning about distributed systems. We give two examples, each of which can be pictured as by the following diagram:

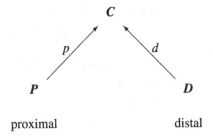

This is a channel involving a proximal classification *P*, a distal classification *D*, and connecting classification *C*.

Example 2.6. For a dramatic example, consider a nuclear reactor. Such a reactor is indeed a very distributed system. An engineer operating such a system is forced to reason about what is going on in the reactor's core from information available to him at the periphery, so to speak, from various monitors, gauges, warning lights, and so forth. In this case, the proximal classification would be a classification of the control room with its monitors, gauges, and so forth. The distal classification would classify the core of the reactor. The connecting classification classifies the whole reactor. (Our terminology "core" is potentially misleading in this example, as the core of our channel is the whole reactor, not its core in the usual sense.)

Example 2.7. For a different sort of example, imagine some real-world phenomenon being studied by scientists using mathematical tools. The proximal classification is the classification of various mathematical objects. The distal classification is that of the real-world phenomenon. The connecting classification is the particular practice of mathematical modeling being employed. Thus in this example we are interested in how reasoning about the mathematical objects can give us information about the real-world phenomenon.

In both examples, we are interested in seeing what kind of a theory of the distal classification is available to someone with complete knowledge of the proximal classification. The diagram suggests breaking this problem into two parts, that of going from P to C and that of going from C to D. Notice that the first step is in the direction of the infomorphism p, whereas the second step is against the direction of the infomorphism d.

We can discuss both steps at once by considering arbitrary classifications A and B and an infomorphism $f : A \rightleftarrows B$. Imagine someone who needs to reason about tokens on either side by using the natural theory of the other side. (In the above, f could be either $p : P \rightleftarrows C$ or $d : C \rightleftarrows D$.) Let's write Γ^f for the set of translations of types in Γ when Γ is a set of types of A. If Γ is a set of types of B, write Γ^{-f} for the set of sentences whose translations are in Γ.

Consider, now, the following "rules of inference": The first of these is a stylized way of saying that from the sequent $\Gamma^{-f} \vdash_A \Delta^{-f}$ we can infer the sequent $\Gamma \vdash_B \Delta$; the second is read similarly.

$$f\text{-Intro: } \frac{\Gamma^{-f} \vdash_A \Delta^{-f}}{\Gamma \vdash_B \Delta}$$

$$f\text{-Elim: } \frac{\Gamma^f \vdash_B \Delta^f}{\Gamma \vdash_A \Delta}$$

The first rule allows one to move from a sequent of A to a sequent of B, whereas the second allows one to go the other way around. These inference rules have very important properties.

Let us think of them in terms of the interpretation of Peano arithmetic (PA) in set theory in Section 2.1. The first rule would allow us to take any valid sequent of PA and translate it into a sequent about models of set theory. The second rule goes the other way around, allowing us to take a sequent in the language of set theory that happens to be the translation of a sequent from number theory and allowing us to infer the latter from the former.

Consider whether these inference rules preserve validity and nonvalidity. Let us think first about whether the rules preserve validity, that is, lead from constraints of A to constraints of B.

The rule f-**Intro** preserves validity. That is, if the sequent $\Gamma^{-f} \vdash_A \Delta^{-f}$ is valid in A, then $\Gamma \vdash_B \Delta$ is valid in B. This follows immediately from the fundamental property of infomorphisms. If c were a counterexample to the latter sequent, then $f(c)$ would be a counterexample to the former.

The rule f-**Elim** does not preserve validity. It is perfectly possible to have a constraint $\Gamma^f \vdash_B \Delta^f$ of B such that $\Gamma \vdash_A \Delta$ has a counterexample. However, no such counterexample can be of the form $f(c)$ for a token c of B, again by the fundamental property of infomorphisms. In other words, the rule is sound as long as one restricts attention to tokens that come from tokens of the classification B. In the case of number theory and set theory, this tells us that theorems of set theory in the language of number theory are reliable as long as we are only interested in models of number theory that are parts of models of set theory. On other models, these theorems are unreliable.

Let us turn now from preservation of validity to preservation of nonvalidity. If the premise sequent of the rule f-**Intro** is not a constraint of A, can we be sure that the conclusion is not a constraint of B? No, not in general. In the case of number theory and set theory, for example, there are many nontheorems about numbers that can be proven in ZFC, Gödel's consistency statement for PA being the most famous. By contrast, the rule f-**Elim** is much better in this regard. If the premise is a nonconstraint of B then the conclusion will be a nonconstraint of A.

Summarizing the above observations, the rule of f-**Intro** preserves validity but not nonvalidity, whereas the rule of f-**Elim** preserves nonvalidity but not validity. Using the f-**Intro** rule, any constraint that holds for a component translates into a constraint about the system. Using the f-**Elim** rule, any constraint about the whole system gives one a constraint about the components but only guarantees that it holds on those tokens that really are the components of some token of the whole system. All bets are off on any other tokens. This is certainly a reasonable rule of inference, even if it might lead one astray were one to apply it to something that was not a component of the system, that is, even though it is not sound.

Now lets return to apply these considerations to the channel depicted earlier:

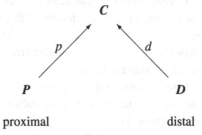

proximal   distal

We wanted to know what happens when we use the complete theory of the proximal classification P to reason about the distal classification D. We have seen that p-**Intro** preserves validities, so the theory we obtain on C is sound, but it may not be complete. That is, there may be constraints about C that we miss. On the other hand, using d-**Elim** means that we lose our guarantee that the resulting theory is either sound or complete. A sequent about distal tokens obtained from a constraint about proximal tokens in this way is guaranteed to apply to distal tokens that are connected to a proximal token in the channel, but about other distal tokens we have no guarantees.

The concept of a local logic tracks what happens when we reason at a distance in this way.

Definition. A *local logic* $\mathfrak{L} = \langle A, \vdash_{\mathfrak{L}}, N_{\mathfrak{L}} \rangle$ consists of a classification A, a set $\vdash_{\mathfrak{L}}$ of sequents (satisfying certain structural rules) involving the types of A, called the *constraints* of $\mathfrak{L}$, and a subset $N_{\mathfrak{L}} \subseteq A$, called the *normal tokens* of $\mathfrak{L}$, which satisfy all the constraints of $\vdash_{\mathfrak{L}}$. A local logic $\mathfrak{L}$ is *sound* if every token is normal; it is *complete* if every sequent that holds of all normal tokens is in the consequence relation $\vdash_{\mathfrak{L}}$.

This is the promised generalization of the notion of the complete theory of a classification. Sound and complete local logics are really nothing more or less than classifications. But infomorphisms allow us to move local logics around from one classification to another, in ways that do not preserve soundness and completeness. Given any infomorphism $f : A \rightleftarrows B$ and a logic $\mathfrak{L}$ on one of these classifications, we obtain a natural logic on the other. If $\mathfrak{L}$ is a logic on A, then $f[\mathfrak{L}]$ is the logic on B obtained from $\mathfrak{L}$ by f-Intro. If $\mathfrak{L}$ is a logic on B, then $f^{-1}[\mathfrak{L}]$ is the logic on A obtained from $\mathfrak{L}$ by f-Elim.

For any binary channel C as above, we define the local logic $\mathrm{Log}_C(D)$ on D induced by that channel as

$$\mathrm{Log}_C(D) = d^{-1}[p[\mathrm{Log}(P)]],$$

where Log(P) is the sound and complete logic of the proximal classification P. This logic builds in the logic implicit in the complete theory of the classification P. As we have seen, Log$_C$(D) may be neither sound nor complete.

In Lecture 15 we will show that *every local logic on a classification D is of the form* Log$_C$ (D) *for some binary channel.* Moreover, the proximal classification of C has a very intuitive interpretation as an idealization of D. This result shows that local logics are very naturally associated with information channels.

We can now go back and generalize our initial proposal concerning information flow. That proposal presupposed knowledge of the complete theory of the core of the channel. We really want to allow the core of the channel to be thought of as the distal classification of some other channel and use the proximal channel to reason about the core and so about the components. Or, equivalently in view of the previous paragraph, we relativize our account of information flow along a channel relative to some local logic $\mathfrak{L}$ on its core.

We mentioned two problems with our initial proposal, one aesthetic, one substantial. We have dwelt at length on the substantial problem, that of complete knowledge of the theory of the core classification. We now turn to the first problem, the fact that we did not end up with constraints about the components of the system, only about their translations into the types of the core. We can solve this problem quite easily with the tools we have developed.

The existence of sums of classifications allows one to turn any information channel into one with a single infomorphism; to do so you simply take the sum of the component classifications and a corresponding sum of the component infomorphisms. If we have any channel $C = \{f_i : A_i \rightleftarrows C\}_{i \in I}$, we can represent it by means of a single infomorphism by simply taking the sum $A = \sum_{i \in I} A_i$ of the A_i and the corresponding sum $f = \sum_{i \in I} f_i$ of the f_i:

$$f : A \rightleftarrows C.$$

Given any logic $\mathfrak{L}$ on the core, we can use the rule f-Elim to obtain a local logic $f^{-1}|\mathfrak{L}|$ on A. It is this logic, with its constraints and its set of normal tokens, that captures the information flow inherent in the channel. Or, to return to the questions posed at the start of this lecture, the local logic $f^{-1}|\mathfrak{L}|$ is the "what" of information flow, the channel is the "why". The closer the logic $\mathfrak{L}$ agrees with the complete theory of C, the better an account we will get of the actual information flow of the system.

Example 2.8. Let's reexamine the flashlight example in light of this discussion. Recall that $f : B \rightleftarrows F$ and $g : S \rightleftarrows F$ represent the part-whole relations between flashlights (tokens of F) classified scientifically, and bulbs (B) and switches (S) classified in commonsense ways. Putting these together, we obtain an infomorphism $h = f + g$ from $\boldsymbol{B} + \boldsymbol{S}$ to $\boldsymbol{F}$. On flashlight tokens x, $h(x) = \langle f(x), g(x) \rangle$, that is, $h(x)$ gives us the bulb and switch connected by x. On types, h is the (disjoint) union of f and g.

Let us suppose that the classification $\boldsymbol{B}$ supports the constraint:

$$\text{LIT} \vdash_{\boldsymbol{B}} \text{LIVE}.$$

It is easy to verify that this will also be a constraint in $\boldsymbol{B} + \boldsymbol{S}$. Now, whatever the classification $\boldsymbol{F}$ of flashlights is and whatever our infomorphism h does to these types, we see that

$$h(\text{LIT}) \vdash_{\boldsymbol{F}} h(\text{LIVE})$$

must be the case. We know from the validity of the one sequent that the other must be valid.

To go the more interesting way around, suppose again that the classification $\boldsymbol{F}$ supports the constraint

$$h(\text{ON}) \vdash_{\boldsymbol{F}} h(\text{LIT}),$$

where the antecedent ON is the type of $\boldsymbol{S}$ of switches that are on. In other words, we suppose that the flashlights that make up the tokens of $\boldsymbol{F}$ are all working normally. In this case, we obtain the sequent

$$\text{ON} \vdash_{\boldsymbol{B}+\boldsymbol{S}} \text{LIT}.$$

This sequent, nice as it is, is not valid! There are pairs $\langle b, s \rangle$ of switches and bulbs such that s is on but b is not lit. Not surprisingly, it only holds of those pairs that happen to be connected by a token of a single flashlight f_i of $\boldsymbol{F}$. The pairs that are so connected are the normal tokens of our the logic obtained by h-Elim. (Notice that this is entirely parallel to the case of number-theoretic theorems of ZFC not holding all models of PA.) This logic gives us a mathematical characterization of the information flow between bulbs and switches made possible by the channel in question.

2.4 Exceptions

We now turn to the most challenging aspect of a theory of information. As explained earlier, an important motivation for developing the details of the theory presented in this book is the severe tension between the reliability and the fallibility of constraints describing distributed systems and the consequent information flow.

Exceptions and Information Channels

On the present account, distributed systems are modeled by means of classifications and infomorphisms. Typically, there are many ways to analyze a particular system as an information channel. Take Judith's flashlight, for example. In the first place, it is up to us as theorists to decide on the level of granularity of analysis. Do we consider just the switch and bulb, or do we want to also take into account the case, the batteries, the spring, the wires, and all the other pieces. In the second place, it is up to us to decide on the types to be used in the analysis. We might have a very simple system or a much more elaborate one. This is true of both the system as a whole and of the constituent parts. Last but far from least, there is the matter of what tokens are present in the classifications. Do we take only tokens of the particular system that happen to have occurred in the past, or do we also allow more idealized tokens to represent possibilities that may not have been realized yet? Do we admit only "normal" instances of the flashlight, where the batteries are working and there is no short circuit, or do we admit other tokens? The decisions here all go into determining what counts as a valid constraint of the classification. We summarize this as our final principle.

Fourth Principle of Information Flow: The regularities of a given distributed system are relative to its analysis in terms of information channels.

This principle includes, among other things, the key insight in Dretske's response to sckepticism, discussed in Lecture 1. Recall that that reply argued that whether or not something counted as a relevant possibility was not an absolute matter, but was dependent on some contextually based standards. In the same way, an analysis of a system as a channel is similarly dependent on contextually based perspectives and standards. Whether or not some sequent is a constraint of a given system is not an absolute matter, but depends on the channel one uses in understanding the system. Such a channel may be explicitly described by a theorist, or it may be implicit in the judgments of a user of the system. But the point is that if one changes the channel, one typically gets different constraints and so different information flow. Thus whether or not a particular token carries information about another token depends in part on the channel under consideration.

Intuitively, the more "refined" the channel used to analyze a system, the more reliable the information flow. But what sort of relation between channels is this notion of being more refined?

Example 2.9. Consider, for simplicity, two analyses of Judith's flashlight in terms of channels $\mathcal{F}$ and $\mathcal{F}'$ with core classifications F and F', respectively. If there is an infomorphism $r : \boldsymbol{F'} \rightleftarrows \boldsymbol{F}$ such that the following diagram commutes, then $\mathcal{F}'$ is said to be a *refinement* of $\mathcal{F}$.

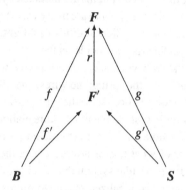

Let us see why this is a reasonable definition.

Consider the rules of inference r-**Intro** and r-**Elim** for the infomorphism r, as discussed earlier. Any constraint of $\boldsymbol{F'}$ will yield a constraint about $\boldsymbol{F}$ using r-**Intro**. This means that any sequent that holds relative to $\mathcal{F}'$ will continue to hold relative to $\mathcal{F}$. However, some sequents that are constraints relative to $\mathcal{F}$ may not be constraints relative to $\mathcal{F}'$, owing to the unsoundness of r-**Elim**.

Let us assume that $\mathcal{F}'$ contains as tokens all actual instances of Judith's flashlight, including those where the batteries are dead. (It might even include wider tokens, so as to take account of whether the flashlight is in air or water, say.) Suppose, however, that $\mathcal{F}$ is just like $\mathcal{F}'$ except that it does not contain any tokens where there are dead batteries. Observe that $\mathcal{F}'$ is a refinement of $\mathcal{F}$; take r to be identity on both types of $\mathcal{F}'$ and tokens of $\mathcal{F}$.

Now suppose Judith's flashlight does indeed have a dead battery. Then b, the bulb, is connected to the switch s by a connection c' in $\mathcal{F}'$ but not relative to any connection in $\mathcal{F}$. Relative to $\mathcal{F}$ there is a constraint that the switch being on involves the bulb being lit. This is not a constraint relative to $\mathcal{F}'$, however, Judith's flashlight is an exception relative to $\mathcal{F}$ but not relative to $\mathcal{F}'$.

Now let us move back to the normal case. Suppose that switch s and bulb b are connected by being components of a normal flashlight y, one where the batteries are in working order. Does s being on carry the information that b is lit or not? Well, it depends. It does relative to the channel with core $\boldsymbol{F}$ but not with respect to the more refined channel $\boldsymbol{F'}$.

The rule of Weakening

$$\frac{\alpha \vdash \gamma}{\alpha, \beta \vdash \gamma}$$

is perfectly valid, as long as one is working with constraints relative to a single information channel. The trouble with the inference from

The switch being on entails the bulb lighting

to

The switch being on and the battery being dead entails the bulb lighting

is that the added antecedent implicitly changes the channel relative to which the sequent is assessed; it does so by changing the standards through raising the issue of whether the battery is dead.

Another way to put it is as follows. The inference is *not* a counterexample to the valid rule of Weakening but rather an application of the invalid rule r-Elim, where $r : F' \rightleftarrows F$ is the refinement described above. The sequent

$$h(\text{ON}) \vdash_F h(\text{LIT})$$

is valid, but the sequent

$$h'(\text{ON}) \vdash_{F'} h'(\text{LIT})$$

(obtained from the former sequent by r-Elim, where $h' = f' + g'$) is not valid; there are tokens in F' that are not in F.

From the present perspective, the reluctance of people to use Weakening in such circumstances does not show that they use nonclassical logic, but rather shows that people are good at changing channels when exceptions arise, re-assessing a situation in terms of a refined channel, and that this is a useful way to think about exceptions.

This suggests that, corresponding to the notion of refinements among channels, there ought to be a notion of refinement in local logics, and there is. More refined logics have fewer constraints but more normal tokens to which they apply.

It is too soon to tell whether these equivalent ways of looking at exceptionality will help in the AI researcher's quest search for computationally tractable logics that cope with exceptions in a graceful way, though we do explore some ideas in this direction in Lecture 19. It would be interesting to reinterpret various nonmonotonic logics as logics of changing channels, but we have not attempted that here. We do feel that it can only help, though, to have an account of distributed systems and their information flow that can, in a principled way, say something sensible about reliability and exceptionality.

2.5 State Spaces

In science, engineering, and applied mathematics the classifications employed are typically derived from state-space models of a system. In the final section of this lecture we want to discuss how these models fit into the framework presented here. In particular, we want to show how any such state space gives rise to a local logic embodying a theory of information flow on the components of the system.

In the framework presented here, a state space S is not just a (possibly structured) set Ω_S of states, but also comes with a function mapping a set S of tokens into the set Ω_S of states. Such a state space S is depicted here as in the diagram below. (When we use the arrow notation and write *state*: $S \to \Omega_S$ horizontally, or vertically as below, we mean that *state* is a function with domain S and range contained in Ω_S.)

State Spaces and Classifications

Every state space is a classification, but this fact is a bit misleading. From an informational point of view, the types associated with a state space are not the states, but rather the events, that is, the sets $\alpha \subseteq \Omega_S$ of states. Thus for any state space S, we let Evt(S) be the classification with the same tokens as S but with types the sets $\alpha \in \mathrm{pow}\, \Omega_S$ (the power set of Ω_S), and with $s \vDash \alpha$ if and only if $state(s) \in \alpha$. Notice that a token is of type $\alpha \cap \beta$ if and only if it is of both types α and β. More generally, using sets of states as types gives rise to a Boolean algebra, where the set-theoretic operations of intersection, union, and complement correspond to conjunction, disjunction, and negation, respectively.

State Spaces and Infomorphisms

Let us now turn to infomorphisms. Suppose we use the earlier state-space analysis of the system that consists of the roll of two dice. Let S consist of all tosses $\langle d_1, d_2, t \rangle$ where $d_1, d_2 \in D$ are distinct and Ω_S is the set used earlier, namely pairs of numbers between 1 and 6; let *state* be a function from S to Ω_S. Now let S_1 consist of all tosses $\langle d_1, t \rangle$ of one die, let Ω_1 be $\{1, 2, 3, 4, 5, 6\}$, and let $state_1$ be a function from S_1 to Ω_1.

If these two state spaces are to sensibly describe a system and one of its parts, they should be related. How? Well, suppose we start with a toss

$x = \langle d_1, d_2, t \rangle$ of two dice, extract a toss $x_1 = \langle d_1, t \rangle$ of the first dice, and determine its state $state_1(x_1)$. We should get the same thing if we determine the state $\langle n, m \rangle = state(x)$ of x and then take its first coordinate n. That is, writing $f^\vee(\langle d_1, d_2, t \rangle) = \langle d_1, t \rangle$ and $f^\wedge(\langle n, m \rangle) = n$, the following diagram should commute:

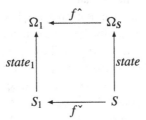

A pair $f = \langle f^\wedge, f^\vee \rangle$ like this is called a *projection* from the state space S for the whole to that for the component S_1. (In this diagram the state space for the system as a whole is written on the right and that for the component is written on the left, for ease of comparison with the notion of infomorphism.)

More generally, suppose one has a state-space analysis of some distributed system, and in addition, a state-space analysis of a component of the system. If both of these are correct, then there should be a way to get from the system to its component, and from the state of the system to the state of the component, in such a way that the above diagram commutes. That is, starting with c (in the lower right-hand corner), one could either determine its state and then see what information that gives one about the state of the component a_1, or one could determine the component and determine its state. These two procedures correspond to the two paths from the lower right to the upper left corner of the diagram. Clearly, the two ways of getting at the state of the component should agree.

The diagram makes it appear there is a problem squaring the notion of state-space projection with the notion of an infomorphism given earlier, because the arrows here both run from right to left rather than in opposite directions. As we have seen, however, when working with information, one works not with single states but with sets of states. The commutativity of the above diagram is equivalent to that of the following:

$$
\begin{array}{ccc}
\text{pow } \Omega_1 & \xrightarrow{\;f^{\wedge -1}\;} & \text{pow } \Omega_S \\
\Big\uparrow{\scriptstyle \models_1} & & \Big\uparrow{\scriptstyle \models} \\
S_1 & \xleftarrow[\;f^\vee\;]{} & S
\end{array}
$$

The function on types is now running the other direction, mapping any set α of states to its inverse image

$$f^{\wedge-1}[\alpha] = \{\sigma \mid f^{\wedge}(\sigma) \in \alpha\}.$$

Thus one has an infomorphism after all.

In Lecture 1 we mentioned the problem of squaring scientific accounts of inference and information flow with the more commonsense accounts actually used by people in going about the world. The use of infomorphisms and classifications also gives us a way to attack this problem by relating commonsense accounts of information flow to the kinds of state-space accounts more common in science and engineering. The basic idea is to obtain an infomorphism $f : A \rightleftarrows \text{Evt}(S)$ from a commonsense classification A to the event classification associated with a state space S. An example of this is worked out in Lecture 3 (and in more detail in Lecture 18) where we show how useful, commonsense, but vague properties can be related to precise, scientific accounts.

State Spaces and Theories

The choice of a given set Ω_S as a set of states for a system implicitly brings with it a theory of that system. Consider, for example, the set Ω_S used in Example 2.3 for classifying throws $x = \langle d_1, d_2, t \rangle$ of a pair of dice. Suppose, for example, that die d_1 is normal but d_2 is abnormal in that it has a face with the numeral 7 (or seven dots) on it. In this case our state space is inadequate to model a toss $\langle d_1, d_2, t \rangle$ because the state of such a toss might not be in our state space. By assuming the set $\{\langle n, m \rangle \mid 1 \leq n, m \leq 6\}$ as our state space, we have implicitly limited ourselves to the analysis of particulars whose state is in this set. If we use this space in the presence of our unusual die, we will make unsound inferences.

On the other hand, imagine that the dice are six-sided dice but with only the numerals 1, 2, 3, and 4 on their faces, some more than once, of course. In this case our state-space model is inappropriate but in a different way. It implicitly assumes that every state $\sigma \in \Omega_S$ is possible, which in this case is not so. Reasoning using such a state space about these tosses will be incomplete. For example, from the information that the state of toss x has a sum of at least seven, it will fail to follow that the state is in $\{\langle 3, 4 \rangle, \langle 4, 3 \rangle\}$, an inference that is in fact warranted in this context.

Definition. For any state space S, $\text{Log}(S)$ is the local logic on the classification Evt (S) with every token normal and with constraints given by

$$\Gamma \vdash \Delta \quad \text{iff} \quad \bigcap \Gamma \subseteq \bigcup \Delta$$

That is, $\Gamma \vdash \Delta$ holds if and only if every state that is in every type in Γ is in at least one type in Δ. Notice that this logic is sound, because we assume that every token a in S has a state state$(a) \in \Omega_S$. But also notice that the logic is given entirely by the set Ω_S of states; it is completely independent of the set of tokens and the state function. This is quite different than the case of the sound and complete logic associated with a classification that depends crucially on the set of tokens and the classification relation.

Suppose we have an information channel with a core of the form Evt(S) for some state space S. The logic Log(S) is then a logic on this core that is suitable for distributing over the sum of the component classifications. This gives us an account of the information flow in the system implicit in the use of the set Ω_S of states of S. We will examine an application of this idea in the next lecture.

Let us now turn to an extended example to illustrate how these ideas can be put to work.

Lecture 3

A Simple Distributed System

In this lecture we investigate a distributed, physical system that is simple enough to explore in some detail but complex enough to illustrate some of the main points of the theory. Readers may work through this lecture as a way of getting a feeling for the motivations behind the mathematics that follow or skip ahead to the theory and come back to this example later. Readers who decide to work through this lecture should accept various assertions on faith, because they are justified by the work that follows.

Informal Description of the Circuit

The example consists of a light circuit LC. The circuit we have in mind is drawn from the home of one of the authors. It consists of a light bulb B connected to two switches, call them SW_1 and SW_2, one upstairs, the other downstairs. The downstairs switch is a simple toggle switch. If the bulb is on, then flipping switch SW_2 turns it off; if it is off, then flipping SW_2 turns it on. The upstairs switch SW_1 is like SW_2 except that it has a slider SL controlling the brightness of the bulb. Full up and the bulb is at maximum brightness (if lit at all); full down and the bulb is at twenty-five percent brightness, if lit, with the change in brightness being linear in between.

We are interested in showing how the theory sketched in the previous lecture and developed in this book handles two kinds of information flow in this system: static and dynamic. The static information we are interested in can be expressed informally by means of statements like the following:

1. If SW_1 is down and SW_2 is up, then B is on.
2. If SL is up and B is on, then B is bright.
3. If B is off, then the switches are both up or both down.

Another phrasing makes the connection with information flow clearer:

1. SW_1 being down and SW_2 being up carry the information that B is on.
2. SL being up and B being on carry the information that B is bright.
3. B being off carries the information that the switches are both up or both down.

Our aim is to see how these sorts of claims can be seen to fall out of an analysis of the circuit connecting the components B, SW_1, SW_2, and SL.

These claims are static because they do not involve any change in the system. The dynamic information that interests us has to do with changes effected by actions taken when someone uses the system by flipping one of the switches or moving the slider to a new position. We want to account for the following sorts of statements:

4. If B is off and SW_1 is flipped, then B will go on.
5. If B is off and SL is slid to the midpoint, then no change will take place in B.
6. If B is dim and SL is slid to the top, then B will be bright.

The aim of this lecture is to build an information channel C_{LC} and an associated local logic $\mathfrak{L}_{LC}$ that captures these regularities. In fact, we will build two such pairs, one for the static case and one for the dynamic. We call the static versions C_s and $\mathfrak{L}_s$ and the dynamic versions C_d and $\mathfrak{L}_d$. The most natural way to study the circuit LC is with state spaces. However, the regularities are phrased in terms of the commonsense conditionals used for talking about such circuits. Thus one of our tasks in analyzing this example is to show how these commonsense conditionals square with a state-space description of the system. The account will explain why these conditionals hold.

Notice, however, that these conditionals are defeasible. If the power to this house is off, then neither (2) nor (3) hold, for example. We want to see how this sort of thing fits into a general account. That is, normal and exceptional cases should be seen as arising from principled considerations involving the circuit. Indeed, they should be seen as following from the mathematical modeling of the principles enunciated in the preceding lecture.

As an added attraction, we note that our constraints involve useful but vague predicates like "dim" and "bright." Working out this example will allow us to see how such predicates can interact with our scientific description of the system by way of infomorphisms.[1]

---

[1] The basic idea here is elaborated in Lecture 18 on vagueness.

Our first task is to construct the classification A on which the local logic $\mathfrak{L}_s$ lives. This classification is the sum of four classifications, one for each of the components; $A = A_B + A_{SW} + A_{SW} + A_{SL}$. These classifications are connected together by a channel as follows:

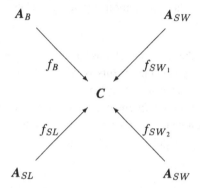

A light bulb classification A_B. There are many different ways one could classify light bulbs at times. We could take into account the state of their vacuums, their filaments, the glass, their metal connectors, the current passing through them, and so on. We will, for now, at least, restrict ourselves to the illumination.

The tokens $b, b', \ldots$ of A_B consist of light bulbs at various times. Types consist of ON, OFF, BRIGHT, MEDIUM, and DIM, with the obvious classification relation. We assume that these types have the obvious meanings but stress that the meanings of the last three are vague and somewhat context dependent. We will see how that works out below.

The switch classification A_{SW}. Just as there are many ways of classifying the bulbs, so are there many ways of classifying the switches. We will keep things simple. The tokens $s, s', \ldots$ of S_{SW} consist of switches at various times. The types consist of UP and DN.

The slider classification A_{SL}. The tokens $sl, sl', \ldots$ of S_{SL} consist of sliders at various times. The types consist of real numbers between 0 and 1, representing the position of the slider, plus two new types UP and DN. The real-number types represent the position of the slider. For example, if $sl \vDash_{A_{SL}} .2$ then sl is exactly two-tenths of the way up. As for the other two types, we declare that sl is of type DN if and only if sl is less than one-tenth of the way up, and is of type UP if it is more than nine-tenths of the way up.

We now define the classification A we are after to be $A_B + A_{SW} + A_{SW} + A_{SL}$. The classification A_{SW} of switches occurs twice because the circuit we are interested in has two switches. The tokens of this classification consist of

4-tuples $\langle b, s_1, s_2, sl \rangle$, where b, s_1, s_2, and sl are instances of a bulb, two switches, and a slider SL. The types of this classification are the disjoint union of the types of the individual classifications. Because A_{SW} occurs twice, and because its types are also types in A_{SL}, the types of $A_B + A_{SW} + A_{SW} + A_{SL}$ contain three copies of UP and DN, one for each copy of A_{SW} and one for A_{SL}. (The other types are distinct from one another.) We denote the copies of UP by UP_1, UP_2, and UP_{SL}, respectively, and analogously define copies for DN.

We want a local logic on A that captures the intuitions about information flow in the system that interests us. Intuitively, this local logic should have as normal tokens those 4-tuples $\langle b, s_1, s_2, sl \rangle$ that are part of a normal instance of our circuit, and it should have as constraints things like

$$\text{DN}_1, \text{UP}_2 \vdash \text{ON}.$$

$$\text{UP}_{SL}, \text{ON} \vdash \text{BRIGHT}.$$

We will obtain such a local logic by finding a natural channel C_s with these four classifications as its component classifications and by looking at a distributed local logic associated with this system.

The most natural way to proceed for this particular example is by way of state spaces. So we first construct state spaces for each of these components together with infomorphisms of these classifications into the event classifications of the state spaces. Because our analysis will make central use of state spaces, we need to say a bit more about them and their relationship to classifications.

First, recall that a state space S consists of a set S of tokens, a set Ω of states, and a function *state* $: S \to \Omega$ assigning a state to each token. We call S *complete* if every state $\sigma \in \Omega$ is the state of some $s \in S$.

Associated with any state space S, there is a classification Evt(S), called the *event classification of* S. The tokens of Evt(S) are the same as those of S but whose types are sets of states from S, interpreted disjunctively. That is, if α is a set of states of S and a is a token of S, then $a \vDash_{\text{Evt}(S)} \alpha$ if and only if the state(a), the state of a, is in α. As we mentioned, in this classification, the types form a Boolean algebra under the operations of intersection (conjunction of types), union (disjunction of types), and complement (negation of types).

There is an intuitive notion of entailment implicit in any classification of the form Evt(S). Recall that type α entails type β if every state in α is in β; that is, if $\alpha \subseteq \beta$. When we combine this with the Boolean operations, we see that, for example, $\alpha_1, \alpha_2 \vdash \beta_1, \beta_2$ if every state in both α_1 and α_2 is in at least one of β_1 or β_2, that is, if $\alpha_1 \cap \alpha_2 \subseteq \beta_1 \cup \beta_2$. More generally, if Γ and Δ are sets of Evt(S) types, then, intuitively,

$$\Gamma \vdash \Delta \quad \text{iff} \quad \bigcap \Gamma \subseteq \bigcup \Delta.$$

This defines a sound entailment relation on Evt(S). We can turn it into a sound local logic by simply taking all the tokens of S to be normal. This logic is called the *local logic induced by the state space S*, and is written Log(S); it is the logic implicit in the use of the state-space model S.

We can now see the rationale for calling a space S complete when every state is the state of some token. For suppose S is complete and consider a sequent $\langle \Gamma, \Delta \rangle$ that holds of every token. It follows that $\Gamma \vdash \Delta$, for if not, there would be a state in $\sigma \in (\bigcap \Gamma - \bigcup \Delta)$. But then let s be a token whose state is σ. This token would be of every type in Γ and of no type in Δ, contradicting the assumption that $\langle \Gamma, \Delta \rangle$ holds of every token. In other words, the logic Log(S) is a complete logic.

In the previous lecture we noted that whenever there is a projection $p : S \rightrightarrows S_1$ of state spaces, there is a natural associated infomorphism $p^* : \text{Evt}(S_1) \rightleftarrows \text{Evt}(S)$ of their associated classifications. On types, this infomorphism takes a set of types to its inverse image under $p^\wedge$; on tokens it is identical to $p^\vee$. We call this infomorphism Evt(p). Thus whenever p is a projection, Evt(p) : Evt(S_1) $\rightleftarrows$ Evt(S) is an infomorphism. We will use this operation repeatedly below.

3.1 The Static Case

We begin by restricting attention to the static case, returning to the dynamic case in the next section, where we will build on the work done here.

The bulb state space S_B. The tokens $b, b', \ldots$ of S_B consist of light bulbs at various times. The states will consist of real numbers between 0 and 1, representing the brightness of the bulb. If $\text{state}_{S_B}(b) = .5$ then b is at half brightness; if $\text{state}_{S_B}(b) = 0$ then b is off. The classification Evt(S_B) has the same tokens as A_B and has types arbitrary subsets of the closed, unit interval $[0, 1]$.

Infomorphisms from A_B to Evt(S_B). The classification A_B is rather subjective. What is considered bright or dim varies from person to person and also with conditions. What seems bright at night may not seem bright at noon on a sunny day. This sort of dependence on the viewer's perspective might seem inimical developing a mathematical theory of information flow, so we want to see how we can handle it.

One way to get at some aspects of this subjectivity is by recognizing that there are many different infomorphisms $g_B : A_B \rightleftarrows \text{Evt}(S_B)$ from A_B into Evt(S_B).

We are interested in those that are the identity on tokens and satisfy the following condition on types:

- $g_B(\text{ON}) = (0, 1]$
- $g_B(\text{OFF}) = \{0\}$
- $g_B(\text{DIM})$ is a left closed subset of $(0, 1]$.[2]
- $g_B(\text{BRIGHT})$ is a right closed subset of $(0, 1]$.
- $g_B(\text{MEDIUM})$ is a convex subset of $(0, 1]$.[3]
- Every member of $g_B(\text{DIM})$ is less than every member of $g_B(\text{MEDIUM})$, which in turn is less than every member of $g_B(\text{BRIGHT})$.

Notice that we have not assumed that the three sets $g_B(\text{MEDIUM})$, $g_B(\text{DIM})$, and $g_B(\text{BRIGHT})$ exhaust the interval $(0, 1]$, because there might be some values that the observer would be reluctant to classify as any of medium, dim, or bright.

The switch state space S_{SW}. The tokens $s, s', \ldots$ of S_{SW} consist of switches at various times. The states will consist of 0 and 1. The state of s is 1 if s is up, 0 if s is down.

Whenever a state space S has exactly two states, say 0 and 1, the event space $\text{Evt}(S)$ will have four types, namely, the empty set $\emptyset$, the set $\{0, 1\}$, and the types $\{0\}$ and $\{1\}$. The empty set is a type with no tokens of that type; it represents impossibility. The type $\{0, 1\}$ represents no information at all, because every token is of that type; it represents necessity. So the only possible but nonnecessary types are $\{0\}$ and $\{1\}$. Thus we see that for such a state space, the only advantage of $\text{Evt}(S)$ over S is that the former has an impossible type and a necessary type.

We define a token-identical infomorphism $g_{SW} : A_{SW} \rightleftarrows \text{Evt}(S)_{SW}$ to capture the relationship between the types and the states. Namely, $g_{SW}(\text{UP}) = \{1\}$ and $g_{SW}(\text{DN}) = \{0\}$.

The slider state space S_{SL}. The tokens $sl, sl', \ldots$ of S_{SL} consist of sliders at various times. The states will consist of real numbers between 0 and 1, representing the position of the slider. If $\text{state}_{S_{SW}}(sl) = .2$ then sl is two-tenths of the way up. The classification $\text{Evt}(S_{SL})$ has arbitrary subsets of $[0, 1]$ as types.

---

[2] A left closed subset X of a set Y of reals is a set such that if $x \in X$ and $y \in Y$ is less than x, then $y \in X$.

[3] A convex subset X of a set Y of reals is a set such that if $x_1, x_2 \in X$, and $y \in Y$ is between x_1 and x_2, then $y \in X$.

We define the obvious infomorphism $g_{SL}: A_{SL} \rightleftarrows \text{Evt}(S_{SL})$ by letting $g_{SL}(r) = \{r\}$ for each real number and letting $g_{SL}(\text{DN}) = [0, .1)$ and $g_{SL}(\text{UP}) = (.9, 1]$.

We have now constructed token identical infomorphisms from each of our classifications into the event classifications of the corresponding state spaces.

The Channel C_s

The information channel consists of a classification of the circuit as a whole, together with infomorphisms from our component classifications into this classification. In coming up with a classification for the circuit, we have to choose what aspects of the circuit to model. Should we take into account the condition of the wiring, the amount of current available, whether or not the house is flooded, or just what? We want our framework to be able to account for such factors and contingencies without getting bogged down by them. We choose to develop a state space S_L to model the system and then take the core of the channel to be the event classification of this state space. Before defining S_L, we define an auxiliary space S_L^*.

The state spaces S_L^*. The tokens $c, c', \ldots$ of S_L^* are arbitrary instances of the circuit at various times. The set Ω^* of states of S_L^* is $[0, 1]^4$, the set of all 4-tuples of real numbers between 0 and 1. This is a very simplified model of the state of the circuit. The circuit c is in state $\langle r_1, r_2, r_3, r_4 \rangle$ if the state of c's bulb is r_1, the state of c's lower switch is r_2, the state of c's upper switch is r_3, and the state of c's slider is r_4.

We have set up our example state spaces so that there are simple, natural projections $p_B: S_L^* \rightrightarrows S_B$, $p_{SW1}: S_L^* \rightrightarrows S_{SW}$, $p_{SW2}: S_L^* \rightrightarrows S_{SW}$, and $p_{SL}: S_L^* \rightrightarrows S_{SL}$ from S_L^* into the state spaces for the bulbs, switches, and slider, respectively.

For example, the projection $p_B: S_L^* \rightrightarrows S_B$ acts as follows. On tokens, $p_B(c)$ is the bulb that is part of the circuit instance c. (We suppose that every circuit instance that is a token of S_L^* has a bulb screwed in.) On states, $p_B(\langle r_1, r_2, r_3, r_4 \rangle) = r_1$. The projection $p_{SW_1}: S_L^* \rightrightarrows S_{SW}$ acts on tokens by $p_{SW1}(c)$ being the instance of the switch SW_1 that is part of the circuit instance c. On states, $p_{SW_1}(\langle r_1, r_2, r_3, r_4 \rangle) = r_2$. The projection $p_{SW_2}: S_L^* \rightrightarrows S_{SW}$ is similar except that it gives an instance of SW_2 on tokens and r_3 on states. The projection $p_{SL}: S_L^* \rightrightarrows S_{SL}$ is defined similarly.

The state space S_L. The constraints we are after are a product of natural laws governing the circuit and the meanings of our types. The latter are built into the infomorphisms defined above. The laws governing the circuit, however, have not yet been built into the model. We do this by looking at a subspace S_L of S_L^*.

Let Ω consist of all those tuples $\sigma = \langle r_1, r_2, r_3, r_4 \rangle$ satisfying:

$$r_2, r_3 \in \{0, 1\}$$

$$r_1 = |r_2 - r_3| \left(\frac{3r_4 + 1}{4} \right)$$

Notice that if $r_2 = r_3$ (that is, if the switches are both up or both down), then $r_1 = 0$. On the other hand, if $r_2 = 1$ and $r_3 = 0$ or vice versa (meaning that the two switches are in opposite positions), then

$$r_1 = \frac{3r_4 + 1}{4}.$$

For example, if $r_4 = 0$, then $r_1 = .25$, meaning that if the slider is all the way down, then the bulb is at twenty-five percent brightness, whereas if $r_4 = 1$, then $r_1 = 1$, meaning that if the slider is all the way up, then the bulb is at full brightness. The dependence of r_1 on r_4 is linear, as specified earlier.

We let S_L be the subspace of S_L^* with Ω as the set of states and tokens those instances of the circuit whose state is in Ω. It is reasonable to suppose that this state space is complete for the following reason. There are only four possible combinations of positions for the switches. We have put the switches in these four positions and, in each of these, run the slider from bottom to top. In this way we have exhausted all the possible states of the system, at least up to the gap between the physical system and its mathematical model.

The core of the channel. The core of our channel C_s is the event classification of S_L, that is, the classification $C = \text{Evt}(S_L)$.

The infomorphisms from the component classifications are defined in the expected manner:

The infomorphism $f_B : A_B \rightleftarrows C$ is the composition of the infomorphisms $g_B : A_B \rightleftarrows \text{Evt}(S_B)$ and $\text{Evt}(p_B) : \text{Evt}(S_B) \rightleftarrows C$.[4]

The infomorphism $f_{SW_1} : A_{SW} \rightleftarrows C$ is the composition of $g_{SW} : A_{SW} \rightleftarrows \text{Evt}(S_{SW})$ and $\text{Evt}(p_{SW_1}) : \text{Evt}(S_{SW}) \rightleftarrows C$.

The infomorphism $f_{SW_2} : A_{SW} \rightleftarrows C$ is the composition of $g_{SW} : A_{SW} \rightleftarrows \text{Evt}(S_{SW})$ and $\text{Evt}(p_{SW_2}) : \text{Evt}(S_{SW}) \rightleftarrows C$.

The infomorphism $f_{SL} : (A_{SL}) \rightleftarrows C$ is the composition of $g_{SL} : A_{SL} \rightleftarrows \text{Evt}(S_{SL})$ and $\text{Evt}(p_{SL}) : \text{Evt} p(S_{SL}) \rightleftarrows C$.

---

[4] Composition of infomorphisms is defined in the obvious manner in the next lecture.

Let the index set $I = \{B, SW_1, SW_2, SL\}$, and let

$$C_s = \{f_i : A_i \rightleftarrows C\}_{i \in I}$$

be the channel as depicted earlier.

The core classification C has a local logic $\mathfrak{L}_C$ that captures the state space classification, namely, the logic $\mathrm{Log}(S_L)$ defined earlier. This local logic has a consequence relation given by

$$\Gamma \vdash \Delta \quad \text{iff} \quad \bigcap \Gamma \subseteq \bigcup \Delta$$

for Γ, Δ sets of sets of states of Ω. It is sound, so its normal tokens are the tokens of S_L, that is, the tokens of S_L^* whose state obey the defining law for Ω. Because the state space is complete, the local logic is also complete.

The local logic $\mathfrak{L}_s$. We can now use the local logic $\mathfrak{L}_C$ on the core C to obtain the desired local logic $\mathfrak{L}_s$ on the sum A using the infomorphisms. Let $f : A \rightleftarrows C$ be the sum infomorphism $\sum_{i \in I} f_i$. This infomorphism allows us to move the logic from C to A, via f-Elim. $\mathfrak{L}_s$ is the resulting local logic. In the lectures that follow, this kind of logic will be denoted by the logic $f^{-1}[\mathfrak{L}_C]$. It is the strongest logic on A such that the infomorphism f is well-behaved. In particular, $\Gamma \vdash_{\mathfrak{L}_s} \Delta$ if and only if $f[\Gamma] \vdash_{\mathfrak{L}_C} f[\Delta]$. (We'll compute some of the constraints in a moment.) This local logic is complete, because the inverse image of a complete local logic is always complete. It is not sound, however. That is, not all tokens are normal. The normal tokens consist of those sequences $\langle b, s_1, s_2, sl \rangle$ of bulb, switches, and slider that are connected by means of a circuit c whose state satisfies the defining law for Ω.

Because the local logic $\mathfrak{L}_s$ is complete, it should give us all the constraints we expect, but let us check the following two constraints in some detail, by way of illustrating this logic:

$$\mathrm{DN}_1, \mathrm{UP}_2 \vdash_{\mathfrak{L}_s} \mathrm{ON},$$

and

$$\mathrm{UP}_{SL}, \mathrm{ON} \vdash_{\mathfrak{L}_s} \mathrm{BRIGHT}.$$

By the definition of $\mathfrak{L}_s$, we need to check that

$$f_{SW_1}(\mathrm{DN}_1), f_{SW_2}(\mathrm{UP}_2) \vdash_{\mathfrak{L}_C} f_B(\mathrm{ON}),$$

and

$$f_{SL}(\mathrm{UP}_{SL}), f_B(\mathrm{ON}) \vdash_{\mathfrak{L}_C} f_B(\mathrm{BRIGHT}).$$

These amount to

$$f_{SW_1}(\text{DN}_1) \cap f_{SW_2}(\text{UP}_2) \subseteq f_B(\text{ON}),$$

and

$$f_{SL}(\text{UP}_{SL}) \cap f_B(\text{ON}) \subseteq f_B(\text{BRIGHT}).$$

These, in turn, say the following: for every for tuple $\langle r_1, r_2, r_3, r_4 \rangle \in [0, 1]^4$ such that $r_2, r_3 \in \{0, 1\}$ and

$$r_1 = |r_2 - r_3| \left(\frac{3r_4 + 1}{4} \right)$$

1. if $r_2 = 0$ and $r_3 = 1$, then $r_1 > 0$;
2. if $r_4 > .9$ and $r_1 > 0$, then $r_1 \in f_B(\text{BRIGHT})$.

The first of these is clear. The second does not actually follow from anything we have said so far. The reason is that in postulating our conditions on the infomorphism g_B we did not assume that $g_B(\text{BRIGHT})$ is nonempty; it might be, for example, that a person might under certain conditions consider the bulb dim even at its brightest. But for such a person, the second constraint would not hold! To get this constraint to hold, we must assume that $g_B(\text{BRIGHT})$ is nonempty. In fact, because anything over nine-tenths of the way up counts as being up, this constraint will hold if and only if we assume that all brightnesses above 92.5% count as being bright, that is, that $(.925, 1] \subseteq f_B(\text{BRIGHT})$ (the reason being that $.925 = (3 \times .9 + 1)/4$).

Let us now consider the third constraint

If B is off, then the switches are both up or both down.

Intuitively, this should be expressed by

$$\text{OFF} \vdash_{\mathfrak{L}_s} \text{UP}_1 \wedge \text{UP}_2, \ \text{DN}_1 \wedge \text{DN}_2.$$

However, our local logic $\mathfrak{L}_s$ does not have a conjunction because A doesn't have one, so this does not make sense in this logic.

The natural thing to do is to enlarge the system of types in A to one that has conjunctions, disjunctions, and negations of types. There is a canonical way to do this, resulting in a classification Boole(A). Because the types of C form a complete Boolean algebra, there is a canonical way to extend the infomorphism f to an infomorphism $f^* = \text{Boole}(f)$ from Boole(A) to C. Let $\mathfrak{L}_s^*$ be the local logic $f^{*-1}[\mathfrak{L}_C]$. This is the natural extension of our logic $\mathfrak{L}_s$ to the Boolean closure Boole(A) of A. We will show that

$$\text{OFF} \vdash_{\mathfrak{L}_s^*} \text{UP}_1 \wedge \text{UP}_2, \quad \text{DN}_1 \wedge \text{DN}_2.$$

This is equivalent to the condition:

$$f_B(\text{OFF}) \subseteq (f_{SW_1}(\text{UP}_1) \cap f_{SW_2}(\text{UP}_2)) \cup (f_{SW_1}(\text{DN}_1) \cap f_{SW_2}(\text{DN}_2))$$

This says the following: for every 4-tuple $\langle r_1, r_2, r_3, r_4 \rangle \in [0, 1]^4$ such that $r_2, r_3 \in \{0, 1\}$ and

$$r_1 = |r_2 - r_3| \left(\frac{3r_4 + 1}{4} \right),$$

if $r_1 = 0$, then either $r_2 = 1$ and $r_3 = 1$ or $r_2 = 0$ and $r_3 = 0$. This is easily checked.

Exceptions

Our model of the circuit made many simplifying assumptions of normality, assumptions that get reflected in our constraints. Let us see what happens if we relax one of these assumptions. Suppose, for example, that we want to model the possibility that the power to the house can go off, during a storm, say. To do this, construct a new state space S'_L using 5-tuples rather than 4-tuples for states, say $\langle r_1, \ldots, r_5 \rangle \in [0, 1]^5$, where the fifth coordinate represents whether there is power ($r_5 = 1$) or not ($r_5 = 0$).

Let Ω' consist of all those tuples $\sigma = \langle r_1, r_2, r_3, r_4, r_5 \rangle$ satisfying

$$r_2, r_3, r_5 \in \{0, 1\}$$

$$r_1 = |r_2 - r_3| \left(\frac{3r_4 + 1}{4} \right) r_5$$

and let S'_L be the space with this set of states and tokens that are all circuits whose state is in Ω'. This will properly include the tokens of our earlier example, which only included circuits where the power is on. Similarly, let $C' = \text{Evt}(S'_L)$ be the event classification of S'_L.

We could run through everything we did before and obtain a channel

$$C'_s = \{f'_i : A_i \rightleftarrows C'\}_{i \in I}.$$

Using this local logic would not give us any of the above constraints, because this channel takes into account the possibility of the power being off. To get some constraints, we would need to devise a classification A_P for the power and put it in as a summand of our classification A and put the assumption that the power was on into the antecedent of the constraint.

The channel C'_s is a refinement of the channel C_s in the precise sense defined in the preceding lecture. This means that its constraints are more reliable than those of C_s, that is, more reliable in that they hold of a wider class of cases. To see that C'_s is a refinement of C_s, first notice that the state space S_L is isomorphic to a subspace of the state space S'_L; the embedding e is the identity on tokens whereas on types $e(\langle r_1, r_2, r_3, r_4 \rangle) = \langle r_1, r_2, r_3, r_4, 1 \rangle$.

Applying this operation to e, we let $r = \text{Evt}(e)$ be the infomorphism that is the identity on tokens and is defined on types by: $r(\alpha) = e^{-1}[\alpha]$. The infomorphism r shows the channel C'_s to be a refinement of the channel C_s.

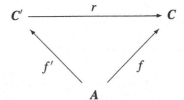

The constraints discussed above hold relative to the channel C_s but not relative to the more refined channel C'_s.

Suppose that one has the information that the light is off and the switch SW_2 is up. Does one have the information that the switch SW_1 is also up? Well, not unless the two are connected by a normal instance c of our circuit, of course, and so are both up at the same time. But even then we see that the constraint depends upon which channel we consider. If we consider the channel C_s, then the answer is "yes," because

$$\text{OFF}, \text{UP}_2 \vdash_{\mathcal{L}_s} \text{UP}_1$$

and because we are dealing with a normal token of the local logic. However, if we are considering the more refined channel C'_s, then the answer is "no," because

$$\text{OFF}, \text{UP}_2 \nvdash_{\mathcal{L}'_s} \text{UP}_1.$$

For example, the state $\sigma = \langle 0, 1, 0, 1, 0 \rangle$ is a counterexample, one where the power is off.

Our general attitude toward defeasible reasoning and its so-called nonmonotonicity is that additional information can alert the reasoner to a shift in channels and so to a shift in local logics. This happens typically by bringing in some issue that is not relevant to the channel under consideration. Thus, for example, suppose one is asked "Does the above constraint hold when the power is off?" In such a case one knows immediately that channel C_s and its associated local logic $\mathfrak{L}_s$ are inappropriate and moves to the local logic $\mathfrak{L}'_s$.

3.2 The Dynamic Case

Recall that we are also concerned with information that involves someone operating the switches and slider, things like the following:

4. If B is off and SW_1 is flipped, then B will go on.
5. If B is off and SL is slid to the midpoint, then no change will take place in B.
6. If B is dim and SL is slid to the top, then B will be bright.

We now want to find a classification B and a local logic $\mathfrak{L}_d$ on B that captures these kinds of constraints.

The constraints are about actions that affect the circuit so we need to classify such actions. We thus define a classification *Act* of actions. The tokens are particular acts $a, a', \ldots$, that involve our circuit. We assume that for each act a there are two instances of the circuit, init(a) and final(a). We posit types FLIP1, FLIP2, RAISE-SL, SLIDER-TO-p (where $0 \leq p \leq 1$), and TURN-OFF with the natural extensions. For example, the extension of FLIP1 is the set of all acts where the first switch is flipped, but the other switch and slider are left unchanged. Similarly, the extension of SLIDER-TO-p is the set of all acts where the slider starts at some position other then p and is positioned at p at the end, with both switches remaining changed.

Our desired classification is the classification $B = A + Act + A$. The tokens consist of 9-tuples of the form

$$\langle b^{init}, s_1^{init}, s_2^{init}, sl^{init}, \; a, \; b^{final}, s_1^{final}, s_2^{final}, sl^{final} \rangle.$$

We interpret such a token as follows: The first four terms will be the initial components, before the action a; the last four will be the final components (after the action a). Because the classification has two copies of A it will have two copies of each of its types in the type set. We use superscripts to indicate these. For example, UP_1^{init} is the copy of UP_1 that goes with the first copy of A, because that copy represents the initial configuration. Our example constraints can now be formulated.

4. OFF^{init}, FLIP1 $\vdash ON^{final}$.

5. OFF^{init}, $\mathrm{SLIDER\text{-}TO\text{-}.5} \vdash \mathrm{OFF}^{final}$.
6. DIM^{init}, $\mathrm{SLIDER\text{-}TO\text{-}1} \vdash \mathrm{BRIGHT}^{final}$.

The next step in our analysis is to translate these types into types in the event space of an appropriate state space. For this we use a state space S_{Act}. The tokens consist of all acts a such that the states of both $\mathrm{init}(a)$ and $\mathrm{final}(a)$ are in the set Ω of normal states discussed in the previous section. The set of states is $\Omega \times \Omega$. The state of an action is defined to be the ordered pair consisting of the states of its initial and final circuits.

Let $p_{init} : S_{Act} \rightrightarrows S_L$ and $p_{final} : S_{Act} \rightrightarrows S_L$ be the projections defined as follows:

$$p_{init}(a) = \mathrm{init}(a)$$
$$p_{init}(\langle \sigma, \sigma' \rangle) = \sigma$$
$$p_{final}(a) = \mathrm{final}(a)$$
$$p_{final}(\langle \sigma, \sigma' \rangle) = \sigma'$$

Our information channel has as its core the event classification $C_{Act} = \mathrm{Evt}(S_{Act})$. This classification has as types subsets of $\Omega \times \Omega$, that is, binary relations on Ω.

Because C_{Act} is the event space of the state space S_{Act}, there is an inherited local logic, namely, $\mathrm{Log}(S_{Act})$. We are going to use this local logic to obtain the local logic $\mathcal{L}_d$ on the classification B by means of an infomorphism $h : B \rightleftarrows C_{Act}$. We construct this infomorphism as follows. First, let $k_{init} = \mathrm{Evt}(p_{init})$ and $k_{final} = \mathrm{Evt}(p_{final})$ so that $k_{init} : C \rightleftarrows C_{Act}$ and $k_{final} : C \rightleftarrows C_{Act}$ are infomorphisms. We let $h_{init} = f k_{init}$ and $h_{final} = f k_{final}$, where $f : A \rightleftarrows C$ is the infomorphism used in the previous section. Thus both h_{init} and h_{final} are infomorphisms from A into C. The first represents the case where the components are considered components of the initial circuit of an action; the latter represents the case where the components are considered components of the final circuit of the action.

There is a token-identical infomorphism $h_{Act} : Act \rightleftarrows C_{Act}$ defined on types α of Act as follows:

α	$h_{Act}(\alpha)$
FLIP1	$\{\langle \sigma, \sigma' \rangle \mid r'_{SW_1} = 1 - r_{SW_1}\}$
FLIP2	$\{\langle \sigma, \sigma' \rangle \mid r'_{SW_2} = 1 - r_{SW_2}\}$
RAISE-SL	$\{\langle \sigma, \sigma' \rangle \mid r'_{SL} > r_{SL}\}$
SLIDER-TO-p	$\{\langle \sigma, \sigma' \rangle \mid r_{SL} \neq p, r'_{SL} = p\}$
TURN-OFF	$\{\langle \sigma, \sigma' \rangle \mid r_B = 1, r'_B = 0\}$

(In the descriptions on the right we have only given the condition on the coordinate that changes under the action. All other coordinates are fixed.)

The local logic $\mathfrak{L}_d$. We are now in a position to define the channel C_d that is going to give us our desired local logic. Namely, it consists of the three infomorphisms displayed below:

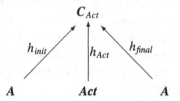

Adding these three infomorphisms together, we obtain an infomorphism $h = h_{init} + h_{Act} + h_{final}$ from $B = A + Act + A$ into C_{Act}. This infomorphism $h: B \rightleftarrows C_{Act}$ is the desired map for obtaining our local logic. Let $\mathfrak{L}_d = h^{-1}[\text{Log}(S_{Act})]$, a local logic on the classification C_{Act}.

The normal tokens of this local logic are those 9-tuples

$$\langle b^{init}, s_1^{init}, s_2^{init}, sl^{init}, a, b^{final}, s_1^{final}, s_2^{final}, sl^{final} \rangle$$

such that a is an action for which both $init(a)$ and $final(a)$ are normal circuit instances and such that the components of $init(a)$ are $b^{init}, s_1^{init}, s_2^{init}, sl^{init}$ and the components of $final(a)$ are $b^{final}, s_1^{final}, s_2^{final}, sl^{final}$.

Let us now check our three sample constraints, to see that they in fact hold in our local logic:

4. OFF^{init}, $\text{FLIP1} \vdash_{\mathfrak{L}_d} \text{ON}^{final}$.
5. OFF^{init}, $\text{SLIDER-TO-}.5 \vdash_{\mathfrak{L}_d} \text{OFF}^{final}$.
6. DIM^{init}, $\text{SLIDER-TO-}1 \vdash_{\mathfrak{L}_d} \text{BRIGHT}^{final}$.

Let $\langle r_B^{init}, r_{SW_1}^{init}, r_{SW_2}^{init}, r_{SL}^{init} \rangle$, $\langle r_B^{final}, r_{SW_1}^{final}, r_{SW_2}^{final}, r_{SL}^{final} \rangle \in [0, 1]^4$ meet the conditions for states in Ω. The three constraints translate into the following conditions:

4. If $r_B^{init} = 0$ and $r_{SW_1}^{final} = 1 - r_{SW_1}^{init}$, then $r_B^{final} > 0$.
5. If $r_B^{init} = 0$ and $r_{SL}^{final} = .5$, then $r_B^{final} = 0$.
6. If $r_{SL}^{init} \in f_B(\text{DIM})$ and $r_{SL}^{final} = 1$, then $r_{SL}^{init} \in f_B(\text{BRIGHT})$.

The first two are readily checked. The last one can be checked if we again assume that $(.925, 1] \subseteq f_B(\text{BRIGHT})$.

Sequences of Actions

The logic $\mathfrak{L}_d$ handles single actions but it does not allow us to express constraints like the following:

7. If B is off and SW_1 is flipped and then SW_2 is flipped, then B will be off.
8. If B is off, SL is slid to the bottom, and then SW_2 is flipped, then B will be dim.

This shortcoming is easily remedied, however.

Assume there is an operation $\circ$ of *composition* of actions, so that if a_1, a_2 are actions with $\mathrm{final}(a_1) = \mathrm{init}(a_2)$ then $a_1 \circ a_2$ is an action with $\mathrm{init}(a_1 \circ a_2) = \mathrm{init}(a_1)$ and $\mathrm{final}(a_1 \circ a_2) = \mathrm{final}(a_2)$. At the level of types, add a binary operation, also denoted by $\circ$, requiring that a is of type $\alpha_1 \circ \alpha_2$ if and only if there are actions a_1 of type α_1 and a_2 of type α_2 such that $a = a_1 \circ a_2$. Finally, we define $h_{Act}(\alpha_1 \circ \alpha_2)$ to the (relational) composition of the relations $h_{Act}(\alpha_1)$ and $h_{Act}(\alpha_2)$. With these elaborations the reader can easily derive the following formal versions of our earlier constraints:

7. OFF^{init}, $\mathrm{FLIP1} \circ \mathrm{FLIP2} \vdash \mathrm{OFF}^{final}$.
8. OFF^{init}, $\mathrm{SLIDER\text{-}TO\text{-}0} \circ \mathrm{FLIP2} \vdash \mathrm{DIM}^{final}$.

Part II

Channel Theory

Lecture 4

Classifications and Infomorphisms

In this lecture, we present the basic theory of classifications, infomorphisms, and information channels, the latter being our basic model of a distributed system. Information flow will be defined relative to an information channel. These notions are used throughout the rest of the book.

4.1 Classifications

Information presupposes a system of classification. Information is only possible where there is a systematic way of classifying some range of things as being this way or that.

Information flow is not restricted to a single on to logical category. The theoretical vocabularies used to describe these different kinds of things can be extremely diverse, so one needs a way to talk about classification that does not favor any particular "vocabulary." This is captured in the following definition.

Definition 4.1. A *classification* $A = \langle \text{tok}(A), \text{typ}(A), \vDash_A \rangle$ consists of

1. a set, $\text{tok}(A)$, of objects to be classified, called the *tokens of A*,
2. a set, $\text{typ}(A)$, of objects used to classify the tokens, called the *types of A*, and
3. a binary relation, $\vDash_A$, between $\text{tok}(A)$ and $\text{typ}(A)$.

If $a \vDash_A \alpha$, then a is said to be *of type α in A*. We sometimes represent a classification by means of a diagram of the following form:

$$\text{typ}(A)$$

$$\vDash_A$$

$$\text{tok}(A)$$

69

Example 4.2. Finite classifications can be conveniently represented by a *classification table*. We write the types along the top of the table, and tokens along the left side. For example, the following table

$A_{4.2}$	α_1	α_2	α_3	α_4	α_5
a_1	1	1	0	1	0
a_2	1	0	1	0	1
a_3	0	1	0	1	0
a_4	1	0	1	0	0
a_5	0	1	0	0	0
a_6	1	0	0	0	1

represents the classification A with tokens $\{a_1, a_2, a_3, a_4, a_5, a_6\}$ and types $\{\alpha_1, \alpha_2, \alpha_3, \alpha_4, \alpha_5\}$, where a_1 is of type α_1, α_2, and α_4, whereas a_2 is of types α_1, α_3, and α_5. Notice that although there are five types, there are $2^5 = 32$ possible distinct sequences of 1s and 0s. Any classification where some of the possible rows do not appear in the table is one where there are patterns or regularities among the types. In the above classification, for example, we see that nothing that is of type α_3 is of type α_4 and that every token of type α_5 is also of type α_1.

Example 4.3. We can represent the classification of English words according to parts of speech as given in Webster's Dictionary using a classification table. We give only a small part of the table representing this classification, of course.

Webster	NOUN	INT VB	TR VB	ADJ
bet	1	1	1	0
eat	0	1	1	0
fit	1	1	1	1
friend	1	0	1	0
square	1	0	1	1
$\vdots$				

Given a classification A, we introduce the following notation and terminology. For any token $a \in \text{tok}(A)$, the *type set* of a is the set

$$\text{typ}(a) = \{\alpha \in \text{typ}(A) \mid a \vDash_A \alpha\}.$$

Similarly, for any type $\alpha \in \text{typ}(A)$, the *token set* of α is the set

$$\text{tok}(\alpha) = \{a \in \text{tok}(A) \mid a \vDash_A \alpha\}.$$

(For example, in the classification **Webster**, the type set of the word "square" is the set {NOUN, TRANSITIVE VERB, ADJECTIVE}. The token set of the type NOUN is the set of all nouns of English.)

Types α_1 and $\alpha_2 \in \text{typ}(A)$ are *coextensive in A*, written $\alpha_1 \sim_A \alpha_2$, if $\text{tok}(\alpha_1) = \text{tok}(\alpha_2)$. Tokens a_1, a_2 are *indistinguishable in A*, written $a_1 \sim_A a_2$, if $\text{typ}(\alpha_1) = \text{typ}(\alpha_2)$. (No pair of distinct types in Example 4.2 or in **Webster** are coextensive. In Example 4.2 it happens that no pair of tokens are indistinguishable. In **Webster** any two words that are of the same parts of speech, like "apple" and "kiwi" are indistinguishable.)

The classification A is *separated* provided there are no distinct indistinguishable tokens, that is, if $a_1 \sim_A a_2$ implies $a_1 = a_2$. The classification A is *extensional* provided that all coextensive types are identical, that is, if $\alpha_1 \sim_A \alpha_2$ implies $\alpha_1 = \alpha_2$. (The classification in Example 4.2 is both separated and extensional whereas **Webster** is extensional.)

Example 4.4. Given any set A, the *powerset classification* associated with A is the classification whose types are subsets of A, whose tokens are elements of A and whose classification relation is defined by $a \vDash \alpha$ if and only if $a \in \alpha$. The classification is both extensional and separated.

Example 4.5. Given any function $f : A \to B$, the *map classification* associated with f is the classification whose types are elements of B, whose tokens are elements of A and whose classification relation is defined by $a \vDash b$ if and only if $b = f(a)$.

Example 4.6. Given a first-order language L, the *truth classification* of L is the classification whose types are sentences of L, whose tokens are L-structures, and whose classification relation is defined by $M \vDash \varphi$ if and only if φ is true in the structure M.[1] The type set of a token M is the set of all sentences of L true in M, usually called the *theory of M*. The token set of a sentence φ is the collection of all models of φ.

Definition 4.7. Classifications A and B are said to be *isomorphic*, written $A \cong B$, if there are one-to-one correspondences between their types and between their tokens such that given corresponding tokens a and b and corresponding types α and β, $a \vDash_A \alpha$ if and only if $b \vDash_B \beta$.

---

[1] Strictly speaking, this is not a classification because every language has a proper class of structures. We shall not be concerned with the matter of size here; with the usual modifications, everything carries over to classifications with classes of tokens and types.

Exercises

4.1.   For Examples 4.4–4.6 what is the type set of each token and the token set of each type? Which of these classifications are in general separated or extensional? For those that are not one or the other, state the conditions under which they would be.

4.2 Infomorphisms

Now that the notion of a classification has been introduced, we turn to the main notion used in this book, that of an infomorphism. Infomorphisms are important relationships between classifications A and B and provide a way of moving information back and forth between them. The classifications can be of the same objects or they can be of different objects. When modeling a distributed system and one of its components, we typically think of the latter. But when we think of one object viewed from different perspectives, that of different people, different linguistic communities, different time zones, or different branches of science, it is the former we have in mind.

   We shall work extensively with pairs $f = \langle f^\wedge, f^\vee \rangle$ of functions, of which $f^\wedge$ is a function from the types of one of these classifications to the types of the other, and $f^\vee$ is a function from the tokens of one of these classifications to the tokens of the other. To remember which function is which, recall that classifications are pictured with the types above the tokens. The function $f^\wedge$ (read "f up") on types has the caret pointing up, the function $f^\vee$ (read "f down") on tokens has the caret pointing down.

   We are primarily interested in the case where the two functions map in opposite directions. We say that f is a *contravariant* pair from A to B, and write $f : A \rightleftarrows B$, if $f^\wedge : \mathrm{typ}(A) \to \mathrm{typ}(B)$ and $f^\vee : \mathrm{tok}(B) \to \mathrm{tok}(A)$. In later lectures we shall explore the *covariant* case, $f : A \rightrightarrows B$, in which the functions both run the same direction: $f^\wedge : \mathrm{typ}(A) \to \mathrm{typ}(B)$ and $f^\vee : \mathrm{tok}(A) \to \mathrm{typ}(B)$.

Definition 4.8. *An* infomorphism $f : A \rightleftarrows B$ *from* A *to* B *is a contravariant pair of functions* $f = \langle f^\wedge, f^\vee \rangle$ *satisfying the following Fundamental Property of Infomorphisms:*

$$ f^\vee(b) \vDash_A \alpha \quad \text{iff} \quad b \vDash_B f^\wedge(\alpha) $$

for each token $b \in \mathrm{tok}(B)$ *and each type* $\alpha \in \mathrm{typ}(A)$.[2]

---

[2] Strictly speaking, an infomorphism consists of two things: a pair of classifications $\langle A, B \rangle$ and a contravariant pair $f = \langle f^\wedge, f^\vee \rangle$ of functions between A and B, satisfying the above condition.

We will omit the "up" and "down" superscripts if no confusion is likely, in which case the fundamental property reads

$$f(b) \vDash_A \alpha \quad \text{iff} \quad b \vDash_B f(\alpha).$$

We use classification diagrams to depict infomorphisms as follows, again leaving off the superscripts on f because it is clear which function is which:

$$
\begin{array}{ccc}
\text{typ}(A) & \xrightarrow{\quad f \quad} & \text{typ}(B) \\
\Big| & & \Big| \\
{\vDash_A} & & {\vDash_B} \\
\Big| & & \Big| \\
\text{tok}(A) & \xleftarrow[\quad f \quad]{} & \text{tok}(B)
\end{array}
$$

Example 4.9. Here is an infomorphism that represents the way that the punctuation at the end of a written sentence carries information about the type of the sentence. We have two classifications, **Punct** and **Sent**. The tokens of **Punct** are written inscriptions of the punctuation marks of English, things like commas, periods, and question marks. We will classify these marks in the way just suggested, by PERIOD, EXCLAMATION MARK, QUESTION MARK, COMMA, and so forth. The tokens of **Sent** are full, written inscriptions of grammatical sentences of English. For types we take three: DECLARATIVE, QUESTION, and OTHER.

Define an infomorphism $f : \textbf{\textit{Punct}} \rightleftarrows \textbf{\textit{Sent}}$ as follows. On tokens, f assigns to each sentence token its own terminating punctuation mark. On types, f assigns DECLARATIVE to EXCLAMATION MARK and PERIOD, QUESTION to QUESTION MARK, and OTHER to the other types of **Punct**. The fundamental property of infomorphisms is the requirement that a written token be of the type indicated by its own punctuation. This condition is satisfied if we treat commands as declarative sentences and if part of what we mean for a written token of an English sentence to be grammatical is that it end with the right punctuation mark.

Example 4.10. Let A and B be power classifications on two sets A and B, respectively. Let us examine the meaning of the infomorphism condition in this case. By definition, an infomorphism $f : A \rightleftarrows B$ consists of a function $f^\vee : B \rightarrow A$ and a function $f^\wedge : \text{pow } A \rightarrow \text{pow } B$ satisfying the condition that for all $b \in B$ and all $\alpha \subseteq A$,

$$f^\vee(b) \vDash_A \alpha \quad \text{iff} \quad b \vDash_B f^\wedge(\alpha),$$

which is to say that

$$f^\vee(b) \in \alpha \quad \text{iff} \quad b \in f^\wedge(\alpha).$$

But this line says that

$$f^\wedge(\alpha) = \{b \in B \mid f^\vee(b) \in \alpha\},$$

which is, by definition, $f^{\vee-1}[\alpha]$. In other words, in the case of power classifications, an infomorphism is nothing but a function from B into A paired with
its inverse, the latter being a function from subsets of A to subsets of B. This
is, of course, a familiar situation in mathematics. For example, in topology we
use open sets to classify points and focus on "continuous" functions, functions
whose inverse takes open sets to open sets.

We said earlier that we think of an infomorphism $f : A \rightleftarrows B$ as going from
A to B. Example 4.10 suggests that this is backward, that it goes from B to A.
The direction of the infomorphism in 4.8 is a terminological decision that could
have gone either way. Our choice was motivated by the following example
from logic.

Example 4.11 (Interpretations in First-Order Logic). Let L and L' be first-
order languages. We assume for simplicity that the basic symbols of L are
relation symbols $R_1, \ldots, R_n$ of arities $\nu(R_1), \ldots, \nu(R_n)$, respectively.[3] An *interpretation* of L into L' is determined by a formula $\psi(x)$ of L' with the one free
variable x (used to define the range of quantification) and formulas $\varphi_1, \ldots, \varphi_n$
of L' such that φ_i has free variables $x_1, \ldots, x_{\nu(R_i)}$, where φ_i is used to interpret
R_i.

Such an interpretation I can be thought of as an infomorphism on the truth
classifications of L and L' in a natural way. On types, that is on L-sentences,
we get a mapping $f^\wedge$ from L-sentences to L'-sentences as follows. Each atomic
formula $R_i(t_1, \ldots, t_{\nu(R_i)})$ is replaced by $\varphi(t_1, \ldots, t_{\nu(R_i)})$ and all quantifiers are
relativized to ψ.[4] For example, the formula

$$\exists y \, R_2(x, y)$$

is mapped to the formula

$$\exists y (\psi(y) \wedge \varphi_2(x, y)),$$

---

[3] The arity of a relation is just its number of places. So, for example, if R is binary, then $\nu(R) = 2$.
[4] Some care has to be taken to avoid clashes of free and bound variables, but we will not worry
about the details here.

and the sentence

$$\forall x[R_1(x) \rightarrow \exists y R_2(x, y)]$$

is mapped to the sentence

$$\forall x[\psi(x) \rightarrow [\varphi_1(x) \rightarrow \exists y(\psi(y) \wedge \varphi_2(x, y))]].$$

On structures, the interpretation works in the opposite direction. Given an L'-structure M', we use the formulas of L' to define a model $f^\vee(M')$. Its domain consists of those objects b of M' that satisfy ψ in M'; for $1 \leq i \leq n$, the interpretation of R_i in $f^\vee(M')$ is the set of $v(R_i)$-ary sequences that satisfy $\varphi_i(x_1, \ldots, x_{v(R_i)})$ in M'.

It is a straightforward matter to check that for each model M' of L' and each sentence φ of L, φ is true in $f^\vee(M')$ if and only if $f^\wedge(\varphi)$ is true in M'. (It would be a good exercise to verify this.) Thus the contravariant pair $\langle f^\wedge, f^\vee \rangle$ is an infomorphism from the truth classification of L to the truth classification of L'.

Definition 4.12. For any classification A, the *identity* infomorphism $1_A : A \rightleftarrows A$ consists of the identity functions on types and tokens, respectively.

Justification. In this definition, we have implicitly made a claim, namely, that 1_A is indeed an infomorphism. In this case, the claim is obvious. In other definitions, we will be making similar implicit claims and so will need to justify them. □

Definition 4.13. Given infomorphisms $f : A \rightleftarrows B$ and $g : B \rightleftarrows C$, the *composition* $gf : A \rightleftarrows C$ of f and g is the infomorphism defined by $(gf)^\wedge = g^\wedge f^\wedge$ and $(gf)^\vee = f^\vee g^\vee$.

Justification. We leave it to the reader to verify that the composition of infomorphisms really is an infomorphism. □

An infomorphism $f : A \rightleftarrows B$ is an *isomorphism* if both $f^\wedge$ and $f^\vee$ are bijections. Classifications A and B are isomorphic if and only if there is an isomorphism between them.

4.3 Information Channels Defined

We now come to our key proposal for modeling information flow in distributed systems.

Definition 4.14. A *channel* C is an indexed family $\{f_i : A_i \rightleftarrows C\}_{i \in I}$ of info-morphisms with a common codomain C, called the *core* of C. The tokens of C are called *connections*; a connection c is said to *connect* the tokens $f_i(c)$ for $i \in I$. A channel with index set $\{0, \ldots, n-1\}$ is called an *n-ary* channel.

When we need a notation for the various parts of a channel C, we write $C = \{h_i^c : A_i \rightleftarrows \text{core}(C)\}_{i \in I}$.

As we have explained in Part I, our proposal is that information flow in a distributed system is relative to some conception of that system as an information channel.

Refinements

We sometimes draw diagrams showing infomorphisms between several classifications. For the sake of graphical simplicity, we draw an arrow only in the direction of the function on types. Think of an infomorphism $f : A \rightleftarrows B$ as a way of translating from the types of A to those of B. For example, the diagram

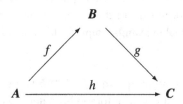

indicates that f, g, and h are contravariant pairs as follows: $f : A \rightleftarrows B$, $g : B \rightleftarrows C$, and $h : A \rightleftarrows C$.

To say that this diagram commutes is to assert that $h = gf$. For types, this means that $h(\alpha) = g(f(\alpha))$, for all $\alpha \in \text{typ}(A)$, whereas for tokens it means that $h(c) = f(g(c))$ for all tokens $c \in \text{tok}(C)$. (Notice the different order of f and g in these two equations.)

We can now define what it means for one channel to refine another.

Definition 4.15. Let $C = \{f_i : A_i \rightleftarrows C\}_{i \in I}$ and $C' = \{g_i : A_i \rightleftarrows C'\}_{i \in I}$ be channels with the same component classifications A_i. A *refinement* infomorphism r from C' to C is an infomorphism $r : C' \rightleftarrows C$ such that for each i, $f_i = rg_i$, that is, such that the following diagram commutes:

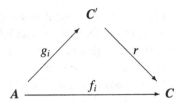

The channel C' is a *refinement* of the channel C if there is a refinement r from C' to C.

Example 4.16. One example of a refinement is where $\text{typ}(C) = \text{typ}(C')$, $\text{tok}(C) \subseteq \text{tok}(C')$, and their classification relations agree on their common tokens. The refinement infomorphism is the identity function on types and the inclusion function on tokens. This refinement amounts to taking more tokens into account in the more refined channel. The more refined channel gives more reliable information, though at a cost, as we will see.

While on the subject of diagrams, we prove a lemma that is useful for determining that a pair of functions is an infomorphism. We say that a pair $f : A \rightleftarrows B$ of functions is *token surjective* (or *type surjective*) if $f^\vee$ (or $f^\wedge$, respectively) is surjective.

Lemma 4.17. *Let $f : A \rightleftarrows B$, $g : B \rightleftarrows C$, and $h : A \rightleftarrows C$ be contravariant pairs such that the following diagram commutes:*

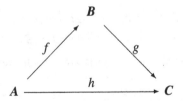

1. *If f and g are infomorphisms, so is h.*
2. *If f and h are infomorphisms, and f is type surjective, then g is an infomorphism.*
3. *If g and h are infomorphisms, and g is token surjective, then f is an infomorphism.*

Proof. (1) is straightforward. To prove (2) let $\beta \in \text{typ}(B)$ and $c \in \text{tok}(C)$. We need to show that $g(c) \vDash_B \beta$ if and only if $c \vDash_C g(\beta)$. Because $f^\wedge$ is surjective, we know that $\beta = f(\alpha)$ for some $\alpha \in \text{typ}(A)$. The following are then equivalent:

$$
\begin{array}{llll}
g(c) \vDash_B \beta & \text{iff} & g(c) \vDash_B f(\alpha) & (\text{because } \beta = f(\alpha)) \\
& \text{iff} & f(g(c)) \vDash_A \alpha & (\text{because } f \text{ is an infomorphism}) \\
& \text{iff} & h(c) \vDash_A \alpha & (\text{because } h = gf) \\
& \text{iff} & c \vDash_C h(\alpha) & (\text{because } h \text{ is an infomorphism}) \\
& \text{iff} & c \vDash_C g(f(\alpha)) & (\text{because } h = gf) \\
& \text{iff} & c \vDash_C g(\beta) & (\text{because } \beta = f(\alpha))
\end{array}
$$

(3) is proved in a similar way. (It also follows from (2) by the duality of types and tokens discussed in the next section.)   □

Exercises

4.2.   If $f : A \rightleftarrows B$ is an infomorphism and b is indistinguishable from b' in B, show that $f(b)$ is indistinguishable from $f(b')$ in A.

4.3.   Let A and B be classifications, and let $g : \text{tok}(B) \to \text{tok}(A)$. Find a necessary and sufficient condition for there to be an infomorphism $f : A \rightleftarrows B$ with $f^{\vee} = g$.

4.4.   There is a special classification $\mathbf{o}$ that plays the role of a zero classification. It has a single token but no types. Show that for any classification A there is a unique infomorphism $f : \mathbf{o} \rightleftarrows A$. (Note that any two classifications with this property are isomorphic, so $\mathbf{o}$ is unique up to isomorphism.)

4.5.   Given a separated classification A and infomorphisms $f : A \rightleftarrows B$ and $g : A \rightleftarrows B$, show that if $f^{\wedge} = g^{\wedge}$, then $f = g$.

4.6.   (†) The category whose objects are classifications and whose morphisms are infomorphisms is sometimes called the *category of Chu spaces*, or the "Chu over Set" category. Show that an infomorphism $f : A \rightleftarrows B$ is
   1. monic in this category if and only if $f^{\wedge}$ is injective and $f^{\vee}$ is surjective and
   2. epi in this category if $f^{\wedge}$ is surjective and $f^{\vee}$ is injective.

4.4 Type-Token Duality

In any classification, we think of the types as classifying the tokens, but it is often useful to think of the tokens as classifying their types. Elements of a set can classify those subsets containing them; models can classify the sentences they make true; objects can be regarded as classifying their properties.

Definition 4.18.

1. For any classification A, the *flip* of A, is the classification $A^\perp$ whose tokens are the types of A, whose types are the tokens of A and such that $\alpha \vDash_{A^\perp} a$ if and only if $a \vDash_A \alpha$.
2. Given any pair of functions $f : A \rightleftarrows B$, define $f^\perp : B^\perp \rightleftarrows A^\perp$ by $f^{\perp\wedge} = f^\vee$ and $f^{\perp\vee} = f^\wedge$.

Pictorially, $A^\perp$ amounts to just flipping A upside down (hence the name "flip" of A, as follows (where $\vDash_A^{-1}$ represents the converse of $\vDash_A$):

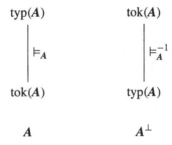

In terms of classification tables, flipping amounts to interchanging rows and columns.

When deciding which way to model a classification we sometimes turn to epistemological considerations. The types are usually considered as "given"; they are things we know about. The tokens are things we want to find out about, i.e., about which we want information. For example, with objects and properties one usually wants to find out about the objects by classifying them in terms of familiar properties. In this case, the objects are taken as tokens and the properties as types. In other circumstances, one might want to learn about some properties by seeing which objects have them. For example, we use paradigmatic objects to explain a concept to a child unfamiliar with it. In this case, we would take the properties or concepts as tokens and the objects to be types. (Chapter 17 contains an application of this idea to the theory of speech acts.)

The observation that the flip of a classification is itself a classification, together with the fact that it behaves nicely with infomorphisms, sets up a duality between types and tokens that can cut certain work we have to do in half, because it means that any definition or notion involving types or tokens has a dual about tokens or types. For example, the dual of "the type set of a token"

is "the token set of a type." The notions of coextensional types and indistinguishable tokens are duals of one another. Similarly, the dual of the notion of
an extensional classification is that of a separated classification.

When we say that flipping is well-behaved with respect to infomorphisms,
what we have in mind is the following:

Proposition 4.19. $f : A \rightleftarrows B$ *is an infomorphism if and only if* $f^{\perp} : B^{\perp} \rightleftarrows A^{\perp}$
is an infomorphism.

Proof. Looking at the following diagrams, we see one is just a redrawing of
the other.

$$
\begin{array}{ccc}
\text{typ}(A) & \xrightarrow{\;f^{\wedge}\;} & \text{typ}(B) \\
\Big| \models_A & & \Big| \models_B \\
\text{tok}(A) & \xleftarrow{\;f^{\vee}\;} & \text{tok}(B)
\end{array}
\qquad
\begin{array}{ccc}
\text{tok}(B) & \xrightarrow{\;f^{\vee}\;} & \text{tok}(A) \\
\Big| \models_B^{-1} & & \Big| \models_A^{-1} \\
\text{typ}(B) & \xleftarrow{\;f^{\wedge}\;} & \text{typ}(A)
\end{array}
$$

$$
\qquad\quad f \qquad\qquad\qquad\qquad f^{\perp}
$$

$\square$

Proposition 4.20.

1. $(A^{\perp})^{\perp} = A$ *and* $(f^{\perp})^{\perp} = f$.
2. $(fg)^{\perp} = g^{\perp} f^{\perp}$.

Proof. This is a routine verification. $\square$

As a simple example of duality at work, we can dualize Exercise 4.2 to obtain
the following:

Proposition 4.21. *Given an infomorphism* $f : A \rightleftarrows B$, *if* α *is coextensive with*
α' *in* A, *then* $f(\alpha)$ *is coextensive with* $f(\alpha')$ *in* B.

Proof. Apply Exercise 4.2 to $A^{\perp}$ and $f^{\perp}$. $\square$

We will make frequent use of such dualities in what follows.

Exercise

4.7.   Dualize Exercise 4.4.

Lecture 5

Operations on Classifications

There are many operations that take classifications and produce new classifications. This lecture discusses two of these operations that are quite important from an information-theoretic perspective. Whenever such an operation is introduced, we will study how it interacts with infomorphisms.

5.1 Sums of Classifications

As should be evident from Part I, the most basic way of combining classifications for our purposes is to add them. In forming a sum of classifications A and B, we classify pairs $\langle a, b \rangle$ of tokens, a from A and b from B, using types that are copies of the types in A and B.

Definition 5.1. Given classifications A and B, the *sum* $A + B$ of A and B is the classification defined as follows:

1. The set $\text{tok}(A + B)$ is the Cartesian product of $\text{tok}(A)$ and $\text{tok}(B)$. Specifically, the tokens of $A + B$ are pairs $\langle a, b \rangle$ of tokens, $a \in \text{tok}(A)$ and $b \in \text{tok}(B)$.
2. The set $\text{typ}(A + B)$ is the disjoint union of $\text{typ}(A)$ and $\text{typ}(B)$. For concreteness, the types of $A + B$ are pairs $\langle i, \alpha \rangle$, where $i = 0$ and $\alpha \in \text{typ}(A)$ or $i = 1$ and $\alpha \in \text{typ}(B)$.
3. The classification relation $\vDash_{A+B}$ of $A + B$ is defined by

$$
\begin{aligned}
\langle a, b \rangle \vDash_{A+B} \langle 0, \alpha \rangle &\quad \text{iff} \quad a \vDash_A \alpha \\
\langle a, b \rangle \vDash_{A+B} \langle 1, \beta \rangle &\quad \text{iff} \quad b \vDash_B \beta.
\end{aligned}
$$

Example 5.2. Suppose that Sw is a classification of light switches using types UP and DN. Then $Sw + Sw$ classifies pairs $\langle s_1, s_2 \rangle$ of switches using four types,

types we write informally as UP_1, UP_2, DN_1, and DN_2. For example, $\langle s_1, s_2 \rangle$ is of type DN_2 if and only if s_2 is down.

Definition 5.3. There are natural infomorphisms $\sigma_A : A \rightleftarrows A + B$ and $\sigma_B : B \rightleftarrows A + B$ defined as follows:

1. $\sigma_A(\alpha) = \langle 0, \alpha \rangle$ for each $\alpha \in \text{typ}(A)$,
2. $\sigma_B(\beta) = \langle 1, \beta \rangle$ for each $\beta \in \text{typ}(B)$, and
3. for each pair $\langle a, b \rangle \in \text{tok}(A + B)$, $\sigma_A(\langle a, b \rangle) = a$ and $\sigma_B(\langle a, b \rangle) = b$.

Justification. It is routine to verify that σ_A and σ_B are infomorphisms. ☐

The following proposition will be used implicitly over and over again in what follows.

Proposition 5.4 (Universal Mapping Property for Sums). *Given infomorphisms* $f : A \rightleftarrows C$ *and* $g : B \rightleftarrows C$, *there is a unique infomorphism* $f + g$ *such that the following diagram commutes:*

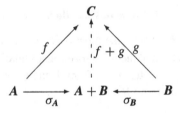

Proof. Let us prove this explicitly, even though it is pretty clear. First, suppose we had such an infomorphism $f + g$. From the fact that the diagram commutes we see that $f + g$ must satisfy the following equations:

$$(f + g)\hat{\ }(\langle 0, \alpha \rangle) = f\hat{\ }(\alpha)$$
$$(f + g)\hat{\ }(\langle 1, \beta \rangle) = g\hat{\ }(\beta)$$
$$(f + g)\check{\ }(c) = \langle f\check{\ }(c), g\check{\ }(c) \rangle$$

But we can use these equations to define $f + g$. If we show that $f + g$ so defined is an infomorphism, we will show both existence and uniqueness. Suppose $c \in \text{tok}(C)$ and that $\langle i, \sigma \rangle \in \text{typ}(A + B)$. We need to check that $(f + g)(c)$ is of type $\langle i, \sigma \rangle$ in $A + B$ if and only if c is of type $(f + g)(\langle i, \sigma \rangle)$ in C. There are two cases to consider, depending on whether $i = 0$ or $i = 1$. They are symmetrical, though, so assume $i = 0$. Then the following are equivalent:

$(f + g)(c)$ is of type $\langle 0, \sigma \rangle$ in $A + B$;
$\langle f(c), g(c) \rangle$ is of type $\langle 0, \sigma \rangle$ in $A + B$ (by the definition of $(f + g)(c)$);

$f(c)$ is of type σ in A (by the definition of $\vDash_{A+B}$);

c is of type $f(\sigma)$ in C (by the fact that f is an infomorphism); and

c is of type $(f+g)(\langle 0, \sigma \rangle)$ in C (because $f(\sigma) = (f+g)(\langle 0, \sigma \rangle)$).

So we have the desired equivalence. □

Many of our constructions extend from two classifications to indexed families of classifications in a straightforward way. We give the details for addition and then are less detailed about others. By an *indexed family* $\{A_i\}_{i \in I}$ of classifications we mean a function on some set I taking classifications as values. We call I the index set of the indexed family.

Definition 5.5. Let $\{A_i\}_{i \in I}$ be an indexed family of classifications. The sum $\sum_{i \in I} A_i$ of the family $\{A_i\}_{i \in I}$ is defined by the following:

1. $\text{tok}(\sum_{i \in I} A_i)$ is the Cartesian product of the sets $\text{tok}(A_i)$ for $i \in I$;
2. $\text{typ}(\sum_{i \in I} A_i)$ is the disjoint union of the sets $\text{typ}(A_i)$ for $i \in I$; and
3. for each $\vec{a} \in \text{tok}(\sum_{i \in I} A_i)$ and each $\alpha \in \text{typ}(A_i)$, writing a_i for the ith component of $\vec{a}$,

$$\vec{a} \vDash \langle i, \alpha \rangle \quad \text{in} \quad \sum_{i \in I} A_i \quad \text{iff} \quad a_i \vDash_{A_i} \alpha.$$

This is a generalization of our previous definition because we can think of a pair A_1, A_2 of classifications as an indexed family $\{A\}_{i \in \{1,2\}}$ for which the index set is $\{1, 2\}$. In this case, $\sum_{i \in \{1,2\}} A_i = A_1 + A_2$.

Definition 5.6. Natural infomorphisms $\sigma_i : A_i \rightleftarrows \sum_{i \in I} A_i$ are defined as follows.

1. For each $\alpha \in \text{typ}(A_i)$, $\sigma_i(\alpha)$ is the copy of α in $\text{typ}(\sum_{i \in I} A_i)$.
2. For each $\vec{a} \in \text{tok}(\sum_{i \in I} A_i)$, $\sigma_i(\vec{a}) = a_i$, where a_i is the ith component of a.

Finally, given a family $\{f_i : A_i \rightleftarrows C\}_{i \in I}$ of infomorphisms, the *sum* $\sum_{i \in I} f_i$ of this family is the unique infomorphism $h : \sum_{i \in I} A_i \rightleftarrows C$ such that $h \sigma_{A_i} = f_i$ for each $i \in I$.

Justification. This is a straightforward generalization of the finite case. □

Sums and Channels. The importance of the addition operation is evident from our examples in Part I. It gives us a way of putting the components of an information channel $\mathcal{C} = \{f_i : A_i \rightleftarrows C\}_{i \in I}$ together into a single classification, $A = \sum_{i \in I} A_i$, and the infomorphisms together into a single infomorphism

$f = \sum_{i \in I} f_i$, with $f : A \rightleftarrows C$. This greatly simplifying the kinds of channels we need to consider as well as giving a single classification on which we will discover a local logic that captures the constraints about the system implicit in the channel.

5.2 Invariants and Quotients

My copy of today's edition of the local newspaper bears much in common with that of my next door neighbor. If mine has a picture of President Clinton on page 2, so does hers. If mine has three sections, so does hers. For some purposes, it is convenient to identify these tokens. On the other hand, they are different, both as tokens and in terms of types. Mine has orange juice spilled on it, hers does not. Hers has the crossword puzzle solved, mine does not.

These observations have clear information-theoretic implications. I can get certain kinds of information about my neighbor's paper by looking at mine, but not other kinds. How can we view this in terms of classifications and infomorphisms?

Definition 5.7. Given a classification A, an *invariant* is a pair $I = \langle \Sigma, R \rangle$ consisting of a set $\Sigma \subseteq \mathrm{typ}(A)$ of types of A and a binary relation R between tokens of A such that if $a R b$, then for each $\alpha \in \Sigma$, $a \vDash_A \alpha$ if and only if $b \vDash_A \alpha$.

Example 5.8. Let A be the classification of newspapers by their physical properties. Let $I = \langle \Sigma, R \rangle$, where $a R b$ hold if and only if a and b are physical copies of the same edition and Σ is the set of those properties that are invariant under R. This is an invariant on A. We want to form a new classification A/I that identifies tokens related by R, using types from Σ.

When we apply the notion of an invariant $I = \langle \Sigma, R \rangle$ the relation R will usually be an equivalence relation on the tokens of A. But it is convenient not to require this. After all, given any relation R on a set A, R is contained in a smallest-equivalence relation $\equiv_R$ on A, the equivalence relation generated by R. This is simply the reflexive, symmetric, transitive closure of R. In the following definition we refer to the equivalence classes under $\equiv_R$ as the R-equivalence classes and write $[a]_R$ for the R-equivalence classes of the token a.

Definition 5.9. Let $I = \langle \Sigma, R \rangle$ be an invariant on the classification A. The *quotient of A by I*, written A/I, is the classification with types Σ, whose tokens are the R-equivalence classes of tokens of A, and with $[a]_R \vDash_{A/I} \alpha$ if and only if $a \vDash_A \alpha$.

Justification. A simple (inductive) proof shows that if $\langle \Sigma, R \rangle$ is an invariant on A, so is $\langle \Sigma, \equiv_R \rangle$. Hence if $a \equiv_R b$ and $\alpha \in \Sigma$, then $a \vDash_A \alpha$ if and only if $b \vDash_A \alpha$. Thus our definition of the relation $\vDash_{A/I}$ is well-defined. □

Here are some examples of this construction. We begin with a very simple example, move on to a more motivating example, and then turn to some important special cases.

Example 5.10. Recall the classification $A_{4.2}$ of Example 4.2. If we restrict attention to the types α_3 and α_4, we can discover a repeated pattern. The third and fourth rows look just like the first and second, respectively, and the sixth looks like the fifth. We can isolate this pattern as a new classification as follows. Let R be the relation given by $a_1 R a_3$, $a_2 R a_4$, and $a_5 R a_6$. There are three R-equivalence classes, one that groups a_1 with a_3, one that groups a_2 with a_4, and one that groups a_5 and a_6. Let us call these equivalence classes b_1, b_2, and b_3, respectively. Let $\Sigma = \{\alpha_3, \alpha_4\}$ and let $I = \langle \Sigma, R \rangle$. Our pattern tells us that I is an invariant so we can form a quotient classification $A_{4.2}/I$. This classification has as tokens b_1, b_2, b_3, types α_3 and α_4, and its classification relation is given by the following table:

	α_3	α_4
b_1	0	1
b_2	1	0
b_3	0	0

Example 5.11. Given a classification A, a binary relation R on $\mathrm{tok}(A)$ is an *indistinguishability relation* if all tokens related by R are indistinguishable in A. In that case, $\langle \mathrm{typ}(A), R \rangle$ is an invariant. The quotient of A by $\langle \mathrm{typ}(A), R \rangle$ is sometimes abbreviated as A/R.

Example 5.12. For any classification A, the pair $\langle \mathrm{typ}(A), \sim_A \rangle$ is an invariant. The corresponding quotient identifies tokens that are indistinguishable from one another in A and so is separated. It is called the *separated quotient* of A, written $\mathrm{Sep}(A)$.

Example 5.13. For any classification A, let $=_A$ be the identity relation on $\mathrm{tok}(A)$. For any set $\Sigma \subseteq \mathrm{typ}(A)$, the pair $\langle \Sigma, =_A \rangle$ is an invariant. The quotient of A by $\langle \Sigma, =_A \rangle$ is called the *restriction* of A to Σ, written as $A \mid \Sigma$.

Example 5.14. Given infomorphisms $f : A \rightleftarrows B$ and $g : A \rightleftarrows B$, we can obtain an invariant on A as follows. Let Σ_{fg} be the set of types $\alpha \in \mathrm{typ}(A)$ such that

$f(\alpha) = g(\alpha)$, and let R_{fg} be the binary relation between tokens of A defined by $a_1 R_{fg} a_2$ if and only if there is some $b \in \text{tok}(B)$ such that $f(b) = a_1$ and $g(b) = a_2$. The pair $\langle \Sigma_{fg}, R_{fg} \rangle$ is easily seen to be an invariant on A.

Definition 5.15. Given a classification A and an invariant $I = \langle \Sigma, R \rangle$ on A, the *canonical quotient infomorphism* $\tau_I : A/I \rightleftarrows A$ is the inclusion function on types, and on tokens, maps each token of A to its R-equivalence class.

Justification. From the definition of A/I, $[a]_R \vDash_{A/I} \alpha$ if and only if $a \vDash_A \alpha$, and so τ_I is an infomorphism.   □

Definition 5.16. Given an invariant $I = \langle \Sigma, R \rangle$ on A, an infomorphism $f : B \rightleftarrows A$ *respects* I if

1. for each $\beta \in \text{typ}(B)$, $f(\beta) \in \Sigma$; and
2. if $a_1 R a_2$, then $f(a_1) = f(a_2)$.

Example 5.17. Let $f : B \rightleftarrows A$ be any infomorphism. There is a natural invariant on A respected by f; namely, the types are the range of $f^{\wedge}$ and the relation is given by $a_1 R a_2$ if and only if $f(a_1) = f(a_2)$. (This invariant is called the *cokernel* of f.)

Given any invariant I, the canonical quotient infomorphism $\tau_I : A/I \rightleftarrows A$ clearly respects I. What is more, it does so canonically in the following sense.

Proposition 5.18. *Let I be an invariant on A. Given any infomorphism $f :$ $B \rightleftarrows A$ that respects I, there is a unique infomorphism $f' : B \rightleftarrows A/I$ such that the following diagram commutes.*

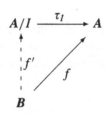

Proof. Let $I = \langle \Sigma, R \rangle$. Notice that if f' is an infomorphism making the above diagram commute then

1. $f'(\beta) = f(\beta)$ for each $\beta \in \text{typ}(B)$, and
2. $f'([a]_R) = f(a)$ for each $a \in \text{tok}(A/I)$.

These conditions give us a definition of f'. That it is a good one follows from the assumption that f respects I: f' maps into the types of A/I because $f(\beta) \in A$ for each $\beta \in \text{typ}(B)$, and is well-defined on tokens because if $[a_1]_R = [a_2]_R$, then $R(a_1, a_2)$, so $f(a_1) = f(a_2)$. □

Definition 5.19. An infomorphism $f : A \rightleftarrows B$ is *token identical* if $\text{tok}(A) = \text{tok}(B)$ and $f^\vee$ is the identity function on this set. Dually, f is *type identical* if $\text{typ}(A) = \text{typ}(B)$ and $f^\wedge$ is the identity.

For example, given any indistinguishability relation R on A, the quotient infomorphism $[]_R : A/R \rightleftarrows A$ is type identical.

Proposition 5.20. *Given classifications A and B, if A is separated, then there is at most one type-identical infomorphism from A to B.*

Proof. The result in an immediate corollary of Exercise 4.5. □

Dualizing Invariants and Quotients

There is a dual notion to that of an invariant and we will need this notion as well. Indeed, it will be quite important. We work through the process of dualizing the above, both because we need the notion and to give us a better feel for the uses of the type-token duality.

Given a classification A, recall that an invariant is a pair $I = \langle \Sigma, R \rangle$ consisting of a set $\Sigma \subseteq \text{typ}(A)$ of types of A and a binary relation R between tokens of A such that if aRb, then for each $\alpha \in \Sigma$, $a \vDash_A \alpha$ if and only if $b \vDash_A \alpha$. By duality, a *dual invariant* is a pair $J = \langle A, R \rangle$ consisting of a set A of tokens and a binary relation R on types such that if $\alpha R \beta$, then for each $a \in A$, $a \vDash_A \alpha$ if and only if $a \vDash_A \beta$. The (dual) quotient of A by J has A for its set of tokens and has as types the R-equivalence classes of types of $\text{typ}(A)$. We write this as A/J.

Continuing this process of dualization, given a classification A and a dual invariant $J = \langle A, R \rangle$ on A, the *canonical quotient infomorphism* $\tau_J : A \rightleftarrows A/J$ is the inclusion function on tokens, and on types, maps each type of A to its R-equivalence class. An infomorphism $f : A \rightleftarrows B$ *respects J* if

1. for each $b \in \text{tok}(B)$, $f(b) \in A$, and
2. if $\alpha_1 R \alpha_2$, then $f(\alpha_1) = f(\alpha_1)$.

Dualizing Proposition 5.18 gives us the following proposition.

Proposition 5.21. *Let J be a dual invariant on A. Given any infomorphism $f : A \rightleftarrows B$ that respects J, there is a unique infomorphism $f' : A/J \rightleftarrows B$ such that the following diagram commutes:*

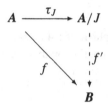

Exercises

5.1. Let A, B, and C be classifications. Prove that $A + \mathbf{o} \cong A$, $A + B \cong B + A$, and $A + (B + C) \cong (A + B) + C$ ($\mathbf{o}$ is the zero classification introduced in Exercise 4.4).

5.2. Show that a classification A is separated if and only if $A \cong \mathrm{Sep}(A)$.

5.3. Define $I_1 \sqsubseteq I_2$ on invariants $I_1 = \langle \Sigma_1, R_1 \rangle$ and $I_2 = \langle \Sigma_2, R_2 \rangle$ if and only if $\Sigma_1 \subseteq \Sigma_2$ and $a R_2 b$ entails $a \equiv_{R_1} b$. Show that this is a preordering and that it is a partial ordering on invariants where the relation on tokens is an equivalence relation. Show that if $I_1 \sqsubseteq I_2$, then there is a natural infomorphism $f : A/I_1 \rightleftarrows A/I_2$.

5.4. Let $f : B \rightleftarrows A$ be an infomorphism. Show that the cokernel of f is the smallest invariant (in the sense of the $\sqsubseteq$-ordering) I such that f respects I.

5.5. (†) Show that the pair $I_{fg} = \langle \Sigma_{fg}, R_{fg} \rangle$ defined in Example 5.14 really is an invariant, and that an infomorphism $h : C \rightleftarrows A$ respects it if and only if $fh = gh$. Conclude that the canonical quotient infomorphism $\tau I_{fg} : A/I_{fg} \rightleftarrows A$ is the equalizer of f and g. Show that every canonical quotient infomorphism is an equalizer.

Lecture 6

Distributed Systems

We introduced the notion of an information channel $\mathcal{C} = \{f_i : A_i \rightleftarrows C\}_{i \in I}$ as a mathematical model of the intuitive idea of a distributed system, a whole made up of parts in a way that supports information flow. The core C of the channel represents the whole, the classifications A_i the parts, and the infomorphisms f_i the relationships between the whole and its parts. When we look at a typical real-world example, however, like that involving Judith from Lecture 1, we see that there are many interacting systems involved in information flow. The question arises as to whether we can put these various systems together and view it as a single channel. The aim of this lecture is to show that we can.

6.1 The Xerox Principle

To initiate the discussion, let us start with a special case, the one needed to justify Dretske's Xerox principle, the principle that says that information flow is transitive. To be more concrete, suppose we have two channels sharing a common component, maps. The first channel will involve people examining maps; this channel is to capture the process whereby a person's perceptual state carries information about the map at which the person is looking. The second channel will involve maps of mountains and other regions, the idea being that a map carries information about the region of which it is a map. Diagrammatically, we have the following picture:

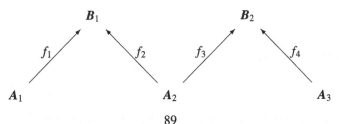

The connections of the first channel (the tokens of B_1) are spatiotemporal perceptual events involving people (tokens in A_1) looking at maps (tokens in A_2). The connections of the second channel (the tokens of B_2) are spatio-temporal events that involve the making of maps (tokens in A_2) of various regions (tokens in A_3).[1] We want to show that under certain circumstances, a person's perceptual state carries information about a particular mountain in virtue of the fact that the person is examining a map of that mountain. To do this, we need to see how to get a channel that puts these together into another channel.

There is a natural set of "connections" connecting people with regions: namely, go first to a person, then to a map she is examining, and then on to the map's region. Mathematically, we can model this with the set of pairs $\langle b_1, b_2 \rangle$ such that $f_2(b_1) = f_3(b_2)$, say; that is, b_1 is to be a perceptual event, b_2 a map-making event, and they involve the same map $a_2 = f_2(b_1) = f_3(b_2)$.

How should we classify such connections $c = \langle b_1, b_2 \rangle$? Because they are combinations of tokens from the classifications B_1 and B_2, we can certainly use the types of these two classifications to classify them. However, this alone misses something very important about their relationship. For suppose we have some type $\alpha_2 \in \mathrm{typ}(A_2)$ about maps. This type translates into some property $\beta_1 = f_2(\alpha_2)$ of perceptual events, but also translates into some other property $\beta_2 = f_3(\alpha_2)$ of mapmakings. If $f_2(b_1) = f_3(b_2) = a_2$, we know that the perceptual event b_1 is of type β_1 if and only if the map a_2 is of type α_2, but this latter holds if and only if the mapmaking event b_2 satisfies β_2. In other words, by restricting attention to connections $c = \langle b_1, b_2 \rangle$ with $f_2(b_1) = f_3(b_2)$, the types β_1 and β_2 are equivalent because they are both "translations" of α_2. We need to build this into our information channel by identifying β_1 and β_2.

Thus we form a new classification C with the above tokens, and whose types are the types of B_1 and B_2, except that we identify types that come from a common type in A_2. We can turn this into a channel connecting B_1 to B_2 by defining the infomorphisms in the obvious way, giving us the following picture:

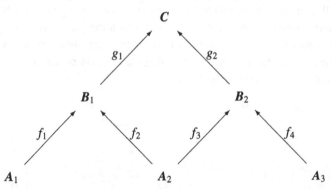

[1] We will have more to say about these channels in the lecture on representations, Lecture 20.

Out of this picture we obtain a derived binary channel with core C linking A_1 to A_3. The infomorphisms of the channel are $h_1 = g_1 f_1$ and $h_3 = g_2 h_4$. This is the *sequential composition* of the original channels. A person a_1 is connected to a region a_3 relative to this channel if a_1 is examining some map of a_3. Of course there is also a ternary channel with the addition classification A_2 and infomorphism $h_2 = g_1 f_2$. (Note that $h_2 = g_2 f_3$ because the diagram commutes.)

Notice that although we have used talk of people, maps, and regions to illustrate this construction, it is all perfectly general and applies to allow us to sequentially compose any pair of channels that line up as depicted in the first diagram above.

6.2 Distributed Systems to Channels

Having seen how to sequentially compose binary channels, we want to generalize this substantially.

Definition 6.1. A *distributed system* $\mathcal{A}$ consists of an indexed family cla$(\mathcal{A}) = \{A_i\}_{i \in I}$ of classifications together with a set inf$(\mathcal{A})$ of infomorphisms all having both domain and codomain in cla$(\mathcal{A})$.

It is possible for A_i to be the same as A_j even if $i \neq j$. In other words, it is possible for one classification to be part of a distributed system in more than one way. This will be important in some of our applications. Also, there is no assumption that any infomorphisms in inf$(\mathcal{A})$ commute. This notion allows us to model distributed systems that are quite disparate, as in the example with Judith in the first lecture. We will show how any such system can be turned into a channel.[2]

Example 6.2. If we have a pair of binary channels as depicted above, it gives us a distributed system with five classifications and four infomorphisms.

Example 6.3. Let Z be the set of time zones. We define a classification A_z, for each $z \in Z$, as follows. The tokens of A_z are times (not their descriptions), the types of A_z are temporal descriptions, things like "12:05 A.M." The classification relation is given by $t \vDash_{A_z} \alpha$ if and only if α is the correct description of t in time zone z. For example, the time right now is of type 12:05 A.M. in A_z

---

[2] The reader versed in category theory will note that we could have required distributed systems to be subcategories of the category of all classifications with infomorphisms; this would not effect anything we do here, because it amounts to throwing in the identity infomorphisms and closing under composition.

if and only if it is now 12:05 A.M. in time zone z. There are lots of infomorphisms between these various classifications. For example, between A_e and A_p ("e" and "p" standing for Eastern and Pacific time zones in the United States, respectively), we have a token identical infomorphism $f_{ep} : A_e \rightleftarrows A_p$ given by subtracting three hours, mod 12, from the description, and changing AM to PM or vice versa when mod 12 is invoked; for example, f_{ep} of "12:05 A.M." is "9:05 P.M."

The relationship between distributed systems in general and channels is given by the following definition.

Definition 6.4. A channel $C = \{h_i : A_i \rightleftarrows C\}_{i \in I}$ *covers* a distributed system $\mathcal{A}$ if $\mathrm{cla}(\mathcal{A}) = \{A_i\}_{i \in I}$ and for each i, $j \in I$ and each infomorphism $f : A_i \rightleftarrows A_j$ in $\mathrm{inf}(\mathcal{A})$, the following diagram commutes:

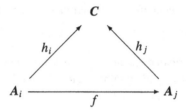

C is a *minimal cover* of $\mathcal{A}$ if it covers $\mathcal{A}$ and for every other channel $\mathcal{D}$ covering $\mathcal{A}$ there is a unique infomorphism from C to D.

A minimal cover of a system $\mathcal{A}$ turns the whole distributed system into a channel. Minimal covers of arbitrary distributed systems may be constructed in a way that generalizes our first example. Minimal covers are known as "colimits" in category theory. The fact that colimits of classifications exist is a result owing to Barr and Chu; see Barr (1991) for a discussion of the history. We state this in the following way:

Theorem 6.5. *Every distributed system has a minimal cover, and it is unique up to isomorphism.*

We are interested not just in the existence of the minimal cover but in understanding its structure, so we take some pains over proving this theorem. We will construct one particular minimal cover of $\mathcal{A}$ and dub it the "limit" of $\mathcal{A}$, written $\lim \mathcal{A}$.[3] We begin with a few simple observations.

---

[3] Strictly speaking, we should call it the colimit of $\mathcal{A}$, of course.

Proposition 6.6. *Any two minimal covers of the same distributed system are isomorphic.*

Proof. For readers familiar with universal algebra or category theory, this proof will be routine. For others, we give an outline. The key to the proof is to realize that if C is a minimal cover, then the identity is the only refinement infomorphism from C to C, because it is one, and there can be only one, by the definition of minimal cover. Now given this, suppose we had another minimal cover $\mathcal{D}$. Then there would be refinements r from C to $\mathcal{D}$ and r' from $\mathcal{D}$ to C. But then the composition $r'r$ is a refinement infomorphism from C to C and so is the identity. Hence r and r' must be inverses of one another and so r is an isomorphism. $\qquad\square$

Example 6.7. The sum of classifications is an example of a minimal cover. Given a family $\{A_i\}_{i \in I}$ of classifications, let $\mathcal{A}$ be the distributed system consisting of these classifications and no infomorphisms. The channel with core $\sum_{i \in I} A_i$ and infomorphisms $\sigma_{A_j} : A_j \rightleftarrows \sum_{i \in I} A_i$ for each $j \in I$ is a minimal cover of $\mathcal{A}$.

Example 6.8. The sequential composition of two binary channels constructed in the preceding section is a minimal cover for the distributed system consisting of five classifications and four infomorphisms.

We now generalize the construction from the special case of binary composition to arbitrary distributed systems. The construction will not yield exactly what we had before, but will yield something isomorphic to it.

Definition 6.9. Let $\mathcal{A}$ be a distributed system with classifications $\{A_i\}_{i \in I}$. The *limit* $\lim \mathcal{A}$ *of* $\mathcal{A}$ is the channel constructed as follows.

1. The core of $\lim \mathcal{A}$ is a (dual) quotient of the *sum* $A = \sum_{i \in I} A_i$ of the classifications of the system. Write c_i for the ith coordinate of a token c of A. Define the dual invariant $J = \langle C, R \rangle$ on A as follows. The set C of tokens consists of those tokens c of A such that $f(c_j) = c_i$ for each infomorphism $f : A_i \rightleftarrows A_j$ in $\inf(\mathcal{A})$. Intuitively, in terms of systems, this says we have a sequence of tokens that respects all possible whole-part relationships of the system. Define the relation R on the types of the sum by $\alpha R \alpha'$ if and only if there is an infomorphism $f : A_i \rightleftarrows A_j$ and a type $\alpha_0 \in \text{typ}(A_i)$ such that $\alpha = \sigma_i(\alpha_0)$ and $\alpha' = \sigma_j(f(\alpha_0))$. Let C be the dual quotient $\sum_{i \in I} A_i / J$.

2. To define the infomorphisms of $\lim \mathcal{A}$, let $g_j : A_j \rightleftarrows C$ (for any $j \in I$) be the pair of functions defined by

$g_j(\alpha)$ is the R-equivalence class of $\sigma_j(\alpha)$ for each $\alpha \in \text{typ}(A_j)$,

and

$g_j(c) = \sigma_j(c)$ for each $c \in \text{tok}(C)$.

This is just a restriction of the usual infomorphism from a classification to its quotient and so g_j is an infomorphism.

Justification. To see that the definition is well defined, we must verify that J is indeed a dual invariant. Suppose that $c \in C$ and that $\alpha R \alpha'$. We need to verify that

$$ c \vDash_A \alpha \quad \text{iff} \quad c \vDash_A \alpha'. $$

Because $\alpha R \alpha'$, there is an infomorphism $f : A_i \rightleftarrows A_j$ and a type $\alpha_0 \in \text{typ}(A_i)$ such that $\alpha = \sigma_i(\alpha_0)$ and $\alpha' = \sigma_j(f(\alpha_0))$. Because $c \in C$, $f(c_j) = c_i$. Thus we have the following chain of equivalences:

$$
\begin{aligned}
c \vDash_A \alpha \quad &\text{iff} \quad c \vDash_A \sigma_i(\alpha_0) \\
&\text{iff} \quad c_i \vDash_{A_i} \alpha_0 \\
&\text{iff} \quad f(c_j) \vDash_{A_i} \alpha_0 \\
&\text{iff} \quad c_j \vDash_{A_j} f(\alpha_0) \\
&\text{iff} \quad c \vDash_A \sigma_j(f(\alpha_0)) \\
&\text{iff} \quad c \vDash_A \alpha'
\end{aligned}
$$

as desired.   □

Theorem 6.10. *Given a distributed system $\mathcal{A}$, its limit $\lim \mathcal{A}$ is a minimal cover of $\mathcal{A}$.*

Proof. To see that $\lim \mathcal{A}$ is a cover, note that for each infomorphism $f : A_i \rightleftarrows A_j$ the following diagram commutes.

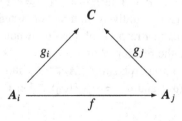

Now suppose $\mathcal{D} = \{h_i : A_i \rightleftarrows D\}_{i \in I}$ is a channel that also covers $\mathcal{A}$. Then for each $j \in I$, the following diagram commutes,

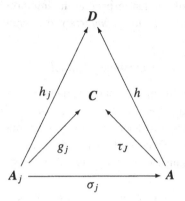

where $A = \sum_{i \in I} A_i$ and h is the sum of the infomorphisms h_j. Because h respects J, it factors uniquely through τ_J by the universal mapping property of the quotient A/J. This gives us the following commuting diagram:

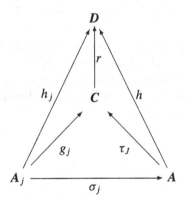

Thus r is the unique refinement infomorphism from $\text{Cha}(\mathcal{A})$ to $\mathcal{D}$, as illustrated by the upper right triangle in the diagram. $\qquad \square$

If one specializes the limit construction to the special case of sequential composition of binary channels considered in the discussion of the Xerox principle, the set of tokens is different. Instead of the pairs $\langle b_1, b_2 \rangle$ satisfying $f_2(b_1) = f_3(b_2)$ that we used there, we now find 5-tuples $\langle a_1, b_1, a_2, b_2, a_3 \rangle$ such that $a_1 = f_1(b_1)$, $f_2(b_1) = a_2 = f_3(b_2)$, and $a_3 = f_2(b_2)$. However, there is clearly a natural one-to-one correspondence between the two sets of tokens. Going one way, just throw out the a_i. Going the other way, insert the a_i as dictated by the f_i.

As a word of warning, we note that it is possible for the core of the limit of a distributed system to have an empty set of tokens. This happens when there are no sequences of tokens that respect all the infomorphisms of the system. Such a distributed system is called *completely incoherent.*

Quotient Channels

We initiated the discussion of invariants and quotients by an example involving the information flow between two copies of the same edition of a newspaper, noting how some information about one carries over intact to the other, but not all information carries. We never did really finish the discussion, though. We can do that now by taking the limit of a suitable distributed system.

Definition 6.11. Given an invariant $I = \langle \Sigma, R \rangle$ on a classification A, the *quotient channel of A by I* is the limit of the distributed system depicted by the following:

$$A \xleftarrow{\;\;\tau_I\;\;} A/I \xrightarrow{\;\;\tau_I\;\;} A$$

Notice that this distributed system has three classifications, not just two, even though two are the same. (This is made possible by the use of indexed families.) Similarly, there are two infomorphisms, each a copy of the canonical quotient infomorphism. The quotient channel makes the following diagram commute and is a refinement of any other such channel:

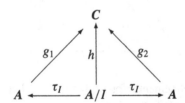

The quotient channel is easily seen to be isomorphic to the following. For each type $\alpha \in \text{typ}(A) - \Sigma$, there are two copies, say α_1 and α_2; let $\text{typ}(C)$ consist of all these types, plus the types in Σ. The tokens of C consist of triples $c = \langle a_1, b, a_2 \rangle$, where $[a_1]_R = b = [a_2]_R$. The classification relation is defined for such $c = \langle a_1, b, a_2 \rangle$ by

$$
\begin{aligned}
c \vDash_C \alpha \quad &\text{iff} \quad b \vDash_{A/I} \alpha \quad &&\text{for} \quad \alpha \in \Sigma \\
c \vDash_C \alpha_1 \quad &\text{iff} \quad a_1 \vDash_A \alpha \quad &&\text{for} \quad \alpha \in \text{typ}(A) - \Sigma \\
c \vDash_C \alpha_2 \quad &\text{iff} \quad a_2 \vDash_A \alpha \quad &&\text{for} \quad \alpha \in \text{typ}(A) - \Sigma
\end{aligned}
$$

The obvious infomorphisms $g_i : A_i \rightleftarrows C$ and $h : A/I \rightleftarrows C$ are defined by the following: each infomorphism is an inclusion on types, whereas on a token $c = \langle a_1, b, a_2 \rangle$, $f_i(c) = a_i$, and $h(c) = b$.

Now suppose that c connects a_1, b, and a_2. Then for any type $\alpha \in \Sigma$, we have $a_1 \vDash_A \alpha$ if and only if $b \vDash_{A/I} \alpha$ if and only if $a_2 \vDash_A \alpha$. On the other hand, if $\alpha \in \text{typ}(A) - \Sigma$, then $a_1 \vDash_A \alpha$ carries no information at all about b or a_2 via this channel.

Example 6.12. To finish up our newspaper example (5.8), let A and $I = \langle \Sigma, R \rangle$ be as in Example 5.8 and let C be its quotient channel. The equivalence class $[a]_R$ models the edition of a so a token $c = \langle a_1, b, a_2 \rangle$ of C is a model of the connection that exists between a_1 and a_2 if they are of the same edition. We see that for types in $\alpha \in \Sigma$, information about a particular newspaper a_1 carries information both about its edition, $[a_1]_R$, as well as about any other token a_2 of that same edition. That is, a_1 being of type α carries the information that a_2 is of the same type, relative to this channel, as long as $\alpha \in \Sigma$. Notice that this does not hold for $\alpha \in \text{typ}(A) - \Sigma$. Having an orange juice stain would be such a type.

Exercises

6.1. What are the infomorphisms g_1 and g_2 in the map example?

6.2. Determine the limit of the time-zone distributed system. Obtain a simpler, isomorphic minimal cover of this system. Interpret your results in terms of time zones.

6.3. Define a notion of *parallel composition* of binary channels.

6.4. Give an example of a completely incoherent distributed system.

Lecture 7

Boolean Operations and Classifications

The notion of a classification does not build in any assumptions about closure under the usual Boolean operations. It is natural to ask What role do the usual Boolean connectives play in information and its flow? This lecture takes an initial step toward answering this question. We will return to this question in later chapters as we develop more tools. It is not a central topic of the book, but it is one that needs to be addressed in a book devoted to the logic of information flow.

Actually, there are two ways of understanding Boolean operations on classifications. There are Boolean operations mapping classifications to classifications, and there are Boolean operations internal to (many) classifications. Because there is a way to explain the latter in terms of the former, we first discuss the Boolean operations on classifications.

7.1 Boolean Operations on Classifications

Given a set Φ of types in a classification, it is often useful to group together the class of tokens that are of *every* type in Φ. In general, there is no type in the classification with this extension. As a remedy, we can always construct a classification in which such a type exists. Likewise, we can construct a classification in which there is a type whose extension consists of all those tokens that are of at least one of the types in Φ.

Definition 7.1. Given a classification A, the *disjunctive power* of A, written $\vee A$, and the *conjunctive power* of A, written $\wedge A$, are classifications specified as follows. Each of these classifications has the same tokens as A and has $\text{pow}(\text{typ}(A))$ as type set. Given $a \in \text{tok}(A)$ and $\Phi \subseteq \text{typ}(A)$,

1. $a \vDash_{\vee A} \Phi$ if and only if $a \vDash_A \sigma$ for some $\sigma \in \Phi$;
2. $a \vDash_{\wedge A} \Phi$ if and only if $a \vDash_A \sigma$ for *every* $\sigma \in \Phi$.

Proposition 7.2. *For each classification A, there are natural embeddings* $\eta_A^d : A \rightleftarrows \vee A$ *and* $\eta_A^c : A \rightleftarrows \wedge A$ *defined by*

1. $\eta_A^d(\alpha) = \eta_A^c(\alpha) = \{\alpha\}$ *for each* $\alpha \in \text{typ}(A)$ *and*
2. $\eta_A^d(a) = \eta_A^c(a) = a$ *for each* $a \in \text{tok}(\vee A) = \text{tok}(\wedge A)$.

Proof. Both η_A^d and η_A^c are clearly injective. They are infomorphisms because $a \vDash_A \alpha$ if and only if $a \vDash_{\vee A} \{\alpha\}$ if and only if $a \vDash_{\wedge A} \{\alpha\}$. $\square$

Another useful operation on classifications is negation.

Definition 7.3. Given a classification A, the *negation of* A, $\neg A$ is the classification with the same tokens and types as A such that for each token a and type α,

$$a \vDash_{\neg A} \alpha \quad \text{iff} \quad a \nvDash_A \alpha.$$

These operations on classifications have counterparts on infomorphisms.

Definition 7.4. Let $f : A \rightleftarrows B$ be an infomorphism. We define infomorphisms $\vee f : \vee A \rightleftarrows \vee B$, $\wedge f : \wedge A \rightleftarrows \wedge B$, and $\neg f : \neg A \rightleftarrows \neg B$ as follows: All three of these agree with f on tokens. On types they are defined by

1. $\vee f(\Theta) = f[\Theta]$ for all $\Theta \subseteq \text{typ}(A)$;
2. $\wedge f(\Theta) = f[\Theta]$ for all $\Theta \subseteq \text{typ}(A)$; and
3. $\neg f(\alpha) = f(\alpha)$

Justification. We need to verify that these are indeed infomorphisms. We check the first. We need to check that for all $b \in \text{tok}(B)$ and all $\Theta \subseteq \text{typ}(A)$, $f(b) \vDash_{\vee A} \Theta$ if and only if $b \vDash_{\vee B} \vee f(\Theta)$. This is seen by the following chain of equivalences:

$$
\begin{aligned}
f(b) \vDash_{\vee A} \Theta \quad &\text{iff} \quad f(b) \vDash_A \alpha \text{ for some } \alpha \in \Theta \\
&\text{iff} \quad b \vDash_B f(\alpha) \text{ for some } \alpha \in \Theta \\
&\text{iff} \quad b \vDash_B \beta \text{ for some } \beta \in f[\Theta] \\
&\text{iff} \quad b \vDash_{\vee B} (\vee f)(\Theta)
\end{aligned}
$$

The others are similar and are left to the reader. $\square$

Another Duality

Notice that for each classification A, $\neg\neg A = A$. Consequently, the negation operation on classifications and infomorphisms gives us a second duality, the classical duality of Boolean algebra. Under this duality conjunction is the dual of disjunction. For example, $\neg(\vee A) = \wedge\neg A$ and $\neg(\wedge A) = \vee\neg A$. Under this duality, unlike the flip duality, the direction of infomorphisms is not reversed.

7.2 Boolean Operations in Classifications

We can use the Boolean operations on classifications to determine what it would mean for an operation on types to be a disjunction, conjunction, or negation in a classification. Recall the notion of a token identical infomorphism from Definition 5.19.

Definition 7.5. Let A be a classification.

1. A *disjunction infomorphism* on A is a token identical infomorphism $d : \vee A \rightleftarrows A$; the corresponding operation $d^\wedge$ is called a disjunction on A. Given a disjunction infomorphism d and a set Θ of types, we often write $\vee\Theta$ for $d^\wedge(\Theta)$.
2. A *conjunction infomorphism* on A is a token identical infomorphism $c : \wedge A \rightleftarrows A$; the corresponding operation $c^\wedge$ is called a conjunction on A. Given a conjunction infomorphism c and a set Θ of types, we often write $\wedge\Theta$ for $c^\wedge(\Theta)$.
3. A *negation infomorphism* on A is a token identical infomorphism $n : \neg A \rightleftarrows A$. Given a negation infomorphism n and a type α, we often write $\neg\alpha$ for $n^\wedge(\alpha)$.

It is easy to see that if d is a token identical infomorphism, then d is a disjunction on A if and only if for every set Θ of types and every token a, $a \vDash_A d(\Theta)$ if and only if $a \vDash_A \alpha$ for some $\alpha \in \Theta$. Likewise, c is a conjunction on A if and only if for every set Θ of types and every token a, $a \vDash_A c(\Theta)$ if and only if $a \vDash_A \alpha$ for all $\alpha \in \Theta$. Similarly, n is a negation if and only if for every $\alpha \in \mathrm{typ}(A)$ and every token a, $a \nvDash_A n(\alpha)$ if and only if $a \vDash_A \alpha$.

7.3 Boolean Classifications

Definition 7.6. A classification B is *Boolean* if it has a disjunction $\bigvee$, conjunction $\bigwedge$, and negation $\neg$.

Boolean classifications are expressively rich. We make this precise in the next result. Call a set $X \subseteq \mathrm{tok}(A)$ *closed under indistinguishability* in A provided that whenever $a_1 \in X$ and $a_1 \sim_A a_2$, then $a_2 \in X$. Clearly every set of tokens of the form $X = \text{tok}(\alpha)$, for $\alpha \in \text{typ}(A)$, is closed under indistinguishability. The Boolean classifications are the classifications in which every set closed under indistinguishability has this form. We leave the proof of the following result to Exercise 7.3. An answer is provided.

Proposition 7.7. *A classification A is Boolean if and only if for every set X of tokens closed under indistinguishability there is a type α such that $X = \text{typ}(\alpha)$.*

Every classification can be canonically embedded in a Boolean classification. We define this classification here. The classification defined will turn out to be important in our discussion of state spaces.

Definition 7.8. A *partition* of a set Σ is a pair $\langle \Gamma, \Delta \rangle$ of subsets of Σ such that $\Gamma \cup \Delta = \Sigma$ and $\Gamma \cap \Delta = \emptyset$.[1] Given a classification A and a token a of A, the *state description* of a is the pair

$$\text{state}_A(a) = \langle \text{typ}(a), \text{typ}(A) - \text{typ}(a) \rangle$$

Notice that such a state description forms a partition of $\text{typ}(A)$.

Definition 7.9. Let A be a classification. The Boolean closure of A, written *Boole*(A), is the classification defined as follows:

1. the tokens of $\text{Boole}(A)$ are the tokens of A;
2. the types of $\text{Boole}(A)$ are arbitrary *sets of* partitions of the types of A; and
3. the classification relation is defined by $a \vDash_{\text{Boole}(A)} \alpha$ if and only if $\text{state}_A(a) \in \alpha$.

We define a token identical, injective infomorphism $\eta_A : A \rightleftarrows \text{Boole}(A)$ by

$$\eta_A(\alpha) = \{\langle \Gamma, \Delta \rangle \text{ a partition} \mid \alpha \in \Gamma\}.$$

Justification. Notice that $\eta_A(\alpha)$ is indeed a set of partitions of the types of A and hence a type of our target classification. It is obvious that $\eta_A : A \rightleftarrows \text{Boole}(A)$ is an injective infomorphism. □

Proposition 7.10. *For any classification A, the operations of union, intersection, and complement are a disjunction, conjunction, and negation, respectively, on* Boole(A).

---

[1] These are sometimes called "quasi-partitions" because it is not assumed that the sets are nonempty. We will be using the notion too frequently to put up with such unpleasant terminology, however.

Proof. This is easy, given the definitions. For example, to see that $\bigcap$ is a conjunction, we need only note that the state description of a token is in every $\alpha \in \Gamma$ if and only if it is in $\bigcap \Gamma$. $\square$

Exercises

7.1.   Prove Proposition 7.7.

7.2.   For any classification A, show that
1. $\neg\neg A = A$
2. $\neg \wedge A = \vee \neg A$
3. $\neg \vee A = \wedge \neg A$

7.3.   Show that for any classifications A and B, $\neg(A + B) = \neg A + \neg B$.
Conclude that $\neg(\neg A + \neg B) = A + B$.

7.4.   Find an infomorphism $f : \wedge\wedge A \rightleftarrows \wedge A$ such that $f \eta^c_{\wedge A} = 1_{\wedge A}$.

7.5.   Investigate the properties of the finite analogs of the Boolean operations studied in the chapter.

Lecture 8

State Spaces

State-space models are one of the most prevalent tools in science and applied mathematics. In this lecture, we show how state spaces are related to classifications and how systems of state spaces are related to information channels. As a result, we will discover that state spaces provide a rich source of information channels. In later lectures, we will exploit the relationship between state spaces and classifications in our study of local logics.

8.1 State Spaces and Projections

Definition 8.1. A *state space* is a classification S for which each token is of exactly one type. The types of a state space are called *states*, and we say that a is *in state* σ if $a \vDash_S \sigma$. The state space S is *complete* if every state is the state of some token.

Example 8.2. In Example 4.5 we pointed out that for any function $f : A \to B$, there is a classification whose types are elements of B and whose tokens are elements of A and such that $a \vDash b$ if and only if $b = f(a)$. This classification is a state space and every state space arises in this way, so another way to put the definition is to say that a state space is a classification S in which the classification relation $\vDash_S$ is a total function. For this reason, we write $\text{state}_S(a)$ for the state σ of a in S. In defining a state space S, we will often proceed by specifying its tokens, types, and the function $\sigma = \text{state}_A(a)$. The state space S is complete if and only if this function is surjective.

Because the classification relation in state spaces is a function, we depict them by diagrams of the following kind:

We call a state space S *ideal* if $\text{typ}(S) = \text{tok}(S)$ and for each $s \in \text{tok}(S)$, $\text{state}_S(s) = s$. For any set S there is exactly one ideal state space S with types and tokens that are the members of S. This is an extremely simple example but it lets us see that we are generalizing the usual notion of a state space, where tokens are ignored. One can simply identify the standard notion of a state space with our notion of an ideal state space. Notice that ideal state spaces are necessarily complete.

We have given a number of examples of state spaces in Lecture 3. We present some additional examples here.

Example 8.3. Let A be a sequence of n gravitating bodies, let T be some ordered set modeling time, and let

$$S = \{\langle A, t \rangle \mid t \in T\}$$

be the set of tokens, with $\langle A, t \rangle$ modeling the bodies at time t. A *Newtonian state space* with tokens S and states $\Omega = R^{6n}$ represents the position and velocity of the bodies at time t.

Example 8.4. If we depict a finite state space as a table, then there must be exactly one "1" in each row, as in the following:

S	α_1	α_2	α_3	α_4	α_5
a_1	1	0	0	0	0
a_2	1	0	0	0	0
a_3	0	1	0	0	0
a_4	0	0	1	0	0

The flip $S^\perp$ of a state space is not in general a state space, of course.

Example 8.5. A molecule of DNA is made up of a long double strand of simpler molecules, called *bases*, and denoted by A, T, C, and G. For example, we might have

```
G   T   A   T   C   C   G   · · ·
‖   |   |   |   ‖   ‖   ‖
C   A   T   A   G   G   C   · · ·
```

Because of the bonding properties of the bases, C and G are always paired together, as are T and A. Information about the genetic makeup of an individual plant or animal is encoded in such a strand. Strings from individuals of a single species will be similar in most regards, and quite different from individuals of other species. Because of the nature of the bonding, any strand of DNA can be characterized by a single string on the alphabet {A, T, C, G}. Thus we can form a state space S_{DNA} whose tokens are strands of DNA and whose types are finite strings on {A, T, C, G}. The state of a strand is the sequence that characterizes it.

In 1953, Crick and Watson observed that if a single strand of DNA were to split and recombine naturally with free molecules of the four bases, two strands would form, each identical in structure to the original. Following up on this idea, Meselson and Stahl showed in 1956 that such splits and recombinations do indeed account for the production of new DNA from old. These connections allow one strand to carry a great deal of information about the other because any two strands of DNA that are connected will normally (mutations being the exceptions) be of the same type. (See Exercise 8.1.)

Example 8.6. In Example 4.6, we defined the truth classification of a language L. This is not a state space as every model will satisfy more than one sentence. However, there is a closely related state space where we take states to be sets of sentences and assign to each model its complete theory, the set of all sentences true in the model.

8.2 Projections and Products

Definition 8.7. A *(state space) projection* $f : S_1 \rightrightarrows S_2$ from state space S_1 to state space S_2 is given by a covariant pair of functions such that for each token $a \in \text{tok}(S_1)$,

$$f(\text{state}_{S_1}(a)) = \text{state}_{S_2}(f(a)).$$

This requirement can be rephrased by saying that the following diagram commutes:

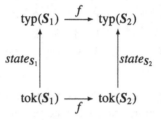

$$\begin{array}{ccc} \text{typ}(S_1) & \xrightarrow{\ f\ } & \text{typ}(S_2) \\ \uparrow {\scriptstyle states_1} & & \uparrow {\scriptstyle states_2} \\ \text{tok}(S_1) & \xrightarrow[f]{} & \text{tok}(S_2) \end{array}$$

(In this diagram we have left off the up and down symbols on f, as we often do when no confusion is likely.)

Example 8.8. Recall the Newtonian state spaces of Example 8.3. Given a sequence A of n gravitating bodies and a set T of times, we took $S = \{\langle A, t \rangle \mid t \in T\}$ as the set of tokens and $\Omega = R^{6n}$ as the set of states. A state space S with these tokens and types models the physical system through time. Now consider a subsequence A_0 of A consisting of, say, $m < n$ objects and consider S_0 to be the analogous state space representing this system of bodies in A_0 through time. There is a natural projection $f : S \rightrightarrows S_0$ defined as follows. For a token $\langle A, t \rangle$ we define $f(\langle A, t \rangle) = x \langle A_0, t \rangle$. This just assigns to the whole system at time t the subsystem at the same time. Given a state $\sigma \in R^{6n}$, $f(\sigma)$ is the vector in R^{6m} that picks out the position and velocity of the bodies in A_0.

Example 8.9. Given projections $f : S_1 \rightrightarrows S_2$ and $g : S_2 \rightrightarrows S_3$, the *composition* $gf : S_1 \rightrightarrows S_3$ of f and g is the projection defined by $(gf)\hat{\ } = g\hat{\ }f\hat{\ }$ and $(gf)\check{\ } = g\check{\ }f\check{\ }$. It is straightforward to see that gf is indeed a projection.

Example 8.10. The *identity* $1_S : S \rightrightarrows S$ on S, which is the identity on both tokens and states, is clearly a projection.

In dealing with classifications, the operation of summation was central. With state spaces, products play the analogous role.

Definition 8.11. Given state spaces S_1 and S_2, the *product* $S_1 \times S_2$ of S_1 and S_2 is the classification defined as follows:

1. The set of tokens of $S_1 \times S_2$ is the Cartesian product of $\text{tok}(S_1)$ and $\text{tok}(S_2)$;
2. the set of types of $S_1 \times S_2$ is the Cartesian product of $\text{typ}(S_1)$ and $\text{typ}(S_2)$; and
3. $\langle a, b \rangle \models_{S_1 \times S_2} \langle \alpha, \beta \rangle$ if and only if $a \models_{S_1} \alpha$ and $b \models_{S_2} \beta$.

There are natural projections $\pi_{S_1} : S_1 \times S_2 \rightrightarrows S_1$ and $\pi_{S_2} : S_1 \times S_2 \rightrightarrows S_2$ defined as follows.

1. For each $\langle \alpha, \beta \rangle \in \text{typ}(S_1 \times S_2)$, $\pi_{S_1}(\langle \alpha, \beta \rangle) = \alpha$ and $\pi_{S_2}(\langle \alpha, \beta \rangle) = \beta$.
2. For each $\langle a, b \rangle \in \text{tok}(S_1 \times S_2)$, $\pi_{S_1}(\langle a, b \rangle) = a$ and $\pi_{S_2}(\langle a, b \rangle) = b$.

Justification. It is clear that $S_1 \times S_2$ is a state space and that $\text{state}_{S_1 \times S_2}(\langle a, b \rangle) = \langle \text{state}_{S_1}(a), \text{state}_{S_2}(b) \rangle$. It is routine to verify that $\pi_{S_1} : S_1 \times S_2 \rightrightarrows S_1$ and $\pi_{S_2} : S_1 \times S_2 \rightrightarrows S_2$ satisfy the defining condition for projections. □

The *product* $\prod_{i \in I} S_i$ of an indexed family $\{S_i\}_{i \in I}$ of state spaces is defined similarly.

8.3 Subspaces

In order to capture the laws of a physical system, we found it convenient in Lecture 3 to carve out a subspace of a state space by means of imposing certain equations of state. Here is the general notion.

Definition 8.12. A state space S_0 is a *subspace* of a state space S_1, written $S_0 \subseteq S_1$, if the pair $\iota = \langle \iota\hat{\ }, \iota\check{\ } \rangle$ of functions that is the identity $\iota\hat{\ }$ on states and $\iota\check{\ }$ on tokens is a projection $\iota : S_0 \rightrightarrows S_1$.

Equivalently, $S_0 \subseteq S_1$ if and only if the tokens of S_0 are a subset of the tokens of S_1, the states of S_0 are a subset of the states of S_1, and the state function of S_0 is the restriction of the state function of S_1 to the tokens of S_0.

Example 8.13. Let R^{6n} be the set of states in the position and momentum state space for n bodies moving through space. The energy of the system of bodies is some (typically differentiable) function of the position and momentum of the bodies, say $E(p_1, x_1, \ldots, p_n, x_n)$. (Here p_i is the triple representing the position of the ith body, x_i its momentum.) If the system is isolated, then its energy remains constant over time, at some value, say e_0. Thus the states the system can actually occupy are the solutions to the equation

$$E(p_1, x_1, \ldots, p_n, x_n) = e_0.$$

If E is differentiable, the solution space is a differential manifold M embedded in R^{6n} and the system will always have a state in M. Restricting the tokens to those whose states are in M will capture the fact that energy is conserved in isolated physical systems.

Definition 8.14. Let $f : S \rightrightarrows S'$ be a state space projection.

1. Given a subspace S_0 of S, the *image* of S_0 under f, written $f[S_0]$, is the subspace of S' whose tokens are those in the range of $f^\vee$ and whose states are those in the range of $f^\wedge$.
2. Similarly, given a subspace S_1 of S', the *inverse image* of S_1 under f, written $f^{-1}[S_1]$, is the subspace of S whose tokens are those in $f^{\vee -1}[\text{tok}(S_1)]$ and whose states are those in $f^{\wedge -1}[\text{typ}(S_1)]$.

Justification. We need to verify that $f[S_0]$ is a subspace of S' and that $f^{-1}[S_1]$ is a subspace of S. We verify the latter and leave the former to the reader. Suppose a is a token of $f^{-1}[S_1]$. We need to make sure that $\text{state}_S(a)$ is a state in $f^{-1}[S_1]$. By definition, $f(a)$ is a token of S_1. Hence $\text{state}_{S'}(f(a))$ is a state of S_1, because $S_1 \subseteq S'$. But $\text{state}_{S'}(f(a)) = f(\text{state}_S(a))$ because f is a projection. Hence $\text{state}_S(a)$ is a state in $f^{-1}[S_1]$, as desired.   □

8.4 Event Classifications

Given a state space S, its states represent total information about the tokens, relative to the classification. Usually, however, we have only partial information about a token. The common way around this is to turn to the "event classification" of S, which we write as Evt(S). (The terminology, not entirely felicitous for reasons explained in Lecture 2, comes from probability theory.) Projections on state spaces correspond to infomorphisms of the associated event classifications.

Definition 8.15. The *event classification* Evt(S) associated with a state space S has as tokens the tokens of S. Its types are arbitrary sets of states of S. The classification relation is given by $a \vDash_{\text{Evt}(S)} \alpha$ if and only if $\text{state}_S(a) \in \alpha$.

As we saw in Lecture 3, these event classifications are a useful tool for understanding the relationship between linguistic accounts of the world, both scientific and common sense accounts, and scientific models of the world.

Example 8.16. Recall the DNA state space S_{DNA} from Example 8.5. The classification Evt(S_{DNA}) is quite useful. Certain sets of states correspond to genetic traits. For example, there will be certain sets of states that correspond to DNA strands from humans with green eyes. This suggests the following infomorphism. Let **Genes** be a classification of humans by their genetic traits. Thus the types of A include things like the gene GREEN-EYES for green eyes, and so forth, with $a \vDash_A \alpha$ if and only if a carries the genetic trait α. Let *hgp*: **Gene** $\rightleftarrows$ Evt(S_{DNA}) be defined on (gene) types by the following: *hgp*(α) is the set of strings that characterize strands of DNA of individuals of type α. On tokens, *hgp*(s) is the individual whose strand of DNA is s. This is an infomorphism because genetic traits are entirely determined by DNA. The famous Human Genome Project can be thought of as attempting to characterize this infomorphism, which is why we have dubbed it "*hgp*."

Let S_1 and S_2 be state spaces and let $f : S_1 \rightrightarrows S_2$ be covariant. Define a contravariant pair Evt(f) : Evt(S_2) $\rightleftarrows$ Evt(S_1) as follows. On tokens, Evt(f) and f are the same: Evt(f)$^\vee(a) = f^\vee(a)$ for $a \in$ tok(Evt(S_1)). On types $\alpha \in$ typ(Evt(S_2)), Evt(f)(α) = $f^{-1}[\alpha]$.

Proposition 8.17. *Given state spaces S_1 and S_2, the following are equivalent:*

1. $f : S_1 \rightrightarrows S_2$ is a projection;
2. Evt(f) : Evt(S_2) $\rightleftarrows$ Evt(S_1) is an infomorphism.

Proof. Assume $f : S_1 \rightrightarrows S_2$ is a state-space projection. To show that Evt(f) is an infomorphism, let $a \in$ tok(Evt(S_1)) and let $\alpha \in$ typ(Evt(S_2)). Then

$$\begin{aligned}
\text{Evt}(f)(a) \vDash_{\text{Evt}(S_2)} \alpha \quad &\text{iff} \quad \text{state}_{S_2}(f(a)) \in \alpha \\
&\text{iff} \quad f(\text{state}_{S_1}(a)) \in \alpha \\
&\text{iff} \quad \text{state}_{S_1}(a) \in f^{-1}[\alpha] \\
&\text{iff} \quad a \vDash_{\text{Evt}(S_1)} f^{-1}[\alpha] \\
&\text{iff} \quad a \vDash_{\text{Evt}(S_1)} \text{Evt}(f)(\alpha)
\end{aligned}$$

To prove the converse, suppose Evt(f) is an infomorphism. We need to check that $\text{state}_{S_2}(f(a)) = f(\text{state}_{S_1}(a))$. Let $\text{state}_{S_1}(a) = \sigma$. We show that $\text{state}_{S_2}(f(a)) = f(\sigma)$. Let $\sigma' = \text{state}_{S_2}(f(a))$, which we can write as $f(a) \vDash_{\text{Evt}(S_2)} \{\sigma'\}$. Because Evt($f$) is an infomorphism,

$$f(a) \vDash_{\text{Evt}(S_2)} \{\sigma'\} \quad \text{iff} \quad a \vDash_{\text{Evt}(S_1)} f^{-1}(\sigma'),$$

so $a \vDash_{\text{Evt}(S_1)} f^{-1}(\sigma')$, which means that $\sigma \in f^{-1}(\sigma')$, that is, $f(\sigma) = \sigma'$, as desired. $\square$

The following makes event classifications especially well behaved.

Proposition 8.18. *For any state space S, the classification Evt(S) is a Boolean classification. Indeed, the operations of intersection, union, and complement are a conjunction, disjunction, and negation, respectively.*

Proof. These are all routine. Let us prove that the complement operation is a negation. For readability, we write $-\alpha$ for typ(A) $-\alpha$. We show that for any set α of states, $a \nvDash_{\text{Evt}(S)} \alpha$ if and only if $a \vDash_{\text{Evt}(S)} -\alpha$. But $a \nvDash_{\text{Evt}(S)} \alpha$ if and only if $\text{state}_S(a) \notin \alpha$ if and only if $\text{state}_S(a) \in -\alpha$ if and only if $a \vDash_{\text{Evt}(S)} -\alpha$, as desired.   □

8.5 State Spaces from Classifications

The classifications naturally associated with first-order logic, where tokens are structures and sentences are types, are not state spaces. We saw in Example 8.6, however, that there is a natural state space associated with each such classification, namely, where we take the state of a structure to be its complete theory. We can do something similar for an arbitrary classification.

Given a classification A and a token a of A, recall from Definition 7.8 that the *state description* of a is the pair

$$\text{state}_A(a) = \langle \text{typ}(a), \text{typ}(A) - \text{typ}(a) \rangle.$$

Thus the state description forms a partition of typ(A).

Definition 8.19. Given a classification A, the *free state space* Ssp(A) of A is defined as follows:

1. The tokens of Ssp(A) are the same as those of A;
2. the states of Ssp(A) are arbitrary partitions $\langle \Gamma, \Delta \rangle$ of the types of A; and
3. $\text{state}_{\text{Ssp}(A)}(a)$ is the state description $\text{state}_A(a)$ of a in A.

Let A and B be classifications, and let $f : A \rightleftarrows B$ be a contravariant pair of functions. Define a covariant pair of functions Ssp(f) : Ssp(B) $\rightrightarrows$ Ssp(A) as follows. On tokens, Ssp(f) and f are the same: $\text{Ssp}(f)^\vee(b) = f^\vee(b)$ for $b \in \text{tok}(B)$. On partitions, Ssp(f) is defined by

$$\text{Ssp}(f)(\langle \Gamma, \Delta \rangle) = \langle f^{\wedge -1}[\Gamma], f^{\wedge -1}[\Delta] \rangle.$$

Proposition 8.20. *Let A and B be classifications, and let $f : A \rightleftarrows B$ be a contravariant pair of functions. The following are equivalent:*

1. *$f : A \rightleftarrows B$ is an infomorphism;*
2. *Ssp(f) : Ssp(B) $\rightrightarrows$ Ssp(A) is a state space projection.*

Proof. To prove the implication from (1) to (2), we need to show that for all $b \in \text{tok}(B)$, $\text{Ssp}(f)(\text{state}_B(b)) = \text{state}_A(\text{Ssp}(f)(b))$. To simplify notation, let

$g = \mathrm{Ssp}(f)$ and let $\mathrm{state}_B(b) = \langle \Gamma, \Delta \rangle$ be the state description of b in B. To show that $g(\langle \Gamma, \Delta \rangle)$ is the state description of $g(b) = f(b)$ in A, we need to show that $\alpha \in f^{\wedge -1}[\Gamma]$ if and only if $f(b) \vDash_A \alpha$ and similarly that $\alpha \in f^{\wedge -1}[\Delta]$ if and only if $f(b) \nvDash_A \alpha$ for every $\alpha \in \mathrm{typ}(A)$. The first of these is verified as follows:

$$\begin{aligned}
\alpha \in f^{\wedge -1}[\Gamma] \quad &\text{iff} \quad f(\alpha) \in \Gamma \\
&\text{iff} \quad b \vDash_B f(\alpha) \\
&\text{iff} \quad f(b) \vDash_A \alpha.
\end{aligned}$$

The second verification is similar.

To prove that (2) implies (1), assume that $\mathrm{Ssp}(f)$ is a state-space projection. We need to check that for $b \in \mathrm{tok}(B)$ and $\alpha \in \mathrm{typ}(A)$, $f(b) \vDash_A \alpha$ if and only if $b \vDash_B f(\alpha)$. Suppose that $b \nvDash_B f(\alpha)$. Then $f(\alpha)$ is in the second coordinate of the state description of b in B. But then because $\mathrm{Ssp}(f)$ is a projection, α is in the second coordinate of the state description of $f(b)$ in A. But that means $f(b) \nvDash_A \alpha$. The proof of the converse is similar, using first coordinates. □

8.6 Back to Boole

The question naturally arises as to what happens if we start with a state space, construct its event classification, and then construct the state space associated with that. Or, to start in the other way, we can begin with a classification, construct its state space, and then construct its event classification. In this section we study this question.

In Lecture 3, we relied at one point on the fact that any infomorphism $f : A \rightleftarrows \mathrm{Evt}(S)$ of a classification into an event classification has a natural extension to the Boolean closure $\mathrm{Boole}(A)$ of A; that is, there is an f^* agreeing with f of A such that $f^* : \mathrm{Boole}(A) \rightleftarrows \mathrm{Evt}(S)$ is an infomorphism. The reason for this will fall out of our discussion.

Proposition 8.21. *For any classification A,*

$$\mathrm{Boole}(A) = \mathrm{Evt}(\mathrm{Ssp}(A)).$$

Proof. This amounts to unwinding the two definitions to see that they come to the same thing. □

The correspondence between state spaces and event classifications is closely related to the Stone representation theorem for Boolean algebras. (If we define the obvious Boolean algebra on the type set of a Boolean classification then the

partitions used in the construction of its state-space are in one-to-one correspondence with the points of the corresponding Stone space. Our main addition
to the Stone representation theorem is in keeping track of the classification
relation throughout the construction. See Davey and Priestlay (1990) for an
excellent introduction to representation theorems.)

Recall the token identical embedding of $\eta_A : A \rightleftarrows \text{Boole}(A)$ of a classification A into its Boolean closure. In view of the above proposition, this means we
have a token identical embedding $\eta_A : A \rightleftarrows \text{Evt}(\text{Ssp}(A))$. On types $\alpha \in \text{typ}(A)$

$$\eta_A(\alpha) = \{\langle \Gamma, \Delta \rangle \text{ a partition} \mid \alpha \in \Gamma\}.$$

In mathematical terms, the next result shows that for any classification A,
the state space $\text{Ssp}(A)$ is "free" on A. It can also be taken as showing that
given a state space S and a classification A, there is a natural bijection between
infomorphisms $f : A \rightleftarrows \text{Evt}(S)$ and projections $g : S \rightrightarrows \text{Ssp}(A)$.

Proposition 8.22. *Let S be a state space and let A be a classification. For every
infomorphism $f : A \rightleftarrows \text{Evt}(S)$ there is a unique projection $g : S \rightrightarrows \text{Ssp}(A)$ such
that the following diagram commutes:*

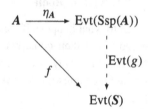

Proof. First, assume $g : S \rightrightarrows \text{Ssp}(A)$ is any projection that makes the diagram
commute. Because η_A is the identity on tokens, it is clear that f and g agree on
tokens. On types, the commuting of the diagram insures that

$$f(\alpha) = \{\sigma \in \text{typ}(S) \mid \alpha \in 1^{st}(g(\sigma))\}.$$

But this means that

$$\sigma \in f(\alpha) \quad \text{iff} \quad \alpha \in 1^{st}(g(\sigma)).$$

Because $g : S \rightrightarrows \text{Ssp}(A)$, this tells us that

$$g\hat{}(\sigma) = \langle \{\alpha \mid \sigma \in f(\alpha)\}, \{\alpha \mid \sigma \notin f(\alpha)\} \rangle.$$

So let us use this equation to define $g\hat{\ }$. It is easy to check that g is a projection and that the diagram commutes. □

This proposition expresses a much simpler idea than it might seem, as is shown by the following example.

Example 8.23. Recall the infomorphism $hgp: \textbf{\textit{Gene}} \rightleftarrows \text{Evt}(S_{DNA})$ encoding genetic traits of humans in terms of strands of their DNA. This infomorphism has the form of f in the proposition, so we are promised a projection $g: S_{DNA} \rightrightarrows \text{Ssp}(\textbf{\textit{Gene}})$ bearing a certain relationship to f. This projection is the same as hgp on tokens; that is, it assigns to each strand of DNA the individual from which it came. On a state $\sigma \in \{A, T, C, G\}^*$, g partitions the genetic traits into those that are compatible with DNA of type σ and those that are not. The infomorphism hgp and the projection g are, up to the embedding of $\textbf{\textit{Gene}}$ in its Boolean closure, two ways of looking at the same coding of human genetic traits by DNA.

As a consequence of the proposition, we obtain the desired ability to lift infomorphisms to Boolean closures of classifications.

Corollary 8.24. *Every infomorphism f of the form $f : A \rightleftarrows \text{Evt}(S)$ of a classification into an event classification has a natural extension to an infomorphism $f^* : \text{Boole}(A) \rightleftarrows \text{Evt}(S)$.*

Proof. In view of Proposition 8.21, we can just let $f^* = \text{Evt}(g)$, where g is given as in Proposition 8.22. □

If we examine the proof of Proposition 8.22, we can get a little more information from it. Namely, we can see how to define the projection g from the infomorphism f. First we need a definition.

Definition 8.25. For any state space S, let $\mu_S : S \rightrightarrows \text{Ssp}(\text{Evt}(S))$ be the injective, token-identical projection defined as follows: for any state $\sigma \in \text{typ}(S)$

$$\mu_S(\sigma) = \langle\{\Gamma \subseteq \text{typ}(S) \mid \sigma \in \Gamma\}, \{\Delta \subseteq \text{typ}(S) \mid \sigma \notin \Delta\}\rangle.$$

Justification. Notice that $\mu_S(\sigma)$ is indeed a partition of the types of $\text{Evt}(S)$ and hence a state of our target state space. It is obvious that $\mu_S : S \rightrightarrows \text{Ssp}(\text{Evt}(S))$ is an injective projection. □

Corollary 8.26. *If the diagram on the left commutes, then so does that on the right.*

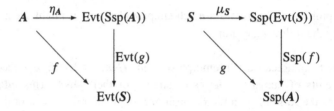

Proof. Recall that $\text{Ssp}(f)$ agrees with f on tokens and on types satisfies

$$\text{Ssp}(f)(\langle \Gamma, \Delta \rangle) = \langle f^{\wedge -1}[\Gamma], f^{\wedge -1}[\Delta] \rangle.$$

On the other hand,

$$\mu_S(\sigma) = \langle \{\Gamma \subseteq \text{typ}(S) \mid \sigma \in \Gamma\}, \{\Delta \subseteq \text{typ}(S) \mid \sigma \notin \Delta\} \rangle.$$

Thus

$$\text{Ssp}(f)(\mu_S(\alpha)) = \langle \{\alpha \mid \sigma \in f(\alpha)\}, \{\alpha \mid \sigma \notin f(\alpha)\} \rangle.$$

Thus to say that the diagram commutes is just to say that f and g agree on tokens and that

$$g(\sigma) = \langle \{\alpha \mid \sigma \in f(\alpha)\}, \{\alpha \mid \sigma \notin f(\alpha)\} \rangle$$

But this is the definition of g in the proof of Proposition 8.22. $\qquad\square$

8.7 State-Space Systems

The state-space model of a complex system consists of a state space for the system as a whole, together with projections into state spaces for each component. Thus we give the following definition.

Definition 8.27. A *state-space system* consists an indexed family $\mathcal{S} = \{f_i : S \rightrightarrows S_i\}_{i \in I}$ of state-space projections with a common domain S, called the *core* of $\mathcal{S}$, to state spaces S_i (for $i \in I$); S_i is called the ith component space of $\mathcal{S}$.

We can transform any state-space system into an information channel by applying the functor Evt. This is particularly obvious if we use diagrams. The system S consists of a family of projections, of which we depict two:

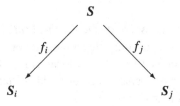

Applying the operator Evt to this diagram gives a family of infomorphisms with a common codomain, Evt(S):

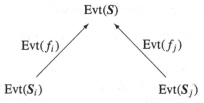

This is an information channel. Using the fundamental property of sums, we get the following commuting diagram, where for the sake of readability, we write σ_i for $\sigma_{\mathrm{Evt}(S_i)}$, and f for $\sum_{k \in I} \mathrm{Evt}(f_k)$:

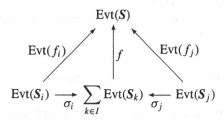

This diagram will be quite useful to us in Lecture 15, once we learn how to move logics along infomorphisms.

We could also go the other way around, turning any channel into a state-space system by means of the functor Ssp.

Exercises

8.1. Construct an information channel representing information flow between two strands of DNA that have the same parent, that is, that arose from the normal splitting of a single strand of DNA.

8.2. Show that state spaces S_1 and S_2 are isomorphic (as classifications) if and only if there is a projection $f : S_1 \rightrightarrows S_2$ such that both $f\hat{}$ and $f\check{}$ are bijections.

8.3.   Show that if state spaces S_1 and S_2 are both complete, so is their product.

8.4.   For any state space S, we define the *idealization* of S to be the state space with types and tokens that are the set of types of S. Show that there is a projection f from S to its idealization. This shows that every state space is the inverse image of an ideal state space under some projection. Note that ideal state spaces are complete, so that we also find that every state space is the inverse image of a complete state space under some projection.

8.5.   Show that for any classifications A and B,

$$\mathrm{Ssp}(A + B) \cong \mathrm{Ssp}(A) \times \mathrm{Ssp}(B).$$

(This result is a consequence of the adjointness results proven above, together with well-known facts about adjoint functors. However, for most of us, it is easier to prove directly.)

8.6.   (†) Verify that Evt() is a functor from the category of state spaces (with projections as morphisms) to classifications (with infomorphisms) by showing the following:
1. If $f : S_1 \rightrightarrows S_2$ and $g : S_2 \rightrightarrows S_3$ are projections of state spaces, then $\mathrm{Evt}(gf) = \mathrm{Evt}(f)\mathrm{Evt}(g)$.
2. If S is any state space, then $\mathrm{Evt}(1_S) = 1_{\mathrm{Evt}(S)}$.

8.7.   (†) Verify that Ssp() is functor from classifications to state spaces by proving the following:
1. If $f : A \rightleftarrows B$ and $g : B \rightleftarrows C$ are infomorphisms, then $\mathrm{Ssp}(gf) = \mathrm{Ssp}(f)\mathrm{Ssp}(g)$.
2. If A is any classification, then $\mathrm{Ssp}(1_A) = 1_{\mathrm{Ssp}(A)}$.

Lecture 9

Regular Theories

In this lecture, we prepare the way for the notion of local logic by studying the ways that classifications give rise to "regular theories." These theories can be seen as an idealized version of the scientific laws supported by a given closed system. The adjective "regular" refers to the purely structural properties that any such theory must satisfy. Any theory with these properties can be obtained from a suitable classification. At the end of the lecture, we will return to the question of how different scientific theories, based on different models of the phenomena under study, can be seen as part of a common theory. We will see conditions under which this obtains.

9.1 Theories

One way to think about information flow in a distributed system is in terms of a "theory" of the system, that is, a set of known laws that describe the system. Usually, these laws are expressed in terms of a set of equations or sentences of some scientific language. In our framework, these expressions are modeled as the types of some classification. However, we will not model a theory by means of a set of types. Because we are not assuming that our types are closed under the Boolean operations, as they are not in many examples, we get a more adequate notion of theory by following Gentzen and using the notion of a sequent.

Given a set Σ, a *sequent* of Σ is a pair $\langle \Gamma, \Delta \rangle$ of subsets of Σ. $\langle \Gamma, \Delta \rangle$ is *finite* if $\Gamma \cup \Delta$ is a finite set. Recall that a sequent $\langle \Gamma, \Delta \rangle$ is a *partition* of a set Σ' if $\Gamma \cup \Delta = \Sigma'$ and $\Gamma \cap \Delta = \emptyset$.

Definition 9.1. A binary relation $\vdash$ between subsets of Σ is called a *(Gentzen) consequence relation on* Σ. A *theory* is a pair $T = \langle \Sigma, \vdash \rangle$, where $\vdash$ is a consequence relation on Σ. A *constraint* of the theory T is a sequent $\langle \Gamma, \Delta \rangle$ of Σ for which, $\Gamma \vdash \Delta$.

We will use the normal notational conventions about consequence relations. For example, we write $\alpha, \beta \vdash \gamma$ for $\{\alpha, \beta\} \vdash \{\gamma\}$ and $\Gamma, \Gamma' \vdash \Delta, \alpha$ for $\Gamma \cup \Gamma' \vdash \Delta \cup \{\alpha\}$. We have already given several examples of constraints in Lecture 2. Here is another.

Example 9.2. Suppose that Σ is the set of polynomials in the variables x and y, and let $\vdash$ be the consequence relation consisting of sequents $\langle \Gamma, \Delta \rangle$ such that every pair $\langle r_1, r_2 \rangle \in R^2$ of real numbers satisfying all the equations in Γ satisfies some equation in Δ. For example, one constraint of the resulting theory is

$$x^2 + y^2 = 25, 3x = 4y \vdash x = 4, x = -4.$$

The point of this example is twofold: to illustrate the way sequents allow us to express certain constraints that would not be expressible without otherwise bringing in logical operations on types, and to stress that the comma on the left has a conjunctive force, whereas that on the right has a disjunctive force.

Example 9.3. Given a first-order language L, recall the truth classification of L given in Example 4.6 whose types are sentences of L and whose tokens are L-structures. The theory of this classification has as constraints just the sequents of first-order logic that are valid in the usual sense. For example, the sequent

$$\forall x \, [A(x) \rightarrow B(x)] \vdash \neg A(c), B(c)$$

is one such constraint.

Our definition of a theory is intended to be neutral between semantic and proof-theoretic notions of theory. Our primary examples of theories come from classifications and from state spaces.

Definition 9.4. Given a classification A, a token $a \in \text{tok}(A)$ *satisfies* a sequent $\langle \Gamma, \Delta \rangle$ of $\text{typ}(A)$ provided that if a is of every type in Γ, then it is of some type in Δ. A token not satisfying a sequent is called a *counterexample* to the sequent. The theory $\text{Th}(A) = \langle \text{typ}(A), \vdash_A \rangle$ *generated by* a classification A is the theory whose types are the types of A and whose constraints are the set of sequents satisfied by every token in A.

Proposition 9.5. *The theory* $\text{Th}(A) = \langle \text{typ}(A), \vdash_A \rangle$ *generated by a classification A satisfies the following for all types* α *and all sets* $\Gamma, \Gamma', \Delta, \Delta', \Sigma', \Sigma_0, \Sigma_1$ *of types:*

> **Identity:** $\alpha \vdash \alpha$.
> **Weakening:** *If* $\Gamma \vdash \Delta$, *then* $\Gamma, \Gamma' \vdash \Delta, \Delta'$.
> **Global Cut:** *If* $\Gamma, \Sigma_0 \vdash \Delta, \Sigma_1$ *for each partition* $\langle \Sigma_0, \Sigma_1 \rangle$ *of* Σ', *then* $\Gamma \vdash \Delta$.

Proof. It is clear that $\vdash_A$ satisfies Identity and Weakening. Let us show that it satisfies Global Cut. Suppose a is a counterexample to $\langle \Gamma, \Delta \rangle$ and that $\Sigma' \subseteq \text{typ}(A)$. Let $\Sigma_0 = \{\alpha \in \Sigma' \,|\, a \vDash \alpha\}$, and let $\Sigma_1 = \{\alpha \in \Sigma' \,|\, a \nvDash \alpha\}$. This gives us a partition of Σ'. Clearly, a is also a counterexample to $\langle \Gamma \cup \Sigma_0, \Delta \cup \Sigma_1 \rangle$. □

We generalize these properties to arbitrary theories.

Definition 9.6. A theory $T = \langle \Sigma, \vdash \rangle$ is *regular* if it satisfies Identity, Weakening, and Global Cut.

It is perhaps worth noting that there are some other structural rules present in some treatments of logic via Gentzen sequents that are made unnecessary by our decision to treat sequents as pairs of sets. For example, the familiar rules of permutation and contraction are not needed, as illustrated by the fact that $\{\alpha, \beta\} = \{\beta, \beta, \alpha\}$. If we were dealing with pairs of sequences, rather than pairs of sets, we would need additional closure conditions in the notion of regular theory.

Readers familiar with the rule of Cut in logic will find our use of this term nonstandard.[1] We call the usual Cut rule "Finite Cut." We will state it in a moment and show it is a consequence of Global Cut and, under certain conditions, is equivalent to it. It is convenient to define the following partial order on sequents of Σ:

$$\langle \Gamma, \Delta \rangle \leq \langle \Gamma', \Delta' \rangle \quad \text{iff} \quad \Gamma \subseteq \Gamma' \quad \text{and} \quad \Delta \subseteq \Delta'.$$

If $\langle \Gamma, \Delta \rangle \leq \langle \Gamma', \Delta' \rangle$, then we say that $\langle \Gamma', \Delta' \rangle$ *extends*, or is an *extension* of, the sequent $\langle \Gamma, \Delta \rangle$.

---

[1] We found Global Cut in the course of characterizing the theories of classifications, only to discover out that it had been previously studied in M. Dunn and G. Hardegree (unpublished manuscript, 1993). The terminology Global Cut is borrowed from their work.

Proposition 9.7. *For every theory $T = \langle \Sigma, \vdash \rangle$, there is a smallest regular theory on Σ containing the sequents in $\vdash$ as constraints. This is called the* regular closure *of T.*

Proof. If we take as a theory all sequents on Σ, it is regular, that is, it satisfies Identity, Weakening, and Global Cut. Now consider the intersection of all regular consequence relations containing $\vdash$. It is easy to see that it too is a regular consequence relation, simply from the general form of the definition.   □

Proposition 9.8. *Any regular theory $T = \langle \Sigma, \vdash \rangle$ satisfies the following conditions:*

Finite Cut: *If $\Gamma, \alpha \vdash \Delta$ and $\Gamma \vdash \Delta, \alpha$ then $\Gamma \vdash \Delta$.*
Partition: *If $\Gamma' \vdash \Delta'$ for each partition of Σ with $\langle \Gamma', \Delta' \rangle \geq \langle \Gamma, \Delta \rangle$, then $\Gamma \vdash \Delta$.*

Proof. Both conditions are special cases of Global Cut, the first with $\Sigma' = \{\alpha\}$, the second with $\Sigma' = \Sigma$.   □

The form of the Finite Cut rule makes it clear why this is called Cut: The type α that appears in both premises is cut out of the conclusion. In practice, we typically use one or the other of these special cases of Global Cut. In the presence of Weakening, Global Cut is equivalent to Partition. We will use this fact repeatedly, so we prove it here.

Proposition 9.9. *Let $T = \langle \Sigma, \vdash \rangle$ be any theory. If T satisfies Weakening and Partition, then T is regular.*

Proof. We need to verify Identity and Global Cut. Identity follows from Partition simply because there are no partitions extending $\langle \{\alpha\}, \{\alpha\} \rangle$. To verify Global Cut, assume the premise of Global Cut; that is, $\Gamma, \Sigma_0 \vdash \Delta, \Sigma_1$ for each partition $\langle \Sigma_0, \Sigma_1 \rangle$ of Σ'. In order to apply Partition, we need only show that $\Gamma, \Sigma_0 \vdash \Delta, \Sigma_1$ for each partition $\langle \Sigma_0, \Sigma_1 \rangle$ of Σ. But any such partition of Σ is an extension of some partition of Σ', so we obtain the result by Weakening.   □

The following definition is going to seem very odd if the sequents mentioned are thought of in terms of constraints. But sequents are not only used in stating constraints, things that must happen, they are also good for talking about what might happen. This definition should be understood in this sense.

Definition 9.10. Given a regular theory $T = \langle \Sigma, \vdash \rangle$, a sequent $\langle \Gamma, \Delta \rangle$ is *T-consistent* if $\Gamma \nvdash \Delta$. The theory T is consistent if it has a consistent sequent.

Example 9.11. If A is a classification, then a sequent of the form $\langle \Gamma, \emptyset \rangle$ is Th(A)-consistent if and only if there is a token $a \in \text{tok}(A)$ such that $a \vDash_A \alpha$ for all $\alpha \in \Gamma$.

Intuitively, $\langle \Gamma, \Delta \rangle$ is consistent if, as far as the theory T knows, it is possible that everything in Γ could hold but, simultaneously everything in Δ could fail. This is clearly the case if our theory is the theory of a classification. If a theory T is fixed, we will omit the "T" and just call a sequent consistent. The following states for the record some obvious equivalences.

Proposition 9.12. *Given a classification A and a sequent $\langle \Gamma, \Delta \rangle$ of* typ(A), *the following are equivalent:*

1. $\langle \Gamma, \Delta \rangle$ *is* Th(A)-*consistent.*
2. $\langle \Gamma, \Delta \rangle$ *is a subsequent of the state description of some a in A.*
3. *There is a token a that is a counterexample to* $\langle \Gamma, \Delta \rangle$.

Hence Th(A) *is consistent if and only if* tok(A) $\neq \emptyset$.

It is sometimes convenient to specify a theory by specifying the set of its consistent partitions. This is a legitimate way to proceed, by virtue of Proposition 9.14. But first we need the following observation.

Proposition 9.13. *Every regular theory satisfies the following condition:*

$\Gamma \vdash \Delta$ *if and only if there is no consistent partition extending* $\langle \Gamma, \Delta \rangle$.

Conversely, any theory satisfying this condition is regular.

Proof. The first claim follows from Weakening in one direction and Partition in the other. As for the second claim, it is easy to check that any theory satisfying the condition satisfies Identity, Weakening, and Partition. For example, to see that $\alpha \vdash \alpha$, suppose it does not. Then by the condition there is a consistent *partition* extending $\langle \{\alpha\}, \{\alpha\} \rangle$. But there can be no such partition. The other rules are checked similarly. $\square$

We can now prove the result that justifies defining a theory by giving a set of consistent partitions.

Proposition 9.14. *Every set P of partitions of* Σ *is the set of consistent partitions of a unique regular theory on* Σ.

Proof. Define

$\Gamma \vdash \Delta$ if and only if there is no partition in P extending $\langle \Gamma, \Delta \rangle$.

By Proposition 9.13, this definition defines a regular theory. But any regular theory with this relation as its set of consistent partitions must also satisfy the above biconditional, so there is only one.   □

Example 9.15. Let $\Sigma = \{\alpha, \beta, \gamma\}$. Think of these types as atomic propositions and construct the truth table that displays all possible assignments of truth values to these three propositions. As with classification tables we use "1" and "0" for truth and falsity, respectively.

α	β	γ
1	1	1
1	1	0
1	0	1
1	0	0
0	1	1
0	1	0
0	0	1
0	0	0

Each row of this truth table corresponds to a partition $\langle \Gamma, \Delta \rangle$ of Σ: put a type into Γ if the type has a 1 under it, and into Δ if it has a 0 under it. Conversely, every partition of Σ arises in this way. Thus giving a set of partitions is nothing more than giving a set of rows of this truth table, those that are possible distributions of truth values among the atomic types.

The following notion will be useful when we turn to characterizing the logical operations on theories.

Definition 9.16. Let A be a classification and $\Sigma \subseteq \mathrm{typ}(A)$. A partition $\langle \Gamma, \Delta \rangle$ of Σ is *realized in A* if there is a token $a \in \mathrm{tok}(A)$ such that

$$\Gamma = \{\alpha \in \Sigma \mid a \vDash_A \alpha\}.$$

Otherwise $\langle \Gamma, \Delta \rangle$ is said to be *spurious in A*. The set Σ is *independent in A* if every partition of Σ is realized in A.

If $\Sigma = \text{typ}(A)$, then a partition $\langle \Gamma, \Delta \rangle$ of Σ is realized in A if it is the state description of some token $a \in \text{tok}(A)$. However, we also want to apply the notions in cases where Σ is a proper subset of $\text{typ}(A)$.

Example 9.17. Suppose we are classifying light bulbs and have among our types the set Σ consisting of LIT, UNLIT, and LIVE. In the everyday classification of bulbs using these types, the types are far from independent. The partitions normally realized correspond to the rows of the following table:

Lit	Unlit	Live
1	0	1
0	1	1
0	1	0

The other partitions are normally spurious. Hence the intuitive theory of light bulbs, at least as far as Σ is concerned, can be specified by the consistent partitions represented by the rows of this truth table.

We can use these ideas to help us compute the theory of a classification A from its classification table. In this way we give substance to the intuition that the regularities of a classification correspond to patterns in the classification table of A. First, note that each row of such a table corresponds to a consistent partition of the types. Hence each such row must satisfy every constraint of T in the following sense: if $\Gamma \vdash_T \Delta$ and every element of Γ has a 1 under it in the given row, then some element of Δ has a 1 under it in the same row. Each missing row corresponds to a spurious partition in the corresponding theory and will thereby falsify some constraint of the theory. We codify this simple but useful observation as follows.

Proposition 9.18. *Let A be a classification and T be a theory on* $\text{typ}(A)$. *The regular closure of T is* $\text{Th}(A)$ *if and only if every row of the classification table of A satisfies each constraint of T and each missing row falsifies some constraint of T.*

Proof. Assume that the regular closure of T is $\text{Th}(A)$. Each token of A must satisfy each constraint of T, so clearly every row of the classification table satisfies each sequent of T. Suppose we have a missing row. This corresponds to an inconsistent partition of $\text{typ}(A)$, that is, a partition $\langle \Gamma, \Delta \rangle$ such that $\Gamma \vdash_A \Delta$. But then the row in question falsifies this constraint of T.

For the converse, assume that every row of the classification table of A satisfies each constraint of T and each missing row falsifies some constraint of T. We want to show that the regular closure of T is Th(A). Because every row of the classification table of A satisfies each constraint of T, and because Identity, Weakening, and Cut are sound, every row of the classification table of A satisfies each constraint of the regular closure of T. Hence every constraint of the regular closure is a constraint of Th(A). To show they are the same, suppose we have a consistent sequent $\Gamma \nvdash_T \Delta$ of the regular closure. By Partition, we can assume that this is a partition. But every partition corresponds to a possible row of the classification table. This row cannot be missing, otherwise it would falsify some constraint of T. Hence the row must correspond to some token of A. Hence $\Gamma \nvdash_A \Delta$. □

Example 9.19. We use Proposition 9.18 to show that the theory defined by the truth table in Example 9.17 is the least regular theory such that

$$\text{LIT} \vdash \text{LIVE}, \quad \vdash \text{LIT}, \text{UNLIT}, \quad \text{LIT}, \text{UNLIT} \vdash .$$

Let A be the classification whose types are those of Example 9.17 and whose tokens are the rows of the truth table, with the natural classification relation. The constraints are satisfied by each of these rows and each missing row falsifies at least one of the constraints.

Exercises

9.1. Let T be a regular theory. Show that T is inconsistent if and only if $\emptyset \vdash_T \emptyset$.

9.2. For any theory T, define an ordering on its types by $\alpha \leq_T \beta$ if and only if $\alpha \vdash_T \beta$. Show that if T is regular, then $\leq_T$ is a preordering, that is, is reflexive and transitive. A theory is said to be *algebraic* if $\leq_T$ is a partial ordering. Show that Th(A) is algebraic if and only if A is extensional.

9.3. Show that every preordering $\leq$ on a set Σ is $\leq_T$ for some regular theory T on Σ.

9.4. Let Σ be a set.
1. Identify the smallest regular theory T on Σ. Is it algebraic?
2. What is the largest regular theory on T? Is it algebraic?

9.5. Given a classification A show that each state description state$_A(a)$ is a partition of the set typ(A) of types of A. Prove that for all $a \in$ tok(A), a is a counterexample to the sequent $\langle \Gamma, \Delta \rangle$ if and only if $\langle \Gamma, \Delta \rangle \leq$ state$_A(a)$.

9.6.   Let Γ and Δ be sets of types of a classification A. Show the following:
1. $\Gamma \vdash_A$ if and only if there is no token of A that is of all types in Γ;
2. $\vdash_A \Delta$ if and only if every token of A is of some type in Δ.

9.7.   Given any set Σ, define a consequence relation on Σ by

$$\Gamma \vdash \Delta \quad \text{iff} \quad \begin{cases} \Gamma \cap \Delta \neq \emptyset, & \text{or} \\ \Gamma \text{ has more than one element,} & \text{or} \\ \Delta = \Sigma. \end{cases}$$

1. Show that $\vdash$ is the closure of the following set of sequents under Identity and Weakening:

   (a) $\langle \emptyset, \Sigma \rangle$.

   (b) $\langle \{\alpha, \beta\}, \emptyset \rangle$ for each pair α, β of distinct elements of Σ.

2. Show that $\vdash$ is closed under Global Cut.

3. Show that a classification A with $\text{typ}(A) = \Sigma$ is a complete state space if and only if for each $\Gamma, \Delta \subseteq \Sigma$, $\Gamma \vdash_A \Delta$ if and only if $\Gamma \vdash \Delta$.

9.2 Finite Cut and Global Cut

The results of this section are not needed in the remainder of the book. We include it in order to connect Global Cut with the more familiar version.

Definition 9.20. A theory $T = \langle \Sigma, \vdash \rangle$ is *compact* if for each constraint $\langle \Gamma, \Delta \rangle$ of T, there is a finite constraint of T such that $\langle \Gamma_0, \Delta_0 \rangle \leq \langle \Gamma, \Delta \rangle$; equivalently, if $\langle \Gamma, \Delta \rangle$ is a sequent and every finite sequent $\langle \Gamma_0, \Delta_0 \rangle \leq \langle \Gamma, \Delta \rangle$ is consistent, then so is $\langle \Gamma, \Delta \rangle$.

Example 9.21. Consider the theory of the truth classification of Example 9.3. The compactness theorem of first-order logic insures that this classification is compact. However, if we restricted the tokens to some class of structures not closed under first-order equivalence, like the class of well-orderings, then the resulting classification would not have a compact theory. Thus, in general, we cannot expect the theories we deal with to be compact.

The following result, whose proof is given as an answer to Exercise 9.8, shows that for compact theories, our notion of regularity agrees with the usual notion of structural rules of classical logic.

Proposition 9.22. *A compact theory T is regular if and only if it is closed under Identity, Weakening, and Finite Cut.*

The following gives an example of a theory that satisfies Identity, Weakening, and Finite Cut, but is far from the theory of any classification with a nonempty set of tokens.

Example 9.23. Let Σ be an infinite set. A subset Γ of Σ is *cofinite* if $\Sigma - \Gamma$ is finite. Define a consequence relation of Σ as follows:

$\Gamma \vdash \Delta$ if and only if either $\Gamma \cap \Delta \neq \emptyset$ or $\Gamma \cup \Delta$ is cofinite.

This relation $\vdash$ satisfies Identity, Weakening, and Finite Cut but is not regular. Indeed, the regular closure of this theory contains the absurd sequent $\vdash$ with both sides empty. (The proof of this claim is left as Exercise 9.9.) These observations show that in the case where a consequence relation is not compact, the rules of Identity, Weakening, and Finite Cut are far from sufficient for having a reasonable consequence relation.

Exercises

9.8.   Prove Proposition 9.22.

9.9.   Prove the claim made in Example 9.23.

9.10.   The rule of *Infinite Cut* asserts that if $\Gamma, \Gamma' \vdash \Delta$ and $\Gamma \vdash \Delta, \alpha$ for each $\alpha \in \Gamma'$, then $\Gamma \vdash \Delta$. (There is also a version of Infinite Cut where the sides of the cut types are reversed. Everything said below about it applies to the other version without change.)
   1. Show that every regular theory satisfies Infinite Cut.
   2. Show that the consequence relation of Example 9.23 satisfies Infinite Cut.
   3. Conclude that Identity, Weakening, and Infinite Cut do not entail Global Cut.

9.3 The Theory of a State Space

Each state space has a regular theory associated with it, because each state space is a classification, and a classification has a theory associated with it. From the informational point of view, however, the most natural classification to associate with a state space S is not the space itself, but its event classification $\mathrm{Evt}(S)$.

By virtue of this classification, we can associate with S the regular theory $\mathrm{Th}(\mathrm{Evt}(S))$ generated by the event classification $\mathrm{Evt}(S)$.

When state spaces are used in science, however, the tokens are not usually considered in any explicit manner. Thus, in order to be able to link up with the state space literature, we study a second regular theory on $\mathrm{pow}(\mathrm{typ}(S))$, one that is independent of the tokens of the state space. By way of introduction, we first note a property of all regular theories of the form $\mathrm{Th}(\mathrm{Evt}(S))$.

Proposition 9.24. *If S is a state space and $T = \mathrm{Th}(\mathrm{Evt}(S))$, then for all $\Gamma, \Delta \subseteq \mathrm{typ}(\mathrm{Evt}(S))$, if $\bigcap \Gamma \subseteq \bigcup \Delta$ then $\Gamma \vdash_T \Delta$.*

Proof. Assume that $\bigcap \Gamma \subseteq \bigcup \Delta$. Let $s \in \mathrm{tok}(S)$. We need to show that s satisfies $\langle \Gamma, \Delta \rangle$. So assume s is of every type $X \in \Gamma$. That is, $\mathrm{state}_S(s) \in X$ for every such X. But then $\mathrm{state}_S(s) \in \bigcap \Gamma$, so $\mathrm{state}_S(s) \in \bigcup \Delta$. But then s is of type some $Y \in \Delta$, so s satisfies $\langle \Gamma, \Delta \rangle$. $\square$

Notice this did not give us a biconditional. To get one, we must bring in the set Ω of "realized" states. A state is *realized* if it is the state of some token of the state space in question.

Proposition 9.25. *Given a state space S, let Ω be the set of realized states of S and let $T = \mathrm{Th}(\mathrm{Evt}(S))$. For each sequent $\langle \Gamma, \Delta \rangle$ of T, $\Gamma \vdash_T \Delta$ if and only if $(\bigcap \Gamma \cap \Omega) \subseteq \bigcup \Delta$.*

Proof. The proof of the direction from right to left is essentially the same as that of Proposition 9.24. To prove the other direction, assume $\Gamma \vdash_T \Delta$ and $\sigma \in (\bigcap \Gamma \cap \Omega)$ and let us prove that $\sigma \in \bigcup \Delta$. Because $\sigma \in \Omega$, σ is realized, so let s be of state σ. Because $\Gamma \vdash_T \Delta$, s satisfies the sequent $\langle \Gamma, \Delta \rangle$. But because s is of every type in Γ, it must be of some type in Δ so $\sigma \in \bigcup \Delta$. $\square$

Corollary 9.26. *If S is a complete state space and $T = \mathrm{Th}(\mathrm{Evt}(S))$, then for all $\Gamma, \Delta \subseteq \mathrm{typ}(T)$, $\bigcap \Gamma \subseteq \bigcup \Delta$ if and only if $\Gamma \vdash_T \Delta$. In particular, this holds for every ideal state space.*

Proof. To say that S is complete is to say that $\mathrm{typ}(S)$ is the set of realized states. $\square$

When working with a state-space model of some phenomena, the default assumption is that the space is complete, that is, that every state is realized. After all, if one knew that some states were not realized, one would throw out those states. Another way to put it is that the following theory is implicit in the use of a state-space model.

Definition 9.27. The regular theory Th(S) associated with a state space S has the same types as Evt(S), that is, arbitrary sets X, Y, ... of states of S, interpreted disjunctively. The theory is given by

$$\Gamma \vdash_{\text{Th}(S)} \Delta \quad \text{iff} \quad \bigcap \Gamma \subseteq \bigcup \Delta.$$

Justification. We need to check that this theory is regular. It suffices to show that it satisfies Partition because it clearly satisfies Weakening. Suppose that $\Gamma \nvdash_{\text{Th}(S)} \Delta$ and let $\sigma \in (\bigcap \Gamma - \bigcup \Delta)$. Let $\Gamma' = \{X \subseteq \text{typ}(S) \mid \sigma \in X\}$ and $\Delta' = \{X \subseteq \text{typ}(S)\sigma \mid \notin X\}$. Then $\langle \Gamma', \Delta' \rangle$ is a partition, $\langle \Gamma, \Delta \rangle \leq \langle \Gamma', \Delta' \rangle$, and $\Gamma' \nvdash_{\text{Th}(S)} \Delta'$.   □

9.4 Theory Interpretations

Just as classifications have infomorphisms and state spaces have projections, theories have their notion of map or morphism. We call it "theory interpretation."

Given a theory T, we write typ(T) for its set of types and $\vdash_T$ for its consequence relation.

Definition 9.28. A *(regular theory) interpretation* $f : T_1 \to T_2$ is a function from typ(T_1) to typ(T_2) such that for each Γ, $\Delta \subseteq \text{typ}(T_1)$

if $\Gamma \vdash_{T_1} \Delta$, then $f[\Gamma] \vdash_{T_2} f[\Delta]$.

The following is sometimes useful for checking that a function is a theory interpretation.

Proposition 9.29. *Given regular theories T_1 and T_2, a function $f : \text{typ}(T_1) \to \text{typ}(T_2)$ is an interpretation if and only if for every consistent partition $\langle \Gamma', \Delta' \rangle$ of T_2, $\langle f^{-1}[\Gamma'], f^{-1}[\Delta'] \rangle$ is consistent in T_1.*

Proof. The routine proof is left as Exercise 9.11.   □

Let us see how theory interpretations arise from infomorphisms and from state-space projections.

Definition 9.30. Given an infomorphism $f : A \rightleftarrows B$, we define

$$\mathrm{Th}(f) : \mathrm{Th}(A) \rightarrow \mathrm{Th}(B)$$

to be the interpretation given by $\mathrm{Th}(f)(\alpha) = f^{\wedge}(\alpha)$.

Justification. In other words, $\mathrm{Th}(f)$ just forgets the action of f on tokens. If b is a counterexample to $\langle f[\Gamma], f[\Delta] \rangle$ in B, then $f(b)$ is a counterexample to $\langle \Gamma, \Delta \rangle$ in A. So, taking contrapositives, $\Gamma \vdash_A \Delta$ entails $f^{\wedge}[\Gamma] \vdash_B f^{\wedge}[\Delta]$. Hence $\mathrm{Th}(f)$ is a interpretation. □

There is a similar operation that turns any state-space projection into a theory interpretation of the corresponding theories. Notice, however, the reversal of arrows.

Definition 9.31. Given a state-space projection $f : S_1 \rightrightarrows S_2$, let

$$\mathrm{Th}(f) : \mathrm{Th}(S_2) \rightarrow \mathrm{Th}(S_1)$$

be the interpretation defined by

$$\mathrm{Th}(f)(X) = f^{-1}[X]$$

for each set X of states of S_2.

Justification. We need to verify that if $f : S_1 \rightrightarrows S_2$ is a projection, then $\mathrm{Th}(f) : \mathrm{Th}(S_2) \rightarrow \mathrm{Th}(S_1)$ is an interpretation. Assume that $\Gamma_2 \vdash_{\mathrm{Th}(S_2)} \Delta_2$. Let $\Gamma_1 = \{f^{-1}(X) \mid X \in \Gamma_2\}$ and define Δ_1 similarly. We need to prove that $\Gamma_1 \vdash_{\mathrm{Th}(S_1)} \Delta_1$. Assume that this is not the case. Then there is a $\sigma_1 \in (\bigcap \Gamma_1 - \bigcup \Delta_1)$. But then $f(\sigma_1) \in (\bigcap \Gamma_2 - \bigcup \Delta_2)$, contradicting $\Gamma_2 \vdash_{\mathrm{Th}(S_2)} \Delta_2$. □

9.5 Representing Regular Theories

We have seen how any classification A gives rise to a regular theory $\mathrm{Th}(A)$. This theory is, of course, very dependent on just what tokens are present in the classification A. The following result shows that any regular theory can be seen as the theory arising from some classification. (We also establish the analogous result for theory interpretations, that they all arise from infomorphisms of classifications.)

Definition 9.32.

1. Given a regular theory T, the classification $\mathrm{Cla}(T)$ *generated* by T is the classification whose

(a) tokens are the consistent partitions $\langle \Gamma, \Delta \rangle$ of $\mathrm{typ}(T)$,

(b) types are the types of T, such that

(c) $\langle \Gamma, \Delta \rangle \models_{\mathrm{Cla}(T)} \alpha$ if and only if $\alpha \in \Gamma$ (equivalently, if and only if $\alpha \notin \Delta$).

2. Given an interpretation $f : T \to T'$, we define an infomorphism

$$\mathrm{Cla}(f) : \mathrm{Cla}(T) \rightleftarrows \mathrm{Cla}(T')$$

by

(a) $\mathrm{Cla}(f)^{\wedge}(\alpha) = f(\alpha)$ for $\alpha \in \mathrm{typ}(T)$, and

(b) $\mathrm{Cla}(f)^{\vee}(\langle \Gamma, \Delta \rangle) = \langle f^{-1}[\Gamma], f^{-1}[\Delta] \rangle$ for any token $\langle \Gamma, \Delta \rangle$ of $\mathrm{Cla}(T')$.

Justification. We need to verify that $\mathrm{Cla}(f) : \mathrm{Cla}(T) \rightleftarrows \mathrm{Cla}(T')$ and that it is an infomorphism. If $\langle \Gamma, \Delta \rangle$ is a token of $\mathrm{Cla}(T')$, then it is a consistent partition of $\mathrm{typ}(T')$. But then $\langle f^{-1}[\Gamma], f^{-1}[\Delta] \rangle$ is a partition of $\mathrm{typ}(T)$; it is consistent because f is an interpretation. Hence $\langle f^{-1}[\Gamma], f^{-1}[\Delta] \rangle$ is a token of $\mathrm{Cla}(T)$, as desired. To see that $\mathrm{Cla}(f)$ is an infomorphism, we need to verify that $\langle \Gamma, \Delta \rangle \models_{\mathrm{Cla}(T')} f(\alpha)$ if and only if $\langle f^{-1}[\Gamma], f^{-1}[\Delta] \rangle \models_{\mathrm{Cla}(T)} \alpha$. But this is clear because the former is equivalent to $f(\alpha) \in \Gamma$ and the latter is equivalent to $\alpha \in f^{-1}[\Gamma]$.   □

Theorem 9.33 (Representation Theorem). *For any regular theory T, $T = \mathrm{Th}(\mathrm{Cla}(T))$. Similarly, for any interpretation f, $f = \mathrm{Th}(\mathrm{Cla}(f))$.*

Proof. Clearly both regular theories have the same set of types. Suppose $\Gamma \vdash_T \Delta$. We need to see that this is satisfied by every token in $\mathrm{Cla}(T)$. Such a token is a partition $\langle \Gamma', \Delta' \rangle$ of $\mathrm{typ}(T)$ such that $\Gamma' \nvdash_T \Delta'$. Suppose token $\langle \Gamma', \Delta' \rangle$ does not satisfy sequent $\langle \Gamma, \Delta \rangle$. Then $\Gamma \subseteq \Gamma'$ but $\Delta \cap \Gamma' = \emptyset$. But then $\langle \Gamma, \Delta \rangle \leq \langle \Gamma', \Delta' \rangle$ because the latter is a partition, but this contradicts Weakening. For the converse, suppose $\Gamma' \nvdash_T \Delta'$. Then by Partition there is a partition $\langle \Gamma', \Delta' \rangle$ of $\mathrm{typ}(T)$ extending $\langle \Gamma, \Delta \rangle$ such that $\Gamma' \nvdash_T \Delta'$. But then $\langle \Gamma', \Delta' \rangle$ is a counterexample to $\langle \Gamma, \Delta \rangle$ in $\mathrm{Cla}(T)$. The second statement is similar.   □

The following is an immediate consequence of this representation theorem. The first sentence of it is equivalent to a theorem proved in Chapter 6 of Dunn and Hardegree's (1993) manuscript.

Corollary 9.34 (Abstract Completeness Theorem). *Every regular theory is $\mathrm{Th}(A)$ for some classification A. Every interpretation is $\mathrm{Th}(f)$ for some infomorphism f.*

We now investigate a related question: Which classifications are isomorphic to those arising from regular theories? It turns out that only very special classifications are of this form, namely, those that are separated, that is, have no indistinguishable tokens.

Recall the definition of the separated quotient Sep(A) of a classification A given in Example 5.12. It is obtained by keeping all types of A while identifying tokens that are indistinguishable from one another.

Proposition 9.35. *For any classification A, Sep(A) is isomorphic to* Cla(Th(A)).

Proof. The isomorphism is the type identical infomorphism that maps the indistinguishability class of each token to its state description. □

Corollary 9.36. *A classification A is isomorphic to* Cla(T) *for some regular theory T if and only if A is separated.*

Proof. The direction from left to right is immediate from Proposition 9.35. For the converse, suppose A is separated. Let $T = \mathrm{Th}(A)$. Then by Proposition 9.35, Cla(T) is isomorphic to Sep(A), that is, isomorphic to A if A is separated. □

Exercises

9.11.   Prove Proposition 9.29.

9.12.   Show that a regular theory T is algebraic if and only if Cla(T) is extensional.

9.13.   (†) Show that the sum of regular theories is the coproduct in the category of regular theories and interpretations.

9.14.   Prove that

$$\mathrm{Cla}(T + T') \cong \mathrm{Cla}(T) + \mathrm{Cla}(T').$$

(The sum of theories is defined in 10.1)

9.15.   (†) Let $f : T \to \mathrm{Th}(A)$ be an interpretation. Show that there is a unique infomorphism $f^* : \mathrm{Cla}(T) \rightleftarrows A$ such that $f = \mathrm{Th}(f^*)$. This shows that the functor Cla is the left adjoint of the functor Th, with the identity as the unit of the adjunction. Because functors that are left adjoints are known to preserve colimits, this result can be viewed as a generalization of Exercise 9.14.

Lecture 10

Operations on Theories

All of the operations on classifications defined earlier have counterparts on local logics. With an eye toward defining these operations, we first explain how the operations work on theories.

10.1 Sums of Theories

Definition 10.1. The *sum* $T + T'$ of regular theories T and T' is the regular theory whose types are the disjoint union of $\text{typ}(T)$ and $\text{typ}(T')$ and whose consequence relation is such that for $\Gamma_1, \Delta_1 \subseteq \text{typ}(T)$ and $\Gamma_2, \Delta_2 \subseteq \text{typ}(T')$,

$$\Gamma_1, \Gamma_2 \vdash_{T+T'} \Delta_1, \Delta_2 \quad \text{iff} \quad \Gamma_1 \vdash_T \Delta_1 \quad \text{or} \quad \Gamma_2 \vdash_{T'} \Delta_2.$$

Justification. We need to check that this theory is regular. To simplify notation, let's assume the types of T and T' are disjoint. Identity and Weakening are clear. We check Partition, or rather, its contrapositive. Suppose $\Gamma_1, \Delta_1 \subseteq \text{typ}(T)$ and $\Gamma_2, \Delta_2 \subseteq \text{typ}(T')$, and that $\Gamma_1, \Gamma_2 \nvdash_{T+T'} \Delta_1, \Delta_2$. We want to show there is a partition $\langle \Gamma, \Delta \rangle$ of the disjoint union of $\text{typ}(T)$ and $\text{typ}(T')$ extending $\langle \Gamma_1 \cup \Gamma_2, \Delta_1 \cup \Delta_2 \rangle$ such that $\Gamma \nvdash_{T+T'} \Delta$. By the definition of $\vdash_{T+T'}$, $\Gamma_1 \nvdash_T \Delta_1$ and $\Gamma_2 \nvdash_{T'} \Delta_2$. Hence, by Partition for each of the theories T and T', there are partitions $\langle \Gamma_1', \Delta_1' \rangle$ of $\text{typ}(T)$ and extending $\langle \Gamma_1, \Delta_1 \rangle$ and a partition $\langle \Gamma_2', \Delta_2' \rangle$ of $\text{typ}(T')$ and extending $\langle \Gamma_2, \Delta_2 \rangle$ such that $\Gamma_1' \nvdash_T \Delta_1'$ and $\Gamma_2' \nvdash_{T'} \Delta_2'$. But then $\langle \Gamma_1' \cup \Gamma_2', \Delta_1' \cup \Delta_2' \rangle$ is a consistent partition of the sum that extends the original sequent. □

Proposition 10.2. *The functions $\sigma_T : T \to T + T'$ and $\sigma_{T'} : T' \to T + T'$ that take types to their copies in the disjoint union are both interpretations.*

Proof. The proof is obvious. □

The sum of theories is a rather trivial operation. For example, if T_1 is a theory of flashlight switches and T_2 is a theory of flashlight bulbs, then $T_1 + T_2$ is a theory of both but without any interactions because there would be no constraints in this theory relating bulbs and switches in any nontrivial manner.

Proposition 10.3. *Given classifications A and B,*

$$\text{Th}(A + B) = \text{Th}(A) + \text{Th}(B).$$

Proof. Without loss of generality we assume the types of the classifications are disjoint. Let $T = \text{Th}(A + B)$, and let $T' = \text{Th}(A) + \text{Th}(B)$. It is immediate that every constraint of T' is a constraint of T. To go the other direction, we prove the contrapositive. Suppose that $\Gamma \nvdash_{T'} \Delta$. Let $\Gamma_A = \Gamma \cap \text{typ}(A)$ and define Δ_A, Γ_B, and Δ_B similarly. Then $\Gamma_A \nvdash_{\text{Th}(A)} \Delta_A$ and $\Gamma_B \nvdash_{\text{Th}(B)} \Delta_B$. Hence there are counterexamples to these sequents, say $a \in \text{tok}(A)$ and $b \in \text{tok}(B)$. But then $\langle a, b \rangle \in \text{tok}(A + B)$ and is a counterexample to the sequent $\langle \Gamma, \Delta \rangle$ in $A + B$. Hence $\Gamma \nvdash_T \Delta$. □

10.2 A Partial Order on Theories

Definition 10.4. Let Σ be fixed. A natural partial order on regular theories on Σ is defined by $T_1 \sqsubseteq T_2$ if and only if each constraint of $\vdash_{T_1}$ is also a constraint of $\vdash_{T_2}$.

This can also be expressed by saying that the inclusion map $\text{typ}(T_1) \subseteq \text{typ}(T_2)$ is a theory interpretation.

Proposition 10.5. *Let T_1 and T_2 be regular theories on Σ. The least upper bound of T_1 and T_2 is the theory $\langle \Sigma, \vdash \rangle$, where $\vdash$ is the smallest regular consequence relation containing $\vdash_{T_1}$ and $\vdash_{T_2}$. The greatest lower bound of T_1 and T_2 in the $\sqsubseteq$-order is the theory $\langle \Sigma, \vdash \rangle$ such that*

$$\Gamma \vdash \Delta \quad \textit{iff} \quad \Gamma \vdash_{T_1} \Delta \quad \textit{and} \quad \Gamma \vdash_{T_2} \Delta.$$

Proof. The proof is straightforward. □

We write the least upper bound of T_1 and T_2 as $T_1 \sqcup T_2$, and also call this the *join* of T_1 and T_2.

The existence of least upper bounds and greatest lower bounds generalizes to show that the set of theories on a fixed set Σ of types is a complete lattice.

10.3 Quotients of Theories

The operation on theories corresponding to quotients of classifications is that of restriction.

Definition 10.6. Let T be a theory on a set Σ of types and let $\Sigma_0 \subseteq \Sigma$. Then $T \upharpoonright \Sigma_0$ is the theory on Σ_0 whose consequence relation is that of T restricted to Σ_0-sequents.

We leave the following proposition to the reader to check. It is entirely routine.

Proposition 10.7. *Let T be a theory on a set Σ of types and let $\Sigma_0 \subseteq \Sigma$.*

1. *If T is regular, so is $T \upharpoonright \Sigma_0$.*
2. *$T \upharpoonright \Sigma_0$ is the largest theory on Σ_0 such that the identity map of Σ_0 into Σ is a theory interpretation.*
3. *If $T = \mathrm{Th}(A)$, then $T \upharpoonright \Sigma_0 = \mathrm{Th}(A \upharpoonright \Sigma_0)$.*

Corresponding to dual invariants on classifications, we have the following operation on theories.

Definition 10.8. Let $T = \langle \Sigma, \vdash \rangle$ be a theory and let R be a binary relation on Σ. The *(dual) quotient of T by R*, written T/R, is the theory defined as follows. Its set of types is the set Σ/R of equivalence classes $[\alpha]_R$ for $\alpha \in \Sigma$. Its consistent partitions are those partitions $\langle \Gamma', \Delta' \rangle$ of Σ/R such that the following is T-consistent:

$$\langle \{\alpha \in \Sigma \mid [\alpha]_R \in \Gamma'\}, \{\beta \in \Sigma \mid [\beta]_R \in \Delta'\} \rangle.$$

Justification. We are using here the fact that we can specify a regular theory by specifying its set of consistent partitions.   □

Example 10.9. Let T be a theory with types α, β_1, β_2, γ and suppose $\alpha \vdash_T \beta_1$ and $\beta_2 \vdash_T \gamma$. If $\beta_1 R \beta_2$, then in the theory T/R we will have $[\alpha]_R \vdash [\gamma]_R$. (Prove this.)

Example 10.10. Given a regular theory T, let $\alpha R \beta$ if and only if $\alpha \vdash_T \beta$. Then $[\alpha]_R = [\beta]_R$ if and only if $\alpha \vdash_T \beta$ and $\beta \vdash_T \alpha$. The quotient T/R is called the *Lindenbaum theory* associated with T and is written $\mathrm{Lind}(T)$. This theory identifies types that are equivalent in T. It is an algebraic theory (in the sense of Exercise 9.2).

We leave the following result as an exercise for the reader, because its parts are very similar to (and simpler than) things we have done earlier.

Proposition 10.11. *Let $T = \langle \Sigma, \vdash \rangle$ be a theory on a set Σ of types and let R be a binary relation on Σ.*

1. *The theory T/R is the least regular theory on Σ/R such that the function $\alpha \mapsto [\alpha]_R$ is a theory interpretation.*
2. *If $J = \langle \text{typ}(A), R \rangle$ is a dual invariant on A and $T = \text{Th}(A)$, then $T/R = \text{Th}(A/J)$.*
3. *Let $f : T \to T'$ be a theory interpretation that respects R in the sense that $f(\alpha) = f(\beta)$ whenever $\alpha R \beta$. There is a unique theory interpretation $f' : T/R \to T'$ such that $f(\alpha) = f'([\alpha]_R)$ for each $\alpha \in \Sigma$.*

Exercises

10.1.   Let A and B be classifications. We say that A is an *informational subclassification* of B, written $A \sqsubseteq B$, if $\text{typ}(A) \subseteq \text{typ}(B)$, $\text{tok}(B) \subseteq \text{tok}(A)$, and the classification relations agree on the types and tokens in common to both.
   1. Prove that if $A \sqsubseteq B$, then $\text{Th}(A) \sqsubseteq \text{Th}(B)$.
   2. Does the converse of (1) hold?

10.4 Moving Theories

A major theme of this book is the idea of reasoning at a distance, that is, using a theory of one or more parts of a distributed system to reason about other parts. This was foreshadowed by our discussion of the rules of f-Intro and f-Elim in Lecture 2. We turn to these rules now, beginning with f-Elim.

Definition 10.12. Let $T' = \langle \Sigma', \vdash_{T'} \rangle$ be a regular theory and let $f : \Sigma \to \Sigma'$. The *inverse image of T' under f*, written $f^{-1}[T']$, is the theory with types Σ and consequence relation given by

$$\Gamma \vdash \Delta \quad \text{iff} \quad f[\Gamma] \vdash_{T'} f[\Delta].$$

Proposition 10.13. *Let $T' = \langle \Sigma', \vdash_{T'} \rangle$ be a regular theory and let $f : \Sigma \to \Sigma'$ be a function. Let T be the inverse image of T' under f. Then T is a regular theory. Indeed, it is the largest regular theory on Σ such that $f : T \to T'$ is an interpretation.*

Proof. Let $T = \langle \Sigma, \vdash \rangle$. We first show that $\vdash$ satisfies Weakening and Partition. The former is obvious. To prove the latter, suppose $\Gamma, \Delta \subseteq \text{typ}(T)$ and $\Gamma \nvdash \Delta$.

We need to show that there is a partition $\langle \Gamma'', \Delta'' \rangle \geq \langle \Gamma, \Delta \rangle$ such that $\Gamma'' \nvdash \Delta''$. By the definition of $\vdash$, $f[\Gamma] \nvdash_{T'} f[\Delta]$. Hence, by Partition in T', there is a partition $\langle \Gamma', \Delta' \rangle \geq \langle f[\Gamma], f[\Delta] \rangle$ such that $\Gamma' \nvdash_{T'} \Delta'$. Let $\Gamma'' = f^{-1}[\Gamma']$ and $\Delta'' = f^{-1}[\Delta']$. It is clear that $\langle \Gamma'', \Delta'' \rangle$ is a partition, that $\langle \Gamma'', \Delta'' \rangle \geq \langle \Gamma, \Delta \rangle$, and that $\Gamma'' \nvdash \Delta''$. It is clear that this is the largest theory that makes $f : T \to T'$ an interpretation.   □

   Images of theories under maps are introduced similarly, but the definition is complicated by the absence of a result analogous to Proposition 10.13. Given a function $f : \mathrm{typ}(T) \to \Sigma'$, there is no guarantee that the consequence relation on Σ' defined by

$$\Gamma' \vdash \Delta' \quad \text{iff} \quad f^{-1}[\Gamma'] \vdash_T f^{-1}[\Delta']$$

is regular. For example, if $\alpha \in \Sigma'$ is a type outside the range of f, then this definition would have $\alpha \nvdash \alpha$. What we want is the smallest regular consequence relation containing the one just defined. Another way to get at the same thing is as follows.

Definition 10.14. Let $T' = \langle \Sigma, \vdash_T \rangle$ be a regular theory and let $f : \Sigma \to \Sigma'$; we define the *image of T under f*, $f[T]$ as follows. Its types are the elements of Σ'. The theory is given by specifying its consistent partitions as follows: a partition $\langle \Gamma, \Delta \rangle$ of Σ' is $f[T]$-consistent if and only if $\langle f^{-1}[\Gamma], f^{-1}[\Delta] \rangle$ is T-consistent.

Proposition 10.15. *Let T be a regular theory and let $f : \mathrm{typ}(T) \to \Sigma'$. $f[T]$ is the smallest regular theory T' on Σ' such that $f : \mathrm{typ}(T) \to T'$ is an interpretation.*

Proof. Let T' be any regular theory on Σ' such that $f : \mathrm{typ}(T) \to T'$ is an interpretation. Assume $\Gamma' \vdash_{f[T]} \Delta'$. We need to prove $\Gamma' \vdash_{T'} \Delta'$. By Partition, it suffices to prove $\Gamma'' \vdash_{T'} \Delta''$ for every partition $\langle \Gamma'', \Delta'' \rangle$ extending $\langle \Gamma', \Delta' \rangle$. Fix such a partition. By Weakening, we have $\Gamma'' \vdash_{f[T]} \Delta''$. Hence, by the definition of $f[T]$, $f^{-1}[\Gamma''] \vdash_T f^{-1}[\Delta'']$. Because $f : \mathrm{typ}(T) \to T'$ is an interpretation, $f[f^{-1}[\Gamma'']] \vdash_{T'} f[f^{-1}[\Delta'']]$. But $f[f^{-1}[\Gamma'']] \subseteq \Gamma''$ and $f[f^{-1}[\Delta'']] \subseteq \Delta''$, so we get the desired $\Gamma'' \vdash_{T'} \Delta''$ by Weakening.   □

10.5 Families of Theories

Science develops partial theories about different phenomena, with the hope that these theories will one day be part of, or interpretable in, some grand, unified theory of everything. In the introduction, we raised the question of how theories fit together. In this section we apply our earlier results to show that there is a sense in which it is always possible to put them together in an optimal manner, as long as the theories are regular. (Every theory has a regular closure, of course.)

Definition 10.16. A *family of theories* T consists of an indexed family $\mathrm{th}(T) = \{T_i\}_{i \in I}$ of regular theories together with a set $\mathrm{inter}(T)$ of interpretations, all of which have both domain and codomain in the family $\mathrm{th}(T)$.

Using some of the results obtained earlier, we can prove the following.

Theorem 10.17. *Every family T of theories has a "limit," that is a weakest regular theory in which each T_i can be interpreted so as to respect whatever interpretations $f : T_i \to T_j$ are present in the family. This theory is unique up to theory isomorphism.*

It turns out to be easier to prove the theorem than to state the definitions needed to make it precise. Because we will not be using the result in what follows, we simply sketch the proof of the result, leaving it to the reader to fill in the details.

Given the family T of regular theories, we use the operation Cla to turn it into a distributed system. The classifications of the system consist of those classifications of the form $\mathrm{Cla}(T_i)$ for $T_i \in \mathrm{th}(T)$. The infomorphisms of the distributed system consist of the infomorphisms of the form $\mathrm{Cla}(f)$ for $f \in \mathrm{inter}(T)$. As we have seen, $f : T_i \to T_j$ is an interpretation if and only if $\mathrm{Cla}(f) : \mathrm{Cla}(T_i) \rightleftarrows \mathrm{Cla}(T_j)$ is an infomorphism, so this turns our family of theories into a distributed system. The limit of this system consists of a classification C and infomorphisms $g_i : \mathrm{Cla}(T_i) \rightleftarrows C$. The limit of our family consists of the theory $\mathrm{Th}(C)$, together with the interpretations $\mathrm{Th}(g_i)$ for $i \in I$.

Lecture 11

Boolean Operations and Theories

In Lecture 7 we discussed the relationship between classifications and the Boolean operations. In this lecture, we study the corresponding relationship for theories. In particular, we discuss Boolean operations that take theories to theories, as well as what it would mean for operations to be Boolean operations in the context of a particular theory. In this way, we begin to see how the traditional rules of inference emerge from an informational perspective. The topic is a natural one but it is not central to the main development so this lecture could be skipped.

11.1 Boolean Operations on Theories

Given a regular theory $T = \langle \Sigma, \vdash \rangle$, one may define a consequence relation on the set $\text{pow}(\Sigma)$ of subsets of Σ in one of two natural ways, depending on whether one thinks of the sets of types disjunctively or conjunctively. This produces two new theories, $\vee T$ and $\wedge T$, respectively.

These operations should fit with the corresponding power operations $\vee A$ and $\wedge A$ on classifications A; we want $\vee \text{Th}(A)$ to be the same as the theory $\text{Th}(\vee A)$, for example. Thus, to motivate our definitions, we begin by investigating the relationship of the theory $\text{Th}(A)$ of a classification to the theories $\text{Th}(\vee A)$ and $\text{Th}(\wedge A)$ of its two power classifications.

Definition 11.1. Given a set Γ of subsets of Σ, a set Y is a *choice set* on Γ if $X \cap Y \neq \emptyset$ for each $X \in \Gamma$.

Proposition 11.2. *Let A be a classification, let $a \in \text{tok}(A)$, and let Γ, Δ be subsets of* $\text{pow}(\text{typ}(A))$:

1. *a satisfies the $\vee A$-sequent $\langle \Gamma, \Delta \rangle$ if and only if for every choice set Y on Γ, a satisfies the A-sequent $\langle Y, \bigcup \Delta \rangle$;*

2. *a satisfies the* ∧*A-sequent* ⟨Γ, Δ⟩ *if and only if for every choice set Y on* Δ, *a satisfies the A-sequent* ⟨⋃Γ, Y⟩.

Similarly, if Γ, Δ *are subsets of* typ(*A*), *then a satisfies* ⟨Γ, Δ⟩ *in* ¬*A if and only if a satisfies* ⟨Δ, Γ⟩ *in A.*

Proof. We prove the contrapositive version of (1). Note that a is a counterexample to the sequent ⟨Γ, Δ⟩ in ∨*A* if and only if

(a) for each $X \in \Gamma$, $a \vDash_{\vee A} X$, and
(b) for each $X \in \Delta$, $a \nvDash_{\vee A} X$.

The clause (a) is equivalent to the statement that for each $X \in \Gamma$ there is a type $\alpha \in X$ such that $a \vDash_A \alpha$, which is just to say that there is a choice set Y for Γ such that $a \vDash_A \alpha$ for each $\alpha \in Y$. Clause (b) is equivalent to the statement that for each $X \in \Delta$ and each type $\alpha \in X$, $a \nvDash_A \alpha$, which is just to say that $a \nvDash_A \alpha$ for each $\alpha \in \bigcup \Delta$. Thus a is a counterexample to ⟨Γ, Δ⟩ if and only if there is a choice set Y for Γ such that

(a′) $a \vDash_A \alpha$ for each $\alpha \in Y$, and
(b′) $a \nvDash_A \alpha$ for each $\alpha \in \bigcup \Delta$.

This just says that a is a counterexample to the sequent ⟨Y, $\bigcup \Delta$⟩ in *A*. Part (2) is proved similarly, and part (3) is straightforward. □

As an immediate consequence, we obtain the following corollary.

Corollary 11.3. *Let A be a classification and let* Γ, Δ *be subsets of* pow(typ(*A*)).

1. $\Gamma \vdash_{\vee A} \Delta$ *if and only if for each choice set Y on* Γ, $Y \vdash_A \bigcup \Delta$.
2. $\Gamma \vdash_{\wedge A} \Delta$ *if and only if for each choice set Y on* Δ, $\bigcup \Gamma \vdash_A Y$.

Similarly, if Γ, Δ *are subsets of* typ(*A*), *then* $\Gamma \vdash_{\neg A} \Delta$ *if and only if* $\Delta \vdash_A \Gamma$.

Observing that the right-hand side of each of these equivalences deals only with the theory of the classification *A*, the following is immediate.

Corollary 11.4. *Let A and B be classifications that have the same theory, that is,* Th(*A*) = Th(*B*). *For any Boolean operation B* (∨, ∧, ¬), Th(*B*(*A*)) = Th(*B*(*B*)).

Recall that the Representation Theorem (Theorem 9.33) associated a canonical classification Cla(*T*) with any theory *T*. Using this and the preceding corollary, we have a convenient way to get at canonical Boolean operations on theories.

Definition 11.5. For any regular theory T, define the theories $\vee T$, $\wedge T$, and $\neg T$ as follows:

1. $\vee T = \text{Th}(\vee \text{Cla}(T))$;
2. $\wedge T = \text{Th}(\wedge \text{Cla}(T))$;
3. $\neg T = \text{Th}(\neg \text{Cla}(T))$.

We unwind this definition as follows.

Corollary 11.6. *Let* $T = \langle \Sigma, \vdash \rangle$ *be a regular theory. The disjunctive power* $\vee T = \langle \text{pow}(\Sigma), \vdash_{\vee} \rangle$ *and conjunctive power* $\wedge T = \langle \text{pow}(\Sigma), \vdash_{\wedge} \rangle$ *of* T *are those regular theories on* $\text{pow}(\Sigma)$ *such that for each* $\Gamma, \Delta \subseteq \text{pow}(\Sigma)$

1. $\Gamma \vdash_{\vee} \Delta$ *if and only if for each choice set* Y *on* Γ, $Y \vdash \bigcup \Delta$, *and*
2. $\Gamma \vdash_{\wedge} \Delta$ *if and only if for each choice set* Y *on* Δ, $\bigcup \Gamma \vdash Y$.

The negation $\neg T = \langle \Sigma, \vdash_{\neg} \rangle$ *is the regular theory on* Σ *such that for each* $\Gamma, \Delta \subseteq \Sigma$, $\Gamma \vdash_{\neg} \Delta$ *if and only if* $\Delta \vdash \Gamma$.

The following shows that these definitions behave properly with respect to the Boolean operations on classifications.

Corollary 11.7. *For any classification A and any Boolean operation* $\mathcal{B}$, $\mathcal{B}$ $(\text{Th}(A)) = \text{Th}(\mathcal{B}(A))$.

Proof. By the Representation Theorem,

$$\text{Th}(A) = \text{Th}(\text{Cla}(\text{Th}(A))).$$

Hence, by Corollary 11.4,

$$\text{Th}(\mathcal{B}(A)) = \text{Th}(\mathcal{B}(\text{Cla}(\text{Th}(A)))).$$

But the right-hand side of this equation is the definition of $\mathcal{B}(\text{Th}(A))$.   □

Exercises

11.1.   Let T be any regular theory. It follows from the definition of $\neg T$ and Proposition 9.35 that $\text{Cla}(\neg T) \cong \neg \text{Cla}(T)$. Find a natural isomorphism.

11.2. Investigate the relationship between the disjunctive classifications $\vee\mathrm{Cla}(T)$ and $\mathrm{Cla}(\vee T)$ and similarly for conjunction.

11.2 Boolean Operations in Theories

We now turn to the question of what it would mean for a theory T to have a conjunction, negation, or disjunction. Because it is in some ways the simplest, we begin with negation to get our bearings.

Negation

To determine what the correct notion of a Boolean connective in a theory should be, we again start the discussion with theories that arise from classifications. Our aim is to find out how Boolean operations behave on such theories and then generalize this to arbitrary regular theories.

Proposition 11.8. *Let A be a classification with a negation $\neg$. The consequence relation $\vdash_A$ generated by A has the following properties:*

$\neg$-**Left:** *If $\Gamma \vdash_A \Delta, \alpha$ then $\Gamma, \neg\alpha \vdash_A \Delta$.*
$\neg$-**Right:** *If $\Gamma, \alpha \vdash_A \Delta$ then $\Gamma \vdash_A \Delta, \neg\alpha$.*

Proof. These are both rather obvious. □

The rules of $\neg$-Left and $\neg$-Right are, of course, simply the standard rules for negation in a classical, Gentzen approach to classical validity.

Definition 11.9. Let $T = \langle \Sigma, \vdash \rangle$ be a regular theory. A function $\neg : \Sigma \to \Sigma$ is a negation on T if and only if T satisfies the following closure conditions:

$$\neg\text{-Left:} \quad \frac{\Gamma \vdash_T \Delta, \alpha}{\Gamma, \neg\alpha \vdash_T \Delta}$$

$$\neg\text{-Right:} \quad \frac{\Gamma, \alpha \vdash_T \Delta}{\Gamma \vdash_T \Delta, \neg\alpha}$$

We have stated this in the rule format that is standard for Gentzen system; they should be read as "if ... then ...," as in the statement of Proposition 11.8.

We have stated this definition only for regular theories on purpose. Without the structural properties insured by regularity, the traditional rules simply do not guarantee that $\neg$ behaves anything like a negation. For example, in the theory defined in Example 9.23, the identity function satisfies $\neg$-Left and

¬-Right. However, for regular theories ¬-Left and ¬-Right are all that are needed to ensure that a function behaves like a negation. This is shown in our Theorem 11.12, the abstract completeness theorem for negation. The following definition provides the key to this result.

Definition 11.10. Let T be a regular theory on Σ and $\neg : \Sigma \to \Sigma$. A partition $\langle \Gamma, \Delta \rangle$ *treats* $\neg$ *as a negation* if for all types α, $\neg\alpha \in \Gamma$ if and only if $\alpha \in \Delta$.

If A is a classification with a negation $\neg$, then any realized partition of the types of A must treat $\neg$ as a negation. Put the other way around, partitions that do not respect $\neg$ are spurious. Consequently, they should not be relevant in using the rule Partition. The following result shows that closure under the negation rules allows us to ignore these spurious partitions in applying Partition.

Proposition 11.11. *Let T be any regular theory on Σ and let $\neg : \Sigma \to \Sigma$. Then T satisfies $\neg$ -Left and $\neg$ -Right if and only if T satisfies the following condition:*

> $\neg$ **-Partition:** *If $\Gamma' \vdash_T \Delta'$ for every partition $\langle \Gamma', \Delta' \rangle \geq \langle \Gamma, \Delta \rangle$ that treats $\neg$ as a negation, then $\Gamma \vdash_T \Delta$.*

Proof. Assume that T is a regular theory on Σ satisfying ¬-Left and ¬-Right. Let us show that it satisfies ¬-Partition. Suppose that $\Gamma' \vdash_T \Delta'$ for every partition that both treats $\neg$ as a negation and extends $\langle \Gamma, \Delta \rangle$. We need to prove that $\Gamma \vdash_T \Delta$. To do this, we use Partition. Thus let $\langle \Gamma', \Delta' \rangle$ be *any* partition extending $\langle \Gamma, \Delta \rangle$. We need to prove that $\Gamma' \vdash_T \Delta'$. If $\langle \Gamma', \Delta' \rangle$ treats $\neg$ as a negation, we are done by our assumption. So we need only consider the case where it does not treat $\neg$ as a negation. There are two cases to consider.

Case 1. There is a $\neg\alpha \in \Gamma'$ such that $\alpha \notin \Delta'$. But then $\alpha \in \Gamma'$. Then we have our desired $\Gamma' \vdash_T \Delta'$ as follows:

$$\frac{\dfrac{\dfrac{\alpha \vdash_T \alpha}{\Gamma' \vdash_T \Delta', \alpha}}{\Gamma', \neg\alpha \vdash_T \Delta'}}{\Gamma' \vdash_T \Delta'}.$$

The first step is an Identity, the second is by Weakening, the third is by ¬-Left. The final step is simply the third step rewritten, in view of the fact that $\neg\alpha \in \Gamma'$.

Case 2. There is a $\neg\alpha \notin \Gamma'$ such that $\alpha \in \Delta'$. But then $(\neg\alpha) \in \Delta'$. The conclusion follows as before, using ¬-Right.

Toward the converse, let us show ¬-Left, the other case being symmetric. Thus we want to show

$$\frac{\Gamma \vdash_T \Delta, \alpha}{\Gamma, \neg\alpha \vdash_T \Delta}.$$

Assume $\Gamma \vdash_T \Delta, \alpha$ but $\Gamma, \neg\alpha \not\vdash_T \Delta$. Then there is a partition $\langle \Gamma', \Delta' \rangle$ extending $\langle \Gamma \cup \{\neg\alpha\}, \Delta \rangle$ such that $\Gamma' \not\vdash_T \Delta'$ and such $\langle \Gamma', \Delta' \rangle$ treats ¬ as a negation. But then $\alpha \in \Delta'$ so we have $\Gamma' \vdash_T \Delta'$ from $\Gamma \vdash_T \Delta, \alpha$ by Weakening. □

This proposition allows us to prove the promised result, justifying the definition of a theory negation for regular theories.

Theorem 11.12 (Abstract Completeness for Negation). *Let* $T = \langle \Sigma, \vdash \rangle$ *be a regular theory and let* $\neg : \Sigma \to \Sigma$. *The following are equivalent:*

1. ¬ *is a negation on* T;
2. *there is a classification* A *and a negation infomorphism* $n : \neg A \rightleftarrows A$ *such that* $T = \text{Th}(A)$ *and* $\neg = n\hat{}$;
3. *let* $A = \text{Cla}(T)$ *and* $n : \neg A \rightleftarrows A$ *be the token identical contravariant pair that agrees with* ¬ *on types. Then* $n : \neg A \rightleftarrows A$ *is a negation infomorphism on* A.

Proof. The implication from (3) to (2) is trivial. That from (2) to (1) follows immediately from Proposition 11.8. To prove that (1) implies (3), assume (1). Recall that the types of A are those of T whereas the tokens of A are the consistent partitions of T. By Proposition 11.11, we know that all consistent partitions treat ¬ as a negation. To establish that n is a negation, we need to prove that for any such consistent partition $\langle \Gamma, \Delta \rangle$ and any type α, $\langle \Gamma, \Delta \rangle \models_{\neg A} \alpha$ if and only if $\langle \Gamma, \Delta \rangle \models_A \neg\alpha$. This is a consequence of the following chain of equivalences:

$$\begin{array}{lll}
\langle \Gamma, \Delta \rangle \models_{\neg A} \alpha & \text{iff} & \langle \Gamma, \Delta \rangle \not\models_A \alpha \\
& \text{iff} & \alpha \notin \Gamma \\
& \text{iff} & \alpha \in \Delta \\
& \text{iff} & \neg\alpha \in \Gamma \\
& \text{iff} & \langle \Gamma, \Delta \rangle \models_A \neg\alpha.
\end{array}$$

□

Corollary 11.13. *If* ¬ *is a negation on the regular theory* T, *then it is a regular theory interpretation from* $\neg T$ *to* T.

Proof. This is an immediate consequence of the previous result. □

One might be tempted to define a negation to be any interpretation from $\neg T$ to T. This, however, is far too weak. In other words, the converse of Corollary 11.13 does not hold.

Example 11.14. It does not follow from the fact that $\neg$ is an interpretation from $\neg T$ to T that a type and its negation are incompatible or that together they exhaust the possibilities. In other words, neither

$$\alpha, \neg\alpha \vdash_T \quad \text{nor} \quad \vdash_T \alpha, \neg\alpha$$

is a consequence of $\neg$ being a interpretation from $\neg T$ to T. To see this, let Σ be any set containing at least two types, say α and β, and let $T = \text{Triv}(\Sigma)$ be the least regular theory on Σ as characterized in Exercise 9.4. As we saw there, $\Gamma \vdash_T \Delta$ if and only if $\Gamma \cap \Delta \neq \emptyset$. Hence this consequence relation is symmetric so $\neg T = T$. Consequently, any permutation of Σ is a interpretation from $\neg T$ to T. For example, simply switching α and β is such an interpretation. However, clearly $\alpha, \beta \nvdash_T$ and $\nvdash_T \alpha, \beta$.

Corollary 11.15. *If T is a regular theory with a negation $\neg$ then*

    Converse of $\neg$-Left: $\Gamma \vdash_T \Delta, \alpha$ *if* $\Gamma, \neg\alpha \vdash_T \Delta$.
    Converse of $\neg$-Right: $\Gamma, \alpha \vdash_T \Delta$ *if* $\Gamma \vdash_T \Delta, \neg\alpha$.

Proof. Any negation on a classification with negation $\neg$ has these properties. □

Disjunction and Conjunction

We now proceed to the parallel considerations for disjunction and conjunction. We will not be as verbose in our discussion, because the main points have already been made with negation.

Proposition 11.16. *Let A be a classification. If A has a disjunction $\vee$, then its theory $\text{Th}(A)$ satisfies the following:*

    $\vee$**-Left:** *If* $\Gamma, \alpha \vdash_A \Delta$ *for each* $\alpha \in \Theta$ *then* $\Gamma, \vee\Theta \vdash_A \Delta$.
    $\vee$**-Right:** *if* $\Gamma \vdash_A \Delta, \Theta$ *then* $\Gamma \vdash_A \Delta, \vee\Theta$.

If A has a conjunction $\wedge$, then its theory $\text{Th}(A)$ satisfies the following:

    $\wedge$**-Left:** *If* $\Gamma, \Theta \vdash_A \Delta$, *then* $\Gamma, \wedge\Theta \vdash_A \Delta$.
    $\wedge$**-Right:** *If* $\Gamma \vdash_A \Delta, \alpha$ *for each* $\alpha \in \Theta$, *then* $\Gamma \vdash_A \Delta, \wedge\Theta$.

Proof. These are all easily proved.   □

Definition 11.17. Let $T = \langle \Sigma, \vdash \rangle$ be a regular theory. A function $\vee : \mathrm{pow}(\Sigma)$ $\to \Sigma$ is a disjunction on T if and only if T satisfies

$$\vee\text{-Left:} \quad \frac{\Gamma, \alpha \vdash \Delta \quad \text{for each } \alpha \in \Theta}{\Gamma, \vee\Theta \vdash \Delta}$$

$$\vee\text{-Right:} \quad \frac{\Gamma \vdash \Delta, \Theta}{\Gamma \vdash \Delta, \vee\Theta}$$

Similarly, a function $\wedge : \mathrm{pow}(\Sigma) \to \Sigma$ is a conjunction on T if and only if T satisfies

$$\wedge\text{-Right:} \quad \frac{\Gamma \vdash \Delta, \alpha \quad \text{for each } \alpha \in \Theta}{\Gamma \vdash \Delta, \wedge\Theta}$$

$$\wedge\text{-Left:} \quad \frac{\Gamma, \Theta \vdash \Delta}{\Gamma, \wedge\Theta \vdash \Delta}$$

Just as with negation, when we have an operation on types that is a disjunction (or conjunction), certain partitions of the types become spurious.

Definition 11.18. Let T be any regular theory on Σ. A partition $\langle \Gamma, \Delta \rangle$ is said to *treat* $\vee$ *as a disjunction* if for all sets Θ of types, $\vee\Theta \in \Delta$ if and only if $\Theta \subseteq \Delta$. The partition $\langle \Gamma, \Delta \rangle$ *treats* $\wedge$ *as a conjunction* if for all sets Θ of types, $\wedge\Theta \in \Gamma$ if and only if $\Theta \subseteq \Gamma$.

Proposition 11.19. *Let T be any regular theory on Σ.*

1. If $\vee : \mathrm{pow}(\Sigma) \to \Sigma$, then T satisfies $\vee$-Left and $\vee$-Right if and only if it satisfies the following condition:

     $\vee$**-Partition:** *If $\Gamma' \vdash_T \Delta'$ for every partition $\langle \Gamma', \Delta' \rangle \geq \langle \Gamma, \Delta \rangle$ that treats $\vee$ as a disjunction, then $\Gamma \vdash_T \Delta$.*

2. Similarly, if $\wedge : \mathrm{pow}(\Sigma) \to \Sigma$, then T satisfies $\wedge$-Left and $\wedge$-Right if and only if it satisfies the following condition:

     $\wedge$**-Partition:** *If $\Gamma' \vdash_T \Delta'$ for every partition $\langle \Gamma', \Delta' \rangle \geq \langle \Gamma, \Delta \rangle$ that treats $\wedge$ as a conjunction, then $\Gamma \vdash_T \Delta$.*

Proof. We prove that if T is a regular theory on Σ satisfying $\vee$-Left and $\vee$-Right, then it satisfies $\vee$-Partition, and leave the rest to the reader. Suppose that $\Gamma \vdash_T \Delta$ for every partition that treats $\vee$ as a disjunction and extends

$\langle \Gamma, \Delta \rangle$. We need to prove that $\Gamma \vdash_T \Delta$. To do this, we use partition. Thus let $\langle \Gamma', \Delta' \rangle$ be any partition extending $\langle \Gamma, \Delta \rangle$. We need to prove that $\Gamma' \vdash_T \Delta'$. If $\langle \Gamma', \Delta' \rangle$ treats $\vee$ as a disjunction, we are done. So we need only consider the case where it does not treat $\vee$ as a disjunction. There are two ways in which this might happen.

Case 1. There is a $\vee\Theta \in \Delta'$ such that $\Theta \nsubseteq \Delta'$. But then there is some $\alpha \in \Theta \cap \Gamma'$. Then we have our desired $\Gamma' \vdash_T \Delta'$ by Identity, Weakening, and $\vee$-Right.

Case 2. There is a $\vee\Theta \notin \Delta'$ such that $\Theta \subseteq \Delta'$. Because $\Theta \subseteq \Delta'$, we have $\alpha \vdash_T \Delta'$ for each $\alpha \in \Theta$. But then by $\vee$-Left, $\vee\Theta \vdash_T \Delta'$. But if $\vee\Theta \notin \Delta'$, then $\vee\Theta \in \Gamma'$, so $\Gamma' \vdash_T \Delta'$ by Weakening.   □

We obtain abstract completeness results for disjunction and conjunction parallel to that for negation. We will only state the one for disjunction.

Theorem 11.20 (Abstract Completeness for Disjunction). *Let* $T = \langle \Sigma, \vdash \rangle$ *be a regular theory and let* $\vee : \mathrm{pow}(\Sigma) \to \Sigma$. *The following are equivalent:*

1. $\vee$ *is a disjunction on* T.
2. *There is a classification* A *and a disjunction infomorphism* $d : \vee A \rightleftarrows A$ *such that* $T = \mathrm{Th}(A)$ *and* $\vee = d\hat{\,}$.
3. *Let* $A = \mathrm{Cla}(T)$ *and* $d : \vee A \rightleftarrows A$ *be the token identical contravariant pair that agrees with* $\vee$ *on types. Then* $d : \vee A \rightleftarrows A$ *is a disjunction infomorphism on* A.

Proof. The proof is similar to the result for negation.   □

Corollary 11.21. *If* T *is a regular theory with a disjunction* $\vee$ *(or conjunction* $\wedge$*) then*

Converse of $\vee$-Left: $\Gamma, \alpha \vdash_T \Delta$ *for each* $\alpha \in \Theta$, *provided* $\Gamma, \vee\Theta \vdash_T \Delta$.
Converse of $\vee$-Right: $\Gamma \vdash_T \Delta, \Theta$ *if* $\Gamma \vdash_T \Delta, \vee\Theta$.

In the case of conjunction, T *has the following properties:*

Converse of $\wedge$-Left: $\Gamma, \Theta \vdash_T \Delta$ *if* $\Gamma, \wedge\Theta \vdash_T \Delta$.
Converse of $\wedge$-Right: $\Gamma \vdash_T \Delta, \alpha$ *for each* $\alpha \in \Theta$, *provided* $\Gamma \vdash_T \Delta, \wedge\Theta$.

Proof. Any consequence relation on a classification with disjunction (conjunction) has these properties.   □

Definition 11.22. A regular theory T is *Boolean* if it has a disjunction, conjunction, and negation.

Corollary 11.23. *Let T be a regular theory. The following are equivalent:*

1. *T is a Boolean theory.*
2. *T is the theory of a Boolean classification.*
3. *$\mathrm{Cla}(T)$ is a Boolean classification.*

Proof. This is an immediate consequence of Theorems 11.12, 11.20, our abstract completeness theorems for negation, disjunction, and conjunction. $\square$

Exercises

11.3. Let T be a regular theory with a negation $\neg$. Show the following infinitary version of $\neg$-Left: for any sets Γ, Δ, Θ, if $\Gamma \vdash_T \Delta, \Theta$ then $\Gamma, \neg[\Theta] \vdash_T \Delta$ ($\neg[\Theta]$ is the image of Θ under $\neg$; note that if Θ is finite, this result follows from a finite number of applications of $\neg$-Left, but this strategy will not work if Θ is infinite). There is a corresponding infinitary version of $\neg$-Right.

11.4. Let T be an algebraic theory with a disjunction $\vee$. Show that for any set Γ of types, $\vee \Gamma$ is the least upper bound of Γ in the partial ordering $\leq_T$. Prove the analogous result for conjunction. What can you prove about $\neg$? Show that if T is a Boolean, algebraic theory, then it is in fact a Boolean algebra under the same operations.

11.5. Give a direct proof of Corollary 11.13, that is, one that does not go through the abstract completeness theorem, 11.12.

11.3 Boolean Inference in State Spaces

Let S be a state space with set of states Ω. Recall from Definition 9.27 the theory $\mathrm{Th}(S)$ associated with S. This theory depends only on the set Ω of states of the state space and captures the idea that these states are exhaustive and mutually incompatible. By Proposition 8.18, $\mathrm{Th}(S)$ is a Boolean theory with union, intersection, and complement acting as disjunction, conjunction, and negation, respectively. Furthermore, $\vdash \Omega$.

We now show that $\mathrm{Th}(S)$ is the smallest such regular theory. Thus $\mathrm{Th}(S)$ is the closure of the "axiom" $\vdash \Omega$ under the classical rules of inference associated with disjunction, conjunction, and negation along with Identity, Weakening, and Global Cut.

Theorem 11.24. *Let S be a state space with set of states Ω. $\mathrm{Th}(S)$ is the smallest regular theory on $\mathrm{pow}(\Omega)$ satisfying the following conditions:*

1. $\vdash \Omega$,
2. *the operation* $\Theta \mapsto \bigcup \Theta$ *is a disjunction,*
3. *the operation* $\Theta \mapsto \bigcap \Theta$ *is a conjunction, and*
4. *the operation* $X \mapsto \Omega - X$ *is a negation.*

Proof. Let $\vdash$ be the smallest consequence relation on $\mathrm{pow}(\Omega)$ such that (1)–(4) hold. Suppose $\Gamma, \Delta \subseteq \mathrm{pow}(\Omega)$ and $\Gamma \vdash_{\mathrm{Th}(S)} \Delta$. We need to prove that $\Gamma \vdash \Delta$. By assumption, we have $\bigcap \Gamma \subseteq \bigcup \Delta$. Hence $\bigcup \Delta \cup -(\bigcap \Gamma) = \Omega$. By (1), then, $\vdash \bigcup \Delta \cup -(\bigcap \Gamma)$. By the converse of $\vee$-Right, we have $\vdash \bigcup \Delta, \Omega - (\bigcap \Gamma)$. By $\neg$-Left, $\bigcap \Gamma \vdash \bigcup \Delta$. By the converse of $\vee$-Right, we obtain $\bigcap \Gamma \vdash \Delta$; and by the converse of $\wedge$-Left, we obtain the desired conclusion $\Gamma \vdash \Delta$.   □

Lecture 12

Local Logics

With the groundwork laid in the preceding lectures, we come to the central material of the book, the idea of a local logic, which will take up the remainder of Part II. In this lecture we introduce local logics and proceed in the lectures that follow to show how local logics are related to channels and so to information flow.

If one is reasoning about a distributed system with components of very different kinds, the components will typically be classified in quite different ways, that is, with quite different types. Along with these different types, it is natural to think of each of the components as having its own logic, expressed in its own system of types. In this way, the distributed system gives rise to a distributed system of local logics. The interactions of the local logics reflect the behavior of the system as a whole.

In order to capture this idea, we introduce and study the notions of "local logic" and "local logic infomorphism" in this lecture. The main notions are introduced in the first two sections and studied throughout this lecture. The important idea of moving a logic along an infomorphism is studied in Lecture 13. In Lecture 14, we show that every local logic can be represented in terms of moving natural logics along binary channels. The idea of moving logics is put to another use in Lecture 15 to define the distributed logic of an information system. It is in this chapter that our picture of information flow is most fully articulated. Finally, in Lecture 16, we explore the relationship between local logics and state spaces in some detail.

12.1 Local Logics Defined

The notion of a local logic puts the idea of a classification together with that of a regular theory, but with an important added twist. In order to model reasonable but unsound inference, we introduce the notion of a "normal token" of a logic.

Definition 12.1. A *local logic* $\mathfrak{L} = \langle \text{tok}(\mathfrak{L}), \text{typ}(\mathfrak{L}), \vDash_{\mathfrak{L}}, \vdash_{\mathfrak{L}}, N_{\mathfrak{L}} \rangle$ consists of

1. a classification $\text{cla}(\mathfrak{L}) = \langle \text{tok}(\mathfrak{L}), \text{typ}(\mathfrak{L}), \vDash_{\mathfrak{L}} \rangle$,
2. a regular theory $\text{th}(\mathfrak{L}) = \langle \text{typ}(\mathfrak{L}), \vdash_{\mathfrak{L}} \rangle$, and
3. a subset $N_{\mathfrak{L}} \subseteq \text{tok}(\mathfrak{L})$, called the *normal tokens* of $\mathfrak{L}$, which satisfy all the constraints of $\text{th}(\mathfrak{L})$.

A token $a \in \text{tok}(\mathfrak{L})$ that fails to satisfy some constraint $\Gamma \vdash_{\mathfrak{L}} \Delta$ of $\mathfrak{L}$ is said to be an *exception* to this constraint. Part of the definition of a local logic insures that normal tokens are not exceptions to any constraints of the logic. Notice, however, that we do not assume that every nonnormal token is an exception to some constraint of the logic. It sometimes happens that a token satisfies all the constraints of a logic, but "by accident" as it were; the tokens in $N_{\mathfrak{L}}$ model the set of tokens that satisfy all the constraints for principled reasons.

Definition 12.2. A logic $\mathfrak{L}$ is *sound* if every token of $\text{tok}(\mathfrak{L})$ is normal. $\mathfrak{L}$ is *complete* if every sequent satisfied by every normal token is a constraint of the logic.

When we come to moving logics via infomorphisms, we will see that there are two natural ways to move logics. One preserves soundness, the other preserves completeness. Both, however, correspond to natural methods of reasoning about distributed systems.

Systematic Examples

We give three important examples of ways in which local logics arise. We will study these logics in detail in what follows.

Definition 12.3. Let A be a classification. The *local logic generated by* A, written $\text{Log}(A)$, has classification A, regular theory $\text{Th}(A)$, and all its tokens are normal. A logic is *natural* if it is generated by some classification.

Definition 12.4. Let S be a state space. The *local logic generated by* S, written $\text{Log}(S)$, has classification $\text{Evt}(S)$, regular theory $\text{Th}(S)$, and all its tokens are normal.

Justification. To see that Log(S) is a local logic, we need to verify that every token of Evt(S), that is, every token of S, satisfies every constraint of Th(S). This is obvious. □

Definition 12.5. Let T be a regular theory. The *local logic generated by* T, written Log(T), has classification Cla(T), regular theory T, and all its tokens are normal. A logic is *formal* if it is generated by some regular theory.

Proposition 12.6. *Every formal logic is natural. Every natural logic* Log(A) *on a separated classification A is isomorphic to a formal logic.*

Proof. The first follows from Log(T) = Log(Cla(T)). The second holds because if A is separated, then $A \cong$ Cla(Th(A)), by Proposition 9.35. □

All of the examples of local logics given so far have been sound. Our main source of unsound local logics arises from moving logics via infomorphisms, a topic we take up in the next chapter. But it is easy enough to give other examples of unsound local logics. One example is given in Exercise 12.1. Others will be given in Lecture 19.

Exercises

12.1. Let $\mathfrak{L}$ be a local logic and let $\Theta \subseteq$ typ($\mathfrak{L}$) be a set of types. Suppose that in reasoning about the tokens in $\mathfrak{L}$ we have, in the course of a great deal of experience, never encountered any token that is not of all types in Θ. It might not be unreasonable to conclude that all tokens are of all the types in Θ and so ignore Θ in our reasoning. The *conditionalization of* $\mathfrak{L}$ *on* Θ is the logic $\mathfrak{L} \mid \Theta$ defined as follows. The classification of $\mathfrak{L} \mid \Theta$ is the same as that of $\mathfrak{L}$. The theory of $\mathfrak{L} \mid \Theta$ is given by

$$\Gamma \vdash_{\mathfrak{L} \mid \Theta} \Delta \quad \text{iff} \quad \Gamma, \Theta \vdash_{\mathfrak{L}} \Delta.$$

The normal tokens of $\mathfrak{L} \mid \Theta$ consist of those normal tokens of $\mathfrak{L}$ that are of all types in Θ. If $\Theta = \{\theta\}$ is a singleton, we write this conditionalized logic as $\mathfrak{L} \mid \theta$.

1. Show that $\mathfrak{L} \mid \Theta$ is indeed a local logic.
2. Give an everyday example of a sound local logic $\mathfrak{L}$ and a type θ such that $\mathfrak{L} \mid \theta$ is not sound.
3. Prove that for every local logic $\mathfrak{L}$ there is a sound local logic $\mathfrak{L}'$ and a type $\theta \in$ typ($\mathfrak{L}'$) such that $\mathfrak{L} = \mathfrak{L}' \mid \theta$.

12.2.   Let S be a state space with set Ω of types. The trivial logic on S, written $\text{Triv}(S)$, is the sound local logic with the classification S and with the consequence relation that is the smallest regular consequence relation such that $\vdash_{\text{Triv}(S)} \Omega$ and, for all distinct states $\sigma_1, \sigma_2 \in \Omega$, $\sigma_1, \sigma_2 \vdash_{\text{Triv}(S)}$.

1. Justify this definition.
2. Show that for any sets $\Gamma, \Delta \subseteq \text{typ}(S)$, $\Gamma \vdash_{\text{Triv}(S)} \Delta$ if and only if one of the following three conditions holds:

   (a) $\Gamma \cap \Delta \neq \emptyset$,

   (b) Γ has at least two elements, or

   (c) $\Delta = \Omega$.

12.2 Soundness and Completeness

In this section we make some simple remarks about sound and complete local logics. Note, though, that most interesting local logics are neither sound nor complete.

Proposition 12.7. *For any local logic $\mathfrak{L}$ on a classification A, the following are equivalent:*

1. *$\mathfrak{L}$ is natural.*
2. *$\mathfrak{L}$ is sound and complete.*
3. *$\mathfrak{L} = \text{Log}(A)$.*

Proof. For any classification A, $\text{Log}(A)$ is the unique sound and complete local logic with classification A.   □

Proposition 12.8. *Let S be a state space. The logic $\text{Log}(S)$ is sound. It is complete if and only if S is complete.*

Proof. This is obvious from the definitions.   □

We turn any logic into one that is sound, complete, or both, as follows.

Definition 12.9. For any local logic $\mathfrak{L}$, the *sound part of $\mathfrak{L}$*, written $\text{Snd}(\mathfrak{L})$, is the local logic obtained by throwing away all the abnormal tokens of $\mathfrak{L}$ and restricting the classification relation accordingly. Everything else is left unchanged.

Example 12.10. Recall the theory of light bulbs from Example 9.17. The consistent partitions were given by the rows of the following truth table:

Lit	Unlit	Live
1	0	1
0	1	1
0	1	0

The theory was characterized in terms of sequents in Example 9.19. Let us turn this into a local logic $\mathfrak{L}$ by specifying the classification as follows:

	Lit	Unlit	Live
b_1	0	1	1
b_2	1	0	1
b_3	0	1	1
b_4	0	0	1

The set of normal tokens of our logic consists of all the tokens that satisfy the constraints, that is, b_1, b_2, and b_3. Token b_4 violates the constraint $\vdash$ LIT, UNLIT. (Perhaps b_4 is burning but extremely dimly.) The sound part $\mathrm{Snd}(\mathfrak{L})$ is the same logic, except on the classification corresponding to the first three rows of the above table, that is, the token b_4 is thrown out.

Definition 12.11. For any local logic $\mathfrak{L}$ the *completion of* $\mathfrak{L}$, written $\mathrm{Cmp}(\mathfrak{L})$, is the local logic obtained by adding a new normal token $n_{\langle \Gamma, \Delta \rangle}$ for each consistent partition $\langle \Gamma, \Delta \rangle$ that is not the state description of a normal token of $\mathfrak{L}$.[1] The new token $n_{\langle \Gamma, \Delta \rangle}$ is classified by type α of $\mathfrak{L}$ if and only if $\alpha \in \Gamma$. Everything else is left unchanged.

Example 12.12. Returning to the logic $\mathfrak{L}$ of Example 12.10, the completion $\mathrm{Cmp}(\mathfrak{L})$ is obtained by adding a normal token n to correspond to the one unrealized consistent partition, as follows:

	Lit	Unlit	Live
b_1	0	1	1
b_2	1	0	1
b_3	0	1	1
b_4	0	0	1
n	0	1	0

---

[1] Under normal circumstances, the most sensible way to do this would be to add the consistent partition $\langle \Gamma, \Delta \rangle$ itself as this new token. This could only be a problem if by some quirk this pair were already a token of the classification.

Someone using the logic $\mathfrak{L}$ is implicitly assuming that tokens like n are possible even if they do not happen to be realized.

Proposition 12.13. *Let $\mathfrak{L}$ be a local logic.*

1. $\text{Snd}(\mathfrak{L})$ *is sound; it is complete if and only if $\mathfrak{L}$ is complete.*
2. $\mathfrak{L}$ *is sound if and only if $\text{Snd}(\mathfrak{L}) = \mathfrak{L}$.*
3. $\text{Cmp}(\mathfrak{L})$ *is complete; it is sound if and only if $\mathfrak{L}$ is sound.*
4. $\mathfrak{L}$ *is complete if and only if $\text{Cmp}(\mathfrak{L}) = \mathfrak{L}$.*

Proof. See Exercise 12.3.   □

Proposition 12.14. $\text{Snd}(\text{Cmp}(\mathfrak{L})) = \text{Cmp}(\text{Snd}(\mathfrak{L}))$

Proof. See Exercise 12.3.   □

Definition 12.15. For any local logic $\mathfrak{L}$, the *sound completion* of $\mathfrak{L}$, written $\text{SC}(\mathfrak{L})$, is $\text{Snd}(\text{Cmp}(\mathfrak{L}))$.

The sound completion of a local logic $\mathfrak{L}$ throws away the nonnormal tokens and adds in tokens to make the logic complete. It is thus a sound and complete logic, one with the same constraints as the original logic. Thus $\text{SC}(\mathfrak{L})$ represents an idealization of the logic $\mathfrak{L}$, how the world would work if the logic were perfect. We will see that there is an important relationship between $\mathfrak{L}$ and $\text{SC}(\mathfrak{L})$ in Lecture 14. For now we simply note that $\mathfrak{L}$ is sound and complete if and only if $\text{SC}(\mathfrak{L}) = \mathfrak{L}$.

Exercise

12.3.   Give proofs of Propositions 12.13 and 12.14.

12.3 Logic Infomorphisms

Suppose we have classifications A and C, representing the possible behaviors of some distributed system C and its components A. The part-whole relationship is modeled by means of an infomorphism $f : A \rightleftarrows C$. If we have local logics on A and C, respectively, we need to ask ourselves under what conditions f respects these logics.

The basic intuition is that if an instance c of the whole system is normal with respect to its logic, then the component $f(c)$ should be normal. Similarly, any constraint that holds of normal components must translate into something that holds of normal instances of the whole system. This is formalized in the following definition.

Definition 12.16. A *logic infomorphism* $f : \mathfrak{L}_1 \rightleftarrows \mathfrak{L}_2$ consists of a contravariant pair $f = \langle f^\wedge, f^\vee \rangle$ of functions such that

1. $f : \text{cla}(\mathfrak{L}_1) \rightleftarrows \text{cla}(\mathfrak{L}_2)$ is an infomorphism of classifications,
2. $f^\wedge : \text{th}(\mathfrak{L}_1) \to \text{th}(\mathfrak{L}_2)$ is a theory interpretation, and
3. $f^\vee[N_{\mathfrak{L}_2}] \subseteq N_{\mathfrak{L}_1}$.

We have seen how to associate a local logic with any classification, state space, or regular theory. The various morphisms between these structures (infomorphisms, projections, and interpretations, respectively) all give rise to logic infomorphisms, as we now show. First, though, we state a lemma that we will use several times.

Lemma 12.17. *Let $f : A \rightleftarrows B$ be an infomorphism, let Γ, Δ be sets of types of A, and let $b \in \text{tok}(B)$. Then $f(b)$ satisfies $\langle \Gamma, \Delta \rangle$ in A if and only if b satisfies $\langle f[\Gamma], f[\Delta] \rangle$ in B.*

Proof. Assume that $f(b)$ satisfies $\langle \Gamma, \Delta \rangle$ in A. To show that b satisfies $\langle f[\Gamma], f[\Delta] \rangle$ in B, assume that b satisfies every $\beta \in f[\Gamma]$. Then, because f is an infomorphism, $f(b)$ satisfies every $\alpha \in \Gamma$. But then $f(b)$ satisfies some $\alpha' \in \Delta$, so b satisfies $f(\alpha')$, an element of $f[\Delta]$, as desired. The converse is similar. □

Definition 12.18. For any (classification) infomorphism $f : A \rightleftarrows B$, let $\text{Log}(f) : \text{Log}(A) \rightleftarrows \text{Log}(B)$ be the logic infomorphism that is the same as f as a pair of functions, but taken to have as domain and codomain the logics, rather than their underlying classification.

Justification. By Lemma 12.17, it is clear that if $\Gamma \vdash_{\text{Log}(A)} \Delta$ then $f[\Gamma] \vdash_{\text{Log}(B)} f[\Delta]$. Because these logics are sound, the condition on normal tokens is trivial. □

Definition 12.19. For any state space projection $f : S_1 \rightleftarrows S_2$ let $\text{Log}(f)$ be the logic infomorphism $\text{Log}(f) : \text{Log}(S_2) \rightleftarrows \text{Log}(S_1)$ that, as a pair of functions, is the same as $\text{Evt}(f)$; that is, $\text{Log}(f)$ is the identity on tokens and takes inverse images of sets of states.

Justification. To see that $\text{Log}(f)$ is a logic infomorphism, we need to check that if $\Gamma_2 \vdash_{\text{Log}(S_2)} \Delta_2$, and if $\Gamma_1 = \{f^{-1}[X] \mid X \in \Gamma_2\}$, and $\Delta_1 = \{f^{-1}[X] \mid X \in \Delta_2\}$, then $\Gamma_1 \vdash_{\text{Log}(S_1)} \Delta_1$. But $\Gamma_i \vdash_{\text{Log}(S_i)} \Delta_i$ just means that every state of S_i that is in every $X \in \Gamma_i$ is in some $Y \in \Delta_i$, so the implication follows from general properties of inverse images of functions.   □

Definition 12.20. For any regular theory interpretation $f : T_1 \rightarrow T_2$, let $\text{Log}(f)$ be the logic infomorphism $\text{Log}(f) : \text{Log}(T_1) \rightleftarrows \text{Log}(T_2)$ defined as follows. On types, $\text{Log}(f)$ is just f. On tokens, $\text{Log}(f)$ maps any consistent partition $\langle \Gamma, \Delta \rangle$ of T_2 to $\langle f^{-1}[\Gamma], f^{-1}[\Delta] \rangle$.

Justification. To see that $\text{Log}(f)$ is a logic infomorphism, we need to check that if $\langle \Gamma, \Delta \rangle$ is a consistent partition of T_2, then $\langle f^{-1}[\Gamma], f^{-1}[\Delta] \rangle$ is a consistent partition of T_1. That it is a partition follows just from set-theoretic properties of functions. That it is consistent follows from the fact that f is a regular theory interpretation.   □

Exercises

12.4.   Let o be the unique sound local logic on the zero classification (cf. Exercise 3). Show that for every local logic $\mathfrak{L}$ there is a unique logic infomorphism $f : \text{o} \rightleftarrows \mathfrak{L}$. Find a local logic $\mathbf{1}$ such that for every local logic $\mathfrak{L}$ there is a unique logic infomorphism $f : \mathfrak{L} \rightleftarrows \mathbf{1}$.

12.5.   (†) Let cla be the forgetful functor from the category of local logics to the category of classifications, taking each logic $\mathfrak{L}$ to its classification $\text{cla}(\mathfrak{L})$ and each logic infomorphism f to the infomorphism f constituted by the same pair of functions. Show that Log is left adjoint to the restriction of cla to complete logics, and right adjoint to the restriction of cla to sound logics.

12.4 Operations on Logics

We have already seen ways of combining classifications and regular theories. It is but a small step from that to combining local logics.

Sums of Logics

Definition 12.21. The sum $\mathfrak{L}_1 + \mathfrak{L}_2$ of local logics $\mathfrak{L}_1$ and $\mathfrak{L}_2$ is the local logic with

1. classification $\text{cla}(\mathfrak{L}_1) + \text{cla}(\mathfrak{L}_2)$,
2. regular theory $\text{th}(\mathfrak{L}_1) + \text{th}(\mathfrak{L}_2)$, and
3. $N_{\mathfrak{L}_1 + \mathfrak{L}_2} = N_{\mathfrak{L}_1} \times N_{\mathfrak{L}_2}$

The *canonical logic infomorphisms* $\sigma_{\mathfrak{L}_1} : \mathfrak{L}_1 \rightleftharpoons \mathfrak{L}_1 + \mathfrak{L}_2$ and $\sigma_{\mathfrak{L}_2} : \mathfrak{L}_2 \rightleftharpoons \mathfrak{L}_1 + \mathfrak{L}_2$ are defined as follows:

1. for each $\alpha \in \text{typ}(\mathfrak{L}_i)$, $\sigma_{\mathfrak{L}_i}(\alpha) = \sigma_{\text{cla}(\mathfrak{L}_i)}(\alpha)$;
2. for each pair $c \in \text{tok}(\mathfrak{L}_1 + \mathfrak{L}_2)$, $\sigma_{\mathfrak{L}_i}^{\,\hat{}}(c) = \sigma_{\text{cla}(\mathfrak{L}_i)}^{\,\hat{}}(c)$.

Justification. To see that $\mathfrak{L}_1 + \mathfrak{L}_2$ is a local logic, we need to see that every token $\langle a, b \rangle \in N_{\mathfrak{L}_1} \times N_{\mathfrak{L}_2}$ satisfies every constraint of $\text{th}(\mathfrak{L}_1) + \text{th}(\mathfrak{L}_2)$. But this is clear from the definitions. To see that $\sigma_{\mathfrak{L}_1} : \mathfrak{L}_1 \rightleftharpoons \mathfrak{L}_1 + \mathfrak{L}_2$ and $\sigma_{\mathfrak{L}_2} : \mathfrak{L}_2 \rightleftharpoons \mathfrak{L}_1 + \mathfrak{L}_2$ are indeed logic infomorphisms, there are three things to check, as follows:

1. $\sigma_{\mathfrak{L}_i}$ is an infomorphism because it is identical to $\sigma_{\text{cla}(\mathfrak{L}_i)}$ on classifications;
2. $\sigma_{\mathfrak{L}_i}^{\,\hat{}}$ is a theory interpretation because it is identical to $\sigma_{\text{th}(\mathfrak{L}_i)}$ on regular theories; and
3. if $b = \langle a_1, a_2 \rangle \in N_{\mathfrak{L}_1 + \mathfrak{L}_2}$, then $\sigma_{\mathfrak{L}_i}^{\,\hat{}}(b) = a_i$, which is a normal token of $\mathfrak{L}_i$. □

The above definition extends from the sum of two local logics to the sum of any indexed families of local logics without incident.

Proposition 12.22. *For any classifications A and B,*

$$\text{Log}(A + B) = \text{Log}(A) + \text{Log}(B).$$

The same holds for arbitrary indexed families of classifications.

Proof. The only part that is not obvious is that the two logics have the same theories. But this is the content of Proposition 10.3. □

Proposition 12.23. *Let $\mathfrak{L}$ be the sum $\sum_{i \in I} \mathfrak{L}_i$ of an indexed family $\{\mathfrak{L}_i\}_{i \in I}$ of local logics. Given a family $\{f_i : \mathfrak{L}_i \rightleftharpoons \mathfrak{L}'\}_{i \in I}$ of logic infomorphisms, the sum $\sum_{i \in I} f_i : \mathfrak{L} \rightleftharpoons \mathfrak{L}'$ is a logic infomorphism.*

Proof. Suppose c is a normal token of $\mathfrak{L}'$. Then $f_i^{\,\hat{}}(c)$ is a normal token of A_i for each $i \in I$, and so $(\sum_{i \in I} f_i)^{\,\hat{}}(c)$ is a normal token of $\mathfrak{L}$. Suppose that $\Gamma \vdash_{\mathfrak{L}} \Delta$. We can write $\langle \Gamma, \Delta \rangle$ as

$$\langle \Gamma, \Delta \rangle = \left\langle \bigcup_{i \in I} \sigma_{\mathfrak{L}_i}[\Gamma_i], \bigcup_{i \in I} \sigma_{\mathfrak{L}_i}[\Delta_i] \right\rangle,$$

where $\langle \Gamma_i, \Delta_i \rangle$ is a sequent of $\mathfrak{L}_i$ for each $i \in I$. Because $\mathfrak{L} = \sum_{i \in I} \mathfrak{L}_i$, it follows that $\Gamma_i \vdash_{\mathfrak{L}_i} \Delta_i$ for some $i \in I$. But f_i is a logic infomorphism, so $f_i[\Gamma_i] \vdash_{\mathfrak{L}'} f_i[\Delta_i]$, and so by Weakening $(\sum_{i \in I} f_i)[\Gamma] \vdash_{\mathfrak{L}'} (\sum_{i \in I} f_i)[\Delta]$. □

Exercises

12.6. Show that $\mathfrak{L}_1 + \mathfrak{L}_2$ is sound if and only if $\mathfrak{L}_1$ and $\mathfrak{L}_2$ are both sound.

12.7. Show that $\mathfrak{L}_1 + \mathfrak{L}_2$ is complete if and only if $\mathfrak{L}_1$ and $\mathfrak{L}_2$ are both complete.

Joins of Logics

Definition 12.24. We define a partial order on local logics on a fixed classification A as follows:

$$\mathfrak{L}_1 \sqsubseteq \mathfrak{L}_2 \quad \text{iff} \quad \text{th}(\mathfrak{L}_1) \sqsubseteq \text{th}(\mathfrak{L}_2) \quad \text{and} \quad N_{\mathfrak{L}_2} \subseteq N_{\mathfrak{L}_1}.$$

Note the difference in the direction of the two inclusions. Stronger logics have more constraints but fewer normal tokens. This "contravariance" is something we have seen repeatedly. This is closely related to the problem of nonmonotonicity. A hint of this is given in Exercise 2.

Definition 12.25. The *join* $\mathfrak{L}_1 \sqcup \mathfrak{L}_2$ of logics $\mathfrak{L}_1$ and $\mathfrak{L}_2$ on A is the local logic with regular theory $\text{th}(\mathfrak{L}_1) \sqcup \text{th}(\mathfrak{L}_2)$ and normal tokens $N_{\mathfrak{L}_1} \cap N_{\mathfrak{L}_2}$. The *meet* of local logics is defined dually.

Justification. We need to check that $\mathfrak{L}_1 \sqcup \mathfrak{L}_2$ is the least upper bound of logics $\mathfrak{L}_1$ and $\mathfrak{L}_2$ in the $\sqsubseteq$-ordering on logics. This follows from the corresponding properties of classifications and regular theories. Greatest lower bounds are justified similarly.   □

A straightforward generalization of the justification of joins and meets gives the following.

Proposition 12.26. *The ordering $\sqsubseteq$ on logics on A is a complete lattice.*

Example 12.27. Let A be a classification. Here are some simple applications of Proposition 12.26.

1. There is a smallest local logic $\mathfrak{L}$ on A. Its theory is given by $\Gamma \vdash_{\mathfrak{L}} \Delta$ if and only if $\Gamma \cap \Delta \neq \emptyset$. $\mathfrak{L}$ is sound. We call $\mathfrak{L}$ the *a priori logic* on A and denote it by $\text{AP}(A)$. This logic looks trivial, but it is of some use.
2. There is a largest local logic on A. Its theory consists of all sequents, and so is inconsistent. It has an empty set of normal tokens. It is tempting to call this the postmodern logic on A.

3. Given any theory T on typ(A), there is a smallest logic $\mathcal{L}$ for which all the constraints of T are constraints of $\mathcal{L}$. Its theory is the regular closure of T and its normal tokens are the set of all tokens satisfying all the constraints of T.

Proposition 12.28. *Let $f : \mathcal{L}_1 \rightleftarrows \mathcal{L}_2$ be a logic infomorphism, and let $\mathcal{L}_1'$ and $\mathcal{L}_2'$ be logics with the same classifications as $\mathcal{L}_1$ and $\mathcal{L}_2$, respectively. If $\mathcal{L}_1' \sqsubseteq \mathcal{L}_1$ and $\mathcal{L}_2 \sqsubseteq \mathcal{L}_2'$, then f is also a logic infomorphism from $\mathcal{L}_1'$ to $\mathcal{L}_2'$.*

Proof. The proof is routine. □

Proposition 12.29. *Let $\mathcal{L}_1$ and $\mathcal{L}_2$ be logics on the classification A. If $f : \mathcal{L}_1 \rightleftarrows \mathcal{L}$ and $f : \mathcal{L}_2 \rightleftarrows \mathcal{L}$ are logic infomorphisms, then f is also a logic infomorphism from $\mathcal{L}_1 \sqcup \mathcal{L}_2$ to $\mathcal{L}$.*

Proof. Recall that the consequence relation of $\mathcal{L}_1 \sqcup \mathcal{L}_2$ is not just the union of the consequence relations of the individual logics but is the result of closing the union under Weakening. So suppose $\Gamma \vdash_{\mathcal{L}_1 \sqcup \mathcal{L}_2} \Delta$. Then for some $i = 1, 2$ and some $\Gamma' \subseteq \Gamma$, $\Delta' \subseteq \Delta$ such that $\Gamma' \vdash_{\mathcal{L}_i} \Delta'$. Because $f : \mathcal{L}_i \rightleftarrows \mathcal{L}$ is a logic infomorphism, $f[\Gamma'] \vdash_{\mathcal{L}} f[\Delta']$ and so $f[\Gamma] \vdash_{\mathcal{L}} f[\Delta]$, by Weakening in $\mathcal{L}$. The condition on normal tokens is clear. □

Quotients of Logics

Just as we had quotients and dual quotient of classifications and theories, so too do we have them for logics.

Definition 12.30. Let $\mathcal{L}$ be a local logic on a classification A and let $I = \langle \Sigma, R \rangle$ be an invariant on A. The *quotient logic of $\mathcal{L}$ by I*, written $\mathcal{L}/I$, is the logic that has

1. classification A/I,
2. theory th($\mathcal{L}$) $\mid \Sigma$, and
3. the set of normal tokens $\{[a]_R \mid a \in N_{\mathcal{L}}\}$.

Justification. We must verify that if $a \in N_{\mathcal{L}}$, then $[a]_R$ satisfies all the constraints of th($\mathcal{L}$) $\mid \Sigma$. This follows from the fact that $\tau_I : A/I \rightleftarrows A$ is an infomorphism. □

This construction is not as important for our purposes as the dual, so we leave some of its properties to the exercises.

Definition 12.31. Let $\mathfrak{L}$ be a local logic on a classification A and let $J = \langle A, R \rangle$ be a dual invariant on A. The *quotient logic of* $\mathfrak{L}$ *by* J, written $\mathfrak{L}/J$, is the logic that has

1. classification A/J,
2. theory $\mathrm{th}(\mathfrak{L})/R$, and
3. the set of normal tokens $N_{\mathfrak{L}} \cap A$.

Justification. We must verify that if $a \in N_{\mathfrak{L}} \cap A$, then a satisfies all the constraints of $\mathrm{th}(\mathfrak{L})/R$. Equivalently, it suffices to show that if $\langle \Gamma, \Delta \rangle$ is the state description of a in A/J, and $\Gamma_0 = \tau_J^{-1}[\Gamma]$, $\Delta_0 = \tau_J^{-1}[\Delta]$, then a satisfies $\langle \Gamma_0, \Delta_0 \rangle$ in A. This follows from the fact that $\tau_J : A \rightleftarrows A/J$ is an infomorphism.   □

Example 12.32. Given a local logic $\mathfrak{L}$, let $\alpha R \beta$ if and only if $\alpha \vdash_T \beta$. Let $J = \langle N_{\mathfrak{L}}, R \rangle$. This is clearly a dual invariant, because all normal tokens satisfy all constraints and hence respect R. The quotient $\mathfrak{L}/J$ is called the *Lindenbaum logic* of $\mathfrak{L}$ and is written Lind $(\mathfrak{L})$. This logic identifies types that are equivalent in $\mathfrak{L}$. Notice that it is always a sound logic. It is complete if and only if $\mathfrak{L}$ is complete.

We say that a partition $\langle \Gamma, \Delta \rangle$ of Σ *respects the relation* R on Σ if for all $\alpha, \beta \in \Sigma$, if $\alpha R \beta$, then $\alpha \in \Gamma$ if and only if $\beta \in \Gamma$. This is equivalent to saying that if $\alpha \in \Gamma$, then $[\alpha]_R \subseteq \Gamma$.

Proposition 12.33. *Let $\mathfrak{L}$ be a local logic on A and let $J = \langle A, R \rangle$ be a dual invariant on A.*

1. *$\mathfrak{L}/J$ is sound if and only if $A \subseteq N_{\mathfrak{L}}$. Hence if $\mathfrak{L}$ is sound, then $\mathfrak{L}/J$ is sound.*
2. *$\mathfrak{L}/J$ is complete if and only if every $\mathfrak{L}$-consistent partition of $\mathrm{typ}(A)$ that respects R is the state description of some $a \in A \cap N_{\mathfrak{L}}$. Hence, if $\mathfrak{L}$ is complete and $N_{\mathfrak{L}} \subseteq A$, then $\mathfrak{L}/J$ is complete.*

Proof. Statement (1) is an immediate consequence of the definition. Statement (2) is almost immediate, given the rule Partition.   □

From this we obtain the following simple but useful characterization of a dual quotient as a natural logic.

Corollary 12.34. *A logic of the form $\mathfrak{L}/J$, where $J = \langle A, R \rangle$ is a dual invariant on $\mathrm{cla}(\mathfrak{L})$, is a natural logic if and only if $A \subseteq N_{\mathfrak{L}}$ and every $\mathfrak{L}$-consistent partition that respects R is the state description of some $a \in A$.*

Proof. Because a logic is natural if and only if it is sound and complete, this result follows immediately from Proposition 12.33. ☐

Proposition 12.35. *Let $\mathcal{L}$ be a local logic on a classification A and let J be a dual invariant on A.*

1. *The logic $\mathcal{L}/J$ is the least logic on A/J such that the function τ_J is a logic infomorphism.*
2. *Let $f : \mathcal{L} \rightleftarrows \mathcal{L}'$ be a logic infomorphism that respects J. There is a unique logic infomorphism $f' : \mathcal{L}/J \rightleftarrows \mathcal{L}'$ such that the following diagram commutes:*

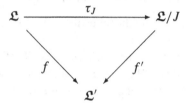

Proof. Statement (1) follows easily from Proposition 10.11. Statement (2) follows directly from Propositions 5.21 and 10.11. ☐

Exercises

12.8. Recall the definition of the conditionalization $\mathcal{L} \mid \Theta$ of a logic to a set of types in Exercise 12.1. Let $\mathcal{L}$ be a local logic and let $\Theta_0 \subseteq \Theta_1 \subseteq \text{typ}(\mathcal{L})$. Show that $\mathcal{L} \mid \Theta_0 \sqsubseteq \mathcal{L} \mid \Theta_1$.

12.9. Let $\mathcal{L}$ be a local logic on a classification A. For any set $B \subseteq \text{tok}(A)$, let $\text{typ}(B) = \bigcap_{b \in B} \text{typ}(b)$. That is, $\alpha \in \text{typ}(B)$ if and only if for all $a \in B$, $a \vDash_A \alpha$. Suppose that B consists of all tokens in $\mathcal{L}$ ever observed in the past, and suppose we are willing to reason on the assumption that anything that has always held true of past tokens will hold true of some future token. We can model this form of reasoning by considering the logic $\mathcal{L} \mid \text{typ}(B)$. The normal tokens of this logic consist of the set of all tokens that satisfy all the types that hold of tokens in B. Prove the following antimonotonicity result: if $B_0 \subseteq B_1$, then $\mathcal{L} \mid \text{typ}(B_1) \sqsubseteq \mathcal{L} \mid \text{typ}(B_0)$.

12.10. Dualize Proposition 12.35.

12.5 Boolean Operations and Logics

Our discussion of Boolean operations, classifications, and theories was prompted by the natural desire to relate Boolean operations and local logics. Readers who have skipped the chapters on Boolean operations will want to skip this section as well.

Again, we break the discussion into two parts. We first discuss Boolean operations on logics and then discuss what it means for an operation on the types of a single logic to be a disjunction, conjunction, or negation. We have done most of the work already, so the discussion will be rather brief.

Boolean Operations on Logics

We have laid the groundwork for the following definition in preceding chapters.

Definition 12.36. Let $\mathfrak{L}$ be a local logic on a classification A with theory T and set N of normal tokens. We define the disjunctive power logic $\vee\mathfrak{L}$, the conjunctive power logic $\wedge\mathfrak{L}$, and the negation $\neg\mathfrak{L}$ of $\mathfrak{L}$ as follows:

1. $\vee\mathfrak{L}$ is the local logic with classification $\vee A$, theory $\vee T$, and normal tokens N;
2. $\wedge\mathfrak{L}$ is the local logic with classification $\wedge A$, theory $\wedge T$, and normal tokens N; and
3. $\neg\mathfrak{L}$ is the local logic with classification $\neg A$, theory $\neg T$, and normal tokens N.

Justification. We need to see that every token in N satisfies the constraints of $\vee T$, $\wedge T$, and $\neg T$ in the classifications $\vee A$, $\wedge A$, and $\neg A$, respectively. This follows immediately from Proposition 11.2.   □

Proposition 12.37. *For any local logic $\mathfrak{L}$, $\mathfrak{L}$ is sound if and only if $\vee\mathfrak{L}$ is sound, if and only if $\wedge\mathfrak{L}$ is sound, and if and only if $\neg\mathfrak{L}$ is sound. Similarly, $\mathfrak{L}$ is complete if and only if $\vee\mathfrak{L}$ is complete, if and only if $\wedge\mathfrak{L}$ is complete, and if and only if $\neg\mathfrak{L}$ is complete.*

Proof. Soundness is trivial. Let us show that $\mathfrak{L}$ is complete iff $\vee\mathfrak{L}$ is complete. First, suppose that $\mathfrak{L}$ is not complete. Thus there is a consistent sequent $\langle \Gamma, \Delta \rangle$ with no normal counterexample in A. Let $\Gamma' = \{\{\alpha\} \mid \alpha \in \Gamma\}$, and let $\Delta' = \{\Delta\}$. Then $\langle \Gamma', \Delta' \rangle$ has no normal counterexample in $\vee A$. We claim that $\langle \Gamma', \Delta' \rangle$ is consistent in $\vee A$. Suppose this is not the case. Then for every choice set Y for Γ', $Y \vdash_{\mathfrak{L}} \bigcup \Delta'$. But Γ is such a choice set and $\bigcup \Delta' = \Delta$, so $\Gamma \vdash_{\mathfrak{L}} \Delta$, contradicting the assumption that $\langle \Gamma, \Delta \rangle$ is consistent. Now let us prove the converse. Suppose $\langle \Gamma', \Delta' \rangle$ is consistent in $\lor A$. Then there is a choice set Y for Γ' such that $Y \nvdash_{\mathfrak{L}} \bigcup \Delta'$. If $\mathfrak{L}$ is complete, then this sequent has a normal counterexample a. But then, by Proposition 11.2, a is a normal counterexample to $\langle \Gamma', \Delta' \rangle$ in $\lor A$. □

Proposition 12.38. *For any Boolean operation $\mathcal{B}$ and any classification A,* $\mathcal{B}(\text{Log}(A)) = \text{Log}(\mathcal{B}(A))$.

Proof. The two logics clearly have the same classification and normal tokens. But they also have the same constraints by Corollary 11.4. □

Boolean Operations in Local Logics

We can define what it means for an operation on types to be a disjunction, conjunction, or negation on a local logic.

Definition 12.39. Let $\mathfrak{L}$ be a local logic on a classification A.

1. A function $\lor : \text{pow}(\text{typ}(A)) \to \text{typ}(A)$ is a *disjunction on* $\mathfrak{L}$ if $\lor$ is a disjunction on A and on $\text{th}(\mathfrak{L})$.
2. A function $\land : \text{pow}(\text{typ}(A)) \to \text{typ}(A)$ is a *conjunction on* $\mathfrak{L}$ if $\land$ is a conjunction on A and on $\text{th}(\mathfrak{L})$.
3. A function $\lnot : \text{typ}(A) \to \text{typ}(A)$ is a *negation on* $\mathfrak{L}$ if $\lnot$ is a negation on A and on $\text{th}(\mathfrak{L})$.

Exercises

12.11. Show that if $\lnot$ is a negation on the regular theory T, then it is also a negation on the sound local logic $\text{Log}(T)$. Prove parallel statements for disjunction and conjunction.

12.12. Let S be an ideal state space, that is, one where the tokens and types are identical and the identity function is the state function. Prove that $\text{Log}(S) = \text{Log}(\text{Evt}(S))$.

12.13. Let S be a state space and its associated trivial logic $\text{Triv}(S)$ from Exercise 2.
1. Show that

$$\text{Log}(S) = \lor\, \text{Triv}(S).$$

2. Prove that the natural embedding $\eta^d_{\mathrm{Triv}(S)} : \mathrm{Triv}(S) \rightleftarrows \mathrm{Log}(S)$ is a logic infomorphism.

12.14. In order to state the following succinctly, let us use the following notation. If A and B are classifications with the same set of tokens and $f : \mathrm{typ}(A) \rightarrow \mathrm{typ}(B)$, let us write f_* for the unique token identical, contravariant pair $f_* : A \rightleftarrows B$ with $f = f_*^\wedge$. Let $\mathfrak{L}$ be a *complete* local logic. Prove the following results:

1. A function $\vee : \mathrm{pow}(\mathrm{typ}(A)) \rightarrow \mathrm{typ}(A)$ is a disjunction on $\mathfrak{L}$ if and only if $\vee_* : \vee \mathfrak{L} \rightleftarrows \mathfrak{L}$ is an infomorphism.

2. A function $\wedge : \mathrm{pow}(\mathrm{typ}(A)) \rightarrow \mathrm{typ}(A)$ is a conjunction on $\mathfrak{L}$ if and only if $\wedge_* : \wedge \mathfrak{L} \rightleftarrows \mathfrak{L}$ is an infomorphism.

3. A function $\neg : \mathrm{typ}(A) \rightarrow \mathrm{typ}(A)$ is a negation on $\mathfrak{L}$ if and only if $\neg_* : \neg \mathfrak{L} \rightleftarrows \mathfrak{L}$ is an infomorphism.

Give an example to show that the assumption of completeness is needed.

Lecture 13

Reasoning at a Distance

Suppose we are given an infomorphism $f : A \rightleftarrows B$. In Lecture 2, we discussed how we often implicitly use a logic on one of these classifications to reason about tokens in the other. There we expressed the idea in terms of inference rules we called f-**Intro** and f-**Elim**. In Section 10.4 we explored the idea in terms of regular theories. In this chapter, we amplify on this by showing how to move local logics. Most of the work has already been done in the discussion of theories.

The rule f-**Intro** corresponds to moving a logic $\mathfrak{L}$ from A to B via f; we call the new logic $f[\mathfrak{L}]$. The rule f-**Elim** corresponds to moving a logic $\mathfrak{L}$ from B to A via f^{-1}; we call the new logic $f^{-1}[\mathfrak{L}]$.

13.1 Moving Logics

We define both of the above logics here and then study them in turn in the subsections that follow. The rules mentioned above are used for motivation. The actual definition is phrased differently.

Definition 13.1. Given an infomorphism $f : A \rightleftarrows B$ and a local logic $\mathfrak{L}$ on A, the *image of $\mathfrak{L}$ under f*, denoted $f[\mathfrak{L}]$, is the local logic on the classification B with theory $f[\text{th}(\mathfrak{L})]$ and with normal tokens

$$\{b \in \text{tok}(B) \mid f(b) \in N_{\mathfrak{L}}\}.$$

Justification. We have seen in Proposition 10.15 that $f[\text{th}(\mathfrak{L})]$ is a regular theory. We need to verify that every normal token satisfies every constraint of this theory. Recall that this theory was specified by giving its consistent partitions. Because closure under Partition is valid, it suffices to show that for

165

each partition $\langle \Gamma, \Delta \rangle$ of typ(B) if $f(b)$ satisfies $f^{-1}[\Gamma] \vdash_{\mathfrak{L}} f^{-1}[\Delta]$, then b satisfies $\Gamma \vdash_{f[\mathfrak{L}]} \Delta$. This follows from Lemma 12.17.   □

We define the inverse image of a logic in a parallel manner.

Definition 13.2. Given an infomorphism $f : A \rightleftarrows B$ and a local logic $\mathfrak{L}$ on B, the *inverse image of $\mathfrak{L}$ under f*, denoted $f^{-1}[\mathfrak{L}]$, is the local logic on A with theory $f^{-1}[\text{th}(\mathfrak{L})]$ and with normal tokens

$$\{a \in \text{tok}(A) \mid a = f(b) \text{ for some } b \in N_{\mathfrak{L}}\}.$$

Justification. We need only check that every normal token satisfies every constraint, but this is clear.   □

13.2 Images of Logics

We begin with the following result showing us that our definition gives us what we want, at least as far as the consequence relation is concerned. By "least" in the following, we mean with respect to the $\sqsubseteq$-partial ordering on local logics.

Theorem 13.3. *Let $\mathfrak{L}$ be a local logic on A and let $f : A \rightleftarrows B$ be an infomorphism. The image of $\mathfrak{L}$ is the least logic $\mathfrak{L}'$ on B such that f is a logic infomorphism from $\mathfrak{L}$ to $\mathfrak{L}'$.*

Proof. To show that f is a logic infomorphism from $\mathfrak{L}$ to $f[\mathfrak{L}]$, suppose that $\Gamma \vdash_{\mathfrak{L}} \Delta$. If $\langle \Gamma', \Delta' \rangle$ is a partition of typ($\mathfrak{L}'$) extending $\langle f[\Gamma], f[\Delta] \rangle$, then $\langle f^{-1}[\Gamma'], f^{-1}[\Delta'] \rangle$ is a partition of typ(A) extending $\langle \Gamma, \Delta \rangle$. Then $f^{-1}[\Gamma'] \vdash_{\mathfrak{L}} f^{-1}[\Delta']$ by Weakening, and so $\Gamma' \vdash_{f[L]} \Delta'$ because $\langle f^{-1}[\Gamma'], f^{-1}[\Delta'] \rangle$ is a partition. Hence by Partition, $f[\Gamma] \vdash_{f[L]} f[\Delta]$. The condition for normal tokens is clearly satisfied.

Now assume that f is a logic infomorphism from $\mathfrak{L}$ to $\mathfrak{L}'$. To show that $f[\mathfrak{L}] \sqsubseteq \mathfrak{L}'$, we recall that f is already known to be a theory interpretation. So suppose that b is a normal token of $\mathfrak{L}'$. Then $f(b)$ is a normal token of $\mathfrak{L}$ because f is a logic infomorphism, and so b is a normal token of $f[\mathfrak{L}]$, by definition. Hence $N_{\mathfrak{L}'} \subseteq N_{f[\mathfrak{L}]}$.   □

We now turn to the soundness and completeness of the f-Intro rule. Recall that a pair $f = \langle f^{\wedge}, f^{\vee} \rangle$ is *token surjective* if $f^{\vee}$ is surjective.

Proposition 13.4. *Let $\mathfrak{L}$ be a local logic on a classification A and let $f : A \rightleftarrows B$ be an infomorphism.*

1. If $\mathfrak{L}$ is sound, then $f[\mathfrak{L}]$ is sound.
2. If f is token surjective and $\mathfrak{L}$ is complete, then $f[\mathfrak{L}]$ is complete.

Proof. For (1), suppose $\mathfrak{L}$ is sound. Then for each token b of $\mathbf{B}$, $f(b)$ is normal in $\mathfrak{L}$, and so b is normal in $f[\mathfrak{L}]$. For (2), suppose $\mathfrak{L}$ is complete and $f^{\vee}$ is surjective. Any consistent sequent $\langle \Gamma, \Delta \rangle$ of $f[\mathfrak{L}]$ is extendable to a consistent partition $\langle \Gamma', \Delta' \rangle$, by Partition, and so $\langle f^{-1}[\Gamma'], f^{-1}[\Delta'] \rangle$ is a consistent partition of $\mathfrak{L}$. By the completeness of $\mathfrak{L}$, there is a normal token a of $\mathfrak{L}$ with state description $\langle f^{-1}[\Gamma'], f^{-1}[\Delta'] \rangle$. By the surjectivity of $f^{\vee}$, there is a token b of $\mathbf{B}$ with $f(b) = a$, and so b has state description $\langle \Gamma', \Delta' \rangle$. Moreover, because a is a normal token of $\mathfrak{L}$, b is a normal token of the image $f[\mathfrak{L}]$. □

The restriction in the second part of Proposition 13.4 is crucial: If the infomorphism is not surjective on tokens, then the image of a complete logic is not necessarily complete. Indeed, we have the following.

Proposition 13.5. *Any logic $\mathfrak{L}$ is the image of the complete logic $\mathrm{Cmp}(\mathfrak{L})$ under the type-identical inclusion infomorphism $\kappa_{\mathfrak{L}} : \mathrm{cla}(\mathrm{Cmp}(\mathfrak{L})) \rightleftarrows \mathrm{cla}(\mathfrak{L})$.*

Proof. That $\kappa_{\mathfrak{L}}$ is an infomorphism and $\mathrm{Cmp}(\mathfrak{L})$ is complete are immediate given their construction. That $\mathfrak{L}$ is $\kappa_{\mathfrak{L}}[\mathrm{Cmp}(\mathfrak{L})]$ follows directly from our characterization of the image of a logic. □

Corollary 13.6. *A local logic is sound if and only if it is an image of a natural logic.*

Proof. By Proposition 12.7, every natural logic is sound and complete, so by Proposition 13.4, its image is sound. Conversely, if $\mathfrak{L}$ is sound then $\mathrm{Cmp}(\mathfrak{L})$ is both sound and complete, by Proposition 12.13, and so is natural by Proposition 12.7 again. Moreover, by Proposition 13.5, $\mathfrak{L}$ is an image of $\mathrm{Cmp}(\mathfrak{L})$, and so we are done. □

13.3 Inverse Images of Logics

We now explore the same set of issues with respect to inverse images of logics, or, if you like, the f-Elim rule. In some ways, this operation is better behaved, in other ways worse. First we have the following characterization of the inverse image of a logic.

Theorem 13.7. *Let $f : A \rightleftarrows B$ be an infomorphism and let $\mathfrak{L}'$ be a logic on $\mathbf{B}$. The inverse image of $\mathfrak{L}'$ under f is the largest logic $\mathfrak{L}$ on A such that f is a logic infomorphism from $\mathfrak{L}$ to $\mathfrak{L}'$.*

Proof. First, f is a logic infomorphism from $f^{-1}[\mathcal{L}']$ to $\mathcal{L}'$ because $f\hat{\ }$ is a regular theory interpretation, by Proposition 10.13, and again the condition for normal tokens is clearly satisfied.

Assume that f is a logic infomorphism from $\mathcal{L}$ to $\mathcal{L}'$. To show that $\mathcal{L} \sqsubseteq f^{-1}[\mathcal{L}']$, suppose that a is a normal token of $f^{-1}[\mathcal{L}']$. Then there is a normal token b of $\mathcal{L}'$ such that $a = f(b)$, and so a is a normal token of $\mathcal{L}$ because f is a logic infomorphism from $\mathcal{L}$ to $\mathcal{L}'$. Hence $N_{f^{-1}[\mathcal{L}']} \subseteq N_{\mathcal{L}}$. Moreover, if $\Gamma \vdash_{\mathcal{L}} \Delta$, then $f[\Gamma] \vdash_{\mathcal{L}'} f[\Delta]$ because f is a logic infomorphism from $\mathcal{L}$ to $\mathcal{L}'$, and then $\Gamma \vdash_{f^{-1}[\mathcal{L}']} \Delta$, by Proposition 10.13. Hence $\mathcal{L} \sqsubseteq f^{-1}[\mathcal{L}']$, and we are done. $\qquad\square$

Example 13.8. A simple application is the relationship between a logic $\mathcal{L}$ on a sum $A + B$ of classifications and the logics on the summand A induced by $\mathcal{L}$ and the canonical embedding $\sigma_A : A \rightleftarrows A + B$ of A into $A + B$. The normal tokens of this logic are those $a \in \mathrm{tok}(A)$ such that for some $b \in \mathrm{tok}(B)$, $\langle a, b \rangle \in N_{\mathcal{L}}$. The constraints of the logic are those sequents $\langle \Gamma, \Delta \rangle$ of A such that $\sigma_A[\Gamma] \vdash_{\mathcal{L}} \sigma_A[\Delta]$. (The reason is simply that both of these logics are the largest logic on A making σ_A a logic infomorphism.) If the types of A and B are disjoint, this is simply the restriction of $\vdash_{\mathcal{L}}$ to the sequents of A.

Proposition 13.9. *Let $\mathcal{L}$ be a local logic on a classification B and let $f : A \rightleftarrows B$ be an infomorphism.*

1. *If $\mathcal{L}$ is complete, then $f^{-1}[\mathcal{L}]$ is complete.*
2. *If f is token surjective and $\mathcal{L}$ is sound, then $f^{-1}[\mathcal{L}]$ is sound.*

Proof. For (1), note that a counterexample to completeness in $f^{-1}[\mathcal{L}]$ would give rise, via f, to a counterexample in $\mathcal{L}$. The second statement follows directly from the definition of inverse images. $\qquad\square$

The restriction in (2) is again crucial: if the infomorphism is not surjective on tokens, then the inverse image of a sound logic is not necessarily sound. Indeed, we have the following result.

Proposition 13.10. *Any local logic $\mathcal{L}$ is the inverse image of the sound local logic $\mathrm{Snd}(\mathcal{L})$ under the type identical inclusion $\iota_{\mathcal{L}} : \mathrm{cla}(\mathcal{L}) \rightleftarrows \mathrm{cla}(\mathrm{Snd}(\mathcal{L}))$.*

Proof. The proof is derived from the definition of inverse images. $\qquad\square$

Proposition 13.11. *A local logic is complete if and only if it is an inverse image of a natural logic.*

Proof. By Proposition 12.7, every natural logic is sound and complete, so by Proposition 13.9, its inverse image is complete. Conversely, if $\mathfrak{L}$ is complete, then $\text{Snd}(\mathfrak{L})$ is both sound and complete, by Proposition 12.13, and so is natural by Proposition 12.7 again. Moreover, by Proposition 13.10, $\mathfrak{L}$ is an inverse image of $\text{Snd}(\mathfrak{L})$ and so we are done. □

Corollary 13.12. *If* $f : A \rightleftarrows B$ *is a token surjective infomorphism, then,* $f^{-1}[\text{Log}(B)] = \text{Log}(A)$ *and* $f[\text{Log}(A)] = \text{Log}(B)$.

Proof. $\text{Log}(B)$ is sound and complete. Completeness is preserved under inverse images and soundness is preserved for token-surjective infomorphisms, so its inverse image is also sound and complete. But by Proposition 12.7, $\text{Log}(A)$ is the only sound and complete logic on A. The second part follows similarly from Proposition 13.4. □

Analytic Truth

To illustrate these notions, let us work out a simple example having to do with the notion of analytic truth, that is, truth by virture of meaning.

We are going to set up two propositional languages as classifications A and B. The language A has as types arbitrary sentences built up from the atomic sentences MOTHER, FATHER, and BACHELOR. For tokens, we take arbitrary truth assignments to these atomic sentences, with $a \vDash_A \alpha$ defined in the usual way. Thus the logic $\text{Log}(A)$ is just the usual classical propositional logic on this set of atomic sentences. The constraints of this logic are those that are classically valid, which, by the completeness theorem for proposition logic, are those derivable in the classical Gentzen calculus. As a schematic example, we have

$$\alpha \rightarrow \neg(\beta \wedge \gamma), \alpha, \beta \vdash_{\text{Log}(A)} \neg\gamma,$$

where α, β and γ are arbitrary sentences.

The language B is similar, but its atomic sentences are FEMALE, MARRIED, PARENT, where the last is intended to connote the property of being a parent. Again, we take all truth assignments as tokens, and the constraints are those derivable in the classical calculus.

There is an important difference between these two classifications. Some of the truth assignments (tokens) of A represent spurious possibilities, things that could not really happen. For example, an assignment that assigned true (1) to both MOTHER and BACHELOR does not represent a real possibility (ignoring the possibility of sex-change operations). As a result, some seeming analytic truths are not constraints in the theory of A. For example, we note that

$$\text{MOTHER} \nvdash_A \neg\text{BACHELOR}$$

By contrast, every truth assignment of B represents a genuine possibility, because the atomic types of this classification are independent. Hence every analytic truth that can be expressed in this language is a constraint of B.

We can use B to see what is wrong with A. There is a natural infomorphism $f : A \rightleftarrows B$. Define f on atomic sentences as follows:

α	$f(\alpha)$
MOTHER	PARENT $\wedge$ FEMALE
FATHER	PARENT $\wedge$ $\neg$FEMALE
BACHELOR	$\neg$(FEMALE $\vee$ MARRIED)

Here f is defined on complex sentences so as to commute with the various logical operations.

On tokens, we define f in the natural way. Thus, given an assignment s for B, we define the assignment $s' = f(s)$ by means of the following:

$$
\begin{aligned}
s'(\text{MOTHER}) = 1 \quad &\text{iff} \quad s \vDash \text{PARENT} \wedge \text{FEMALE} \\
s'(\text{FATHER}) = 1 \quad &\text{iff} \quad s \vDash \text{PARENT} \wedge \neg\text{FEMALE} \\
s'(\text{BACHELOR}) = 1 \quad &\text{iff} \quad s \vDash \neg(\text{FEMALE} \vee \text{MARRIED})
\end{aligned}
$$

We can use the infomorphism f to move the natural logic $\text{Log}(A)$ to B or to move the natural logic $\text{Log}(B)$ to A. By our general results, we see that $f[\text{Log}(A)]$ is sound on B and $f^{-1}[\text{Log}(B)]$ is a complete logic on A.

The infomorphism f is *not* token surjective, however, because if a is one of the spurious truth assignments mentioned above, it is not in the range of f. Consequently, we do not expect $f[\text{Log}(A)]$ to be complete. And, indeed, we see that

$$f(\text{MOTHER}) \nvdash_{f[\text{Log}(A)]} f(\neg\text{BACHELOR}),$$

whereas

$$f(\text{MOTHER}) \vdash_{\text{Log}(B)} f(\neg\text{BACHELOR}).$$

Similarly, because f is not token surjective, we know that $f^{-1}[\text{Log}(B)]$ cannot be sound, because the normal tokens of this logic are just those in the range of f. Note, however, that these are exactly the nonspurious truth assignments. In other words, the normal tokens of $f^{-1}[\text{Log}(B)]$ are just those tokens that represent genuine possibilities.

13.4 More About Moving Logics

In this section we collect together some simple but useful observations about the operations of taking images and inverse images of local logics.

Proposition 13.13. *Let $f : A \rightleftarrows B$ and $g : B \rightleftarrows C$ be infomorphisms.*

1. *For any logic $\mathfrak{L}$ on A, $gf[\mathfrak{L}] = g[f[\mathfrak{L}]]$.*
2. *For any logic $\mathfrak{L}$ on C, $(gf)^{-1}[\mathfrak{L}] = f^{-1}[g^{-1}[\mathfrak{L}]]$.*

Proof. The proof is immediate from the definitions. □

Proposition 13.14. *The operations of taking images and inverse images of logics are both order-preserving (with respect to $\sqsubseteq$).*

Proof. Let $f : A \rightleftarrows B$ be an infomorphism. We need to show the following:

1. For logics $\mathfrak{L}_1$ and $\mathfrak{L}_2$ on A, if $\mathfrak{L}_1 \sqsubseteq \mathfrak{L}_2$ then $f[\mathfrak{L}_1] \sqsubseteq f[\mathfrak{L}_2]$.
2. For logics $\mathfrak{L}_1$ and $\mathfrak{L}_2$ on B, if $\mathfrak{L}_1 \sqsubseteq \mathfrak{L}_2$ then $f^{-1}[\mathfrak{L}_1] \sqsubseteq f^{-1}[\mathfrak{L}_2]$.

For (1), note that by Theorem 13.7, f is a logic infomorphism from $\mathfrak{L}_2$ to $f[\mathfrak{L}_2]$ and so is also a logic infomorphism from $\mathfrak{L}_1$ to $f[\mathfrak{L}_2]$ by Proposition 12.28. By Theorem 13.7 again, $f[\mathfrak{L}_1]$ is the smallest logic making f a logic infomorphism from $\mathfrak{L}_1$, and so $f[\mathfrak{L}_1] \sqsubseteq f[\mathfrak{L}_2]$. Part (2) is proved similarly. □

Proposition 13.15. *The operations of taking images and inverse images of logics preserves joins in the $\sqsubseteq$ ordering.*

Proof. Let $f : A \rightleftarrows B$ be an infomorphism. We need to show the following:

1. If $\mathfrak{L}_1$ and $\mathfrak{L}_2$ are both logics on A, then $f[\mathfrak{L}_1 \sqcup \mathfrak{L}_2] = f[\mathfrak{L}_1] \sqcup f[\mathfrak{L}_2]$.
2. If $\mathfrak{L}_1$ and $\mathfrak{L}_2$ are both logics on B, then $f^{-1}[\mathfrak{L}_1 \sqcup \mathfrak{L}_2] = f^{-1}[\mathfrak{L}_1] \sqcup f^{-1}[\mathfrak{L}_2]$.

For (1), first note that by Corollary 13.14, $f[\mathfrak{L}_1] \sqsubseteq f[\mathfrak{L}_1 \sqcup \mathfrak{L}_2]$ and $f[\mathfrak{L}_2] \sqsubseteq f[\mathfrak{L}_1 \sqcup \mathfrak{L}_2]$. Therefore $f[\mathfrak{L}_1] \sqcup f[\mathfrak{L}_2] \sqsubseteq f[\mathfrak{L}_1 \sqcup \mathfrak{L}_2]$. For the other direction, note that by Theorem 13.7, f is a logic infomorphism from $\mathfrak{L}_i$ to $f[\mathfrak{L}_i]$, for $i = 1, 2$, and so also from $\mathfrak{L}_i$ to $f[\mathfrak{L}_1] \sqcup f[\mathfrak{L}_2]$, by Proposition 12.28. Thus by

Proposition 12.29, f is a logic infomorphism from $\mathfrak{L}_1 \sqcup \mathfrak{L}_2$ to $f[\mathfrak{L}_1] \sqcup f[\mathfrak{L}_2]$, and so by Theorem 13.7 again, $f[\mathfrak{L}_1 \sqcup \mathfrak{L}_2] \sqsubseteq f[\mathfrak{L}_1] \sqcup f[\mathfrak{L}_2]$. The proof of (2) is similar. $\qquad\square$

Corollary 13.16. *Let $f : A \rightleftarrows B$ be an infomorphism.*

1. *For any logic $\mathfrak{L}$ on A, $\mathfrak{L} \sqsubseteq f^{-1}[f[\mathfrak{L}]]$.*
2. *For any logic $\mathfrak{L}$ on B, $f[f^{-1}[\mathfrak{L}]] \sqsubseteq \mathfrak{L}$.*

Proof. For (1), by Theorem 13.7, $f^{-1}[f[\mathfrak{L}]]$ is the largest logic on A such that f is a logic infomorphism from $f^{-1}[f[\mathfrak{L}]]$ to $f[\mathfrak{L}]$. But also by Theorem 13.7, f is a logic infomorphism from $\mathfrak{L}$ to $f[\mathfrak{L}]$, and so the result follows. The proof of (2) is similar. $\qquad\square$

Corollary 13.17. $\mathfrak{L}_1 + \mathfrak{L}_2 = \sigma_{\mathfrak{L}_1}[\mathfrak{L}_1] \sqcup \sigma_{\mathfrak{L}_2}[\mathfrak{L}_2]$.

Proof. By Theorem 13.7, $\sigma_{\mathfrak{L}_1}[\mathfrak{L}_1] \sqsubseteq \mathfrak{L}_1 + \mathfrak{L}_2$ and $\sigma_{\mathfrak{L}_2}[\mathfrak{L}_2] \sqsubseteq \mathfrak{L}_1 + \mathfrak{L}_2$ because $\sigma_{\mathfrak{L}_1} : \mathfrak{L}_1 \rightleftarrows \mathfrak{L}_1 + \mathfrak{L}_2$ and $\sigma_{\mathfrak{L}_2} : \mathfrak{L}_2 \rightleftarrows \mathfrak{L}_1 + \mathfrak{L}_2$ are logic infomorphisms. Thus $\sigma_{\mathfrak{L}_1}[\mathfrak{L}_1] \sqcup \sigma_{\mathfrak{L}_2}[\mathfrak{L}_2] \sqsubseteq \mathfrak{L}_1 + \mathfrak{L}_2$.

For the other inequality, we must check that every normal token of $\sigma_{\mathfrak{L}_1}[\mathfrak{L}_1] \sqcup \sigma_{\mathfrak{L}_2}[\mathfrak{L}_2]$ is a normal token of $\mathfrak{L}_1 + \mathfrak{L}_2$ and that if $\Gamma \vdash_{\mathfrak{L}_1 + \mathfrak{L}_2} \Delta$, then $\Gamma \vdash_{\sigma_{\mathfrak{L}_1}[\mathfrak{L}_1] \sqcup \sigma_{\mathfrak{L}_2}[\mathfrak{L}_2]} \Delta$. This is sufficient, because the classification of both sides is just $\text{cla}(\mathfrak{L}_1) + \text{cla}(\mathfrak{L}_2)$.

Suppose $\langle a, b \rangle$ is normal in $\sigma_{\mathfrak{L}_1}[\mathfrak{L}_1] \sqcup \sigma_{\mathfrak{L}_2}[\mathfrak{L}_2]$. Then it is normal in both $\sigma_{\mathfrak{L}_1}[\mathfrak{L}_1]$ and $\sigma_{\mathfrak{L}_2}[\mathfrak{L}_2]$, so a is normal in $\mathfrak{L}_1$ and b is normal in $\mathfrak{L}_2$. But $N_{\mathfrak{L}_1 + \mathfrak{L}_2} = N_{\mathfrak{L}_1} \times N_{\mathfrak{L}_2}$, and so $\langle a, b \rangle$ is normal in $\mathfrak{L}_1 + \mathfrak{L}_2$.

Now suppose that $\Gamma \vdash_{\mathfrak{L}_1 + \mathfrak{L}_2} \Delta$. We can write $\langle \Gamma, \Delta \rangle$ uniquely as

$$\langle \sigma_{\mathfrak{L}_1}\Gamma_1 \cup \sigma_{\mathfrak{L}_2}\Gamma_2, \sigma_{\mathfrak{L}_1}\Delta_1 \cup \sigma_{\mathfrak{L}_2}\Delta_2 \rangle,$$

where $\Gamma_1, \Delta_1 \subseteq \text{typ}(\mathfrak{L}_1)$ and $\Gamma_2, \Delta_2 \subseteq \text{typ}(\mathfrak{L}_2)$. So either $\Gamma_1 \vdash_{\mathfrak{L}_1} \Delta_1$ or $\Gamma_2 \vdash_{\mathfrak{L}_2} \Delta_2$, by the definition of $\mathfrak{L}_1 + \mathfrak{L}_2$. Thus $\sigma_{\mathfrak{L}_1}\Gamma_1 \vdash_{\sigma_{\mathfrak{L}_1}[\mathfrak{L}_1]} \sigma_{\mathfrak{L}_1}\Delta_1$ or $\sigma_{\mathfrak{L}_2}\Gamma_2 \vdash_{\sigma_{\mathfrak{L}_2}[\mathfrak{L}_2]} \sigma_{\mathfrak{L}_2}\Delta_2$. In either case, $\Gamma \vdash_{\sigma_{\mathfrak{L}_1}[\mathfrak{L}_1] \sqcup \sigma_{\mathfrak{L}_2}[\mathfrak{L}_2]} \Delta$ by weakening. $\qquad\square$

Corollary 13.18. *Given an indexed family $\{ f_i : \mathfrak{L}_i \rightleftarrows \mathfrak{L} \}_{i \in I}$ of logic infomorphisms,*

$$\sum_{i \in I} f_i \left[\sum_{i \in I} \mathfrak{L}_i \right] = \bigsqcup_{i \in I} f_i[\mathfrak{L}_i].$$

Proof. This is a straightforward computation given the above results:

$$\left(\sum_{i\in I} f_i\right)\left[\sum_{i\in I}\mathfrak{L}_i\right] = \left(\sum_{i\in I} f_i\right)\left[\bigcup_{i\in I}\sigma_{\mathfrak{L}_i}[\mathfrak{L}_i]\right] \quad \text{(Cor. 13.17)}$$

$$= \bigcup_{i\in I}\left(\sum_{i\in I} f_i\right)[\sigma_{\mathfrak{L}_i}[\mathfrak{L}_i]] \quad \text{(Cor. 13.15)}$$

$$= \bigcup_{i\in I}\left(\sum_{i\in I} f_i\right)\sigma_{\mathfrak{L}_i}[\mathfrak{L}_i] \quad \text{(Prop. 13.13)}$$

$$= \bigcup_{i\in I} f_i[\mathfrak{L}_i]$$

The final identity follows from the definition of $\sum_{i\in I} f_i$. □

Proposition 13.19.

$$\left(\sum_{i\in I} f_i\right)^{-1}[\mathfrak{L}] = \sum_{i\in I}\left(f_i^{-1}[\mathfrak{L}]\right).$$

Proof. The proof is similar to that of 13.18. □

Exercises

13.1. Characterize the *a priori* logic AP(**A**) on **A** by moving the logic **o** of Exercise 12.4.

13.2. Given an infomorphism $f : A \rightleftarrows B$ and a local logic $\mathfrak{L}$ on **A**, show that if f is surjective on types, then for all sequents $\langle \Gamma, \Delta \rangle$ of **B**, $\Gamma \vdash_{f[\mathfrak{L}]} \Delta$ if and only if $f^{-1}[\Gamma] \vdash_{\mathfrak{L}} f^{-1}\Delta$. Give an example showing that the surjectivity condition is necessary.

Lecture 14

Representing Local Logics

We have now presented two mathematical models of information flow in distributed systems, information channels, and local logics. In this lecture we explore the relationship between these models.

14.1 Idealization

An old problem in the philosophy of mathematics and science has to do with the efficacy of mathematics in understanding the real world. This can be put as a question of information flow. How is it that science, with its use of abstract mathematical models, carries any information at all about the real world? We want to look at this question in terms of information channels as a way to motivate our discussion of the relation between local logics and binary information channels.

Suppose we have a binary channel C relating P and D as depicted below.

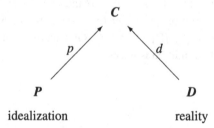

Here the classification D is a domain under scientific investigation, in all its real-world complexity, and P is some specific scientific idealization or model of the domain D. (The "P" and "D" stand for "proximal" and "distal", respectively, as in Lecture 2.) The channel C models the idealization or modeling process being used. A token c of C connects some particular situation $a = d(c)$ in D and an idealized token or model $b = p(c)$ in P, often some mathematical object. This channel C is itself a model of the use of the idealized domain P to reason about the reality D in terms of moving the natural logic $\text{Log}(P)$ on P to D along this channel. This prompts the following definition.

Definition 14.1. Given a binary channel C from P to D, the local logic on D *induced by* C is the logic

$$\text{Log}_C(D) = d^{-1}[p[\text{Log}(P)]].$$

The concept of a local logic gives us the wherewithal to capture the structure of reasoning by means of idealizations. The logic $\text{Log}_C(D)$ on D is not guaranteed to be complete; that assurance is lost by taking the image under p. Neither is it guaranteed to be sound; that assurance is lost by taking the inverse image under d. The constraints of $\text{Log}_C(D)$ are those that come from the idealization process from some law that holds in the idealized domain. The normal tokens of $\text{Log}_C(D)$ are those real-world tokens that are "appropriately connected" to some idealized token. The better the scientific model is, the better this logic is, better in the sense of having fewer exceptional tokens and more constraints.

As a theory of idealization, scientific modeling, and the efficacy of applied mathematics this sketch is at best highly programmatic. Some further thoughts related to this sketch are presented in Lecture 20. Its purpose here is to introduce the definition of the logic induced by a binary channel. We can characterize this induced logic in the following way.

Proposition 14.2. *Let C be a binary channel from P to D as depicted above.*

1. *A partition $\langle \Gamma, \Delta \rangle$ of $\text{typ}(D)$ is consistent in $\text{Log}_C(D)$ if and only if $\langle p^{-1}[d[\Gamma]], p^{-1}[d[\Delta]] \rangle$ is the state description of some $b \in \text{tok}(P)$.*
2. *A token $a \in \text{tok}(D)$ is normal in $\text{Log}_C(D)$ if and only if it is connected to a token of P.*

Proof. This characterization is obtained by applying the definitions of images and inverse images in Definitions 13.1 and 13.2. ☐

Example 14.3. Recall that for any logic $\mathfrak{L}$ on any classification A, the sound completion $\text{SC}(\mathfrak{L})$ is the logic that is obtained by throwing away exceptional tokens and adding in idealized tokens for the consistent partitions that are not realized. This is clearly some kind of idealization process. Let us see that it fits the above picture.

Because $SC(\mathfrak{L})$ is sound and complete, it is a natural logic. In other words, if we let P be the classification of $SC(\mathfrak{L})$, then $SC(\mathfrak{L}) = Log(P)$. Recalling the inclusion infomorphisms $\iota_{\mathfrak{L}} : \mathfrak{L} \rightleftarrows Snd(\mathfrak{L})$ and $\kappa_{Snd(\mathfrak{L})} : SC(\mathfrak{L}) \rightleftarrows Snd(\mathfrak{L})$, we have the following channel C:

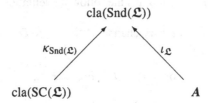

With this channel, we have $\mathfrak{L} = Log_C(A)$.

We can summarize this discussion as follows.

Theorem 14.4. *Every local logic $\mathfrak{L}$ on a classification A is of the form $Log_C(A)$ for a binary channel C linking A to the classification of the sound completion of $\mathfrak{L}$.*

This shows that all local logics are induced by binary channels. The sound completion of $\mathfrak{L}$ is not well behaved with regard to infomorphisms, however. That is, logic infomorphisms do not give us the right kind of morphisms between their associated channels when one uses the sound completion as an idealization. There is a closely related idealization associated with the local logic $\mathfrak{L}$ that works out better.

Definition 14.5. Given a local logic $\mathfrak{L}$, the *idealization of $\mathfrak{L}$* is the classification $Idl(\mathfrak{L})$ with the same types as $\mathfrak{L}$, whose tokens are the consistent partitions of $\mathfrak{L}$, and such that $\langle \Gamma, \Delta \rangle \vDash_{Idl(\mathfrak{L})} \alpha$ if and only if $\alpha \in \Gamma$ (equivalently, if and only if $\alpha \notin \Delta$).

We have seen this classification earlier in various guises.

Proposition 14.6. *For any logic $\mathfrak{L}$,*

1. $Idl(\mathfrak{L}) = Cla(th(\mathfrak{L}))$, *and*
2. $Idl(\mathfrak{L}) \cong Sep(cla(SC(\mathfrak{L})))$.

Proof. The first part is clear from the definitions of the two sides. For the second part, let $g : Idl(\mathfrak{L}) \rightleftarrows cla(SC(\mathfrak{L}))$ be the type-identical infomorphism such that

$g(a)$ is the state description of a in $\mathrm{cla}(\mathrm{SC}(\mathfrak{L}))$, which is a consistent partition (by the soundness of $\mathrm{SC}(\mathfrak{L})$) and so is in $\mathrm{tok}(\mathrm{Idl}(\mathfrak{L}))$. This is clearly a bijection on tokens. It is easy to check that g is an infomorphism. □

Definition 14.7. Given a local logic $\mathfrak{L}$, the channel *representing* $\mathfrak{L}$ is the binary channel $\mathrm{Cha}(\mathfrak{L}) = \langle h_{\mathrm{cla}(\mathfrak{L})}, h_{\mathrm{Idl}(\mathfrak{L})} \rangle$ from $\mathrm{cla}(\mathfrak{L})$ to $\mathrm{Idl}(\mathfrak{L})$ with core $\mathrm{cla}(\mathrm{Snd}(\mathfrak{L}))$ and type-identical infomorphisms given by

1. $h_{\mathrm{cla}(\mathfrak{L})}(a) = a$, and
2. $h_{\mathrm{Idl}(\mathfrak{L})}(a) = \mathrm{state}_{\mathfrak{L}}(a)$

for each token $a \in \mathrm{tok}(\mathrm{Snd}(\mathfrak{L}))$.

Justification. These are indeed infomorphisms: $h_{\mathrm{cla}(\mathfrak{L})}$ is just the inclusion infomorphism $\iota_{\mathrm{cla}(\mathrm{Snd}(\mathfrak{L}))}$ from Proposition 13.10, and $h_{\mathrm{Idl}(\mathfrak{L})}$ is an infomorphism because the state description of every token of $\mathrm{Snd}(\mathfrak{L})$ is consistent and so is a token of $\mathrm{Idl}(\mathfrak{L})$, by the soundness of $\mathrm{Snd}(\mathfrak{L})$. □

Theorem 14.8. *Every local logic $\mathfrak{L}$ on a classification A is the derived logic of its associated channel; that is,* $\mathrm{Log}_{\mathrm{Cha}(\mathfrak{L})}(A) = \mathfrak{L}$.

Proof. Let $B = \mathrm{cla}(\mathrm{SC}(\mathfrak{L}))$. By Proposition 14.6, there is an isomorphism $f : \mathrm{Idl}(\mathfrak{L}) \rightleftarrows \mathrm{Sep}(B)$. Thus we have the following diagram:

$$
\begin{array}{ccccc}
A & \xrightarrow[\iota_{\mathfrak{L}}]{h_A} & \mathrm{cla}(\mathrm{Snd}(\mathfrak{L})) & \xleftarrow{h_{\mathrm{Idl}(\mathfrak{L})}} & \mathrm{Idl}(\mathfrak{L}) \\
& & \Big\uparrow{\scriptstyle \kappa_{\mathrm{Snd}(\mathfrak{L})}} & & \Big\downarrow{\scriptstyle f} \\
& & B & \xleftarrow{\tau_B} & \mathrm{Sep}(B)
\end{array}
$$

The diagram commutes, by Exercise 4.5, because all the infomorphisms are type identical, and so the image of $\mathrm{Log}(\mathrm{Idl}(\mathfrak{L}))$ under $h_{\mathrm{Idl}(\mathfrak{L})}$ is the same as its image under $\kappa_{\mathrm{Snd}(\mathfrak{L})} \tau_B f$. Thus

$$h_{\mathrm{Idl}(\mathfrak{L})}[\mathrm{Log}(\mathrm{Idl}(\mathfrak{L}))] = \kappa_{\mathrm{Snd}(\mathfrak{L})}[\tau_B[f[\mathrm{Log}(\mathrm{Idl}(\mathfrak{L}))]]]$$

by Proposition 13.13. Note that

1. $f[\mathrm{Log}(\mathrm{Idl}(\mathfrak{L}))] = \mathrm{Log}(\mathrm{Sep}(B))$ because f is an isomorphism, and

2. $\tau_B[\text{Log}(\text{Sep}(\boldsymbol{B}))] = \text{Log}(\boldsymbol{B})$ because τ_B is surjective on tokens, by Proposition 13.12,

and so $h_{\text{Idl}(\mathfrak{L})}[\text{Log}(\text{Idl}(\mathfrak{L}))] = \kappa_{\text{Snd}(\mathfrak{L})}[\text{Log}(\boldsymbol{B})]$. But then $\text{Log}(\text{Cha}(\mathfrak{L}))$ is $\iota_A^{-1}[\kappa_{\text{Snd}(\mathfrak{L})}[\text{Log}(\boldsymbol{B})]]$, which is just $\mathfrak{L}$. ◻

Corollary 14.9. *Every sound local logic $\mathfrak{L}$ is the image of its idealization* $\text{Idl}(\mathfrak{L})$ *under the infomorphism* $h_{\text{Idl}(\mathfrak{L})}$.

Proof. If $\mathfrak{L}$ is sound, then the other half of the channel $\text{Cha}(\mathfrak{L})$ is the identity. ◻

14.2 Channel Infomorphisms

We have associated an information channel $\text{Cha}(\mathfrak{L})$ with each local logic $\mathfrak{L}$. If this association is natural, there should be a correspondence between logic infomorphisms and channel infomorphisms. We have not defined the latter notion, though it is in some sense implicit in our notion of a refinement between channels. We define this notion now in order to show that logic infomorphisms do indeed naturally correspond to channel infomorphisms. The material in this section will not be needed in for the following lectures.

Definition 14.10. Given channels

$$C = \{h_i : A_i \rightleftarrows C\}_{i \in I}$$

and

$$C' = \{h'_i : A'_i \rightleftarrows C'\}_{i \in I}$$

on an index set I, a *channel infomorphism* $f : C \rightleftarrows C'$ consists of infomorphisms $f : C \rightleftarrows C'$ and $f_i : A_i \rightleftarrows A'_i$ such that for each $i \in I$ the following diagram commutes:

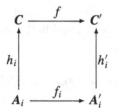

Thus a channel refinement is essentially a channel infomorphism $f : C \rightleftarrows C'$, where $A_i = A'_i$ and $f_i = 1_{A_i}$ for each $i \in I$.

Proposition 14.11. *Suppose we have a channel infomorphism* $f : C \rightleftarrows C'$ *between binary channels as depicted by the following diagram:*

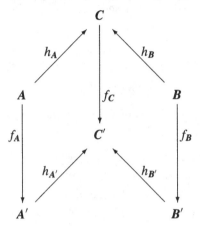

Then f_A, *considered as a map of logics, is a logic infomorphism of the induced logics* $f_A : \mathrm{Log}_C(A) \rightleftarrows \mathrm{Log}_{C'}(A)$.

Proof. First we show that f_A on types is a regular theory interpretation. Suppose $\langle \Gamma', \Delta' \rangle$ is a consistent partition of $\mathrm{Log}_{C'}(A')$. By Proposition 14.2, there is a $b' \in \mathrm{tok}(B'$ whose state description is $\langle h_{B'}^{-1}[h_{A'}[\Gamma]], h_{B'}^{-1}[h_{A'}[\Delta]] \rangle$. Then $f_B(b')$ has state description $\langle f_B^{-1}[h_{B'}^{-1}[h_{A'}[\Gamma]]], f_B^{-1}[h_{B'}^{-1}[h_{A'}[\Delta]]] \rangle$. From the diagram, we see that

$$f_B^{-1} h_{B'}^{-1} h_{A'} = h_B^{-1} f_C^{-1} h_{A'} = h_B^{-1} h_A f_A^{-1}.$$

Thus $f_B(b')$ has state description $\langle h_B^{-1}[h_A[f_A^{-1}[\Gamma']]], h_B^{-1}[h_A f_A^{-1}[\Delta']] \rangle$. Applying Proposition 14.2 again, $\langle f_A^{-1}[\Gamma'], f_A^{-1}[\Delta'] \rangle$ is consistent and so f_A is a theory interpretation, as required.

Let us check that if a' is a normal token of $\mathrm{Log}_{C'}(A')$, then $f_A(a')$ is a normal token of $\mathrm{Log}_C(A)$. By Proposition 14.2, if a' is a normal token of $\mathrm{Log}_{C'}(A')$, then there is a connection c' of C' connecting a' to some token b' of B'. But then $f_C(c')$ is a connection of C connecting $f_A(a')$ to $f_B(b')$. Hence by Proposition 14.2, $f_A(a')$ is a normal token of $\mathrm{Log}_C(A)$. □

The preceding result shows that channel infomorphisms give rise to logic infomorphisms. We now prove that every logic infomorphism can be obtained in this way when we restrict attention to channels that represent logics.

Proposition 14.12. *Given a logic infomorphism* $f : \mathfrak{L} \rightleftarrows \mathfrak{L}'$, *there are unique infomorphisms* $f_{\mathrm{Snd}(\mathfrak{L})} : \mathrm{cla}(\mathrm{Snd}(\mathfrak{L})) \rightleftarrows \mathrm{cla}(\mathrm{Snd}(\mathfrak{L}'))$ *and* $f_{\mathrm{Idl}(\mathfrak{L})} : \mathrm{Idl}(\mathfrak{L}) \rightleftarrows$

$Idl(\mathcal{L}')$ *such that the following diagram commutes:*

$$
\begin{array}{ccccc}
\mathrm{cla}(\mathcal{L}) & \xrightarrow{\ h_{\mathrm{cla}(\mathcal{L})}\ } & \mathrm{cla}(\mathrm{Snd}(\mathcal{L})) & \xleftarrow{\ h_{\mathrm{Idl}(\mathcal{L})}\ } & \mathrm{Idl}(\mathcal{L}) \\
\Big\downarrow{f} & & \Big\downarrow{f_{\mathrm{Snd}(\mathcal{L})}} & & \Big\downarrow{f_{\mathrm{Idl}(\mathcal{L})}} \\
\mathrm{cla}(\mathcal{L}') & \xrightarrow{\ h_{\mathrm{cla}(\mathcal{L}')}\ } & \mathrm{cla}(\mathrm{Snd}(\mathcal{L}')) & \xleftarrow{\ h_{\mathrm{Idl}(\mathcal{L})}\ } & \mathrm{Idl}(\mathcal{L}')
\end{array}
$$

Proof. To satisfy the conditions of the proposition, $f_{\mathrm{Snd}(\mathcal{L})}$ and $f_{\mathrm{Idl}(\mathcal{L})}$ must satisfy the following:

1. $f_{\mathrm{Snd}(\mathcal{L})}(\alpha) = f(\alpha)$ for each $\alpha \in \mathrm{typ}(\mathrm{Snd}(\mathcal{L}))$,
2. $f_{\mathrm{Snd}(\mathcal{L})}(b) = f(b)$ for each $b \in \mathrm{tok}(\mathrm{Snd}(\mathcal{L}'))$,
3. $f_{\mathrm{Idl}(\mathcal{L})}(\alpha) = f(\alpha)$ for each $\alpha \in \mathrm{typ}(\mathrm{Idl}(\mathcal{L}))$, and
4. $f_{\mathrm{Idl}(\mathcal{L})}(\langle \Gamma, \Delta \rangle) = \langle f^{-1}[\Gamma], f^{-1}[\Delta] \rangle$ for each $\langle \Gamma, \Delta \rangle \in \mathrm{tok}(\mathrm{Idl}(\mathcal{L}'))$.

But these amount to a definition of $f_{\mathrm{Snd}(\mathcal{L})}$ and $f_{\mathrm{Idl}(\mathcal{L})}$, so ensuring the existence and uniqueness of these infomorphisms. □

Definition 14.13. Given a logic infomorphism $f : \mathcal{L} \rightleftarrows \mathcal{L}'$, let

$$\mathrm{Cha}(f) : \mathrm{Cha}(\mathcal{L}) \rightleftarrows \mathrm{Cha}(\mathcal{L}')$$

be the channel infomorphism given by $f : \mathrm{cla}(\mathcal{L}) \rightleftarrows \mathrm{cla}(\mathcal{L}')$, $f_{\mathrm{Snd}(\mathcal{L})} : \mathrm{cla}(\mathrm{Snd}(\mathcal{L})) \rightleftarrows \mathrm{cla}(\mathrm{Snd}\mathcal{L}'))$, and $f_{\mathrm{Idl}(\mathcal{L})} : \mathrm{Idl}(\mathcal{L}) \rightleftarrows \mathrm{Idl}(\mathcal{L}')$.

Justification. This is a channel infomorphism by Proposition 14.12. □

Proposition 14.14. *For any logic infomorphism* $f : \mathcal{L} \rightleftarrows \mathcal{L}'$,

$$\mathrm{Log}(\mathrm{Cha}(f)) = f.$$

Proof. This is immediate from the definitions. □

We take these results to show that we have the "right" information-theoretic definition of morphism between channels, but we do not pursue this topic further here.

Exercises

14.1. Show that the identity function from the types of $\mathrm{th}(\mathcal{L})$ to the types of $\mathrm{Th}(\mathrm{cla}(\mathrm{Snd}(\mathcal{L})))$ is a theory interpretation and that the infomorphism $h_{\mathrm{Idl}(\mathcal{L})}$ in Definition 14.7 is its image under Cla.

14.2. (†) Call a binary channel C from A to B *special* if there is a function $f : \text{typ}(A) \to \text{typ}(B)$ such that $h_B f = h_A$.

1. Show that for any special channel C and logic infomorphism $f : \mathfrak{L} \rightleftarrows \text{Log}_C(A)$, there is a unique channel infomorphism $f^* : \text{Cha}(\mathfrak{L}) \rightleftarrows C$ such that $\text{Log}(f^*) = f$.

2. Use (1) to show that Cha is left adjoint to the functor Log restricted to special channels.

3. What is the counit of this adjoint pair?

Lecture 15

Distributed Logics

The view of information put forward here associates information flow with distributed systems. Such a system $\mathcal{A}$, we recall, consists of an indexed family $\text{cla}(\mathcal{A}) = \{A_i\}_{i \in I}$ of classifications together with a set $\text{inf}(\mathcal{A})$ of infomorphisms, all of which have both a domain and a codomain in $\text{cla}(\mathcal{A})$. With any such a system we want to associate a systemwide logic $\text{Log}(\mathcal{A})$ on the sum $\sum_{i \in I} A_i$ of the classifications in the system. The constraints of $\text{Log}(\mathcal{A})$ should use the lawlike regularities represented by the system as a whole. The normal tokens of $\text{Log}(\mathcal{A})$ model those indexed families of tokens to which the constraints are guaranteed to apply, by virtue of the structure of the system.

If we consider a given component classification A_i of $\mathcal{A}$, there are at least two sensible logics on A_i that we might want to incorporate into $\text{Log}(\mathcal{A})$, the *a priori* logic $\text{AP}(A_i)$ and the natural logic $\text{Log}(A_i)$. The former assumes we are given no information about the constraints of A_i except for the trivial constraints. The latter assumes perfect information about the constraints of A_i. There is typically quite a difference. But really these are just two extremes in our ordering of sound local logics on A_i. After all, in dealing with a distributed system, we may have not just the component classifications and their informorphisms, but also local logics on the component classifications. We want the systemwide logic to incorporate these local logics. To this end, we generalize the notion of a distributed system to that of an information system.

15.1 Information Systems

Definition 15.1. An *information system* $\mathcal{L}$ consists of an indexed family $\log(\mathcal{L}) = \{\mathfrak{L}_i\}_{i \in I}$ of local logics together with a set $\text{inf}(\mathcal{L})$ of logic informorphisms, all of which have both a domain and a codomain in $\log(\mathcal{L})$.

We associate with any information system $\mathcal{L}$ a systemwide logic Log($\mathcal{L}$), one that is the "limit" of the logics of the system and the way they fit together.

Before defining this logic, it is worthwhile to remind ourselves that once we have a logic on a sum $\sum_{i \in I} A_i$, we get an associated logic on any smaller sum $\sum_{i \in I_0} A_i$, for $I_0 \subset I$, as in Example 13.8, by simply restricting the constraints to those of the smaller sum and taking as normal tokens those that are projections of normal tokens in the larger sum. We will often be interested in some such restricted logic of the system.

Definition 15.2. Let $\mathcal{L}$ be an information system, that is, an indexed family log($\mathcal{L}$) = $\{\mathfrak{L}_i\}_{i \in I}$ of local logics together with a set inf($\mathcal{L}$) of logic infomorphisms, all of which have both a domain and a codomain in log($\mathcal{L}$). Let $A_i = \text{cla}(\mathfrak{L}_i)$, and let $\mathcal{A}$ be the associated distributed system with the same set of infomorphisms. Let $\mathcal{C} = \lim \mathcal{A}$ be the limit of this distributed system; write this channel as an indexed family $\{g_i : A_i \rightleftarrows C\}_{i \in I}$. There is a least logic $\mathfrak{L}$ on C such that each g_i is a logic infomorphism. Namely, $\mathfrak{L} = \bigsqcup_{i \in I} g_i[\mathfrak{L}_i]$. The logic Log($\mathcal{L}$) has classification $A = \sum_{i \in I} A_i$. If we let $g = \sum_{i \in I} g_i$, where we think of these as classification infomorphisms, then $g : A \rightleftarrows C$ is an infomorphism. We define Log($\mathcal{L}$) = $g^{-1}[L]$; that is, it is the largest logic on A that makes g a logic infomorphism. In summary, then, the *distributed logic* of the information system $\mathcal{L}$ is the local logic on $\sum_{i \in I} A_i$ given by

$$\text{Log}(\mathcal{L}) = \left(\sum_{i \in I} g_i \right)^{-1} \left[\bigsqcup_{i \in I} g_i[\mathfrak{L}_i] \right].$$

This definition gives us a way to state our basic proposal for an understanding of information flow in a distributed system.

Basic Proposal

In modeling information flow in a distributed system, the system itself is to be modeled as a information system $\mathcal{L}$. The constraints of the distributed logic Log($\mathcal{L}$) model the available regularities of the system. The normal tokens of Log($\mathcal{L}$) model the instances of the system to which the constraints are guaranteed to apply by virtue of the structure of the system.

It is difficult to say anything very informative about the theory of Log($\mathcal{L}$) in general, because the various logics can interact in complicated ways. We can, however, describe the normal tokens of the logic.

Proposition 15.3. *A token* $\{c_i\}_{i \in I}$ *of* Log($\mathcal{L}$) *is normal if and only if each* c_i *is a normal token of* $\mathfrak{L}_i$ *and* $c_i = f(c_j)$ *whenever there is an informorphism of the system of the form* $f : A_i \rightleftarrows A_j$.

Proof. Using the notation of Definition 15.2, we first note that the normal tokens
of $\mathfrak{L}$ consist of those tokens c of C such that $g_i(c) \in N_{\mathfrak{L}_i}$ for each i. From the
definition of limit, the tokens of C are those $\{c_i\}_{i \in I}$ such that $c_i = f(c_j)$ for each
infomorphism $f : A_i \rightleftarrows A_j$ of the system. But the normal tokens of $\mathrm{Log}(\mathcal{L})$
consist of the tokens $\{c_i\}_{i \in I} \in \mathrm{tok}(A)$ of the form $g^{\vee}(c)$ such that $c \in N_{\mathfrak{L}}$ and
$g^{\vee}$ is the identity on the tokens of C.   □

In applying this definition to a distributed system, we typically have a single
logic on either the core of a channel or on one of its components. In such a case,
we use the *a priori* logics on the other classifications of the system in order to
be able to consider the distributed system as an information system. (One can
think of the logic $\mathrm{Log}_C(D)$, studied in Lecture 14, as a special case of the latter;
use $\mathrm{Log}(P)$ together with $\mathrm{AP}(D)$ and $\mathrm{AP}(C)$ to get a logic on the sum, and then
restrict the result to the classification D.)

15.2 File Copying: An Example

If Judith copies a file, say, `adventure.tex`, from the Macintosh in her office
to the one at home, using Apple Remote Access, she expects the copied file to
have many of the same properties as the file copied. It should have the same
contents, the same time stamp, the same icon, and so forth. Other properties
will be different, like where it is in memory or what color of label it is given. Of
course sometimes things go wrong and file copying does not work as expected.
Our goal in this section is to show how we can look at this kind of information
flow in terms of distributed logics. We will greatly simplify things, of course,
as befits an illustrative example.

The distributed system $\mathcal{FC}_0$ ("$\mathcal{FC}$" for "file copying") that interests us is
depicted as follows:

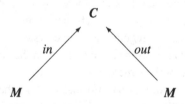

The tokens of M are instances of files on computers spread around the campus
network. The tokens of C are events of successfully copying a file from one
computer to another. The types of M consist of three types α, β, and γ, the
first two of which are supposed to represent typical properties of files such as
contents, time stamp, icon type, the kinds of things one wants preserved from a

file to any copy of the file. We assume that α and β are independent properties of file tokens, things like contents and time stamp. The type γ is the type of being protected. Protected files should be prevented from being copied. The types of C include α^{in}, α^{out}, β^{in}, β^{out}, γ^{in}, γ^{out}, as well as some other types, typified by the type δ, that are not definable as properties of the input or output. These classifications are specified below, along with their infomorphisms. (We should really have a lot more tokens around to get the full flavor of the idea. Also, having more tokens around would help alleviate another problem that will come up. But having hundreds, thousands, or millions of tokens would make the classification tables hard to print, let alone read, so we ask the reader to imagine a lot more tokens in both classifications.)

$\vDash_M$	α	β	γ
m_1	0	1	0
m_2	1	1	1
m_3	1	0	1
m_4	1	1	1
m_5	1	0	1
m_6	0	1	1

$\vDash_C$	α^{in}	α^{out}	β^{in}	β^{out}	γ^{in}	γ^{out}	δ
c_1	1	1	1	1	1	1	1
c_2	1	1	0	0	1	1	0
c_3	1	0	1	1	1	1	1

transaction c	file copied ($=in^{\smile}(c)$)	resulting file ($=out^{\smile}(c)$)
c_1	m_2	m_4
c_2	m_3	m_5
c_3	m_4	m_6

The infomorphisms *in* and *out* are as suggested by the names we have given the types. It is clear from examination of these tables that these functions are indeed infomorphisms, and so the result is a channel. We think of it as a channel from the M on the left to that on the right, though we could equally well use it as a channel in the opposite direction. The table of connections (transactions) shows that the file token m_4 is a copy of m_2, m_5 is a copy of m_3, and m_6 is a copy of m_4. Notice also that the protected file token m_1 is not connected to anything, so is not copied nor is it a copy of any other file. One would have to unprotect it, thereby getting a different file token, before it could be copied. Notice also that the transaction c_3 was not totally successful; it produced the file m_6, but the property α of the copied file m_4 does not hold of m_6. We want to be able to account for facts like

$m_2 \vDash_M \beta$ carries the information that $m_4 \vDash_M \beta$.

According to our proposal, this should be possible to explain in terms of a canonical logic on $M + M$ such that $\langle m_2, m_4 \rangle$ is a normal token of the logic, and $\beta^{in} \vdash \beta^{out}$ is a constraint of the logic.[1]

Given this channel, we can distribute any logic $\mathfrak{L}$ on C to the sum $M + M$. At this point, though, there are only two obvious logics available to us, the *a priori* logic $AP(C)$ and the natural logic $Log(C)$. Let us examine in turn what happens if we distribute these logics.

Example 15.4. Distributing the *a priori* logic $AP(C)$ does not give the desired results. The resulting logic on $M + M$ has as normal tokens the pairs $\langle m_2, m_4 \rangle$, $\langle m_3, m_5 \rangle$, and $\langle m_4, m_6 \rangle$. Because the infomorphisms *in* and *out* of the system have disjoint ranges in typ(C), the theory of this logic is just the smallest regular theory on the types of $M + M$. Hence $\beta^{in} \nvdash \beta^{out}$ so we do not have $m_2 \vDash_M \beta$ carrying the information about its copy m_4 that $m_4 \vDash_M \beta$, let alone any of the more subtle results we are after.

Example 15.5. Distributing the sound and complete $Log(C)$ to $M + M$ is more successful. The normal tokens are the same as before, but the theory is much richer. Recalling that the rows of the classification table for A can be thought of as specifying its set of consistent partitions, we see that this logic contains the following constraints:

$$\beta^{in} \vdash_C \beta^{out}, \quad \beta^{out} \vdash_C \beta^{in}, \quad \vdash_C \gamma^{in}, \quad \vdash_C \gamma^{out}.$$

Consequently, relative to this logic we *do* have $m_2 \vDash_M \beta$ carrying the information that $m_4 \vDash_M \beta$ (and vice versa), and we get for free the information that both tokens are of type γ.

There are some disturbing features of the logic obtained by distributing $Log(C)$, however, features that come from assuming complete information about the classification C. First, because of the faulty transaction c_3, $\alpha^{in} \nvdash_C \alpha^{out}$, so $m_4 \vDash_M \alpha$ does not carry the (mis)information that $m_6 \vDash_M \alpha$, and thus fails to reflect a mistake that users may justifiably make. Worse, we also do not find that $m_2 \vDash_M \alpha$ carries the information that $m_4 \vDash_M \alpha$. Using this logic, even one exceptional transaction out of millions can wreck information flow even for successful transactions. This is just the kind of result we want to avoid.

A different sort of problem comes from accidental generalizations captured by $Log(C)$. For example, looking at the classification table, we see that as it happens $\beta^{in} \vdash_C \alpha^{in}$. This would imply, for example, that $m_2 \vDash_M \beta$ carries

---

[1] We are here using the same notation β^{in} for the copy of β in the sum and for the translation of β into the types of C. This should not cause any confusion.

the information that $m_2 \vDash_M \alpha$, which seems wrong. This information is carried by $m_4 \vDash_M \alpha$ but surely not by $m_2 \vDash_M \beta$; look at m_1. The problem, of course, is that although we said that α and β were independent properties of files, there are no tokens in the classification of transactions that bear witness to this independence.

To rectify these problems, we can modify our distributed system $\mathcal{FC}_0$, either by postulating a third logic on $\mathbf{C}$ or by adding classifications and infomorphisms to the system. We pursue the latter approach first. Expand $\mathcal{FC}_0$ to a larger system $\mathcal{FC}$ by adding two classifications A and B as depicted below.

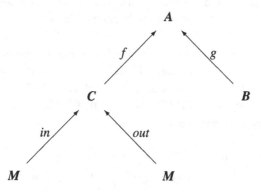

The classification A is the same as C except it throws out the faulty connection c_3:

$\vDash_A$	α^{in}	α^{out}	β^{in}	β^{out}	γ^{in}	γ^{out}	δ
c_1	1	1	1	1	1	1	0
c_2	1	1	0	0	1	1	1

Here f is the identity on types and on the tokens of A. Before describing B, let us see what happens if we distribute $\mathrm{Log}(A)$.

Example 15.6. If we distribute $\mathrm{Log}(A)$, the normal tokens are what we want: $\langle m_2, m_4 \rangle$ and $\langle m_3, m_5 \rangle$. Also, looking at the classification table, we see that

$$\alpha^{in} \vdash_A \alpha^{out}$$

so that relative to this logic, $m_2 \vDash_M \alpha$ carries the information that $m_4 \vDash_M \alpha$, as desired. Moreover, having this constraint does not mean that $m_4 \vDash_M \alpha$ carries the information that $m_6 \vDash_M \alpha$ because $\langle m_4, m_6 \rangle$ is not a normal token. However, distributing $\mathrm{Log}(A)$ still makes the false claim concerning information flow that $m_2 \vDash_M \beta$ carries the information that $m_2 \vDash_M \alpha$.

To take care of the overgeneration due to accidental generalizations, we add idealized tokens in the classification B defined below:

$\vDash_B$	α^{in}	α^{out}	β^{in}	β^{out}	γ^{in}	γ^{out}
c_1	1	1	1	1	1	1
c_2	1	1	0	0	1	1
n_1	0	0	1	1	1	1
n_2	0	0	0	0	1	1

The tokens n_1 and n_2 are idealized tokens used to represent unactualized possibilities embodied in our claim of the independence of α and β. The infomorphism g is the identity on types of B and on tokens of A.

Example 15.7. Consider the logic on $M + M$ obtained by distributing $\text{Log}(B)$. We compute this logic in two steps. First, let $\mathfrak{L} = f^{-1}[g[\text{Log}(B)]]$. This is a local logic on C with normal tokens c_1 and c_2. Because both f and g are type-identical, the theory of $\mathfrak{L}$ is $\text{Th}(B)$. We claim that $\text{Th}(B)$ is the regular closure of the following six constraints:

$$\alpha^{in} \vdash_C \alpha^{out}, \quad \alpha^{out} \vdash_C \alpha^{in}, \quad \vdash_C \gamma^{in},$$

$$\beta^{in} \vdash_C \beta^{out}, \quad \beta^{out} \vdash_C \beta^{in}, \quad \vdash_C \gamma^{out}.$$

To see this, we apply Proposition 9.18. First note that each of these constraints is valid in B. Next, note that any row of 0s and 1s that disagrees with those present in the classification table for B invalidates at least one of these constraints. For example, the row

$\vDash_B$	α^{in}	α^{out}	β^{in}	β^{out}	γ^{in}	γ^{out}
c_1	1	1	1	0	1	1

violates the constraint $\beta^{in} \vdash_B \beta^{out}$. If we now distribute $\mathfrak{L}$ over $M + M$, we get just the intuitively valid constraints; the normal tokens consist of the pairs $\langle m_2, m_4 \rangle$ and $\langle m_3, m_5 \rangle$.

We see that there are two ways to get at what seems like the natural information-theoretic logic on $M + M$. One is by distributing the natural logic $\text{Log}(B)$ over the system $\mathcal{F}C$. The other is by distributing the logic $\mathfrak{L}$ $(= f^{-1}[g[\text{Log}(B)]])$ over $\mathcal{F}C_0$. This corresponds to a information system with $\mathfrak{L}$ on C and $\text{AP}(M)$ on each copy of M. These approaches give us the same logic on $M + M$, but they give us somewhat different ways of looking at information flow.

15.3 The Distributed Logic of a Distributed System

We now turn from our little example to some special cases of the general construction. We begin with the pure case, where we have a distributed system $\mathcal{A}$ with no logics on any of the classifications. Put in terms of information systems, we are assuming that we have an information system where each classification has its *a priori* logic.

Proposition 15.8. *Let $\mathcal{A}$ be a distributed system with classifications $\mathrm{cla}(\mathcal{A}) = \{A_i\}_{i \in I}$ and infomorphisms $\mathrm{inf}(\mathcal{A})$. The systemwide logic $\mathrm{Log}(\mathcal{A})$ can be characterized as follows.*

1. *The classification of the logic is $\sum_{i \in I} A_i$.*
2. *The theory of the logic is the regular closure of the set of constraints of the forms*

$$\alpha \vdash f(\alpha) \quad and \quad f(\alpha) \vdash \alpha$$

   for each $f : A_i \rightleftarrows A_j$ of the system and each $\alpha \in \mathrm{typ}(A_i)$.
3. *The normal tokens are just those indexed families $c = \{c_i\}_{i \in I}$ of tokens that correspond to a global choice of a token from each component so that the pieces respect the whole-part relationships of the system. That is, $c \in N_{\mathfrak{L}}$ if and only if whenever $f : A_i \rightleftarrows A_j$ and $c_j \in \mathrm{tok}(A_j)$, then $c_i = f(c_j)$.*

Proof. In stating this result we have tacitly assumed that the types of the various component classifications are disjoint. If not, they need to be replaced by their disjoint copies. We continue to make this notationally simplifying assumption in the remainder of this lecture. The proof is just a matter of unwinding our earlier definition where all the component logics are *a priori* logics. □

Let us depict the limit $\lim \mathcal{A}$ of our distributed system $\mathcal{A}$ as follows:

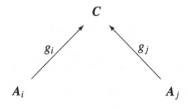

Using the fundamental property of sums, we obtain the following commuting diagram, where we write σ_i for σ_{A_i} and g for $\sum_{k \in I} g_k$:

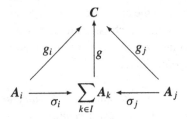

Using this notation, we can now explicate the relationship between the limit and the systemwide logic.

Theorem 15.9. *Let $\mathcal{A}$ be a distributed system as above and let $\mathfrak{L} = \mathrm{AP}(C)$ on the core of $\lim \mathcal{A}$.*

1. *$\mathfrak{L} = \mathrm{Lind}(\mathrm{Log}(\mathcal{A}))$.*
2. *If $\tau : \mathrm{Log}(\mathcal{A}) \rightleftarrows \mathrm{Lind}(\mathrm{Log}(\mathcal{A}))$ is the quotient logic infomorphism, then for each i, $g_i = \tau \sigma_i$.*
3. *$\mathrm{Log}(\mathcal{A}) = g^{-1}[\mathfrak{L}]$.*

Proof. The proofs of (1) and (2) are clear by examining the definition of the limit in Lecture 6 and of the Lindenbaum logic in Lecture 12. To prove (3), we first recall that $g^{-1}[\mathfrak{L}]$ is the largest logic $\mathfrak{L}'$ on A such that $g : \mathfrak{L}' \rightleftarrows \mathfrak{L}$ is a logic infomorphism. However, it is clear that $g : \mathrm{Log}(\mathcal{A}) \rightleftarrows \mathfrak{L}$ is a logic infomorphism, so $\mathrm{Log}(\mathcal{A}) \sqsubseteq g^{-1}[\mathfrak{L}]$. Thus we need only show that $g^{-1}[\mathfrak{L}] \sqsubseteq \mathrm{Log}(\mathcal{A})$. Because $\mathfrak{L}$ is sound, the condition on tokens is trivial. So we need only show that if $\Gamma \vdash_{g^{-1}[\mathfrak{L}]} \Delta$, then $\Gamma \vdash_{\mathrm{Log}(\mathcal{A})} \Delta$, for all $\Gamma, \Delta \subseteq \mathrm{typ}(A)$. Assume $\Gamma \vdash_{g^{-1}[\mathfrak{L}]} \Delta$. Then $g[\Gamma] \vdash_{\mathfrak{L}} g[\Delta]$. Thus there are types $\alpha \in \Gamma, \beta \in \Delta$ such that $F(\alpha) = F(\beta)$, because $\mathfrak{L}$ is the *a priori* logic on C. But this means that $[\alpha]_R = [\beta]_R$, where R is the relation used in taking the quotient in the construction of C. But then an inductive proof (on the length of a chain of types from α to β using R and R^{-1}) shows that $\alpha \vdash_{\mathrm{Log}(\mathcal{A})} \beta$, as desired. $\square$

15.4 Distributing a Logic Along a Channel

Suppose we are given an information channel $C = \{f_i : A_i \rightleftarrows C\}_{i \in I}$ and a logic $\mathfrak{L}$ on the core classification C. We want to define a local logic on the sum $\sum_{i \in I} A_i$ that represents the reasoning about relations among the components justified by the logic $\mathfrak{L}$ on the core. We call this the distributed logic of C generated by $\mathfrak{L}$ and denote it by $\mathrm{DLog}_C(\mathfrak{L})$.

To define this logic, recall the diagram of the channel together with the canonical embedding of the sum into the core of the channel.

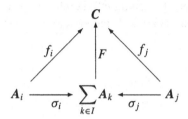

We can characterize this logic in terms of our previous construction by considering the whole channel as a distributed system. However, this gives us a logic on $\sum_{k \in I} A_k + C$, whereas what we want is a logic on $\sum_{k \in I} A_k$. Of course we can easily extract a logic on the first summand from that on the sum. We can characterize the logic directly as $F^{-1}[\mathfrak{L}]$, where F is as above.

If the logic $\mathfrak{L}$ on the core of a channel C is complete, then the distributed logic $\mathrm{DLog}_C(\mathfrak{L})$ is complete, simply because taking inverse images preserves completeness. Note, though, that $\mathrm{DLog}_C(\mathfrak{L})$ is not in general a sound logic, even if $\mathfrak{L}$ is sound. It is only guaranteed to be sound on the range $F^{\vee}$, that is, on those tokens of the sum that are sequences of projections of a normal token of $\mathfrak{L}$. In other words, the normal tokens of the distributed logic $\mathrm{DLog}_C(\mathfrak{L})$ consist of those sequences of components that are connected together by some normal token of the whole system.

15.5 The Distributed Logic of a State-Space System

In Lecture 3, we investigated an example of an information channel whose core was the event classification of a state space S. There we were using the state-space logic $\mathrm{Log}(S)$. This is frequently a very convenient tool. In this section, we explore what it means to distribute this logic over a state-space system.

Suppose we are given a state-space system $S = \{f_i : S \rightrightarrows S_i\}_{i \in I}$. We want to define a local logic on the sum $\sum_{i \in I} \mathrm{Evt}(S_i)$ that captures the way we can infer partial information about the state of some components given partial information about the state of some other components and the fact that they are connected by some token of the system. We call this the distributed logic generated by S, and denote it by $\mathrm{DLog}_C(S)$.

We already have one logic on the sum $\sum_{i \in I} \text{Evt}(S_i)$ of course, namely, the sum of the logics generated by the component state spaces, that is, $\sum_{i \in I} \text{Log}(S_i)$. This logic ignores the connections furnished by the core state space S, however. To take advantage of this state space, we simply distribute the logic $\text{Log}(S)$ to $\sum_{i \in I} \text{Evt}(S_i)$ by means of a natural infomorphism. Recall from Lecture 8 the following construction. Start with the system S depicted by the following diagram:

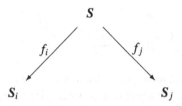

Applying the operator Evt to this diagram and using the fundamental property of sums, we obtained the following commuting diagram, where for the sake of readability, we write σ_i for $\sigma_{\text{Evt}(S_i)}$ and F for $\sum_{k \in I} \text{Evt}(f_k)$:

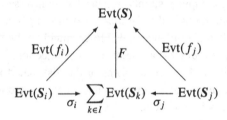

The infomorphism F allows us to pull back any logic $\mathfrak{L}$ on $\text{Evt}(S)$ to a logic $F^{-1}[\mathfrak{L}]$ on the classification $\sum_{k \in I} \text{Evt}(S_k)$.

Definition 15.10. Given a state-space system $S = \{f_i : S \rightrightarrows S_i\}_{i \in I}$, the *distributed logic* $\text{DLog}(S)$ of S is $F^{-1}[\text{Log}(S)]$, where F is as above.

Notice that if the core state space S of S is complete, then this logic is complete, simply because taking inverse images preserves completeness. When using any state space the presumption is that it is complete; hence the presumption carries over to the distributed logic $\text{DLog}(S)$.

Note also, though, that $\text{DLog}(S)$ is not in general a sound logic. It is only guaranteed to be sound on the range of $F^{\vee}$, that is, on those tokens of $\text{DLog}(S)$ that are sequences of projections of a token of S. In other words, the normal tokens of the distributed logic $\text{DLog}(S)$ consist of those sequences of components that are connected together by some token of the whole system. These tokens satisfy all the constraints of the logic for principled reasons: they have to by virtue of the state-space logic on their connections. There might be other tokens around that satisfy the constraint of the logic, but if so, they do so by accident.

There is a simple, explicit characterization of the consequence relation of DLog(S). To make it easier to read, we adopt the following notation. Given any set Γ of types in our logic, write $\Gamma_k = \{X \in \Gamma \mid X \in \text{typ}(\text{Evt}(S_k))\}$, a set of types in Evt($S_k$). Thus $\Gamma = \bigcup_{k \in I} \Gamma_k$.

Theorem 15.11. *Let $S = \{f_i : S \rightrightarrows S_i\}_{i \in I}$ be a state-space system. For any sets Γ, Δ of types of the distributed logic DLog(S), the following are equivalent:*

1. *$\Gamma \vdash_{\text{DLog}(S)} \Delta$.*
2. *For each state σ of the core of S and each $k \in I$, $\Gamma_k, \{f_k(\sigma)\} \vdash_{\text{Log}(S_k)} \Delta_k$.*
3. *For each state σ of the core of S and each $k \in I$, if $f_k(\sigma) \in \bigcap \Gamma_k$, then $f_k(\sigma) \in \bigcup \Delta_k$.*

The normal tokens of DLog(S) consist of those sequences of components that are connected by some token c of the the core S of S. The logic is complete if the state space S is complete.

Proof. To prove the first claim, note that the following are equivalent:

$$\Gamma \vdash_{\text{DLog}(S)} \Delta.$$

$$F[\Gamma] \vdash_{\text{Log}(S)} F[\Delta].$$

$$\{F(X) \mid X \in \Gamma\} \vdash_{\text{Log}(S)} \{F(Y) \mid Y \in \Delta\}.$$

$$\bigcup_{k \in I} \{F(X) \mid X \in \Gamma_k\} \vdash_{\text{Log}(S)} \bigcup_{k \in I} \{F(Y) \mid Y \in \Delta_k\}.$$

$$\bigcup_{k \in I} \{f_k^{-1}[X] \mid X \in \Gamma_k\} \vdash_{\text{Log}(S)} \bigcup_{k \in I} \{f_k^{-1}[Y] \mid Y \in \Delta_k\}.$$

For each state σ of the core of S and each $k \in I$, if $f_k(\sigma) \in \bigcap \Gamma_k$, then $f_k(\sigma) \in \bigcup \Delta_k$

For each state σ of the core of S and each $k \in I$, $\Gamma_k, \{f_k(\sigma)\} \vdash_{\text{Log}(S_k)} \Delta_k$.

Each item in our theorem is in this list. The final two sentences merely summarize the earlier discussion. □

Exercises

15.1. The fundamental dogma of molecular biology asserts that information flows from DNA to RNA to protein but not in the reverse direction. Model this information flow as an information system and explain a sense in which information flow is one directional.

15.2. Using the results on moving logics, generalize the results on limits of distributed systems to information systems. The first step is to generalize our previous notions from classifications (essentially natural logics) to arbitrary local logics.

Lecture 16

Logics and State Spaces

In Lecture 8 we saw how to construct state spaces from classifications and vice versa. In Lecture 12 we saw how to associate a canonical logic Log(S) with any state space S. In this lecture we study the relation between logics and state spaces in more detail. Our aim is to try to understand how the phenomena of incompleteness and unsoundness get reflected in the state-space framework. We will put our analysis to work by exploring the problem of nonmonotonicity in Lecture 19.

16.1 Subspaces of State Spaces

Our first goal is to show that there is a natural correspondence between the subspaces of a state space S and logics on the event classification of S. We develop this correspondence in the next few results.

Definition 16.1. Let S be a state space. An S-logic is a logic $\mathfrak{L}$ on the event classification Evt(S) such that Log(S) $\sqsubseteq \mathfrak{L}$.

The basic intuition here is that an S-logic should build in at least the theory implicit in the state-space structure of S. We call a state σ of S $\mathfrak{L}$-consistent if $\{\sigma\} \nvdash_{\mathfrak{L}}$ and let $\Omega_{\mathfrak{L}}$ be the set of $\mathfrak{L}$-consistent states.

Proposition 16.2. If S is a state space and $\mathfrak{L}$ is an S-logic, then $\vdash_{\mathfrak{L}} \Omega_{\mathfrak{L}}$. Indeed, $\Omega_{\mathfrak{L}}$ is the smallest set of states such that $\vdash_{\mathfrak{L}} \Omega_{\mathfrak{L}}$.

Proof. To prove the first claim, let $\langle \Gamma, \Delta \rangle$ be any partition of the types of Evt(S) with $\Omega_{\mathfrak{L}} \in \Delta$. We need to see that $\Gamma \vdash_{\mathfrak{L}} \Delta$. Because Log($S$) $\sqsubseteq \mathfrak{L}$, we need only check that every state σ that is in every $X \in \Gamma$ is in some $X \in \Delta$. If not,

195

then $\sigma \notin \Omega_{\mathfrak{L}}$, because $\Omega_{\mathfrak{L}} \in \Delta$. Hence σ is inconsistent in $\mathfrak{L}$. But $\{\sigma\} \in \Gamma$ because it cannot be in Δ, so $\Gamma \vdash_{\mathfrak{L}} \Delta$ by Weakening. To prove the second claim, suppose that $\vdash_{\mathfrak{L}} \Omega'$. We want to prove that $\Omega_{\mathfrak{L}} \subseteq \Omega'$. Supposing this is not the case, let $\sigma \in \Omega_{\mathfrak{L}} - \Omega'$. If we can prove $\{\sigma\} \vdash_{\mathfrak{L}}$, we will have our desired contradiction. We want to use Partition, so let $\langle \Gamma, \Delta \rangle$ be a partition with $\{\sigma\} \in \Gamma$. We want to show that $\Gamma \vdash_{\mathfrak{L}} \Delta$. Because $\vdash_{\mathfrak{L}} \Omega'$, it suffices, by Cut, to prove that $\Gamma, \Omega' \vdash_{\mathfrak{L}} \Delta$. Because $\mathfrak{L}$ is an S-logic, it suffices to show $\Gamma, \Omega' \vdash_{\mathrm{Log}(S)} \Delta$. But this is obvious, because Γ contains an element disjoint from Ω', namely $\{\sigma\}$. $\square$

Definition 16.3. Let S be a state space and let $\mathfrak{L}$ be an S-logic. The *subspace* $S_{\mathfrak{L}}$ *of S determined by $\mathfrak{L}$* has $\Omega_{\mathfrak{L}}$ for its set of states and has as tokens the set $N_{\mathfrak{L}}$ of normal tokens of $\mathfrak{L}$.

Justification. We need to check that the state of each normal token of $\mathfrak{L}$ is a member of $\Omega_{\mathfrak{L}}$. This follows from $\vdash_{\mathfrak{L}} \Omega_{\mathfrak{L}}$. $\square$

Proposition 16.4. *Let S be a state space and let $\mathfrak{L}$ be an S-logic. Then $\Gamma \vdash_{\mathfrak{L}} \Delta$ if and only if $\Gamma, \Omega_{\mathfrak{L}} \vdash_{\mathrm{Log}(S)} \Delta$.*

Proof. The direction from right to left follows from Proposition 16.2 and Finite Cut. To prove the converse, suppose that $\Gamma \vdash_{\mathfrak{L}} \Delta$. We need to prove that every state $\sigma \in \Omega_{\mathfrak{L}}$, if $\sigma \in X$ for every $X \in \Gamma$, then $\sigma \in Y$ for some $Y \in \Delta$. Suppose σ is a counterexample. We want to show that σ is inconsistent in $\mathfrak{L}$, contradicting the fact that it is in $\Omega_{\mathfrak{L}}$. To prove this, let $\langle \Gamma', \Delta' \rangle$ be a partition with $\{\sigma\} \in \Gamma'$ such that $\Gamma' \nvdash_{\mathfrak{L}} \Delta'$. From this it is easy to see that

$$\Gamma' = \{X \mid \sigma \in X\},$$
$$\Delta' = \{X \mid \sigma \notin X\}.$$

But then $\Gamma \subseteq \Gamma'$ and $\Delta \subseteq \Delta'$, so $\Gamma' \vdash_{\mathfrak{L}} \Delta'$ by Weakening. $\square$

Proposition 16.5. *If S is a state space and $\mathfrak{L}_1, \mathfrak{L}_2$ are S-logics, then $\mathfrak{L}_1 \sqsubseteq \mathfrak{L}_2$ if and only if $S_{\mathfrak{L}_2} \subseteq S_{\mathfrak{L}_1}$. Hence $\mathfrak{L}_1 = \mathfrak{L}_2$ if and only if $S_{\mathfrak{L}_2} = S_{\mathfrak{L}_1}$.*

Proof. The second claim clearly follows from the first. To prove the first, assume $\mathfrak{L}_1 \sqsubseteq \mathfrak{L}_2$. Because $S_{\mathfrak{L}_1}$ and $S_{\mathfrak{L}_2}$ are both subspaces of S, all we need to check is that the tokens of the latter are a subset of the tokens of the former and that the states of the latter are a subset of the states of the former. The first is immediate from the assumption and the definitions of these spaces. As for states, the claim is almost as obvious. If $\sigma \in \Omega_{\mathcal{L}_2}$, then $\sigma \nvdash_{\mathcal{L}_2}$. But by our assumption, $\sigma \nvdash_{\mathcal{L}_1}$, and so $\sigma \in \Omega_{\mathcal{L}_1}$.

Now assume $S_{\mathcal{L}_2} \subseteq S_{\mathcal{L}_1}$. Again, the inclusion of normal tokens is trivial, so we need only verify the inclusion of constraints. Suppose $\Gamma \vdash_{\mathcal{L}_1} \Delta$. By the previous result, $\Gamma, \Omega_{\mathcal{L}_1} \vdash_{\text{Log}(S)} \Delta$. Hence $\bigcap \Gamma \cap \Omega_{\mathcal{L}_1} \subseteq \bigcup \Delta$. But $\Omega_{\mathcal{L}_2} \subseteq \Omega_{\mathcal{L}_1}$ by assumption, so $\bigcap \Gamma \cap \Omega_{\mathcal{L}_2} \subseteq \bigcup \Delta$. Hence $\Gamma, \Omega_{\mathcal{L}_2} \vdash_{\text{Log}(S)} \Delta$, and so $\Gamma \vdash_{\mathcal{L}_2} \Delta$. $\qquad\qquad\square$

Theorem 16.6. *Let S be any state space. The mapping*

$$\mathcal{L} \mapsto S_{\mathcal{L}}$$

is an order inverting bijection between the family of all S-logics and the family of all subspaces of S.

Proof. Given Proposition 16.5, all we need establish is that every subspace S_0 of S is of the form $S_{\mathcal{L}}$ for some logic extending $\text{Log}(S)$. Let the normal tokens of $\mathcal{L}$ be the tokens of S_0. Define a consequence relation on $\text{Evt}(S)$ by $\Gamma \vdash_{\mathcal{L}} \Delta$ if and only if $\Gamma, \text{typ}(S_0) \vdash_{\text{Log}(S)} \Delta$. This is easily seen to be regular. All we need do is to check that for any state σ of S, $\sigma \vdash_{\mathcal{L}}$ if and only if $\sigma \notin \text{typ}(S_0)$. This is routine. $\qquad\qquad\square$

These results show that the state-space analog of a logic on a classification is that of a subspace of the given state space. The tokens of the subspace correspond to normal tokens of the logic, the states of the subspace correspond to the constraints of the logic. Here is another way in which this analogy holds.

Definition 16.7. Let S be a state space, S_0 a subspace of S. S_0 is *sound* in S if $\text{tok}(S_0) = \text{tok}(S)$.

Proposition 16.8. *Let S be a state space. An S-logic $\mathcal{L}$ is sound if and only if the associated state space $S_{\mathcal{L}}$ is sound.*

Proof. We leave this as an exercise. $\qquad\qquad\square$

The following shows that the concepts of completeness and soundness for state spaces behave as one would expect, given the above correspondence.

Proposition 16.9. *Let $f : S \rightrightarrows S'$ be a state-space projection.*

1. If S_0 is a complete subspace of S, then $f[S_0]$ is a complete subspace of S'.

2. *If S_1 is a sound subspace of S', then $f^{-1}[S_1]$ is a sound subspace of S.*

Proof. The proof is a routine verification. ☐

16.2 From Local Logics to State Spaces

We now complete the correspondence between local logics and state spaces by showing how any local logic $\mathfrak{L}$ gives rise to a canonical state space $\mathrm{Ssp}(\mathfrak{L})$. Recall (from Lecture 8) the state space $\mathrm{Ssp}(A)$ generated by a classification A. This space has the same tokens as A; states are arbitrary partitions of the types of A. The state of a token is its state description.

Definition 16.10. Let $\mathfrak{L}$ be a local logic on a classification A.

1. The state space $\mathrm{Ssp}(\mathfrak{L})$ *generated by* $\mathfrak{L}$ is the subspace of $\mathrm{Ssp}(A)$ whose tokens are the normal tokens of $\mathfrak{L}$ and whose types are the $\mathfrak{L}$-consistent partitions.
2. Given a logic infomorphism $f : \mathfrak{L}_1 \rightleftarrows \mathfrak{L}_2$, let $\mathrm{Ssp}(f)$ be the state-space projection from $\mathrm{Ssp}(\mathfrak{L}_2)$ to $\mathrm{Ssp}(\mathfrak{L}_1)$ that is the restriction of $\mathrm{Cla}(f)$ to $\mathrm{Ssp}(\mathfrak{L}_2)$.

Justification. Because every normal token has a consistent state description, this does indeed define a subspace of $\mathrm{Ssp}(A)$. It is easy to check that things work properly on maps. ☐

Proposition 16.11. *Let $\mathfrak{L}$ be a local logic on a classification A.*

1. *$\mathfrak{L}$ is sound if and only if $\mathrm{Ssp}(\mathfrak{L})$ is a sound subspace of $\mathrm{Ssp}(A)$.*
2. *$\mathfrak{L}$ is complete if and only if $\mathrm{Ssp}(\mathfrak{L})$ is a complete state space.*

We have the following analog of Theorem 16.6.

Theorem 16.12. *Let A be any classification and let $S = \mathrm{Ssp}(A)$ be its associated state space. The mapping*

$$\mathfrak{L} \mapsto \mathrm{Ssp}(\mathfrak{L})$$

is an order inverting bijection between the set of logics on A and the set of subspaces of S.

Proof. The proof is very similar to the proof of Theorem 16.6 and is entirely straightforward. ☐

Exercises

16.1. By Theorem 16.6, different subspaces correspond to different logics. This raises a question as to the relationship between images and inverse images of subspaces, on the one hand, and logics, on the other. Let $f : S \rightrightarrows S'$ be a projection, and let S_1 and S_2 be subspaces of S and S', respectively. Recall that $\text{Evt}(f) : \text{Evt}(S') \rightleftarrows \text{Evt}(S)$ is an infomorphism. Hence the image under $\text{Evt}(f)$ of a logic on $\text{Evt}(S')$ is a logic on $\text{Evt}(S)$ and the inverse image of a logic on $\text{Evt}(S)$ is a logic on $\text{Evt}(S')$. Prove the following identities, where we write $\text{Log}(S_1)$ for the S-logic $\mathfrak{L}$ that corresponds to S_1 under the bijection of Theorem 16.6:

1.

$$\text{Log}(f[S_1]) = \text{Evt}(f)^{-1}[\text{Log}(S_1)].$$

2.

$$\text{Log}(f^{-1}[S_2]) = \text{Evt}(f)[\text{Log}(S_2)].$$

16.2. Prove Proposition 16.11.

16.3. Let $f : A \rightleftarrows B$ be an infomorphism. By Theorem 16.12, subspaces of these state spaces correspond to logics on A and B, respectively. This raises a question as to the relationship between images and inverse images of subspaces, on the one hand, and logics, on the other. Recall that $\text{Ssp}(f) : \text{Ssp}(B) \rightrightarrows \text{Ssp}(A)$ is a state-space projection. Hence the image under $\text{Ssp}(f)$ of a subspace of $\text{Ssp}(B)$ is a subspace of $\text{Ssp}(A)$ and the inverse image of a subspace of $\text{Ssp}(A)$ is a subspace of $\text{Ssp}(B)$. Let $\mathfrak{L}_1$ and $\mathfrak{L}_2$ be logics on A and B, respectively. Prove the following identities:

1.

$$\text{Ssp}(f[\mathfrak{L}_1]) = \text{Ssp}(f)^{-1}[\text{Ssp}(\mathfrak{L}_1)].$$

2.

$$\text{Ssp}(f^{-1}[\mathfrak{L}_2]) = \text{Ssp}(f)^{-1}[\text{Ssp}(\mathfrak{L}_2)].$$

Part III

Explorations

Lecture 17

Speech Acts

In this lecture we want to give a simple application of classifications and infomorphisms to analyze J. L. Austin's four-way distinction in "How to talk: Some simple ways" (Austin, 1961). The material in this lecture follows Lecture 4 and is not needed elsewhere in the book.

17.1 Truth-Conditional Semantics and Speech Acts

The theory of speech acts owes its origins to Austin's (1961) work. This theory is challenging in a couple of ways. First, Austin's paper is one of his more difficult. It is just hard to figure out what he is saying. Second, the theory of speech acts poses a challenge to certain kinds of semantic theories, and the types of speech acts discussed by Austin in his paper illustrate the challenge very clearly. Austin is saying that there are at least four distinct things a person can be doing with a true utterance as simple as "Figure 4 is a triangle." One might say that he is arguing that such an utterance can have at least four distinct types of content. The difference is not reflected in the truth conditions of the utterance, but in something else entirely. If this is right, it seems to pose a special problem for semantic theories that try to explicate sentence meaning in terms of truth conditions.

Austin's paper has a special relevance to our project, as well. This work grew out of attempting to flesh out ideas about constraints presented in *Situations and Attitudes* (Barwise and Perry, 1983), a book that owes much to Austin's general approach to language. It thus seems appropriate to try to bring our insights back to bear on Austin's theory.

Our hope, then, is to do two things in this lecture. One is to try to repay a debt to Austin by using the theory of classifications and infomorphisms to shed some light on his difficult paper. More importantly, though, we hope to suggest initial directions for how channel theory might be used to contribute to a logical approach to speech acts. We emphasize that this lecture, like all of Part III, is intended to be thought provoking and highly tentative and not anything like a full theory of speech acts.

17.2 Austin's Model

In order to elucidate the distinctions he wants to make, Austin begins with a very simplified model of language in use, what he calls the model S_0. Having made the distinctions, he goes on to complicate the model in various ways. We will stick to Austin's S_0 model. Austin assumes the following setup.

The Described Situation

On the world side of the his language/world model, Austin assumes there is a set of *items* and that each item is of a unique *type*. Austin uses two running examples to illustrate his observations, one where items are particular color patches and types are colors, the other where items are drawn figures on a page and the types are geometric shapes like circle, triangle, square, rhombus, and so on. We will restrict our attention to the latter example. Thus, from our perspective, Austin assumes that the world consists of a classification *Fig*, and his items are our tokens.

Language

Austin uses a very simple language to illustrate the ways we can talk about the described situation. In particular, in the S_0 model, Austin allows only sentences S of the form

$$t \text{ is a } N,$$

where t is a term that refers to some item and N is a word whose sense is some type. That is, Austin essentially assumes we are given a set *Names*, a set *Nouns*, a reference function $ref: Names \to tok(Fig)$, and a sense function $sense: Nouns \to typ(Fig)$. An object may have more than one name, and a type may be the sense of more than one noun, but in this model, at least, each name refers to a unique item in *Fig* and each noun has a unique sense, a type of *Fig*.

To make things a little more definite, we assume that every name has the form Figure n for some numeral n. We assume that the set of nouns contains the expressions triangle, square, rhombus, pentagon, hexagon, septagon, and circle and that the function *sense* assigns these nouns their usual geometric senses. We assume that the set of sentences consists of the expressions

Figure n is a N,

where n is a numeral and N is any of the above nouns.

17.3 Austin's Four Speech Acts

In Austin's theory, utterances are more fundamental than sentences. In *Situations and Attitudes* (Barwise and Perry, 1983) this distinction was exploited to handle matters like tense, indexicals, who is being referred to by a given name, what sense of a noun is being used, which described situation is intended, and the like. In Austin's S_0, though, all such matters have been avoided, so one might think that we could deal simply with sentences. But this is not possible. Austin's model shows that even without the intrusion of these complexities, it is still possible to do more than one thing with a given sentence, necessitating the classification of utterances into different types of speech acts.

We thus suppose that there is another classification U of utterances. Each token is, intuitively, an utterance. The types of U are of two kinds, sentence types and speech-act types. The sentence types consist of all sentences of the displayed form, where $t \in Names$ and $N \in Nouns$. It is assumed that each token u is of a unique type. The speech-act types consist of four types: *placing*, *stating*, *instancing*, and *casting*. (That is all we need here, though for more sophisticated analyses one would add types to pick out the speaker, addressee, and so on.) Our aim here is to associate with each of these four types something it would be reasonable to call the "content" of a given utterance of that type.

Statings and Castings

We begin with the simplest of Austin's distinctions, statings versus castings.

Statings

If the sentence type of u is

t is a N,

we write t_u for the name and N_u for the noun used in the utterance. At first sight, it would seem that an utterance u of "t is a N" could make only a single claim: that the item $ref(t_u)$ referred to is of the type $sense(N_u)$ in the world

Fig, that is, that

$$ref(t_u) \vDash_{\textit{Fig}} sense(N_u).$$

Austin calls utterances that make this sort of claim *statings*, reasonably enough. Such a stating u is *true* if and only if $ref(t_u) \vDash_{\textit{Fig}} sense(N_u)$. What other sorts of utterances could there be?

Austin discusses utterances in which names and nouns are misused, names to refer to items that they do not name, or nouns to connote a sense they do not have. But he discusses this only to set it aside as not being relevant to the four-way distinction he is after.

Castings

There are two ways of thinking of classifications. One may think of tokens as somehow more firmly anchored in the physical world and types as more abstract. But the tokens of a classification can be thought of as the givens, the things that need classifying. Types are the things we use to classify the tokens. Often these two notions march in step because it is more typical for the given to be given physically, but sometimes they do not. For example, if a classification A has physical tokens and abstract types, then the dual classification $A^{\perp}$ (where types and tokens are interchanged) has physical types and abstract tokens.

Austin's notion of a casting is one where the tokens are more abstract. The basic idea of a casting is that one is given a type and is trying to "cast" it, as in a play; that is, one is looking for a token of that type. As Austin puts it, "To *cast* we have to find a sample to match this pattern to." If we think of the tokens of a classification as the givens, then this amounts to using the dual classification $\textit{Fig}^{\perp}$. That is, an utterance u is a *casting* if it asserts that

$$sense(N_u) \vDash_{\textit{Fig}^{\perp}} ref(t_u).$$

Note that

$$ref(t_u) \vDash_{\textit{Fig}} sense(N_u) \text{ if and only if } sense(N_u) \vDash_{\textit{Fig}^{\perp}} ref(t_u),$$

so there is no difference of truth between a stating and a casting that use the same names and nouns. There is a difference in what the speaker is doing.

Placings and Instancings

Placings and instancings are like statings and castings, respectively, except in one key regard. In the latter pair, Austin says, the sense of the noun is taken for granted, whereas in the former pair it is not. The difference is most easily seen with examples of error. We look first at placings.

Placings

Suppose Tom says "Figure 3 is a square." One sort of error (misstating) is that Tom has gotten the shape of Figure 3 wrong, perhaps by misperceiving it. If Tom misstates that Figure 3 is a square, then he has mistaken the shape of Figure 3. By contrast, he misplaces Figure 3 in saying "Figure 3 is a square" if he has mistaken what one means by "square."

An easy way to capture this distinction is to use an induced classification. Consider the following diagram:

$$Nouns \xrightarrow{\ sense\ } \text{typ}(\textit{Fig})$$
$$\Big\vert \models_{\textit{Fig}}$$
$$\text{tok}(\textit{Fig})$$

From these ingredients we obtain an induced classification $\textit{Fig}_s$ (the "s" to remind us that it is induced by $\textit{Fig}$ and the function *sense*) of the items by nouns as follows:

$$a \models_{\textit{Fig}_s} N \quad \text{iff} \quad a \models_{\textit{Fig}} sense(N)$$

This says that a figure is called an N if it has the shape $sense(N)$. This can be pictured as follows:

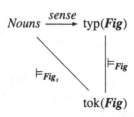

Another way of putting this is to require that *sense* (paired with the identity function on items) be an infomorphism $sense: \textit{Fig}_s \rightleftarrows \textit{Fig}$.

Using this classification, we say that an utterance u is a *placing* if it asserts that

$$ref(t_u) \models_{\textit{Fig}_s} N_u.$$

Again, the difference between this placing and the corresponding stating is not one of truth, because $ref(t_u) \vDash_{Fig_s} N_u$ if and only if $ref(t_u) \vDash_{Fig} sense(N_u)$, but of what the speaker is doing.

Instancing

Given the resources at hand, one possibility is left open to us, namely, using the dual $Fig_s^{\perp}$ of the induced classification. We would hope that Austin's fourth type of assertion would assert

$$N_u \vDash_{Fig_s^{\perp}} ref(t_u).$$

Of the four, instancing is the speech act to which Austin pays least attention. He says merely that to instance is to cite t as an instance of N.

Is This What Austin Had in Mind?

Using the framework of classifications and infomorphisms, we have come up with four possible things one can do with a sentence of the form "t is a N." Let us summarize these by means of the following diagram:

$$ref(t_u) \vDash_{Fig_s} N_u \quad\text{------}\quad ref(t_u) \vDash_{Fig} sense(N_u)$$

$$N_u \vDash_{Fig_s^{\perp}} ref(t_u) \quad\text{------}\quad sense(N_u) \vDash_{Fig^{\perp}} ref(t_u)$$

Each corner of the square represents a distinct possible content for an utterance u of

$$t \text{ is a } N,$$

depending on just what the speaker is doing with the utterance, that is, depending on its type as a speech act. The four contents are true or false together, but informationally they represent four distinct claims.

On the left side of this diagram, we are dealing with the classification Fig_s and its dual, relating items in the world and nouns in the language. On the right side, we are dealing with the classification Fig relating items in the world with their types. The top row of the diagram has to do with classifying items, either by nouns or by their senses. The bottom row has to do with finding items that are examples of nouns or their senses. Our diagram is put forward as an explication of the following diagram from Austin:

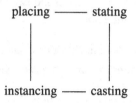

If this analysis is correct, it seems we could say, in a bit clearer way, just what the four speech acts are:

- In placing, one says what an object is called.
- In stating, one says what an object is.
- In instancing, one gives an example to which a given noun applies.
- In casting, one gives an example of a given type.

Let us stress once more that all four speech acts have equivalent truth conditions; where they differ is in what things they are classifying and what they are classifying these things with.

It is not clear from Austin's account why he treats names and noun phrases so asymmetrically. We could use the diagram

$$\text{typ}(\textbf{Fig})$$

$$\Big\vert \models_{\textbf{Fig}}$$

$$\textit{Names} \xrightarrow[\textit{ref}]{} \text{tok}(\textbf{Fig})$$

to induce a different classification W_r, namely, of names by the types of $\textbf{Fig}$.

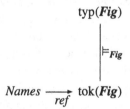

If we use this classification, two more possibilities arise, corresponding to a different kind of information; information about the reference of names. Perhaps Austin used numerals for names just to avoid adding this sort of complication to his already complicated picture. But surely there are times when this is just what one is after. One is thus tempted to add two more assertive speech acts, let us call them *identifying* and *naming*.

- In identifying, one tells what kind of thing a name denotes: $t \vDash_{W_r} sense(N)$.
- In naming, one gives a name of something of a given kind: $sense(N) \vDash_{W_{r\perp}} t$.

There is yet another induced classification C, namely, of names by nouns, given by $t \vDash_C N$ if and only if $ref(t) \vDash_{Fig} sense(N)$. This brings up two more theoretical possibilities. Here the world does not really enter at all, except by the back door, so it is hard to see the point of using language in the two ways suggested by this classification and its dual. But with language use, it seems that anything that is possible is realized somewhere, so it would not surprise us to find real examples of this sort.

What are Propositions?

We have not used the notion of a proposition in this book. There are many different things one might mean by a proposition. If one wants to develop a theory of speech act contents, the above analysis suggests that one model a proposition as a triple $p = \langle A, a, \alpha \rangle$, where A is a classification, $a \in tok(A)$, and $\alpha \in typ(A)$. Then p would be *true* if $a \vDash_A \alpha$. What we have seen in this lecture is that, with this understanding of a proposition, there can be many distinct propositions associated with an utterance u, propositions that are linked to one another in systematic ways and have the same truth conditions. Which of these propositions should be assigned to u depends on us speech act type. This is far from a worked out theory of speech acts and how they would fit in a theory of information flow. But it shows, at least, that taking classifications seriously gives one the tools to make some distinctions that need to be developed for such a theory.

Lecture 18

Vagueness

A standard objection to classical logic has been its failure to come to grips with vague predicates and their associated problems and paradoxes. An analysis of the vague predicates "low," "medium,"and "high" (as applied to brightness of light bulbs) was implicit in Lecture 3. In this lecture we want to make the idea behind this treatment more explicit, thereby suggesting an information-theoretic line of research into vagueness. At best, this line of development would allow the information-flow perspective to contribute to the study of vagueness. At the very least, it should show that vagueness is not an insurmountable problem to the perspective offered in this book.

In this lecture we explore a different family of related vague predicates, "short," "medium," "tall," "taller," and "same height as." This family is simple enough to treat in some detail but complicated enough to exhibit three problems that are typical of vague predicates.

Information Flow Between Perspectives

The first problem is that different people, with differing circumstances, often have different standards in regard to what counts as being short or tall. In spite of the lack of any absolute standard, though, information flow is possible between people using these predicates. If Jane informs me that Mary is of medium height while she, Jane, is short, and if I consider Jane to be tall, then I know that I would consider Mary as tall as well. How is such reliable information flow possible between people with quite different standards of what counts as being tall?

The Logic of Vague Predicates

The second problem takes place within a fixed perspective. A given person may use vague predicates and know that certain cases are indeterminate. For a

given person on the tallish side, Judith may not choose to decide whether that
person is tall or of medium height. Thus she is not willing to grant that everyone
is either short, medium, or tall. Thus it might seem that it would be hard to
reason with vague predicates, but this does not seem to be the case. Judith, for
example, maintains that the following are unproblematic:

> If x is short then x is not tall.
> If x is tall and y is taller than x then y is tall.
> If x is of medium height and y is tall then y is taller than x.
> If x is taller than y and y is taller than z then x is taller than z.

How can one give a principled semantic account of vague predicates that respects these intuitions?

The Sorites Paradox

The third problem, known as the sorites paradox, goes more directly to the
heart of vagueness. One version of it, having to do with our predicates, runs as
follows. Given the physical limits of human perceptual abilities, there is some
positive number ϵ so that if the heights of two people x and y differ by less
than ϵ, then x and y will of necessity be judged to be the same height by any
accurate human observer. But now consider Billy, who was short but grew tall
over the last year. Divide this year up into intervals $t_1 < \cdots < t_N$, where t_1 is
the start of the year and t_N its end and where the intervals are chosen so that
Billy's growth from t_i to t_{i+1} was less than ϵ. Then Billy would of necessity be
judged to be the same height at t_{i+1} as at t_i for each $i < N$. But surely if he is
short at t_i and the same height at t_{i+1} he is short at t_{i+1}. But then by induction
it follows that Billy is short at each t_i and so is short at the end of the year.

18.1 Height Classifications

In this section, we propose that the vague predicates under discussion have
a family of reasonable classifications, what we call "height" classifications.
Within this framework, we will address the three problems raised above.

  In order to be able to express interesting constraints, let Σ consist of the
propositional formulas built up from

SHORT(X), MEDIUM(X), TALL(X), TALLER(X, Y), SAMEHT(X, Y),

using the usual propositional operators, where X, Y, . . . are variables in some set
Var of variables. Let B be some fixed set of instantaneous physical objects. We
will usually be interested in the case where B is finite. Let $A = B^{Var}$ consist of

all variable assignments taking values in B. We are interested in classifications A with typ(A) = Σ and tok(A) = A. We will call such a classification *finite* if the set B is finite.[1] Intuitively,

$$a \vDash_A \text{TALL(X)} \wedge \text{TALLER(Y, X)}$$

if and only if the object a(X) assigned to X is classified as tall in A but the object a(Y) is even taller.

Let Ht be a state space that has as tokens the elements of B. The states of Ht consist of all nonnegative real numbers. We write $ht(b) = \text{state}_{Ht}(b)$ and call $ht(b)$ the *height* of b. We take this state space to model the heights of the objects in B using some standard unit of measurement.

Let $S = Ht^{Var}$. In other words, S is the product $\prod_{i \in I} Ht_i$, where $I = Var$ is the set of variables and $H_i = Ht$ for every i. Thus the tokens of S are functions from Var into B. This is the set of variable assignments taking values in B, that is, elements of A. The states are variable assignments taking values in the nonnegative real numbers.

We define what we mean by a height classification in terms of the notion of a "(height) regimentation," the idea being that any reasonable classification using these predicates must be compatible with one or more regimentations.

Definition 18.1. A *(height) regimentation* consists of a 4-tuple $r = \langle \epsilon, I_s, I_m, I_t \rangle$ satisfying the following conditions:

1. $\epsilon \geq 0$ is a real number in the set I_s, called the *tolerance* of r;
2. I_s, I_m, and I_t are mutually disjoint intervals of nonnegative real numbers such that I_t is closed upward, and I_s is closed downward;
3. if $r_t \in I_t$, $r_m \in I_m$, and $r_s \in I_s$, then $r_t - r_m \geq \epsilon$ and $r_m - r_s \geq \epsilon$.

The intervals I_s, I_m, and I_t of the regimentation r are the heights that are considered short, medium, and tall, respectively, under this regimentation. The tolerance of r is the least amount such that if $ht(b_1)$ is more than ϵ greater than $ht(b_2)$, then b_1 is considered taller than b_2. We allow for the possibility that $\epsilon = 0$, but we do not insist on it. The following result is obvious.

Proposition 18.2. *For any regimentation r, there is a unique token-identical contravariant pair of maps $f_r : A \rightleftarrows \text{Evt}(S)$ satisfying the following condition. (Here σ ranges over the states of S.)*

---

[1] Although Barwise is assumes responsibility for the explorations in Part III, he acknowledges Seligman's help in stressing the importance of finite classifications in response to an earlier version of this lecture.

1. $f_r(\text{SHORT}(\text{X})) = \{\sigma \mid \sigma(\text{X}) \in I_s\}$
2. $f_r(\text{MEDIUM}(\text{X})) = \{\sigma \mid \sigma(\text{X}) \in I_m\}$
3. $f_r(\text{TALL}(\text{X})) = \{\sigma \mid \sigma(\text{X}) \in I_t\}$
4. $f_r(\text{TALLER}(\text{X},\text{Y})) = \{\sigma \mid \sigma(\text{X}) - \sigma(\text{Y}) > \epsilon\}$
5. $f_r(\text{SAMEHT}(\text{X},\text{Y})) = \{\sigma \mid |\sigma(\text{X}) - \sigma(\text{Y})| \leq \epsilon\}$
6. $f_r(\varphi \wedge \psi) = f_r(\varphi) \cap f_r(\psi)$
7. $f_r(\varphi \vee \psi) = f_r(\varphi) \cup f_r(\psi)$
8. $f_r(\neg\varphi) = -f_r(\varphi)$

Moreover, distinct regimentations give rise to distinct contravariant pairs.

Definition 18.3. A classification A with types and tokens as above is a *height classification* if there exists a regimentation r such that $f_r : A \rightleftarrows \text{Evt}(S)$ is an infomorphism. In this case, we say that r is a *regimentation of A*.

We suggest that height classifications and their associated logics are good models of the way we use the vague predicates in question.

The first thing to notice is that a height classification classifies things according to their heights in the following precise sense. For variable assignments $a_1, a_2 \in A$, define $a_1 \equiv a_2$ if for each variable X, $ht(a_1(\text{X})) = ht(a_2(\text{X}))$.

Proposition 18.4. *If $a_1 \equiv a_2$, then a_1 and a_2 are indistinguishable in every height classification. If a is an assignment assigning individuals of the same height to the variables X and Y, then*

$$a \vDash_A \text{SHORT}(\text{X}) \quad \textit{iff} \quad a \vDash_A \text{SHORT}(\text{Y})$$

for every height classification A, and with parallel biconditionals for the other predicates.

In order for A to be a height classification, it must have at least one regimentation. But importantly, it will typically have many different regimentations. For example, we have the following proposition.

Proposition 18.5. *Let A be a height classification. If A is finite, then A has uncountably many distinct regimentations.*

Proof. Given an interval I of real numbers and finitely many distinct real numbers $h_1, \ldots, h_n$, there are uncountably many intervals I such that $h_i \in I$ if and only if $h_i \in I'$, for each $i = 1, \ldots, n$. From this it follows that given any regimentation r, we can adjust the lower endpoint of the upper range of I_t in uncountably many ways and end up with the same classification. $\square$

This result shows that we do not need to assume a specific regimentation in order to have a height classification. Rather, we can think of there being a nonempty class of regimentations implicit in any height classification. The same proof shows the following corollary.

Corollary 18.6. *Every finite height classification has a regimentation with tolerance $\epsilon > 0$.*

18.2 Information Flow

We can now address the first problem mentioned, that of information flow between different height classifications. Suppose A_1 and A_2 are both height classifications over our fixed set B of tokens. Although A_1 and A_2 may well show disagreement on how different objects are classified, there will typically be information flow between them because they are related by a channel as depicted below. Here r_1 and r_2 are any regimentations of A_1 and A_2.

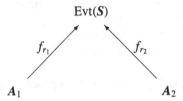

Just exactly what information flow exists between A_1 and A_2 will depend on the properties of the channel, hence on what regimentations are compatible with each of the classifications. But no matter what regimentations are used it is easy to see the following (where we write A $\rightarrow$ B for $\neg$A $\vee$ B as usual):

$$f_1(\text{SHORT}(X) \wedge \text{MEDIUM}(Y)) \vdash_{\text{Log}(S)} f_2(\text{TALL}(X) \rightarrow \text{TALL}(Y)).$$

Consequently, $a \vDash_{A_1} \text{SHORT}(X) \wedge \text{MEDIUM}(Y)$ carries the information that $a \vDash_{A_2}$ TALL(X) $\rightarrow$ TALL(Y). Hence

$$a \vDash_{A_1} \text{SHORT}(X) \wedge \text{MEDIUM}(Y) \quad \text{and} \quad a \vDash_{A_2} \text{TALL}(X)$$

carry the information that

$$a \vDash_{A_2} \text{TALL}(Y).$$

This is just one of infinitely many examples that could be given.

18.3 An Intensional Logic

What logic should we consider to be "given" with the height classification A? One possibility, of course, is to take Log(A); this is sound and complete. This logic is a kind of extensionally given logic, extensional in that its constraints are entirely determined by the extensions of the types of A, regardless of what they mean.

A second possibility, one that is more intensional, is to take $\text{Log}_r^\circ(A) = f_r^{-1}[\text{Log}(S)]$ for some particular regimentation r. By calling $\text{Log}_r^\circ(A)$ "intensional," we mean that the constraints of $\text{Log}_r^\circ(A)$ are determined by the meaning of the types rather than by what their extension in A happens to be. This logic is also sound, being the inverse image of a sound logic under a token surjective infomorphism.

As we have seen, however, there are typically infinitely many different regimentations compatible with a given height classification. A particular regimentation r may well have properties that result in some constraints holding in $\text{Log}_r^\circ(A)$ that would not hold in some other $\text{Log}_{r'}^\circ(A)$. A more canonical choice is to take the meet (i.e., greatest lower bound) of these logics.

Definition 18.7. Let A be a height classification. The extensional height logic of A is just Log(A). The *intensional logic* of A is

$$\text{Log}^\circ(A) = \bigsqcap \{\text{Log}_r^\circ(A) \mid r \text{ a regimentation of } A\}.$$

We write $\vdash_A^\circ$ for the consequence relation of $\text{Log}^\circ(A)$. Being the meet of sound logics, this logic is also sound.

Proposition 18.8. *For any height classification A, the following are constraints of* $\text{Log}^\circ(A)$. *(Because* $\text{Log}^\circ(A) \sqsubseteq \text{Log}(A)$, *they are* a fortiori *constraints of the latter.)*

$$\text{SHORT}(X) \vdash_A^\circ \neg\text{TALL}(X)$$

$$\text{TALL}(X), \text{TALLER}(Y, X) \vdash_A^\circ \text{TALL}(Y)$$

$$\text{MEDIUM}(X), \text{TALL}(Y) \vdash_A^\circ \text{TALLER}(Y, X)$$

$$\text{TALLER}(X, Y) \wedge \text{TALLER}(Y, Z) \vdash_A^\circ \text{TALLER}(X, Z)$$

Proof. Each of these is easily verified to hold in each $\text{Log}_r^\circ(A)$, hence in their meet $\text{Log}^\circ(A)$. □

The constraints listed in the above propositions are, of course, just a small, representative sample. More interestingly, let us turn to some of the differences between the intensional and extensional logics. We call a height classification *A determinate* if each object *b* is classified as one of short, medium, or tall in *A*.

Proposition 18.9. *Let A be a height classification.*

1. If A is determinate, then

$$\vdash_A \text{SHORT(X)} \lor \text{MEDIUM(X)} \lor \text{TALL(X)}.$$

2. If A is finite, then

$$\nvdash_A^{\circ} \text{SHORT(X)} \lor \text{MEDIUM(X)} \lor \text{TALL(X)}.$$

Proof. Here (1) is practically a restatement of the definition of determinate. For (2), we note that if *A* is finite, then it will always have a regimentation *r* of *A* where the intervals of the regimentation do not exhaust the nonnegative real numbers. Then $f_r(\text{SHORT(X)} \lor \text{MEDIUM(X)} \lor \text{TALL(X)})$ does not exhaust the set of states so

$$\nvdash_{\text{Log}_r^{\circ}(A)} \text{SHORT(X)} \lor \text{MEDIUM(X)} \lor \text{TALL(X)}.$$

But $\text{Log}^{\circ}(A) \sqsubseteq \text{Log}_r^{\circ}(A)$, so the result follows. $\qquad\square$

Corollary 18.10. *If A is finite and determinate, then the logic* $\text{Log}^{\circ}(A)$ *is strictly weaker than the logic* $\text{Log}(A)$.

This proposition gives a rigorous form to the intuition that even if it happens to be the case that everything we are classifying is clearly one of the three sizes, short, medium, or tall, there could have been borderline cases too close to call.

18.4 The Sorites Paradox

We now turn to the third and final problem about vague predicates raised earlier, the sorites paradox. We start with a divergence between the intensional and extensional logics that is clearly relevant to this paradox. Call a classification *A precise* if $a \vDash_A \text{SAMEHT(X,Y)}$ implies $ht(a(\text{X})) = ht(a(\text{Y}))$, for all $a \in A$. (The converse is automatic.) It is clear that *A* is precise if it has a regimentation with zero tolerance.

Proposition 18.11. *Let A be a height assignment.*

1. *If A is precise, then*

$$\text{SAMEHT}(X, Y) \wedge \text{SAMEHT}(Y, Z) \vdash_A \text{SAMEHT}(X, Z).$$

2. *If A is finite, then*

$$\text{SAMEHT}(X, Y) \wedge \text{SAMEHT}(Y, Z) \nvdash^\circ_A \text{SAMEHT}(X, Z).$$

Proof. The proof of (1) is clear. To prove (2), note that because A is finite, it has a regimentation r with tolerance $\epsilon > 0$ by Corollary 18.6. Let σ be any state with $\sigma(Y) = \sigma(X) + .6\epsilon$ and $\sigma(Z) = \sigma(Y) + .6\epsilon$. Such states will be in f_r of the left-hand side but not in f_r of the right-hand side because $\sigma(Z) - \sigma(X) = 1.2\epsilon > \epsilon$. $\square$

The relationship to the sorites paradox should be evident. The intensional logic does not provide us with the constraint telling us that being the same height is transitive, even if our classification happens to be precise. (Notice that there will be many imprecise height classifications A that also have this constraint in their extensional logic.) Let us make the connection with the paradox more transparent by means of the following result.

Theorem 18.12. *Let A be a height classification.*

1. *If A is precise, then for all integers $N \geq 2$:*

$$\text{SHORT}(X_1) \wedge \text{SAMEHT}(X_1, X_2) \wedge \cdots \wedge \text{SAMEHT}(X_{N-1}, X_N) \vdash_A \text{SHORT}(X_N),$$

   and so

$$\text{SHORT}(X_1) \wedge \text{SAMEHT}(X_1, X_2) \wedge \cdots \wedge \text{SAMEHT}(X_{N-1}, X_N) \vdash_A \neg\text{TALL}(X_N).$$

2. *Whether or not A is precise, if it is finite then for sufficiently large integers N,*

$$\text{SHORT}(X_1) \wedge \text{SAMEHT}(X_1, X_2) \wedge \cdots \wedge \text{SAMEHT}(X_{N-1}, X_N) \nvdash^\circ_A \neg\text{TALL}(X_N)$$

Proof. Again, the first statement is trivial. For the second, pick a regimentation r of A with tolerance $\epsilon > 0$ and I_t nonempty. Let K be the least integer such that $K\epsilon/2 \in I_t$; such a K must exist because I_t is nonempty and closed upward. Let σ be any state satisfying the following: $\sigma(x_1) = \epsilon/2$ and $\sigma(X_{i+1}) = \sigma(X_i) + \epsilon/2$ for every i. Then

$$\sigma(X_N) = N\epsilon/2 \geq K\epsilon/2$$

for every $N \geq K$. Hence $\sigma(\mathrm{X}_N) \in I_t$ because $K\epsilon/2 \in I_t$ and I_t is closed upward. Consequently, σ is in the translation via f_r of the type on the left of the sequent but not of the type on the right. □

Definition 18.13. Let A be a height classification. The *sorites number* of a regimentation r is the least integer N such that

$$\mathrm{SHORT}(\mathrm{X}_1) \wedge \mathrm{SAMEHT}(\mathrm{X}_1, \mathrm{X}_2) \wedge \cdots \wedge \mathrm{SAMEHT}(\mathrm{X}_{N-1}, \mathrm{X}_N) \wedge \mathrm{TALL}(\mathrm{X}_N)$$

is consistent in $\mathrm{Log}_r^{\circ}(A)$, if it exists. The sorites number of A is the least N such that the above is consistent in $\mathrm{Log}^{\circ}(A)$, if it exists.

The theorem says every finite classification has a sorites number. (We show how to calculate this number in Exercise 18.5.) What this means is that it would be entirely possible to have a chain of individuals, $b_1, \ldots, b_N$, where N is the sorites number of A, such that b_1 is classified as short, each b_i is classified as being the same height as b_{i+1}, for $i < N$, and yet for b_N to be tall, even if this does not happen in the classification A.

Let us go back and analyze the argument in the sorites paradox. The first step is to assert there is a number $\epsilon > 0$ so that the sequent

$$\mathrm{SHORT}(\mathrm{X}) \wedge \mathrm{SAMEHT}(\mathrm{X,Y}) \vdash \mathrm{SHORT}(\mathrm{Y})$$

holds of all tokens a with $|ht(a(\mathrm{X})) - ht(a(\mathrm{Y}))| < \epsilon$. This is possible as long as the height classification A is finite (and for many infinite classifications as well). But the conclusion of the argument deals not just with this classification but with what would happen if we were to use the fixed regimentation and add N new tokens to the classification, where N is the sorites number of A. This would result in a different classification and in that classification the above sequent would fail to hold for many tokens a with $|ht(a(\mathrm{X})) - ht(a(\mathrm{Y}))| < \epsilon$.

Non-Archimedian Regimentations

We have required that our regimentations live in the field of real numbers. An alternative suggestion would allow them to live in non-Archimedian fields, like the fields of nonstandard real numbers. One could then allow the tolerance to be infinitesimal, and sorites numbers could be infinite. This goes along with the discovery in recent years that nonstandard analysis often gives an elegant way to model the differences between the very small and the very large.

Exercises

18.1. Is it consistent with the framework presented here for a short office building be taller than a tall person?

The exercises below all assume the following setup. In a sixth grade gym class having twenty students, the coach has classified students by height before dividing them up into basketball teams so that she can put the same number of short, medium, and tall girls on each of the four teams. The shortest student is $3'8''$, the tallest is $5'6''$, and the smallest difference in heights between students of different heights is $.25''$. The coach classified all the girls less than four feet tall as short, those five feet or over as tall, and those in between as medium height. The coach used measuring tools that have a precision of $.1''$.

18.2. Assuming a unit of measure of $1''$, describe a regimentation of A.

18.3. Is the classification determinate? Is it precise?

18.4. Give an upper bound for the sorites number of A.

18.5. Determine the sorites numbers exact value assuming that the shortest girl of medium height is $4'1''$ and the tallest girl of medium height is $4'10.5''$.

Lecture 19

Commonsense Reasoning

Among the problems that have beset the field of artificial intelligence, or AI, two have a particularly logical flavor. One is the problem of nonmonotonicity referred to in Part I. The other is the so-called frame problem. In this lecture, we suggest that ideas from the theory presented here, combined with ideas and techniques routinely used in state-space modeling in the sciences, suggest a new approach to these problems.

Nonmonotonicity

The rule of Weakening implies what is often called monotonicity:

If $\Gamma \vdash \Delta$ then $\Gamma, \alpha \vdash \Delta$.

The problem of nonmonotonicity, we recall, has to do with cases where one is disinclined to accept a constraint of the form $\Gamma, \alpha \vdash \Delta$ even though one accepts as a constraint $\Gamma \vdash \Delta$. The following is an example we will discuss in this lecture.

Example 19.1. Judith has a certain commonsense understanding of her home's heating system – the furnace, thermostat, vents, and the way they function to keep her house warm. Her understanding gives rise to inferences like the following.

(α_1) The thermostat is set between sixty-five and seventy degrees.
(α_2) The room temperature is fifty-eight degrees.
$\vdash$ (β) Hot air is coming out of the vents.

It seems that $\alpha_1, \alpha_2 \vdash \beta$ is a constraint that Judith uses quite regularly and unproblematically in reasoning about her heating system. However, during a recent blizzard she was forced to add the premise

(α_3) The power is off.

Monotonicity (Weakening) seems to fail, because surely

$$\alpha_1, \alpha_2, \alpha_3 \nvdash \beta.$$

In fact, we would expect Judith to realize that

$$\alpha_1, \alpha_2, \alpha_3 \vdash \neg\beta.$$

The problem of nonmonotonicity has been a major area of research in AI since the late 1970s. Because nonmonotonicity clearly violates the classically valid law of Weakening, a property of all local logics, the problem might be seen as a major one for our account. It seems, though, to be closely related to a problem we have already addressed in this book, that of accounting for exceptions to lawlike regularities. This suggests that implicit in our account of exceptionality is some sort of proposal about how to solve the problem of nonmonotonicity. In this lecture, we propose a solution that involves shifting between local logics, which is, as we have seen, equivalent to shifting between information channels.

The Frame Problem

The "frame" problem has to do with inferring the consequences of a change in a system. We can get a feeling for the problem by means of an example.

Example 19.2. Suppose the temperature at Judith's thermostat is seventy-two degrees and the thermostat is set at sixty-eight degrees. Thus there is no hot air coming out. Now the temperature drops to sixty-five degrees. We want to infer that the furnace comes on and hot air comes out of the vents. The difficulty in obtaining this inference stems from the fact that one change (the temperature dropping) produces other changes, like the furnace coming on, but leaves many other things unaffected. For example, the temperature dropping does not cause the thermostat setting to drop. If it did, the heat would not come on after all.

People are reasonably good at inferring the immediate consequences of basic actions, what other things will change, and how, and what will remain unaffected. In trying to model this sort of inference using axiomatic theories and logical inference, AI researchers have found it very difficult to mimic this performance. The problem is not so much in stating what other changes follow from some basic action, like a drop in the temperature. The difficulty is that it is not feasible to state an explicit axiom that says that a drop in the room's temperature does not cause the furnace to explode or the stock market to crash, and so on.

19.1 The Dimension of a State Space

In Lecture 1, we reviewed the standard scientific practice of treating the state of any system as determined by the values taken on by various attributes, the so-called observables of the system. These values are typically taken to be measurable quantities and so take on values in the set $\mathbb{R}$ of real numbers. Consequently, the total state of the system is modeled by a vector $\sigma \in \mathbb{R}^n$ for some n, the "dimension" of the state space. We saw in Lecture 8 that projections, the natural morphisms that go with state spaces, are covariant and that, consequently, products play the information-theoretic role in state spaces that sums play in classifications. This shows that the traditional use of product spaces as the set of possible states of a system goes with the turf – it is not an accident of history.

Definition 19.3. A *real-valued state space* is a state space S such that $\Omega \subseteq \mathbb{R}^n$, for some natural number n, called the *dimension* of the space.[1] The set $n = \{0, 1, \ldots, n-1\}$ is called the set of *observables* and the projection function $\pi_i(\sigma) = \sigma_i$, the ith coordinate of σ, is called the ith *observation function* of the system. If σ is the state of s, then σ_i is called the value of the ith observable on s. We assume that the set of observables is partitioned into two sets:

$$Observables = J \cup O,$$

where J is the set of input observables and O is the set of output observables. Each output observable $o \in O$ is assumed to be of the form

$$\sigma_o = F_o(\vec{\sigma}_j)$$

for some function F_o of the input observables $\vec{\sigma}_j$.

We are taught to think of the world as being three or four dimensional, but scientific practice shows this to be a vast oversimplification. The spatial-temporal

---

[1] An interesting and useful introduction to real-valued state spaces can be found in the first chapter of Casti (1992). It is worth distinguishing two decisions implicit in the definition of a real-valued state space. One is to be cognizant of the product structure of the set of states of the system. The other is to restrict to those observables whose values are determined by magnitude, and so nicely modeled by real numbers. For the purposes of this lecture, the first decision is the important one. At the cost of being a bit more wordy, we could generalize everything we do here to a setting where we allowed each observable i to take values in a set V_i. This would probably be important in areas like linguistics where the structure of the state has much more to it than mere magnitude.

location of an object is a region in four-space, but its total state typically has more degrees of freedom. We saw, for example, that the Newtonian state of a system consisting of n bodies is classically modeled by a state space of dimension $6n$. In Lecture 3, we modeled the light circuit with a four-dimensional state space, completely setting aside issues of time and space. We then modeled actions on the light circuit with an eight-dimensional state space. Here we suggest ways of exploiting the dimensionality of state spaces for addressing nonmonotonicity and the frame problem.

Example 19.4. We use Judith's heating system as a running example and so start by building a real-valued state space S_{hs} of dimension 7 for describing this system. For tokens, take some set of objects without additional mathematical structure. Intuitively, these are to be instances of Judith's complete heating system at various times, including the vents, the thermostat, the furnace, the ambient air in the room where the thermostat is located, and so forth. We assume that each state is determined by a combination of the following seven "observables" of the system:

> **Thermostat setting:** some real σ_1 between 55 and 80;
> **Room temperature:** (in Fahrenheit) a real σ_2 between 20 and 110;
> **Power:** $\sigma_3 = 1$ (on) or 0 (off);
> **Exhaust vents:** $\sigma_4 = 0$ (blocked) or 1 (clear);
> **Operating condition:** $\sigma_5 = -1$ (cooling), 0 (off), or 1 (heating);
> **Running:** $\sigma_6 = 1$ (on) or 0 (not on);
> **Output air temperature:** a real σ_7 between 20 and 110.

Thus for states we let Ω be the set of vectors $B = \langle \sigma_1, \ldots, \sigma_7 \rangle \in \mathbb{R}^7$. We take $\sigma_1, \ldots, \sigma_5$ as inputs and σ_6 and σ_7 as outputs. We restrict the states to those satisfying the following equations:

$$\sigma_6 = pos(\sigma_5 \cdot sg(\sigma_1 - \sigma_2)) \cdot \sigma_3 \cdot \sigma_4$$

$$\sigma_7 = \begin{cases} 55 & \text{if } \sigma_5 \cdot \sigma_6 = -1 \\ 80 & \text{if } \sigma_5 \cdot \sigma_6 = +1 \\ \sigma_2 & \text{otherwise,} \end{cases}$$

where

$$sg(r) = \begin{cases} +1 & \text{if } r \geq 2 \\ 0 & \text{if } |r| < 2 \\ -1 & \text{if } r \leq -2 \end{cases}$$

$$pos(r) = \begin{cases} 1 & \text{if } r > 0 \\ 0 & \text{if } r \leq 0. \end{cases}$$

We let S_{hs} consist of these tokens and states, with some total function *state* mapping the tokens into the states.

The types used in our nonmonotonicity example are represented in $\text{Evt}(S_{hs})$ by

$$\alpha_1 = \{\sigma \in \Omega_{hs} \mid 65 \leq \sigma_1 \leq 70\}$$
$$\alpha_2 = \{\sigma \in \Omega_{hs} \mid \sigma_2 = 58\}$$
$$\alpha_3 = \{\sigma \in \Omega_{hs} \mid \sigma_3 = 0\}$$
$$\beta \ = \{\sigma \in \Omega_{hs} \mid \sigma_6 = 1 \text{ and } \sigma_7 > \sigma_2\}.$$

It is usually assumed that the input observables are *independent* in that the observer can vary the inputs independently. This amounts to the following requirement: if σ is some state, $i \in J$ is some input observable, and r is a value of σ_i' for some state σ', then there is a state σ'' such that $\sigma_i'' = r$ and $\sigma_j'' = \sigma_j$ for all $j \neq i$. One might think of this as a precondition as to what it would mean for an observable to be an input to the system.

This assumption is clearly related to the frame problem. When we make a change to a system, we typically change one of the inputs, with concommitant changes in output observables; we do not expect a change in one input to produce a change in any other inputs. We will make this idea more explicit later in the lecture. We will not assume that the input observables are independent, preferring to state explicitly where the assumption plays a role in our proposals.

When working with a state-space model, it is customary to partition the inputs into two, $J = I \cup P$. The input observables in I are called the *explicit inputs* of the system and those in P the *parameters* of the system. Intuitively, the parameters are those inputs that are held fixed in any given computation or discussion. We will not make a permanent division into explicit inputs and parameters, but will instead build it into our notion of a background condition in the next section.

Example 19.5. In our heating system example S_{hs}, it is natural to take to take σ_1, σ_2 as explicit inputs, and σ_3, σ_4, and σ_5 as parameters. The inputs are clearly independent.

19.2 Nonmonotonicity

The proposal made here was inspired by the following claim:

"...error or surprise always involves a discrepancy between the objects [tokens] *open* to interaction and the abstractions [states] *closed* to those same interactions. In principle, the remedy for closing this gap is equally clear: augment the description by including more observables to account for the unmodeled interactions (Casti, 1992, p. 25)."

Modeling Background Conditions

Definition 19.6.

1. A *background condition B* is a function with domain some set P of input observables, taking real numbers as values. It is required that $B(i)$ be a number in the range of the ith observation function of the state space. The domain P is called the set of *parameters* of B.
2. A *state* σ satisfies B if $\sigma_i = B(i)$ for each $i \in P$. A *token s satisfies B* if *state*(s) satisfies B.
3. The set of background conditions is partially ordered by inclusion: $B_1 \leq B_2$ if and only if the domain of B_1 is a subset of that of B_2 and the two functions agree on this domain.

Every nonempty set of background conditions has a greatest lower bound under the ordering $\leq$. Also, if a state or token satisfies B, then it clearly satisfies every $B_0 \leq B$. The empty function is the least background condition: It imposes no conditions on states.

In working with a given state space, one assumes one has a fixed background condition B, that one is only concerned with tokens that satisfy this background condition, and hence that all computations and inferences take place relative to that background condition. We can make this precise as follows.

Given a set Q of input observables, define $\sigma \equiv_Q \sigma'$ if $\sigma_i = \sigma_i'$ for all $i \notin Q$. This is an equivalence relation on states. We say that a type $\alpha \subseteq \Omega$ is *silent on* Q if for all states $\sigma, \sigma' \in \Omega$, if $\sigma \equiv_Q \sigma'$ and $\sigma \in \alpha$, then $\sigma' \in \alpha$. We say that α is silent on an input observable i if it is silent on $\{i\}$. Finally, a type α is *silent on B* if α is silent on the set P of parameters of B. If one is given a premise or purported conclusion that is *not* silent on an observable i, it is safe to assume i is *not* a parameter of the system. Put another other way, *if we are reasoning about an observable i, then i must be either an explicit input or output of the system.*

Example 19.7. In our heating system example S_{hs}, the types α_1, α_2, and β are silent on the parameters, as can be seen from their definitions. The type α_3, by contrast, says that $\sigma_3 = 0$ and so is not silent on σ_3. The natural background condition B in the winter is $\sigma_3 = \sigma_4 = \sigma_5 = 1$, representing the case where the power switch is on, the vents are not blocked, and the setting is on "heat." (This is our informal way of indicating the background condition B with domain $\{3, 4, 5\}$ and constant value 1.) In the summer the default background condition is $\sigma_3 = \sigma_4 = 1$ and $\sigma_5 = -1$.

Definition 19.8. Given a background condition B and a set Γ of types, the *weakening of B by Γ*, written $B \!\upharpoonright\! \Gamma$ is the greatest lower bound (in the $\leq$ ordering) of all $B_0 \leq B$ such that every type $\alpha \in \Gamma$ is silent on B_0.

When $\Gamma = \{\alpha\}$, we write $B \!\upharpoonright\! \alpha$ for $B \!\upharpoonright\! \Gamma$. The function $B \!\upharpoonright\! \alpha$ models the intuitive idea of dropping background assumptions of B on the parameters that are critical to the content of the type α. If the input observables of our state space are independent, then this definition is guaranteed to behave the way one would hope.

Theorem 19.9. *Let Γ be a set of types. Assume the input observables of the state space S are independent. Then each type in Γ is silent on $B \!\upharpoonright\! \Gamma$, and this is the greatest such background condition $\leq B$.*

Proof. This follows easily from the following lemma, of independent use in computing $B \!\upharpoonright\! \Gamma$.   □

Lemma 19.10. *If the input observables of the state space S are independent, then a type α is silent on Q if and only if it is silent on each $i \in Q$. Hence, under these conditions, there is a largest set Q of input observables such that α is silent on Q.*

Proof. The left to right half of the first claim is trivial. The converse claim is proved by induction on the size of Q. The second claim follows from the first by taking Q to consist of all the input observables i such that α is silent on i.   □

Given a background condition B with parameters P, the lemma tells us that $B \!\upharpoonright\! \alpha$ is simply the restriction of B to the set of input observables $i \in P$ such that p is silent on i.

Example 19.11. The inputs of our example S_{hs} are independent so the lemma and theorem apply. The type α_3 is silent on each observable except for σ_3. Hence if B is $\{\sigma_3 = \sigma_4 = \sigma_5 = 1\}$, then Weakening B by α_3 gives $B \!\upharpoonright\! \alpha_3 = \{\sigma_4 = \sigma_5 = 1\}$.

Relativizing to a Background Condition

Each background condition B determines a subspace $S_B \subseteq S$ as follows.

Definition 19.12. Let B be a background condition for the state space S. The *relativization S_B of S to B* is the subspace of S whose states are those states σ

of S that satisfy the background condition B and whose tokens are the tokens that satisfy B.

By relativizing, the output equations are simplified because the parameters become constants in the equations in S_B.

Example 19.13. In our example, the output equations simplify to

$$\sigma_6 = pos(sg(\sigma_1 - \sigma_2))$$
$$\sigma_7 = \begin{cases} 80 & \text{if } \sigma_6 = +1, \\ \sigma_2 & \text{otherwise.} \end{cases}$$

Recall the correspondence between subspaces of S and S-logics from Lecture 16. Because $S_B \subseteq S$, this gives us a $\text{Log}(S_B)$ with $\text{Log}(S) \sqsubseteq \text{Log}(S_B)$. We call this the *local logic* $\text{Log}(S_B)$ *supported by the background condition* B.

Proposition 19.14. *For each background condition B, the local logic $\text{Log}(S_B)$ supported by B is the logic on $\text{Evt}(S)$ given by the following:*

1. *The $\text{Log}(S_B)$-consistent states σ are those satisfying B.*
2. *If Γ, Δ are sets of types of S, then $\Gamma \vdash_B \Delta$ if and only if for every state σ satisfying B, if $\sigma \in p$ for all $p \in \Gamma$, then $\sigma \in q$ for some $q \in \Delta$.*
3. *The normal tokens are those tokens satisfying B.*

Proof. The proof of (1) follows immediately from the definition and (2) and (3) follow from (1) and Theorem 16.6.   □

Because $\text{Log}(S) \sqsubseteq \text{Log}(S_B)$, we know that $\text{Log}(S_B)$ typically has more constraints but fewer normal tokens than $\text{Log}(S)$, as one would expect. The logic $\text{Log}(S_B)$ is not in general sound, because there may well be tokens not satisfying the background condition B. Indeed, $\text{Log}(S_B)$ is sound if and only if every token satisfies B. $\text{Log}(S_B)$ is complete if and only if every state that satisfies B is the state of some token.

Example 19.15. In our running example, the sequent $\alpha_1, \alpha_2 \vdash \beta$ is a constraint in the logic $\text{Log}(S_{\sigma_3 = \sigma_4 = \sigma_5 = 1})$ with background condition $\sigma_3 = \sigma_4 = \sigma_5 = 1$. (To see this we need only show that if σ is a state with $65 \leq \sigma_1 \leq 70$ and $\sigma_2 = 58$, then $\sigma_6 = 1$ and $\sigma_7 > \sigma_2$. Using the state equations for $S_{\sigma_3 = \sigma_4 = \sigma_5 = 1}$ displayed above, we calculate that $\sigma_1 - \sigma_2 > 2$ so $sg(\sigma_1 - \sigma_2) = 1$. Hence $\sigma_6 = 1$ and $\sigma_7 = 80$, in which case $\sigma_7 > \sigma_2$, as desired.) On the other hand this constraint does not hold in the full logic $\text{Log}(S_{hs})$, as can be seen by looking at, say, the state $\sigma = \langle 67, 58, 0, 1, 1, 0, 58 \rangle$. This state satisfies the defining equations of our large space; it satisfies α_1 and α_2 but not β.

The following shows that as the background conditions increase in restrictiveness, so do the associated logics.

Corollary 19.16. *If $B_1 \leq B_2$, then $\mathrm{Log}(S_{B_1}) \sqsubseteq \mathrm{Log}(S_{B_2})$.*

Putting this the other way around, if the background conditions decrease in strength, so do the associated logics. As remarked earlier, in reasoning about a system we expect to be given information that is silent on the parameters of the system, because when we are given information that is not silent on some input observable, it is no longer a parameter but an explicit input of the system. In particular, if we are given explicit information about the value of some observable, these observables cannot be parameters, which means that the background is weakened according to the new information. But weakening the background weakens the logic. Thus additional information that is not silent on the parameters weakens the logic.

Example 19.17. The information in α_3 is about the observable σ_3, the power to the system. Not only is α_3 not silent on the background condition B of the first sequent, it directly conflicts with it. Thus the natural understanding of the claim that $\alpha_1, \alpha_2, \alpha_3 \vdash \beta$ is as being relative to the weakened $B \upharpoonright \alpha_3$. Relative to the local logic $\mathrm{Log}(S_{B \upharpoonright \alpha_3})$, this is not a valid constraint. Indeed, in this logic a routine calculation similar to the above shows that $\alpha_1, \alpha_2, \alpha_3 \vdash \neg\beta$, as desired.

We summarize the above discussion by putting forward a pragmatic model of the way people intuitively reason against background conditions. First we present the following definition.

Definition 19.18. Γ *strictly entails* Δ relative to the background condition B, written $\Gamma \Rightarrow_B \Delta$, if the following four conditions hold:

1. $\Gamma \vdash_{\mathrm{Log}(S_B)} \Delta 0$;
2. all types in $\Gamma \cup \Delta$ are silent on B;
3. $\bigcap \Gamma \neq \emptyset$;
4. $\bigcup \Delta \neq \Omega$;

The first two conditions have been extensively discussed above. The third and fourth are not important for this discussion, but we include them for the sake of completeness because they do capture intuitions about the way people reason.

The third condition is that the information in the sequent is consistent in that there should be some possible state of the system compatible with everything in Γ. The last condition is that the information in sequent is nonvacuous in that not every possible state of the system should satisfy Δ.

Our observations can now be put as follows:

1. The consequence relation $\Gamma \Rightarrow_B \Delta$ is a better model of human reasoning against the background condition B than is $\Gamma \vdash_B \Delta$.
2. The relation $\Gamma \Rightarrow_B \Delta$ is monotonic in Γ and Δ, but only as long as you weaken using types that are silent on B and do not make the sequent hold for trivial reasons.
3. If one is given a type α that is not silent on B, the natural thing to do is to weaken the background condition B by α, thereby obtaining $B\lceil\alpha$.
4. But $\Gamma \Rightarrow_B \Delta$ does not entail $\Gamma, \alpha \Rightarrow_{B\lceil\alpha} \Delta$ or $\Gamma \Rightarrow_{B\lceil\alpha} \Delta, \alpha$.

Logic Infomorphisms and Nonmonotonicity

A reasonable objection to our presentation so far would be to point out that we have systematically exploited an ambiguity by using "$\alpha_1, \alpha_2, \alpha_3$" and "$\beta$" for both symbolic expressions (like the English sentences where they were introduced at the start of this lecture) as well as for the "corresponding" state space types, which are, after all, sets of states, not exactly the sort of thing people reason with in ordinary life. We need to discuss this relationship between the symbolic expressions and said types.

The solution, of course, is our notion of a logic infomorphism. To see what this has to do with our problem, let us return to our example and set up a symbolic Boolean classification A. The types of A are symbolic expressions $\varphi, \psi, \eta, \ldots$, either the English expressions used in the introduction and Boolean combinations of them or some sort of more formal counterparts of the sort used in an elementary logic course. We use $\varphi_1, \varphi_2, \varphi_3$, and ψ for the premises and conclusions of our classification. The tokens of A are instances of Judith's heating system. Let B be the classification Evt(S) associated with the state space S as above. The map $\varphi_i \mapsto \alpha_i$, and $\psi \mapsto \beta$, extended in the natural way to the Boolean combinations, defines a map $f^\wedge$ from the types of A to the types of Log(S), whereas the identity map on tokens can be thought of as a map of the tokens of Log(S). This gives us a classification infomorphism from A to the classification Evt(S),

$$f : A \rightleftarrows B.$$

We know that any infomorphism $f : A \rightleftarrows B$ and local logic $\mathfrak{L}$ on B gives rise to a $\sqsubseteq$-largest local logic $f^{-1}[\mathfrak{L}]$ on A such that f is a logic infomorphism from this logic to $\mathfrak{L}$. This gives us a host of logics on the classification A. There is the logic $f^{-1}[\text{Log}(S)]$, but also, for each subspace of S, there is the inverse image of the logic associated with this subspace. In particular, for each background condition B, there is a local logic $f^{-1}[\text{Log}(S_B)]$. Let us write these logics as $\mathfrak{L}$ and $\mathfrak{L}_B$, respectively, and write $\Gamma \vdash \Delta$ and $\Gamma \vdash_B \Delta$ for their entailment relations.[2]

The logic $\mathfrak{L}$ is sound, that is, all its tokens are normal. The constraints of this logic are just those sequents of A whose validity is insured by our state-space model. The logics of the form $\mathfrak{L}_B$, however, are not sound; the normal tokens of $\mathfrak{L}_B$ are those that satisfy the background condition B. For example, the normal tokens of $\mathfrak{L}_{\sigma_3=\sigma_4=\sigma_5=1}$ are those in which the power is on, vents are unblocked, and the controls are in heating mode.

The Ineffability Principle

In the model given in the previous section, a background condition B could be packaged into a type γ_B, namely,

$$\gamma_B = \{\sigma \in \Omega \mid \sigma \text{ satisfies } B\}.$$

This type could, in principle, be made explicit as an additional premise of an inference. But this type will typically lie outside of the range of $f^\wedge$. Put differently, *there is in general no way to capture the background condition B by a symbolic type of A*. We call this the "ineffability principle" because it seems to model the fact that it is seldom, if ever, possible to say exactly what background assumptions are in force when we reason in ordinary life.

Turtles All the Way Down

Having seen the relationship between state spaces, local logics, and nonmonotonicity, let us return to state spaces.

As a start, let us note that if S is a real-valued state space of dimension n and B is a background condition on k parameters, then S_B is isomorphic to a real-valued state space S_B^* of dimension $m = n - k$. The isomorphism is the identity on types whereas on tokens it projects $\langle \vec{\sigma}_i, \vec{\sigma}_p, \vec{\sigma}_o \rangle$ to $\langle \vec{\sigma}_i, \vec{\sigma}_o \rangle$. (In our example, the new space would have as states those 4-tuples $\langle \sigma_1, \sigma_2, \sigma_3, \sigma_4 \rangle$ such that $\langle \sigma_1, \sigma_2, 1, 1, 1, \sigma_3, \sigma_4 \rangle \in \Omega$.) The move from the

---

[2] We would actually propose combining this proposal with the ideas in Lecture 18 in a full development.

n-dimensional S to the m-dimensional S_B^* results from setting k parameters as dictated by B.

Now let us look at it the other way around. Suppose we had begun with an m-dimensional state space S and later learned of k additional parameters that we had not taken into account. Letting $n = m + k$, we would then see our space S as projecting onto a subspace S'' of an n-dimensional state space S'. Because $S'' \subseteq S'$, taking the associated local logics and recalling the order reversal that takes place, we have $\text{Log}(S') \sqsubseteq \text{Log}(S'')$. That is, the logic associated with the new state space is weaker, in that it has fewer constraints, but more reliable, in that it has more normal tokens, which is just what we have seen.

Example 19.19. Suppose instead of the information α_3, we had been faced with the following new information:

(α_4) The gas line has been broken and there is no gas getting to the furnace.

We would like to get $\alpha_1, \alpha_2, \alpha_4 \vdash \neg\beta$, but we do not. In fact, the type α_4 does not even make sense in our state space, because the gas pressure and gas line have not been taken into account in our seven-dimensional state space S_{hs}. To take these into account, we would need to see S as isomorphic to a subspace of a nine-dimensional state space S', one where the additional observables are the state of the gas line and the gas pressure. Then as we have seen, we would have $\text{Log}(S') \sqsubseteq \text{Log}(S)$.

One should not think that there is ever an "ultimate" completely perfect state space. In general, it seems it is almost always possible in real-life systems to further refine a state-space model of some system by introducing more observables. That, of course, is what we mean by saying it is turtles all the way down.

The example makes an additional point, though. Once we introduce the new observables, we have also implicitly changed the set of tokens under consideration. Our tokens were just instances of Judith's heating system, something located entirely in Judith's house. But the gas lines run from the house out under the streets of Bloomington. Our tokens have greatly expanded. Each of our old tokens s is part of a token $s' = f^{\vee}(s)$ in S'. In other words, our isomorphism is no longer the identity on tokens. When we look at this in terms of the associated classifications $\text{Evt}(S')$ and $\text{Evt}(S)$, what we have is an infomorphism $f : \text{Evt}(S') \rightleftarrows \text{Evt}(S)$ that is not the identity on tokens. Rather, it takes each token to a richer token. And again, there typically seems to be no end to this. As we reason in greater detail, there seems no end to the richness that may have to be considered.[3]

19.3 The Frame Problem

We view the frame problem as the problem of specifying the immediate consequences of a basic action a taken by an agent, what changes and what doesn't change. Given a state space S as above, following the example in Lecture 3, we define a new state space S_{Act}. Its tokens consist of basic actions. We assume that for each such act a there are two tokens init(a) and final(a) of S. We take as states the pairs $\langle \sigma_1, \sigma_2 \rangle$ of states of S. We say that a token of S_{Act} has state $\langle \sigma_1, \sigma_2 \rangle$ if init(a) has state σ_1 and final(a) has state σ_2. Now any sort of change to the circuit can be modeled in Evt(S).

The frame problem and the problem of nonmonotonicity interact with one another, so one would hope that the machinery developed here would help with the frame problem. Suppose that the temperature is seventy-two degrees and the thermostat is set at sixty-eight degrees, so no hot air is coming out of the vents. But now suppose we are told that the temperature drops to sixty-eight degrees. It seems we want to conclude that the furnace comes on and hot air comes out of the vents. But of course this would not be valid if, in the meantime, the setting was changed to the summer setting. Our proposal for handling the frame problem in this context is quite simple: described actions only involve changes to output observables and to input observables about which the descriptions are not silent. Otherwise one has to weaken the background as before.

19.4 Conclusions

In spite of their ubiquity in science and applied mathematics, state spaces as models for human reasoning have been largely ignored. But there are a couple of reasons why such a move might prove fruitful.

Feasibility

In those applications where the equations

$$\sigma_o = F_o(\vec{\sigma_i})$$

---

[3] This is not a new observation, it has been known to those working in nonmonotonic logic for a decade or so. The point here is just to see how this realization fits into the picture presented here.

really can be computed, the state-space/local-logic approach might give us an interesting alternative to traditional theorem-proving methods, one where fixed numerical calculations could be used in place of more symbolic approaches. This is the antithesis of Pat Hayes' thesis in his famous manifesto (Hayes, 1985). The proposal here is to *exploit* the sciences in modeling commonsense reasoning rather than replace it with a parallel symbolic framework.

In this regard, Tarski's decision procedure for the real numbers suggests itself as potentially a useful tool.[4] As long as the output functions F_o, the types in Γ, Δ, and the background condition B are first-order definable over the field of real numbers, as they are in our example, Tarski's decision procedure gives us a mechanical way to determine whether or not $\Gamma \vdash_B \Delta$.

Logic and Cognition

Much more speculatively, the proposal made here suggests a way out of the box that logic has been put into by some of its detractors. Within the recent cognitive-science literature, logic is often seen as irrevocably wed to what is perceived to be an outdated symbol-processing model of cognition. From there, it is but a short step to the conclusion that the study of logic is irrelevant for cognitive science. This step is often taken in spite of the fact that human reasoning is a cognitive activity and so must be part of cognitive science. Perhaps the use of state spaces might allow a marriage of logic with continuous methods like those used in dynamical systems and so provide a toehold for those who envision a distinctively different model of human reasoning (see Chapter 10 of Barwise and Perry (1983), for example). The (admittedly wild) idea is that the input and output of reasoning could be symbolic, at least sometimes, whereas reasoning itself might be better modeled by state-space equations, with the two linked together by means of something like infomorphisms.

---

[4] See Rabin (1974) for a brief exposition of Paul Cohen's improved proof of Tarski's theorem.

Lecture 20

Representation

The concepts of information and representation are, of course, closely related. Indeed, Jerry Fodor feels that they are so closely related as to justify the slogan "No information without representation." Though we do no go that far, we do think of the two as intimately connected, as should be clear from our account. In this lecture, we sketch the beginnings of a theory of representation within the framework presented in Part II. We have three motives for doing so. One is to suggest what we think such a theory might look like. The second is to explain some interesting recent work on inference by Shimojima. The third is to show that Shimojima's work has a natural setting in the theory presented here.[1]

20.1 Modeling Representational Systems

When we think of information flow involving humans, some sort of representational system is typically, if not always, involved: Spoken or written language, pictures, maps, diagrams, and the like are all examples of representations. So representations should fit into our general picture of information flow.

A theory of representation must be compatible with the fact that representation is not always veridical. People often misrepresent things, inadvertently or otherwise. For this reason, we model representation systems as certain special kinds of information systems where unsound logics can appear. We begin with our model of a representational system.

Definition 20.1.

1. A *representation system* $\mathcal{R} = \langle \mathcal{C}, \mathfrak{L} \rangle$ consists of a binary channel $\mathcal{C} = \{f :$

---

[1] Representation is such a big and important topic that it surely deserves a book of its own. We hope one of our readers will write a book that further develops the ideas sketched here.

$A \rightleftarrows C$, $g : B \rightleftarrows C$}, with one of the classifications designated as *source* (say A) and the other as *target*, together with a local logic $\mathfrak{L}$ on the core C of this channel.

2. The *representations* of $\mathcal{R}$ are the tokens of A. If $a \in$ tok(A) and $b \in$ tok(B), a is a *representation of* b, written $a \leadsto_{\mathcal{R}} b$, if a and b are connected by some $c \in C$. The token a is an *accurate representation of* b if a and b are connected by some normal token, that is, some $c \in N_{\mathfrak{L}}$.

3. A set of types Γ of the source classification *indicates* a type β of the target classification, written $\Gamma \Rightarrow_{\mathcal{R}} \beta$, if the translations of the types into the core gives us a constraint of the logic $\mathfrak{L}$, that is, if $f[\Gamma] \vdash_{\mathfrak{L}} g(\beta)$. The *content* of a token a is the set of all types indicated by its type set. The representation a *represents* b *as being of type* β if a represents b and β is in the content of a.

We can depict a representational system as follows:

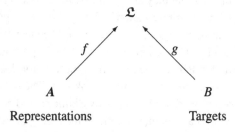

The connections between the representations and their targets model the particular spatial-temporal process whereby the representation comes to represent what it does. The constraints of the logic model the various sort of constraints on this process. When dealing with conventional representation systems like writing or map making, the constraints will typically involve a wide variety of constraints of different types, from conventional to physically necessary, all the way to logic constraints. In this sketch, we simply group them all together.

With our definition, not every representation of $\mathcal{R}$ is a representation of some token in the target. (Novels are representations, but not necessarily of anything real.) Also note that a representation may be a representation of more than one token. For example, the picture of Ben taken on his third birthday represents him as he was then, but it also represents the Ben of today, two years later, though not as accurately as it represents the younger Ben.

Example 20.2. Let us see how we can view the practice of mapmaking as a representation system under this definition. The source classification A is a classification of maps (the tokens) by means of their syntactic types, that is, types that classify maps according to what is printed or drawn on them. The target classification consists of regions classified by properties of and relations between the things in the regions. Thus a typical source type might be something roughly like "a school icon labeled 'Harmony' is next to road line labeled '2nd' " and a target type might be "Harmony School is located on 2nd street." The core of this classification models the actual practice of mapmaking. The connections are causal links between maps and what they are maps of. The types are ways of classifying these links. The logic on this classification models the understanding of users of these maps. Thus the constraints of the system represent the assumptions users of the maps make about the links between maps and what they are maps of. The normal tokens of the logic are the normal links, which must satisfy the constraints. Note, however, that there may be links that do not satisfy all of the constraints of the logic.

Assume the map a is a representation of Mt. Ateb. Suppose that looking at a we observe that $\Gamma \subseteq \mathrm{typ}(a)$, that is, that a of every type in Γ. If $\Gamma \Rightarrow_{\mathcal{R}} \beta$, we would be justified in saying that the map a represents Mt. Ateb as being of type β, whether or not Mt. Ateb is of type β.

The next result shows that our definition of an accurate representation behaves properly.

Proposition 20.3. *If a is an accurate representation of b and a represents b as being of type β, then $b \vDash_B \beta$.*

Proof. Because a is an accurate representation of b, there is a normal connection c between a and b, so $f(c) = a$ and $g(c) = b$. Because a represents b as being of type β, $f[\mathrm{typ}(a)] \vdash_{\mathcal{L}} g(\beta)$. Because f is an infomorphism, $c \vDash_C f(\alpha)$ for each $\alpha \in \mathrm{typ}(a)$. Because c is normal, c satisfies all constraints of the logic, so $c \vDash_C g(\beta)$. Because g is an infomorphism, $b \vDash_B \beta$. $\qquad\square$

20.2 Imperfect Representations

In this section, we sketch our solution to a potentially troublesome fact about information and representation. Suppose we have a map of Mt. Ateb but the mountain has changed in small ways since the map was produced. Maybe a portion of a path has been obliterated by a landslide. There is clearly a sense in which the map is no longer accurate. After all, it represents the existence of a path where there is in fact none. Still, the map does carry a lot of valid information about the mountain. Any informational theory of representation should be compatible with this commonplace phenomenon.

Recall that our tokens in the target classifications are really regions at times, not just regions outside of time. Let us suppose that the original connection c_0 between the map and the mountain was normal, and connected the map a to m_0. Thus a was a representation of m_0. But when the path was destroyed, this changed m_0 to m_1 and, as a result, the connection c_0 between a and m_0 gave rise to a new connection c_1 between a and m_1. Thus a represents both m_0 and m_1. The new connection supports most of the constraints of the representation system but not all of them. In particular, it fails to support the constraint that says that a path icon at location l indicates a path at position p.

Whether or not a representation a is an *accurate* representation of b depends on the connections and the representation system in question; in particular, it depends on the local logic $\mathfrak{L}$ at the core of the system. It may be inaccurate with respect to a logic $\mathfrak{L}$ but accurate with respect to a slightly weaker logic $\mathfrak{L}_0 \sqsubseteq \mathfrak{L}$. The connection c between a and b is not normal with respect to $\mathfrak{L}$ but is normal with respect to a slightly weaker logic $\mathfrak{L}_0$. Relative to this logic, and the associated representation system, a is accurate.

20.3 Shimojima's Thesis

When we use representations to reason about some domain, the nature of the representations can greatly affect the form of the reasoning. The choice of a good representation system for the problem at hand can make the reasoning much easier. Conversely, the choice of a poor representation system can make the reasoning more difficult or even impossible.

There have been many attempts made to explain the various properties of different kinds of representation systems. One common intuition is that the better a fit there is between the representing domain and the represented domain, the better the representational system is. Atsushi Shimojima (1996) has used the basic notions of classification and constraint to give a rigorous formulation of this basic intuition, and has used it to investigate a wide range of representational phenomena. With various case studies, Shiomjima makes a strong case for the following:

Shimojima's Constraint Thesis

The inferential advantages and disadvantages between representation systems with a common target classification can be understood in terms of the kinds of constraints that the system projects from representations to targets.[2]

---

[2] Shimojima never goes quite so far as to call this a thesis. Rather, he calls it an hypothesis. We think his dissertation makes such a strong case, however, that we promote it to a thesis here.

In this section, we give a brief introduction to Shimojima's (1996) work after first setting it in the framework of representation systems as modeled in this chapter.

For a rigorous treatment of the thesis, Shimojima must first give an analysis of what it means for one constraint to project to another constraint.[3] Recall we have a representation system $\mathcal{R}$ with source classification A and target classification B. For sets $\Gamma \subseteq \text{typ}(A)$ and $\Theta \subseteq \text{typ}(B)$, we say that $\mathcal{R}$ *projects* Γ *to* Θ, and write $\Gamma \Rightarrow^* \Theta$, if every $\beta \in \Theta$ is indicated by some $\alpha \in \Gamma$ and every $\alpha \in \Gamma$ indicates some $\beta \in \Theta$. Here are some simple properties of this relation. Recall that $a \vDash_{\wedge A} \Gamma$ means that $a \vDash_A \alpha$ for every $\alpha \in \Gamma$, and dually for disjunction. The following is easy to verify.

Proposition 20.4. *Let a be an accurate representation of b and assume that $\mathcal{R}$ projects Γ to Θ.*

1. *If $a \vDash_{\wedge A} \Gamma$, then $b \vDash_{\wedge B} \Theta$.*
2. *If $a \vDash_{\vee A} \Gamma$, then $b \vDash_{\vee B} \Theta$.*
3. *$\Gamma = \emptyset$ if and only if $\Theta = \emptyset$.*

Furthermore, if $\Gamma = \{\alpha\}$ and $\Theta = \{\beta\}$, then $\Gamma \Rightarrow^* \Theta$ if and only if $\alpha \Rightarrow_{\mathcal{R}} \beta$.

Definition 20.5. Let $S = \langle \Gamma, \Delta \rangle$ and $S' = \langle \Theta, \Psi \rangle$ be sequents of A and B, respectively. We say that $\mathcal{R}$ *projects* S to S' if $\Gamma \Rightarrow^* \Theta$ and $\Delta \Rightarrow^* \Psi$. If S is a constraint of A, then this relationship is said to be an instance of *constraint projection*.

Let a be an accurate representation of b and assume that $\mathcal{R}$ projects S to S'. One might be tempted to think that if a satisfies the sequent S, then b satisfies the sequent S'. A moment's thought shows that this is not in general the case. Indeed, part of Shimojima's argument in favor of his thesis comes from exploring cases where projected constraints are not in fact satisfied. We give a hint as to his argument by examining three cases of projection: where the consequent of S is empty, where it is a singleton, and where it has more than one element.

Free Rides

Shimojima defines a *free ride* to be any case of constraint projection $S \Rightarrow S'$ where both S and S' have a single type in the succedent of the sequent. That is,

---

[3] Actually, Shimojima did not use the framework of channel theory, but instead used the notions of signaling and indicating as primitives.

S is of the form $\langle \Gamma, \{\alpha\} \rangle$ and $S' = \langle \Theta, \{\beta\} \rangle$. In other words, a free ride occurs if $\Gamma \Rightarrow^* \Theta$, $\Gamma \vdash_A \alpha$, and $\alpha \vDash_R \beta$.

Suppose we want to represent the information (or misinformation) Θ about some b by means of a representation a whose type set includes Γ. Any such representation will represent its target b as being of all the types in Θ. Note, however, that because $\Gamma \vdash_A \alpha$, a will also be of type α. But then because $\alpha \Rightarrow_R \beta$, a will also represent b as being of type β. In other words, any attempt to represent b as satisfying all the types in Θ by means of a representation satisfying Γ will automatically represent b as being of type β. This can be a good or a bad thing.

Positive Free Rides

If $\Theta \vdash_B \beta$, then this is called a positive free ride, because the conclusion β automatically generated by creating a representation satisfying Γ is in fact warranted. One of the advantages of various forms of diagrammatic representations is that one gets various forms of positive free rides.

Example 20.6. Let us go back to the example of maps. The cartographer places the line l_1 representing Atwater Street above the line l_2 representing Second Street so the map represents Atwater as being north of Second. The cartographer similarly places the line l_3 representing University Street below l_2 so the map represents University as being south of Second. By virtue of placing l_1 above l_2 and l_3 below l_2, the cartographer also places l_1 above l_3, by virtue of a constraint S of A. As a result, the map automatically represents Atwater as being north of University. This is a legitimate piece of information because the constraint S projects to a matching constraint S' on B.

Negative Free Rides

If $\Theta \nvdash_A \beta$, then this is called a negative free ride, because the conclusion β generated automatically by creating a representation satisfying Γ is not warranted. The mismatch between distances between points on a planar map of a curved surface (like the earth) and the distances between the points they represent gives rise to examples of this.

Overdetermined Alternatives

By a case of *overdetermined alternatives* Shimojima means any case of constraint projection $S \Rightarrow S'$ where both S and S' have more than one type in the succedent, say $S = \langle \Gamma, \Delta \rangle$ and $S' = \langle \Theta, \Psi \rangle$, where Ψ has more than one element but where for each $\beta \in \Psi$, $\Theta \nvdash_B \beta$.

Suppose we were to represent b as satisfying all the types in Θ by means of a representation a satisfying all types in Γ. Because S is a constraint, a must satisfy some $\alpha \in \Delta$. But then by Proposition 20.4.2, there would be some $\beta \in \Psi$ such that a represents b as being of type β. But because $\Theta \nvdash_B \beta$, our representation would have represented b as being of some type that does not follow from the information Θ from which we started. That is, any representation a we choose that represents b as satisfying all the types in Θ by means of Γ has the unfortunate effect of representing b as satisfying some β that does not follow from Θ.

Example 20.7. Suppose the cartographer knows there is new high school being planned for south of town and that the school will be built quite soon. Thus he or she would like to indicate it on the map. However, if he places a school icon at any particular place on the map, it will indicate that the school is at a particular location. Although one of the locations is the right one, which one does not follow from the information Θ at the cartographer's command, that there will be a school south of town.

As with the case of free rides, there are two subcases to consider, depending on whether or not S' is a constraint of $\boldsymbol{B}$. If S' is not a constraint of $\boldsymbol{B}$, then overdetermined alternatives are a potential source of serious error when using the representation system. However, if S' is a constraint, there is a way to get around the problem.

Cases Exhaustive

If S' is a constraint, that is, if $\Theta \vdash_B \Psi$, then one can work around the difficulty by using multiple representations in a disjunctive fashion. To simplify the discussion, let us suppose that $\Delta = \{\alpha_1, \alpha_2\}$ has two types. Suppose that we find representations a_1 and a_2 of b satisfying all types in Γ with $a_1 \vDash_A \alpha_1$ and $a_2 \vDash_A \alpha_2$. These will be called a set of *exhaustive alternatives* for $S \Rightarrow^* S'$. Because each type in Ψ is indicated by at least one of these two, and because both possibilities in Δ are covered, between them they legitimately represent b as satisfying at least one type in Δ without representing b as being of any particular type in Δ.

Example 20.8. Cases exhaustive is one of the main methods of reasoning with simple diagrammatic systems, where one has to break a piece of reasoning into a number of distinct cases. Suppose, for example, we were given a representation

G	M	B

representing a seating arrangement involving Greg, Mary, Bill, Ann, and Toni and we were given the information that Ann was seated next to Mary. If we place an A in the first empty box, it will represent one alternative and represent Ann as sitting next to Greg, in the second a different alternative will represent Ann as sitting next to Bill. We need to break into two exhaustive cases, from which it will follow that Ann is next to either Greg or Bill. For further discussion of the importance of this rule, see the discussion of the Hyperproof system's rule of Cases Exhaustive in Barwise and Etchemendy (1995).

The validity of the method of cases exhaustive depends crucially on the validity of the projected constraint, as Shimojima's analysis makes clear.

Autoconsistent Systems

One of the advantages of certain kinds of representations is that it is difficult, sometimes impossible, to use them to represent inconsistent information. This means that one can demonstrate consistency of some purported information simply by producing a representation of it in such a system. For example, a drawing might be used to show that a certain placement of furniture in the room is possible.

The system $\mathcal{R}$ is said to be *autoconsistent* if whenever $\mathcal{R}$ projects a sequent S of the form $\langle \Gamma, \emptyset \rangle$ to some sequent $S' = \langle \Theta, \emptyset \rangle$, if S' is a constraint, so is S.

Example 20.9. The representation system employed in Hyperproof is autoconsistent. The standard Euler circle system is also autoconsistent.

Proposition 20.10. *Suppose $\mathcal{R}$ is autoconsistent. For every $a \in$ tok(A), the content of a holds for some token $b \in$ tok(B).*

Proof. Let $\Gamma = \text{typ}(a)$ and Θ be the content of a. By definition of content, $\Gamma \Rightarrow^* \Theta$. If Θ holds for no token of B, then $\Theta \vdash_B$. By autoconsistency, $\Gamma \vdash_A$, which contradicts the fact that a satisfies every type in Γ. □

Shimojima (1996) goes into these ideas in much greater depth and with many more examples. He also has an interesting discussion of the roles that different types of constraints, say nomic versus conventional, play in different kinds of representational systems. We recommend it to the reader.

Lecture 21

Quantum Logic

Quantum theory is well known for having a nonclassical and somewhat peculiar logic. One approach to trying to make this logic comprehensible is by means of what is called a "manual of experiments." This is the approach taken, for example, in the book *An Introduction to Hilbert Space and Quantum Logic* (Cohen, 1989), which we use as our main reference. A manual is thought of as describing a variety of different tests of a system, but where the making of one test may, for some reason, preclude the making of some other test of the same system at the same time. Still, it can happen that from performing one kind of experiment we may get information about what the outcome would have been had we performed another kind of experiment.

Example 21.1. Here is an example taken from 17). Imagine a firefly trapped inside a box, and two kinds of experiments, FRONT and SIDE, one can perform when observing this box at a given instant. In a FRONT experiment one looks in the box from the front, whereas in SIDE one looks from the right-hand side. In FRONT there are three possible outcomes: one may see the firefly light lit up on the right (R), lit up on the left (L), or not lit up at all (N). Similarly, in SIDE there are three possible outcomes: one may see the firefly light at the front (F), at the back (B), or not at all (N). Suppose an observer examines the box using FRONT and observes an outcome of L. Then the firefly was lit, so if the observer had performed the experiment SIDE, one would have obtained an outcome in the set {F, B}. Thus we have a constraint L ⊢ F, B, and associated information flow.

We want to see how this kind of information flow fits into the picture presented in this book. We also want to see how well the framework of this book fits with that of quantum logic.

243

21.1 The Theory of a Manual

Definition 21.2. A *manual of experiments* is an indexed family $M = \{\Omega_E\}_{E\in\mathcal{E}}$ of sets. Each $E \in \mathcal{E}$ is called an experiment (or kind of experiment). The set Ω_E is called the set of *possible outcomes* of E.

Cohen calls this a "quasi-manual." What he calls a manual we will call a standard manual (Definition 21.17). Each set Ω_E can be thought of as the set of states of a state-space S_E. To make things canonical, we take S_E to be the ideal state space with Ω_E as states. Thus Ω_E is the set of types and the set of tokens of S_E, and each token is its own type. In this way, each E gives rise to a theory, namely, the $\text{Th}(S_E)$. The types of this theory are arbitrary subsets of Ω_E and $\Gamma \vdash_{\text{Th}(S_E)} \Delta$ if and only if $\bigcap \Gamma \subseteq \bigcup \Delta$.

We want to associate a sound and complete local logic $\text{Log}(M)$ with any manual M. We start with the manual's theory $\text{Th}(M)$, which has an obvious natural definition. From that, we work toward a definition of a classification $\text{Cla}(M)$ associated with M and then show that $\text{Th}(M)$ is the theory of the classification $\text{Cla}(M)$.

Definition 21.3. For any manual $M = \{\Omega_E\}_{E\in\mathcal{E}}$, $\text{Th}(M)$ is the theory whose set of types is

$$\Sigma_M = \bigcup_{E\in\mathcal{E}} \text{pow}\,\Omega_E$$

and whose consequence relation is the smallest regular consequence relation containing the consequence relation $\vdash_{S_E}$ of $\text{Log}(S_E)$, for each $E \in \mathcal{E}$.

Example 21.4. In the firefly manual M, the set $\mathcal{E}$ of experiments is {FRONT, SIDE}, $\Omega_{\text{FRONT}} = \{\text{L, R, N}\}$ and $\Omega_{\text{SIDE}} = \{\text{F, B, N}\}$. Σ_M consists of all subsets of either of these sets. It does not contain a set like {F, L}. Because {L}, {N} $\vdash_{S_{\text{FRONT}}}$ and $\vdash_{S_{\text{SIDE}}}$ {N}, {F}, {B}, both sequents hold in $\text{Th}(M)$. Hence by Cut and Weakening, we obtain the constraint

$$\{\text{L}\} \vdash_{\text{Th}(M)} \{\text{F}\}, \{\text{B}\}$$

as desired.

We want to show that the theory $\text{Th}(M)$ of a manual M is the complete theory of a classification naturally associated with M. To motivate the choice of tokens, we first present some definitions from quantum logic.

Operationally Perspective Types

Let M be a manual and let Σ_M be the associated set of types. A pair of types α, β are said to be *comeasurable* if there is an experiment E of the manual so that $\alpha \cup \beta \subseteq \Omega_E$. That is, they are comeasurable if you can test for them both with a single experiment E. In the firefly example, $\{L\}$ and $\{R\}$ are comeasurable but not consistent. On the other hand, $\{L, N\}$ and $\{B, N\}$ are not comeasurable, even though they could both hold in a given situation.

Types α and β are *orthogonal*, written $\alpha \perp \beta$, if they are comeasurable and disjoint. In the firefly example, $\{L, R\} \perp \{N\}$. Types α and β are *orthogonal compliments*, written α oc β, provided they are orthogonal and their union is an Ω_E, that is, if the two events partition the set Ω_E of possible outcomes of some experiment $E \in \mathcal{E}$. Intuitively, this means that exactly one of the two events would be seen to hold were we to perform an experiment of type E. (In the firefly example, $\{L, R\}$ and $\{N\}$ are orthogonal compliments.)

Types α_1 and α_2 are *operationally perspective*, α_1 op α_2, if there is a type β such that α_1 oc β and α_2 oc β. Intuitively, operationally perspective types are equivalent, because they have a common compliment. (In the firefly example, $\{L, R\}$ op $\{F, B\}$ because they are both orthogonal complements of $\{N\}$.)

In the approach to quantum logic using manuals, it is assumed that operationally perspective types are equivalent. We adopt this assumption and see where it leads us in our search for a classification to go along with the theory $\mathrm{Th}(M)$. First, though, note the following result.

Proposition 21.5. *Let M be a manual and let $\mathrm{Th}(M) = \langle \Sigma_M, \vdash \rangle$ be its theory. For all $\alpha, \beta \in \Sigma_M$:*

1. *If $\alpha \perp \beta$, then $\alpha, \beta \vdash$.*
2. *If α oc β, then $\alpha, \beta \vdash$ and $\vdash \alpha, \beta$.*
3. *If α op β, then $\alpha \vdash \beta$ and $\beta \vdash \alpha$.*

Proof. To prove (1), assume $\alpha \perp \beta$. Then α, β are disjoint but are both subsets of Ω_E for some E. But then $\alpha, \beta \vdash_{S_E}$ so $\alpha, \beta \vdash$. The proof of (2) is similar so we prove (3). Because op is a symmetric relation, it suffices to prove one of the two conclusions. Assume that α op β. Let θ be such that α oc θ and θ oc β. By (2), $\alpha, \theta \vdash$ and $\vdash \theta, \beta$. But then by Finite Cut, we have $\alpha \vdash \beta$. $\qquad\square$

Let

$$A = \sum_{E \in \mathcal{E}} \mathrm{Evt}(S_E)$$

and let

$$\mathfrak{L} = \sum_{E \in \mathcal{E}} \text{Log}(S_E),$$

the corresponding sum of logics. Being a sum of sound and complete logics, $\mathfrak{L}$ is a sound and complete logic on A. The tokens are functions c that assign to each E some element $c_E \in \Omega_E$. We can think of such a token as representing the possible outcomes of performing the different experiments in $\mathcal{E}$: c_E is the outcome one would get were one to perform an experiment of kind E. The types are the disjoint union of the types of the various state spaces.

Recall that $\text{typ}(A)$ is the *disjoint* union of $\text{pow} \, \Omega_E$, for $E \in \mathcal{E}$. But if $\alpha \in \text{pow} \, \Omega_E$ and $\beta \in \text{pow} \, \Omega_F$, they are already distinct objects unless they are identical, in which case they are subsets of $\Omega_E \cap \Omega_F$. But these are exactly the types that give rise to op relationships; that is, if $\alpha = \beta$, then $\Omega_E - \alpha$ is operationally perspective to $\Omega_F - \beta$. So in this case we do not really want to make α and β distinct.

We need, then, to undo the disjointness caused by taking the sum. This is easily accomplished by taking the appropriate (dual) quotient. Define a dual invariant $J = \langle C, R \rangle$ on A as follows. The relation R relates exactly those types that are copies of the same set. The set C consists of those tokens of A that respect the relation R.

Lemma 21.6. *A token of A respects R if and only if for all types $E, F \in \mathcal{E}$, if $c_E \in \Omega_F$ then $c_E = c_F$.*

With this in mind, we make the following important definition.

Definition 21.7. An *idealized token* of M is an element $c \in \text{tok}(A)$ such that for all experiments $E, F \in \mathcal{E}$, if $c_E \in \Omega_F$ then $c_E = c_F$.

Proposition 21.8. *The logic $\mathfrak{L}/J$ is a sound and complete logic on the classification A/J.*

Proof. This is an immediate consequence of Corollary 12.34.   □

Classification A/J has the idealized tokens for tokens. Its types are (up to isomorphism) just the types Σ_M of $\text{Th}(M)$. This suggests that $\text{Th}(M)$ is the theory of the sound and complete logic with idealized tokens as tokens and Σ_M as types.

Definition 21.9. Given a manual M, the *classification* $\mathrm{Cla}(M)$ of M is the classification whose types are the set Σ_M, whose tokens are the M-idealized tokens, and whose classification relation is given by $c \vDash \alpha$ if and only if $c_E \in \alpha$ for some (hence every) E such that $\alpha \subseteq \Omega_E$.

Justification. The classification relation is well defined by the definition of idealized tokens. □

Theorem 21.10. *For any manual M, the theory $\mathrm{Th}(M)$ is the sound and complete theory of $\mathrm{Cla}(M)$. Thus, for any sequent $\langle \Gamma, \Delta \rangle$ of Σ_M, $\Gamma \vdash_{\mathrm{Th}(M)} \Delta$ if and only if every idealized token satisfies $\langle \Gamma, \Delta \rangle$.*

Proof. Let $f : \mathrm{Cla}(M) \rightleftarrows A/J$ be the obvious token-identical infomorphism. It is clear that this is also a theory infomorphism taking $\mathrm{Th}(M)$ into the theory of $\mathfrak{L}/J$. Thus $\mathrm{Th}(M) \sqsubseteq f^{-1}[\mathrm{Th}(\mathfrak{L}/J)]$. To prove they are equal, we need only check that if $\langle \Gamma, \Delta \rangle$ is a consistent partition of $\mathrm{Th}(M)$, then there is an idealized token that is a counterexample to it. Define c_E to be the unique $\alpha \in \Omega_E$ such that $\{\alpha\} \in \Gamma$. It is easy to verify that if $c_E \in \Omega_F$, then $c_E = c_F$, because otherwise the restriction of the sequent to Ω_F would not be consistent in $\mathrm{Log}(S_F)$. □

This theorem shows that the theory $\mathrm{Th}(M)$ is sound as long as it is used with tokens that give rise to idealized tokens. It will be complete as long as every idealized token corresponds to a real token of the classification.

The theory $\mathrm{Th}(M)$ does not in general have a disjunction or a conjunction, as the firefly example shows. It does have a negation, however.

Corollary 21.11. *Suppose that α is both an E-type and an F-type. Then $\Omega_E - \alpha \vdash_{\mathrm{Th}(M)} \Omega_F - \alpha$ and $\Omega_F - \alpha \vdash_{\mathrm{Th}(M)} \Omega_E - \alpha$.*

Proof. See Exercise 21.2. □

We can use this corollary to show that the theory $\mathrm{Th}(M)$ has a negation. Define $\neg\alpha$ to be $\Omega_E - \alpha$ for some E such that α is an E-type. By 21.11, it does not matter which E we choose, they will all be equivalent. The theory obeys the usual rules for negation. This negation is usually called the "orthocomplement" in quantum logic.

Finally, we note the following disquieting possibility. Recall that a logic $\mathfrak{L}$ is coherent if not every sequent is a constraint, which is equivalent to saying that the empty sequent is not a constraint. If a logic has even a single normal token, then it is coherent.

Corollary 21.12. *Let M be a manual. There are idealized tokens for M if and only if the theory $\mathrm{Th}(M)$ is coherent.*

This corollary implies that if there are no idealized tokens for M, then the least logic obtained from putting together the state-space logics from the individual experiments is incoherent! We will see that there are manuals of use in quantum mechanics where this happens.

21.2 A Comparison with Quantum Logic

We have used our general framework to define a notion of consequence between the types in a manual and established an understanding of this logic in terms of idealized tokens. The usual notion of consequence from quantum logic proceeds rather differently. We review this development here and then compare it with that from above.

Definition 21.13. Given a manual M, α_1 is said to *M-entail* α_2, written $\alpha_1 \leq_M \alpha_2$, if and only if there is some β such that $\alpha_1 \perp \beta$ and $\alpha_1 \cup \beta$ op α_2.

Proposition 21.14. *Let M be a manual. If $\alpha_1 \leq_M \alpha_2$, then $\alpha_1 \vdash_{\mathrm{Th}(M)} \alpha_2$.*

Proof. Assume $\alpha_1 \perp \beta$ and $\alpha_1 \cup \beta$ op α_2. Because $\alpha_1 \perp \beta$, $\alpha_1 \cup \beta \subseteq \Omega_E$, for some $E \in \mathcal{E}$, so we have $\alpha_1 \vdash_{\mathrm{Log}(S_E)} \alpha_1 \cup \beta$, and hence $\alpha_1 \vdash_{\mathrm{Th}(M)} \alpha_1 \cup \beta$. But because $\alpha_1 \cup \beta$ op α_2, we have $\alpha_1 \cup \beta \vdash_{\mathrm{Th}(M)} \alpha_2$, by Proposition 21.5.3. We obtain $\alpha_1 \vdash_{\mathrm{Th}(M)} \alpha_2$ by Cut.   □

Two-Experiment Manuals

The following result shows that in the case of a manual with two experiments, the notion of entailment from quantum logic coincides with that in the logic of the manual. We will turn to the more general question in the next section.

Theorem 21.15. *Suppose the manual M has only two experiments, E and F. If $\alpha \subseteq \Omega_E$ and $\beta \subseteq \Omega_F$ are types in α, then $\alpha \leq_M \beta$ if and only if $\alpha \vdash \beta$.*

Proof. We will show the following are equivalent:

1. $\alpha \leq_M \beta$;
2. $\alpha \vdash \beta$;
3. either $\alpha \subseteq \beta$ or $\alpha \cap \Omega_F \subseteq \beta$ and $\Omega_F \subseteq \beta \cup \Omega_E$.

We have already established (1) implies (2), so we need only show (2) implies

(3) and (3) implies (1). Let us first establish the latter implication. Because (3) is a disjunction, there are two cases to consider. If $\alpha \subseteq \beta \subseteq \Omega_F$, then let $\theta = \beta - \alpha$ and $\gamma = \Omega_F - \beta$. Then $\alpha \perp \theta$ and $\alpha \cup \theta$ op β because $\alpha \cup \theta = \beta$ and β oc γ. The other case to consider is when $\alpha \cap \Omega_F \subseteq \beta$ and $\Omega_F \subseteq \beta \cup \Omega_E$. In this case, let $\gamma = \Omega_F - \beta$ so that γ is an orthogonal complement of β. Notice that $\gamma \subseteq \Omega_E$ because $\Omega_F \subseteq \beta \cup \Omega_E$. Now let θ consist of those states in Ω_E that are in neither α nor γ. Clearly, $\alpha \perp \theta$. We want to show that $\alpha \cup \theta$ op β by showing that γ is an orthogonal complement to $\alpha \cup \theta$ (as well as to β, as we saw). Notice that $\gamma \cap \alpha = \emptyset$ because $\alpha \cap \Omega_F \subseteq \beta$. Hence $\Omega_E - \gamma = \alpha \cup \theta$ as desired.

Now assume (2). We show that $\alpha \subseteq \beta$ or that $\alpha \cap \Omega_F \subseteq \beta$ and $\Omega_F \subseteq \beta \cup \Omega_E$. It is convenient to split the proof into two cases, depending on whether or not $\Omega_F \subseteq \beta \cup \Omega_E$.

Case 1. $\Omega_F \subseteq \beta \cup \Omega_E$. We prove that $\alpha \cap \Omega_F \subseteq \beta$ (and hence (3)). Suppose this is not the case. Let $\sigma \in \alpha \cap \Omega_F$, $\sigma \notin \beta$. Notice σ is an outcome in both E and F, because $\sigma \in \alpha \subseteq \Omega_E$. Hence there is an idealized token c that assigns σ to both E and F. But this token is of type α and not of type β, which contradicts (2).

Case 2. $\Omega_F \nsubseteq \beta \cup \Omega_E$. In this case we want to show that $\alpha \subseteq \beta$. Suppose this were not the case. Let $\sigma \in \alpha - \beta$ and let $\tau \in \Omega_F - (\beta \cup \Omega_E)$. If $\sigma \in \Omega_F$, then consider the idealized token c that assigns σ to both E and F. This shows that $\alpha \nvdash_{\text{Th}(M)} \beta$. If $\sigma \notin \Omega_F$, then consider the idealized token c that assigns σ to E and τ to F. This idealized token shows that $\alpha \nvdash_{\text{Th}(M)} \beta$. □

More Than Two Experiments

In Theorem 21.15, the assumption that the manual have only two experiments is crucial, as the following example shows.

Example 21.16. Here is a simple example with four experiments, each with two possible outcomes, where $\leq_M$ is weaker than $\vdash$. Let E have outcomes $\{1, 2\}$, F have outcomes $\{2, 3\}$, G have outcomes $\{3, 4\}$, and H have outcomes $\{4, 5\}$. Then $\{1\} \vdash \{5\}$ because the only idealized token that has $c_E = 1$ must also have $c_F = 3$ so $c_G = 3$ so $c_H = 5$. But it is also clear that $\{1\} \nleq_M \{5\}$. This example also shows that the ordering $\leq_M$ is not even transitive, because $\{1\} \leq_M \{3\}$ and $\{3\} \leq_M \{5\}$.

This example shows that, in general, the quantum logic relation $\alpha \leq_M \beta$ is too weak to be reasonable, it is not even transitive. Hence it does not satisfy even Finite Cut. One approach would be to close the logic under such rules. However, a different approach is taken in the quantum logic literature, where it is standard practice to postulate additional structure on the manual.

Definition 21.17. A manual M is *standard* if it satisfies the following conditions:

1. If $E, F \in \mathcal{E}$, and $\Omega_E \subseteq \Omega_F$, then $\Omega_E = \Omega_F$.
2. If α_1 oc α_2, α_2 oc α_3, and α_3 oc α_4, then $\alpha_1 \perp \alpha_4$.
3. If $x \perp y$, $y \perp z$, and $z \perp x$, then the set $\{x, y, z\}$ is a type, that is, it is a subset of Ω_E for some $E \in \mathcal{E}$.

The manual of Example 21.16 does not satisfy condition (2) so it is not standard.

The first condition seems reasonable enough. After all, why have F in your manual if in fact some of its outcomes are impossible and can be eliminated by E?[1]

Why (2) is reasonable from an intuitive point of view is not at all obvious. It requires that we be able to combine experiments in a certain way. In particular, it rules out a manual of the kind described in Example 21.16, a manual that seems perfectly reasonable from an intuitive point of view. Here is what Cohen (1989, p. 23) has to say by way of justification. Read $\alpha_1, \alpha_2, \alpha_3$, and α_4 for A, B, C, and D, respectively.

Suppose we test for event A by performing experiment E, and A occurs. Then we know that B did not occur. Thus, if we had performed experiment F [an experiment with both B and C as events] then C would have occurred; so, if we had performed experiment G [an experiment with both C and D as events] then D would *not* have occurred. In summary, if we test for A, and A occurs, then testing for D would result in D not occurring. [The reverse is then observed.] Hence A and D are events that bear a special relationship to each other through E, F, and G, and it is not unnatural to require that there be a single experiment H that contains both A and D so that $A \perp D$ in M.

The first step of the argument clearly assumes that if A op C and A occurred under E, then C would have occurred under F, that is, that A and C are equivalent. It is this condition that led to our notion of an idealized token. The assumption is basically that the outcome of an experiment is completely determined by the state of the system, not other factors of the experimental event itself. For a case where this does not hold, consider the following example.

---

[1] Of course it could be that E is much more expensive in time or effort than F. That is why we have book reviews.

Example 21.18. A coin c stands on its edge on a table. We can perform two experiments on this coin. We can pick it up and flip it, with the outcomes of heads or tails: $\Omega_{\text{FLIP}} = \{H, T\}$. Or we can bang the tabletop to see which way the coin falls: $\Omega_{\text{BANG}} = \{H, T\}$. (With a U.S. penny, the probability of an H in the second experiment is close to 1.) Notice that this is a standard manual. Let $A = \{$T$\} = C$ and $B = \{$H$\}$. Thus A op C, but clearly there is no reason to suppose that just because A occurred in an experiment of kind FLIP, that C would have occurred under BANG. So even though we have a standard manual M, its theory is completely inappropriate for understanding information flow with regard to this system.

This example shows that if the outcome of an experimental event is partially determined by the event itself, rather than being completely determined by the state of the system, then op types do not bear a special relationship to one another. To put it the other way around, making operationally perspective types equivalent presupposes that the instantaneous state of the system can be adequately modeled by an idealized token.

A secondary point is that even if the physicist is in a context where the argument up to the final step ("... it is not unnatural to require... ") seems justified, that is, where the system can be modeled by an idealized token, the final step seems unmotivated. It seems likely that the real motivation is that the condition is needed to guarantee the transitivity of the entailment relation $\leq_M$, something we can achieve more gracefully by means of regular theories.

Condition (3), the so-called "ortho-coherence condition," asserts that given any three pairwise incompatible mutual outcomes, each of which can be tested against the others, there is a single experiment that can decide among all three. This seems even less natural than the second condition. (Cohen remarks that this condition is not always assumed.)

These requirements on standard manuals, unnatural as they may appear in general, do hold in the manual naturally associated with a Hilbert space.

Given a Hilbert space H, an *orthonormal base* of H is a maximal orthogonal set E of unit vectors. An orthonormal basis E is the set of eigenstates of a commuting set of Hermitian operators where these operators are used to model experiments. We can think of the total state of a particle as modeled by a unit vector $\xi \in H$. Given an orthonormal basis E, $\xi = \sum_{v \in E} r_v v$ for some choice of scalars whose sum is 1. Performing the experiment modeled by E yields one of these vectors $v_\xi \in E$; intuitively, the outcome depends on the weights: the larger the weight, the more likely that vector is the outcome.

Definition 21.19. Let H be a Hilbert space. The *frame manual of H*, written $\mathcal{F}(H)$, is the manual defined as follows. The experiments E of $\mathcal{F}(H)$ consist of the maximal orthonormal subsets of H. The possible outcomes of E consist of the elements of E.

Proposition 21.20. *For any separable Hilbert space (which includes all finite-dimensional Hilbert spaces), the frame manual $\mathcal{F}(H)$ is standard.*

Proof. This is a standard result; see Example 3.4A of 17).   □

The natural question to ask, in view of this result, is whether the consequence relation of $\text{Th}(M)$ agrees with the entailment relation $\leq_M$ for standard manuals M. That is, can Theorem 21.15 be extended to arbitrary standard manuals? A very strong negative answer to this question was obtained by Kenneth Kunen. Michael Dickson observed that this is equivalent to the famous Kochen–Specker Theorem (29).

Theorem 21.21. *If H is a (real or complex) Hilbert space of dimension at least three, then the frame manual $\mathcal{F}(H)$ has no idealized tokens. In other words, for any function g such that $g(E) \in E$ for each orthonormal base E, there are two orthonormal bases E, F with $g(E) \in F$ but $g(E) \neq g(F)$.*

Proof. Because the theorem for complex Hilbert spaces easily follows from the theorem for real Hilbert spaces, we assume that H is a real Hilbert space. Suppose we had such an idealized token g. Let $\mathcal{E}$ be the set of all $g(E)$ such that E is an orthonormal base (the set of chosen vectors). Note that no two vectors in $\mathcal{E}$ are orthogonal and $E \cap \mathcal{E}$ is a singleton for each orthonormal base E.

Let $\angle(\vec{v}, \vec{w})$ denote the angle between two nonzero vectors, $\vec{v}, \vec{w}$. Because the unit sphere is connected, let $\vec{v}_1$ and $\vec{w}_1$ be unit vectors such that $\vec{w}_1 \in \mathcal{E}$ and $\vec{v}_1 \notin \mathcal{E}$ and $\angle(\vec{v}_1, \vec{w}_1) \leq 1°$. Now, $\mathcal{E}$ contains some, but not all, unit vectors in the complementary space $\vec{v}_1^{\perp}$, so again by connectedness, choose unit vectors $\vec{v}_2$ and $\vec{w}_2$, both orthogonal to v_1, such that $\vec{w}_2 \in \mathcal{E}$ and $\vec{v}_2 \notin \mathcal{E}$ and $\angle(\vec{v}_2, \vec{w}_2) \leq 1°$. Finally, because $\vec{v}_1, \vec{v}_2$ are orthogonal and not in $\mathcal{E}$, there is a unit vector $\vec{w}_3$ orthogonal to them both and in $\mathcal{E}$. So the $\vec{w}_i$ are all in $\mathcal{E}$ $(i = 1, 2, 3)$, and $89° \leq \angle(\vec{w}_i, \vec{w}_j) \leq 91°$ whenever $i \neq j$.   □

Lemma 21.22. *If H is a real Hilbert space, the $\vec{w}_i$ are all nonzero vectors $(i = 1, 2, 3)$, and $89° \leq \angle(\vec{w}_i, \vec{w}_j) \leq 91°$ whenever $i \neq j$, then there is an orthonormal base E for H such that each vector in E is orthogonal to at least one of the $\vec{w}_i$.*

Assuming the lemma, we have a contradiction, because $g(E)$ and some $\vec{w}_i$ will yield two orthogonal vectors in $\mathcal{E}$.

To prove the lemma, note that it is sufficient to prove the lemma for three-dimensional Euclidian space (whence E will have size three), because in the general case, we can produce three orthogonal vectors in the linear span of the $\vec{w}_i$ and extend them arbitrarily to an orthonormal base. Now E will be $\{\vec{p}_1, \vec{p}_2, \vec{p}_3\}$.

Before obtaining E, we fix an orthonormal base, $\{\vec{e}_1, \vec{e}_2, \vec{e}_3\}$ "close to" to $\{\vec{w}_1, \vec{w}_2, \vec{w}_3\}$ as follows. Choose $\vec{e}_1$ parallel to $\vec{w}_1$. Obtain $\vec{e}_2 \perp \vec{e}_1$ in the $(\vec{w}_1, \vec{w}_2)$ plane by rotating $\vec{w}_2$ by $\leq 1°$, so $\angle(\vec{w}_2, \vec{e}_2) \leq 1°$. Then, obtain $\vec{e}_3$ by rotating $\vec{w}_3$ by $\leq 3°$.

Because the lengths of the $\vec{w}_i$ are irrelevant here, we may assume that

$$\vec{w}_1 = \vec{e}_1,$$
$$\vec{w}_2 = a\vec{e}_1 + \vec{e}_2,$$
$$\vec{w}_3 = b\vec{e}_1 + c\vec{e}_2 + \vec{e}_3,$$

where $|a|, |b|, |c| \leq \tan(3°) \leq 0.1$. Let $E = \{\vec{p}_1, \vec{p}_2, \vec{p}_3\}$, where

$$\vec{p}_1 = 0\vec{e}_1 + \cos(\theta)\vec{e}_2 + \sin(\theta)\vec{e}_3,$$
$$\vec{p}_2 = \sin(\varphi)\vec{e}_1 - \cos(\varphi)\sin(\theta)\vec{e}_2 + \cos(\varphi)\cos(\theta)\vec{e}_3,$$
$$\vec{p}_3 = \cos(\varphi)\vec{e}_1 + \sin(\varphi)\sin(\theta)\vec{e}_2 - \sin(\varphi)\cos(\theta)\vec{e}_3,$$

where θ and φ will be determined so that each $\vec{p}_i \perp \vec{w}_i$. Note that if $a = b = c = 0$, then we may take $\theta = \varphi = 0$, whence $\vec{p}_1 = \vec{e}_2$, $\vec{p}_2 = \vec{e}_3$ and $\vec{p}_3 = \vec{e}_1$. In the general case, the fact that a, b, c are small means that we may find small θ, φ that work.

For any values of θ, φ, our E is an orthonormal base and $\vec{p}_1 \perp \vec{w}_1$, so we must choose θ, φ to satisfy

$$a\sin(\varphi) - \cos(\varphi)\sin(\theta) = 0$$

$$b\cos(\varphi) + c\sin(\varphi)\sin(\theta) - \sin(\varphi)\cos(\theta) = 0$$

If $a = 0$, set $\theta = 0$ and choose φ so that $\tan(\varphi) = b$. If $a \neq 0$, choose θ so that $-45° \leq \theta \leq 45°$ and $f(\theta) = ab + c\sin^2(\theta) - \sin(\theta)\cos(\theta) = 0$; this is possible because $f(-45°) > 0 > f(45°)$. Then choose φ such that $a\sin(\varphi) - \cos(\varphi)\sin(\theta) = 0$ (i.e., $\tan(\varphi) = \sin(\theta)/a$). So, $0 = f(\theta)\cos(\varphi)/a = b\cos(\varphi) + c\sin(\varphi)\sin(\theta) - \sin(\varphi)\cos(\theta)$. For small a, b, c, we have (in radians) $\theta \approx ab$ and $\varphi \approx b$.

Corollary 21.23. *If H is a Hilbert space of dimension ≥ 3, then the local logic* $\mathrm{Th}(\mathcal{F}(H))$ *of the frame manual is incoherent.*

Proof. This is an immediate consequence of the theorem and Corollary 21.12. In particular, $\alpha \vdash \beta$ for all α, β whereas there are α, β such that $\alpha \not\leq_M \beta$.   □

This result shows that the Hilbert-space model of quantum mechanics is, in general, incompatible with the view of experiments as represented in our notion of the theory of a manual. Notice that the conflict has nothing at all to do with the meaning of any logical connectives. It has instead to do with two interacting decisions: the decision to have operationally perspective types be equivalent, and the decision to look at only regular theories, thereby building in the principle of Global Cut.

For lack of a better name, let us call a system *deterministic* with respect to a manual M if a token of the system partitions each set of types into those types the token is of and those types it is not of, and if which way a type common to more than one experiment falls is independent of the experiment performed. If we reexamine the proof of soundness of Global Cut in the present context, we see that it depends strongly on the assumption that the system is deterministic in this sense. Our example of the two-experiment manual involving a penny should make this clear. Using this terminology, we see that we cannot think of the set of all orthonormal bases of a Hilbert space (of dimension ≥ 3) as a manual for any deterministic system at all. Hence if the manual of a Hilbert space is a good model of the space of states of fundamental particles, then these particles are not deterministic.

Example 21.24. Recall the manual M for flipping and banging pennies. We can think of a penny c as having a state $\xi(c)$, something that characterizes the distribution of copper in the penny. If we perform either experiment, FLIP or BANG, the outcome will be strongly affected by $\xi(c)$. But it will also be effected by many other factors, like how hard we flip the coin, or at what rate it spins, or how hard we bang the table. These experiments can give us evidence about the state $\xi(c)$ but the outcome of these experiments neither determines nor is completely determined by $\xi(c)$.

Conclusion

It seems like the notion of operationally perspective types is basic to the project of using manuals to give an intuitive account of the logic of quantum mechanics. But it also seems that this notion presupposes that the system under investigation is deterministic in the sense defined above: that its total state can be modeled by an idealized token. For deterministic systems, we have characterized the resulting logic in two different ways, and everything seems quite sensible. But we have also seen that the family of orthonormal bases of a Hilbert space (of dimension ≥ 3) cannot be the manual of a deterministic system.

Exercises

21.1. What are the idealized tokens of the firefly manual and the penny manual?

21.2. Prove Corollary 21.11.

Answers to Selected Exercises

Lecture 4

4.1. The three classifications are discussed in turn.

> **4.4.** In this example typ$(a) =$ the sets of which a is a member, tok$(\alpha) = \alpha$, extensional and separated.
>
> **4.5.** In this example typ$(a) = \{f(a)\}$, tok$(b) = f^{-1}\{b\}$, extensional if f is surjective (or almost surjective: $B - \text{rng}(f)$ is a singleton), separated if f is injective.
>
> **4.6.** Finally, typ$(M) =$ truths of L in M, tok$(\varphi) =$ models making φ true. This is never extensional only because $\varphi \wedge \varphi$ is coextensive with but not identical to φ and never separated because isomorphic structures are indistinguishable.

4.2. For each type α of A, $f(b) \vDash_A \alpha$ if and only if $b \vDash_B f(\alpha)$, by the infomorphism condition, if and only if $b' \vDash_B f(\alpha)$, by indistinguishability, if and only if $f(b') \vDash_A \alpha$, again by the infomorphism condition.

4.3. The condition is that for every type $\alpha \in$ typ(A) there is a type $\beta \in$ typ(B) such that tok$(\alpha) = g\,[\text{tok}(\beta)]$.

4.5. For any token $b \in$ tok(B), $f(b)$ and $g(b)$ have the same types, by the infomorphism condition, and so $f(b) = g(b)$, because A is separated.

4.7. Let $\mathbf{1}$ be a classification with a single type and no tokens. Then for every A there is a unique infomorphism $f : A \rightleftarrows \mathbf{1}$.

Lecture 5

5.1. The isomorphism between $A + \mathbf{o}$ and A is the identity on types. On tokens it takes $\langle a, u \rangle$ to a, where u is the unique token of A. The

256

isomorphism between $A + B$ and $B + A$ is defined on types by taking $\langle 0, \alpha \rangle$ to $\langle 1, \alpha \rangle$ and $\langle 1, \beta \rangle$ to $\langle 0, \beta \rangle$. On tokens it takes $\langle a, b \rangle$ to $\langle b, a \rangle$. It is easy to see that this is an isomorphism. Associativity is similar, if notationally messy.

5.2.   Note that if A is separated, then the identity infomorphism on A respects the invariant $\langle \mathrm{typ}(A), \sim_A \rangle$. Thus, by Proposition 5.18, there is a unique infomorphism $f' : A \rightleftarrows \mathrm{Sep}(A)$ making the following diagram commute:

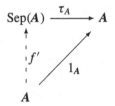

But that implies that f' is the inverse of τ_A, and so τ_A is an isomorphism. The converse is obvious.

5.3.   Suppose that $a_1 \vDash_A \alpha$ and $R_{f,g}(a_1, a_2)$ and $\alpha \in A_{f,g}$. Then there is a token b such that $f(b) = a_1$ and $g(b) = a_2$, and so $b \vDash_B f(\alpha)$ by the infomorphism condition on f. But $f(\alpha) = g(\alpha)$ because $\alpha \in A$, and so $a_2 \vDash_A \alpha$, by the infomorphism condition on g. Hence $I_{f,g}$ is an invariant of A.

To show that $h : C \rightleftarrows A$ respects $\langle A_{f,g}, R_{f,g} \rangle$ if and only if $fh = gh$, note the following equivalences:

1. $h(\gamma) \in A_{f,g}$ iff $f\hat{\ }(h\hat{\ }(\gamma)) = g\hat{\ }(h\hat{\ }(\gamma))$
                  iff $fh(\gamma) = gh(\gamma)$.
2. $R_{f,g}(a_1, a_2)$ iff $\exists b \ f(b) = a_1$ and $g(b) = a_2$
                  iff $\exists b \ fh(b) = h\check{\ }(f\check{\ }(b)) = h\check{\ }(a_1)$ and
                            $gh(b) = h\check{\ }(g\check{\ }(b)) = h\check{\ }(a_2)$.

If $fh = gh$, then by (1) $h(\gamma) \in A_{f,g}$ for all $\gamma \in \mathrm{typ}(C)$; and if $R_{f,g}$ (a_1, a_2), then $h(a_1) = h(a_2)$ by (2), as required. If, on the other hand $fh \neq gh$, then either there is a $\gamma \in \mathrm{typ}(C)$ such that $f\hat{\ }(h\hat{\ }(\gamma)) \neq g\hat{\ }(h\hat{\ }(\gamma))$ and so by (1) $h(\gamma) \neq A_{f,g}$, or there is a $b \in \mathrm{tok}(B)$ such that $fh(b) \neq gh(b)$, so that $h\check{\ }(f\check{\ }(b)) \neq h\check{\ }(g\check{\ }(b))$; but $R_{f,g}(f\check{\ }(b), g\check{\ }(b))$ by definition of $R_{f,g}$, and so h does not respect $\langle A_{f,g}, R_{f,g} \rangle$.

To show that $\tau_{I_{f,g}}$ is the equalizer of f and g, we must show that for every infomorphism $h : C \rightleftarrows A$ for which $fh = gh$ there is a unique infomorphism $h' : C \rightleftarrows A/I_{f,g}$ making the following diagram commute:

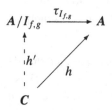

Given the equivalence just proved, this is just a restatement of Proposition 5.18.

Finally, for any invariant $I = \langle \Sigma, R \rangle$ of a classification A, we can define a classification B and infomorphisms $f_0 : A \rightleftarrows B$ and $f_1 : A \rightleftarrows B$ such that τ_I is the equalizer of f_0 and f_1. First, let $A' = \{\langle i, \alpha \rangle \mid i \in \{0, 1\}, \alpha \in \text{typ}(A) - A\}$ be the disjoint union of $\text{typ}(A) - A$ with itself. Now define B to be the classification whose types are members of $A \cup A'$, whose tokens are the pairs $\langle a_0, a_1 \rangle$ for which $R(a_0, a_1)$, and such that

1. for $\alpha \in A$, $\langle a_0, a_1 \rangle \vDash_{A'} \alpha$ if and only if $a_0 \vDash_A \alpha$, and
2. for $\langle i, \alpha \rangle \in A'$, $\langle a_0, a_1 \rangle \vDash_{A'} \langle i, \alpha \rangle$ if and only if $a_i \vDash_A \alpha$.

Define $f_i : A \rightleftarrows B$ by $f_i \langle a_0, a_1 \rangle = a_i$ and

$$f_i(\alpha) = \begin{cases} \alpha & \text{if } \alpha \in A \\ \langle i, \alpha \rangle & \text{if } \alpha \notin A \end{cases}.$$

It is easy to see that $A_{f_0, f_1} = A$ and $R_{f_0, f_1} = R$.

Lecture 6

6.3. Hint: In the first section we showed how to take a sequential composition of channels. The limit construction can also be used to take a parallel composition of channels. Suppose we have two separate channels connecting A_1 and A_2, say $\mathcal{C}_1 = \{f_i : A_i \rightleftarrows B_1\}_{i \in \{1,2,\}}$ and $\mathcal{C}_2 = \{g_i : A_i \rightleftarrows B_2\}_{i \in \{1,2,\}}$. This can be seen as a distributed system with four classifications and four infomorphisms. Determine its minimal cover. Simplify it by obtaining an isomorphic structure that has less redundant structure. Interpret this cover in informational terms.

Lecture 7

7.1. Suppose A is Boolean and that X is closed under indistinguishability. Show that X is represented by the type

$$\alpha = \bigvee_{a \in X} \bigwedge \text{typ}(a).$$

Clearly, every $a \in X$ is of type α. For the converse, suppose that $a' \vDash_A \alpha$. Then there is some $a \in X$ such that $a' \vDash_A \bigwedge \text{typ}(a)$. We show that a' is indistinguishable from a and so is in X, because X is closed under indistinguishability. Clearly, every type of a is a type of a'. Suppose $a' \vDash_A \alpha'$. Then $a' \nvDash_A \neg\alpha'$, so $a \nvDash_A \neg\alpha'$. Hence $a \vDash_A \alpha$. Thus a is indistinguishable from a'.

For the converse, suppose that for every set X closed under indistinguishablity there is a type α such that $X = \text{typ}(\alpha)$. We show that A has a conjunction, disjunction, and negation. Let us start by showing negation. Let $\beta \in \text{typ}(A)$ be arbitrary. The set $\text{tok}(A) - \text{tok}(\beta)$ is closed under indistinguishablity so it is definable by some type. Choose one and let that be the negation of β. This clearly has the desired properties. Now suppose that Θ is an arbitrary set of types. Let $X = \bigcup_{\beta \in \Theta} \text{tok}(\beta)$. Clearly, X is closed under indistinguishablity. Hence it is definable by some type α. Pick such an α and let that be the disjunction of Θ. Conjunction is similar or can be defined in terms of disjunction and negation.

Lecture 8

8.1. Let $A = B = \text{Evt}(S_{DNA})$, and let C be the restriction of $\text{Evt}(S_{DNA})$ to those tokens that have successfully split. Let $f : A \rightleftarrows C$ and $b : B \rightleftarrows C$ be type-identical infomorphisms that on tokens are defined so that $f(c)$ is one of c's offspring and $g(c)$ is the other. The infomorphism condition on c is the condition that the splitting is normal, that is, that no mutation takes place.

8.2. If $f : S_1 \rightleftarrows S_2$ is an isomorphism, then $\langle f^\wedge, f^{\vee-1} \rangle$ is a projection satisfying the above conditions. Conversely, if $f : S_1 \rightrightarrows S_2$ is a projection and both $f^\wedge$ and $f^\vee$ are bijections, we show that $\langle f^\wedge, f^{\vee-1} \rangle$ is an isomorphism. The only thing that needs to be checked is that it is an infomorphism. Let $b \in \text{tok}(S_2)$ and $\alpha \in \text{typ}(S_1)$. The following are equivalent:

$$
\begin{aligned}
f(b) \vDash_{S_1} \alpha \quad &\text{iff} \quad \text{state}_{S_1}(f(b)) = \alpha && \text{(by definition of } state_{S_1}) \\
&\text{iff} \quad f(\text{state}_{S_2}(b)) = \alpha && \text{(because } f \text{ is a projection)} \\
&\text{iff} \quad \text{state}_{S_2}(b) = f^{-1}(\alpha) && \text{(because } f\hat{} \text{ is a bijection)} \\
&\text{iff} \quad b \vDash_{S_2} f^{-1}(\alpha) && \text{(by definition of } state_{S_2})
\end{aligned}
$$

8.4.   Here f is the identity on types and is $f(s) = \text{state}_S(s)$ on tokens s.

Lecture 9

9.1.   The direction from left to right is immediate; if T is inconsistent, then $\Gamma \vdash_T \Delta$ for all sequents. The other direction follows from the fact that regular theories satisfy Weakening.

9.2.   The reflexivity of $\leq_T$ follows from Identity. The transitivity follows from Finite Cut. Saying that T is algebraic is equivalent to

if $\alpha \vdash_T \beta$ and $\beta \vdash_T \alpha$ then $\alpha = \beta$.

If $T = \text{Th}(A)$, then this is equivalent to

$\text{tok}(\alpha) \subseteq \text{tok}(\beta)$ and $\text{tok}(\beta) \subseteq \text{tok}(\alpha)$ implies $\alpha = \beta$.

But this is equivalent to

$\text{tok}(\alpha) = \text{tok}(\beta)$ implies $\alpha = \beta$,

which is the definition of extensionality.

9.3.   Define $\Gamma \vdash_T \Delta$ if and only if $\alpha \leq \beta$ for some $\alpha \in \Gamma$ and some $\beta \in \Delta$. Verify that this theory is regular.

9.4.   (1) The consequence relation is given by

$$\Gamma \vdash \Delta \quad \text{iff} \quad \Gamma \cap \Delta \neq \emptyset$$

for all sequents $\langle \Gamma, \Delta \rangle$ of Σ. Check that this is a regular theory. It is clearly contained in every such theory. Its ordering $\leq_T$ is the identity relation on Σ, which is a partial ordering, so the theory is algebraic. (2) The largest regular consequence relation is simply the set of all sequents. It is not algebraic if there is more than one type in Σ.

9.5.   Let $\text{state}_A(a) = \langle \Gamma_a, \Delta_a \rangle$. The following are equivalent:

> a is a counterexample to $\langle \Gamma, \Delta \rangle$
>
> $\Gamma \subseteq \Gamma_a$ but $\Delta \cap \Gamma_a = \emptyset$ (defn. satisfaction)
>
> $\Gamma \subseteq \Gamma_a$ and $\Delta \subseteq \Delta_a$ ($\langle \Gamma_a, \Delta_a \rangle$ a partition)
>
> $\langle \Gamma, \Delta \le \langle \Gamma_a, \Delta_a \rangle$ (defn. $\le$)

9.8.   The direction from left to right is immediate. For the converse, suppose $\vdash$ is closed under Identity, Weakening, and Finite Cut. Show that the relation satisfies Partition and hence Global Cut. To show Partition, show that every consistent sequent can be extended to a consistent partition. Suppose that $\langle \Gamma, \Delta \rangle$ is consistent. Let X be the set of consistent extensions of $\langle \Gamma, \Delta \rangle$. By compactness, $\langle X, \le \rangle$ is closed under unions of chains, so, by Zorn's Lemma, it has a maximal element, say $\langle \Gamma', \Delta' \rangle$. This sequent must be a consistent partition extending $\langle \Gamma, \Delta \rangle$. To see this, note that $\Gamma' \cap \Delta' = \emptyset$ by Identity. To see that $\Gamma' \cup \Delta' = \Sigma$, suppose $\alpha \in \Sigma$ but $\alpha \notin \Gamma' \cup \Delta'$. By maximality, the sequents $\langle \Gamma', \Delta' \cup \{\alpha\} \rangle$ and $\langle \{\alpha\} \cup \Gamma', \Delta' \rangle$ are constraints. In other words, $\Gamma' \vdash \Delta', \alpha$ and $\Gamma', \alpha \vdash \Delta'$. Then by Finite Cut, $\Gamma' \vdash \Delta'$, contradicting the consistency of $\langle \Gamma', \Delta' \rangle$.

9.9.   It is straightforward to check that $\vdash$ satisfies Identity, Weakening, and Finite Cut. To prove that it is not regular, let $\Gamma = \Delta = \emptyset$. Notice that every partition of Σ extending $\langle \Gamma, \Delta \rangle$ is a constraint of $\vdash$. By Partition, $\Gamma \vdash \Delta$. But this violates the definition of $\vdash$.

9.10.   Part (1) follows easily using Partition. For Part (2), suppose $\Gamma, \Gamma' \vdash \Delta$ and for each $\alpha \in \Gamma'$, $\Gamma \vdash \Delta, \alpha$ but $\Gamma \nvdash \Delta$. Then $\Gamma \cap \Delta = \emptyset$ and $\Gamma \cup \Delta$ has an infinite complement. Thus either Γ' contains infinite many types not in $\Gamma \cup \Delta$ or it contains an element $\alpha_0 \in \Delta$. The latter can't be true because $\Gamma \vdash \Delta, \alpha_0$ and the right side of this is just Δ. But if the former is the case, pick some such $\alpha_1 \in \Gamma'$. Then $\Gamma \vdash \Delta, \alpha_1$. But this cannot be because both sides are disjoint but the complement of their union is still infinite. Part (3) follows immediately from parts (1) and (2) and the fact that this consequence relation is not regular.

9.12.   This is an easy consequence of the observation that $\alpha \not\le_T \beta$ if and only if there is a consistent partition $\langle \Gamma, \Delta \rangle$ with $\alpha \in \Gamma$ and $\beta \in \Delta$.

9.15.   Define $f^{*\wedge} = f$ and $f^{*\vee}(a) = \langle f^{-1}[\Gamma_a], f^{-1}[\Delta_a] \rangle$ where $\langle \Gamma_a, \Delta_a \rangle$ is state description of a in A.

Lecture 10

10.1.   (1) If $A \sqsubseteq B$, then typ(A) $\subseteq$ typ(B). Also, if $\langle \Gamma, \Delta \rangle$ is a sequent of typ(A) and $\Gamma \nvdash_B \Delta$, then $\langle \Gamma, \Delta \rangle$ has a counterexample $b \in$ tok(B), so b must also be a counterexample to $\langle \Gamma, \Delta \rangle$ in A because $A \sqsubseteq B$; hence $\Gamma \nvdash_A \Delta$. (2) If the converse of (1) holds, then $A = B$ if and only if Th(A) = Th(B). But that can't be. Just take some nontrival classification A and a similar classification with an additional token that is indistinguishable from some token of A. They have the same theories.

Lecture 11

11.1.   Let f be type identical and on tokens be defined by

$$f(\langle \Gamma, \Delta \rangle) = \langle \Delta, \Gamma \rangle.$$

It is easy to check that this is an isomorphism.

11.4.   These results are easy consequences of the rules for the connectives. For negation, what follows is that $\neg\neg\alpha = \alpha$ and that $\alpha \leq_T \beta$ if and only if $\neg\beta \leq_T \neg\alpha$.

Lecture 12

12.1.   (1) It is clear that every normal token of $\mathfrak{L} \mid \Theta$ satisfies every constraint of $\mathfrak{L} \mid \Theta$. We also need to check that the theory of $\mathfrak{L} \mid \Theta$ is regular. Weakening is clear. To show Partition, suppose $\Gamma \nvdash_{\mathfrak{L}\mid\Theta} \Delta$. Then $\Gamma, \Theta \nvdash_{\mathfrak{L}} \Delta$. Let $\langle \Gamma', \Delta' \rangle$ be a consistent partition of typ($\mathfrak{L}$) extending $\langle \Gamma \cup \Theta, \Delta \rangle$. Then $\langle \Gamma' - \Theta, \Delta' \rangle$ is an extension of $\langle \Gamma, \Delta \rangle$ that is a consistent partition in $\mathfrak{L} \mid \Theta$. (3) Let θ be a new type not in typ($\mathfrak{L}$) and let A be the classification that is just like cla($\mathfrak{L}$) except that A has the additional type θ with typ(θ) $= N_{\mathfrak{L}}$. Our sound local logic will have A for its classification. Because the logic is to be sound, we need only specify its theory. Let $\Gamma \vdash_{\mathfrak{L}'} \Delta$ if and only if one of the following conditions hold:

1. $\theta \notin \Gamma$ and $\Gamma \cap \Delta \neq \emptyset$.
2. $\theta \in \Gamma \cap \Delta$.
3. $\theta \in \Gamma - \Delta$ and $\Gamma - \{\theta\} \vdash_{\mathfrak{L}} \Delta$.

Clearly every token of A satisfies all these constraints; they satisfy the constraints in (3) because $\mathfrak{L}$ is a local logic and typ(θ) $= N_{\mathfrak{L}}$. So we need only verify that this is indeed a regular theory. We check Partition, leaving Weakening to the reader. Suppose $\Gamma \nvdash_{\mathfrak{L}'} \Delta$. There are two cases to consider. If $\theta \notin \Gamma$, then $\Gamma \cap \Delta = \emptyset$ by (1). Let $\Gamma' = \Gamma$ and $\Delta' = \text{typ}(\mathfrak{L}') - \Gamma$. Then $\langle \Gamma', \Delta' \rangle$ is a consistent partition extending $\langle \Gamma, \Delta \rangle$. So suppose $\theta \in \Gamma$. Then $\theta \notin \Delta$ by (2) and $\Gamma - \{\theta\} \nvdash_{\mathfrak{L}} \Delta$ by (3). Because th($\mathfrak{L}$) is regular, there is a consistent partition $\langle \Gamma', \Delta' \rangle$ of $\mathfrak{L}$ extending $\langle \Gamma - \{\theta\}, \Delta \rangle$. But then $\langle \Gamma' \cup \{\theta\}, \Delta' \rangle$ is a consistent partition of $\mathfrak{L}'$ extending $\langle \Gamma, \Delta \rangle$. Hence every consistent sequent of $\mathfrak{L}'$ has a consistent partition extending it. It is easy to check that $\mathfrak{L} = \mathfrak{L} | \theta$.

12.2.   Let us write $\Gamma \vdash \Delta$ if and only if one of the conditions (a)–(c) holds. We first check that this is a regular consequence relation. It clearly satisfies Weakening. To see that it satisfies Partition, suppose that $\Gamma \nvdash \Delta$. We want to find a consistent partition $\langle \Gamma', \Delta' \rangle$ extending $\langle \Gamma, \Delta \rangle$, that is, such that $\Gamma' \nvdash \Delta'$. By (a), Γ and Δ are disjoint. By (b), Γ contains at most one state. There are now two cases to consider, depending on whether Γ is empty or a singleton. If $\Gamma = \{\sigma\}$, then we let $\Gamma' = \Gamma$ and let $\Delta' = \Omega - \{\sigma\}$, and we have our desired consistent partition. If $\Gamma = \emptyset$, then we apply (c) to find some $\sigma \notin \Delta$ and let $\Gamma' = \{\sigma\}$ and let $\Delta' = \Omega - \{\sigma\}$, again finding a consistent partition. This shows that $\vdash$ is a regular consequence relation. It is clear that every token satisfies every constraint of this relation, so we have a sound logic. Hence the logic it must contain the logic Triv(S). On the other hand, by Weakening, each of the sequents above is a constraint of Triv(S).

12.4   The logic $\mathbf{1}$ is Log($\mathbf{1}$), where $\mathbf{1} = \mathbf{0}^{\perp}$.

12.3   In each case the bijection between Hom-sets is obvious. For the left adjointness, one just needs to check that an infomorphism $f : A \rightleftarrows \text{cla}(\mathfrak{L})$ preserves constraints and so becomes a logic infomorphism from Log(A) to $\mathfrak{L}$; this uses the completeness of $\mathfrak{L}$. For the right adjointness, we need to know that the pair of identity functions on tok($\mathfrak{L}$) and typ($\mathfrak{L}$) preserves normal tokens and so is a logic infomorphism from $\mathfrak{L}$ to Log(cla($\mathfrak{L}$)); this uses the soundness of $\mathfrak{L}$.

12.7.   The direction from left to right is immediate. That from right to left is almost as immediate. It is basically the proof of Proposition 10.3.

12.9.   First prove that if $B_0 \subseteq B_1$, then $\text{typ}(B_1) \subseteq \text{typ}(B_0)$. Use this, plus Exercise 1, to prove the result.

12.10.   Let $\mathcal{L}$ be a local logic on a classification A of types and let J be an invariant on A.

1. The logic $\mathcal{L}/I$ is the largest logic on A/I such that the function τ_I is a logic infomorphism.

2. Let $f : \mathcal{L} \rightleftarrows \mathcal{L}'$ be a logic infomorphism that respects I. There is a unique logic infomorphism $f' : \mathcal{L}' \rightleftarrows \mathcal{L}/I$ such that the following diagram commutes:

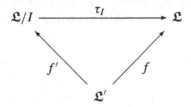

12.12.   This is just definition unwinding.

Lecture 13

13.1.   Let f be the unque infomorphism from o to A. Then $\mathrm{AP}(A) = f[o]$, where this o is the zero logic.

Lecture 15

15.1.   Sketch: The information system has the same shape as that used to illustrate the Xerox principle in Lecture 6. We need five classifications, three for classifying molecules and two for classifying processes. First, we need the classification $\mathrm{Evt}(S_{DNA})$ introduced in Example 8.16 We need a second classification for RNA molecules and a third for classifying protein molecules. As for the process classifications, we need one to classify events where a piece of DNA gives rise to a molecule of messenger RNA (notice the informational vocabulary) and one to classify the process whereby an RNA molecule gives rise to a protein. We can turn this into an information system by imposing a logic on each of these classifications, namely, the logics that represent our current understanding of these classifications. Taking the distributed logic of the system gives us a theory of information flow linking all five. As for the one-way flow posulated by the fundamental dogma, we can see that complete information about the strand of DNA gives rise to complete information about the molecule of RNA but that the converse is not the case and similarly, complete information about the molecule of RNA gives rise to complete information about the protein, but the converse is not the case.

15.2. **Definition A.1.** A *logic channel* C is an indexed family $\{h_i^c : \mathfrak{L}_i \rightleftarrows$ core$(C)\}_{i \in I}$ of logic infomorphisms with a common codomain, called the *core* of C.

Definition A.2.

1. Given an index set I and logic channels $C = \{h_i : \mathfrak{L}_i \rightleftarrows \mathfrak{L}\}_{i \in I}$ and $C' = \{h_i' : \mathfrak{L}_i' \rightleftarrows \mathfrak{L}'\}_{i \in I}$, a *logic channel infomorphism* $f : C \rightleftarrows C'$ consists of logic infomorphisms $f : \mathfrak{L} \rightleftarrows \mathfrak{L}'$ and $f_i : \mathfrak{L}_i \rightleftarrows \mathfrak{L}_i'$ such that for each $i \in I$, the following diagram commutes:

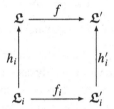

If $\mathfrak{L}_i = \mathfrak{L}_i'$ and $f_i = 1_{\mathfrak{L}_i}$ for each $i \in I$, then f is called a *logic refinement infomorphism* and C is said to be a *logic refinement* of C'.

2. A logic channel $C = \{h_i : \mathfrak{L}_i \rightleftarrows \mathfrak{L}\}_{i \in I}$ *covers* an information system $\mathcal{L}$ if log$(\mathcal{L}) = \{\mathfrak{L}_i\}_{i \in I}$ and for each $i, j \in I$ and each infomorphism $f : \mathfrak{L}_i \rightleftarrows \mathfrak{L}_j$ in inf$(\mathcal{L})$, the following diagram commutes:

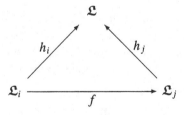

C is a *minimal cover* of $\mathcal{L}$ if it covers $\mathcal{L}$ and for every other channel $\mathcal{D}$ covering $\mathcal{L}$ there is a unique logic refinement infomorphism from C to $\mathcal{D}$.

Theorem A.3. *Every information system has a minimal cover. It is unique up to isomorphism.*

To prove this, let $\mathcal{L}$ be an information system with the indexed family $\log(\mathcal{L}) = \{\mathfrak{L}_i\}_{i \in I}$ of local logics together with the set $\inf(\mathcal{L})$ of logic infomorphisms. From it, extract the obvious distributed system with classifications $\mathrm{cla}(\mathfrak{L})_i$ and infomorphisms $\mathrm{Cla}(f)$, for $f \in \inf(\mathcal{L})$. Let $\mathcal{C} = \{h_i^c : \mathrm{cla}(\mathfrak{L})_i \rightleftarrows C\}_{i \in I}$ be the information channel that is the minimal cover of this system. We turn this into a logic channel by taking $\mathfrak{L} = \bigsqcup_{i \in I} h_i^c[\mathfrak{L}_i]$. By earlier results, this is the smallest logic on C making all of the infomorphisms h_i^c into logic infomorphisms. It is easy to verify that this is the minimal cover of the information system. Uniqueness is routine.

Lecture 16

16.2. This proof is just definition unwinding.

16.3. We prove (1) and leave (2) to the reader. Both state spaces are subspaces of $\mathrm{Ssp}(A)$, so we need only check that they have the same sets of tokens and same states. It is clear that both state spaces have as sets of tokens the set $f^{\smile}[N_{\mathfrak{L}_2}]$, so we need only check that they have the same set of states. The states of $\mathrm{Ssp}(f^{-1}[\mathfrak{L}_2])$ consist of those partitions of $\mathrm{typ}(A)$ that are consistent in $f^{-1}[\mathfrak{L}_2]$. These are exactly the set of partitions of the form $\langle f^{-1}[\Gamma_2], f^{-1}[\Delta_2]\rangle$ for some consistent partition $\langle \Gamma_2, \Delta_2 \rangle$ of $\mathfrak{L}_2$. These, in turn, are exactly the states of $\mathrm{Ssp}(f)[\mathrm{Ssp}(\mathfrak{L}_2)]$.

Lecture 18

18.1. The answer is "No" if the building and person are both tokens of the the same height classification and the building is taller than the person. However, if we allow that the classification of buildings by height is a different classification than that of people by height, then there is no problem.

18.2. Let $r = \langle .1, [0, 48), [48, 60), [60, +\infty)\rangle$. This is the most natural regimentation for A, given the way the problem was stated.

18.3. The classification is determinate, because $.1 \leq .25$, and it is precise because these three intervals exhaust the positive real numbers.

18.4. The sorites number of $\mathrm{Log}_r^{\circ}(A)$ is $(.1)^{-1} \times (60 - 48) + 1 = 121$, so this provides a natural upper bound for the Sorites number of A.

18.5. The sorites number of A depends only on the resulting classification, not on any particular regimentation. Another regimentation that would yield the same classification, the one with the largest possible tolerance, is $r' = \langle .25, [0, 48), [48, 60), [60, +\infty) \rangle$. The sorites number of $\text{Log}^{\circ}_{r'}(A)$ is $(.25)^{-1} \times (60 - 48) + 1 = 49$. To find the Sorites number of A we must minimize the distance between the upper endpoint of I_s and the lower endpoint of I_t, while making the tolerance as large as possible. Let h_1 and h_2 be the heights of the shortest and tallest students of medium height. Thus $h_1 \geq 48$ and $h_2 < 60$. This results in a third regimentation $r'' = \langle .25, [0, h_1), [h_1, h_2], (h_2, +\infty) \rangle$. For this logic the number is the least integer $N > (.25)^{-1} \times (h_2 - h_1)$. Thus, given the information about the shortest and tallest girls of medium height, the sorites number of the classification is $4 \times (58.5 - 49) + 1 = 39$.

Lecture 21

21.1. The idealized tokens of the fire fly manual and the penny manual correspond to the rows of the following tables, respectively:

FRONT	SIDE	FLIP	BANG
L	F	H	H
L	B	T	T
R	F		
R	B		
N	N		

21.2. This is a consequence of Theorem 21.10 Let c be an idealized token of type $\Omega_E - \sigma$ and not of type $\Omega_F - \sigma$. In other words, $c_F \in \sigma$ but $c_E \notin \sigma$. However, this contradicts the fact that c is an idealized token, because σ is a subset of both Ω_E and Ω_F.

Bibliography

Auster, P. (1982). *The Invention of Solitude*. London and Boston: Faber and Faber.

Austin, J. L. (1961). How to talk: Some simple ways. In *Philosophical Papers*. J. O. Urmson and G. J. Warnock, eds. Oxford University Press, Oxford.

Barr, M. (1979). **-Autonomous Categories*. Lecture Notes in Mathematics, 752. Springer-Verlag, Heidelberg.

Barr, M. (1991). *-Autonomous categories and linear logic. *Mathematical Structures in Computer Science*, **1**, 159–178.

Barwise, J. (1983). Information and semantics. *The Behavioral and Brain Sciences*, **6**, 65.

Barwise, J. (1986). Information and circumstance: A reply to Fodor. *Notre Dame Journal of Formal Logic*, **27**(3), 324–338.

Barwise, J. (1989). *The Situation in Logic*. Number 17, CSLI Lecture Notes. CSLI Publications, Stanford, Calif.

Barwise, J. (1991). Information links in domain theory. In *Proceedings of the Mathematical Foundations of Programming Semantics Conference (1991)*, S. Brookes, ed., pp. 168–192. Springer-Verlag, Heidelberg.

Barwise, J. (1993). Constraints, channels, and the flow of information. In *Situation Theory and Its Applications, II*, Number 22, CSLI Lecture Notes. P. Aczel et al., eds., pp. 3–27. CSLI Publications, Stanford, Calif.

Barwise, J., and J. Etchemendy (1990). Information, infons, and inference. In *Situation Theory and Its Applications, I*, Number 22, CSLI Lecture Notes. R. Cooper, K. Mukai, and J. Perry, eds., pp. 33–78. CSLI Publications, Stanford, Calif.

Barwise, J., and J. Etchemendy (1995). *Hyperproof*. Number 42, CSLI Lecture Notes. CSLI Publications, Stanford, Calif.

Barwise, J., and J. Perry (1983). *Situations and Attitudes*. MIT Press, Cambridge, Mass.

Barwise, J., and J. Seligman (1994). The rights and wrongs of natural regularity. In *Perspectives in Philosophy, 8*, J. Tomberlin, ed., pp. 331–364. Ridgeview, Atascadero, Calif.

Barwise, J., D. Gabbay, and C. Hartonas (1996). Information flow and the Lambek calculus. In Logic, Language and Computation. Number 26, CSLI Lecture Notes. J. Seligman and D. Westerståhl, eds., pp. 47–62. CSLI Publications, Stanford, Calif.

Birkhoff, G. (1940). *Lattice Theory*. Colloquium Publications. American Math Society, Providence, R.I.

Casti, J. (1992). *Reality Rules, I*. Wiley Interscience, New York.

Cohen, D. W. (1989). *An Introduction to Hilbert Space and Quantum Logic*. Problem Books in Mathematics. Springer-Verlag, New York.

Davey, B., and H. Priestley (1990). *Introduction to Lattices and Order*. Cambridge Mathematical Textbooks, Cambridge, U.K.

Devlin, K. (1991). *Logic and Information*. Cambridge, U.K.: Cambridge University Press.

Dretske, F. (1970). Epistemic operators. *Journal of Philosophy*, **67**, 1007–1023.

Dretske, F. (1971). Conclusive reason. *Australasian Journal of Philosophy*, **49**, 1–22.

Dretske, F. (1981). *Knowledge and the Flow of Information*. MIT Press, Cambridge, Mass.

Gettier, E. (1963). Is justified true belief knowledge? *Analysis*, **43**, 181–4.

Goldman, A. (1979). What is justified belief? In *Justification and Knowledge*. G. Papas, ed. 1–23. Reidel, Dordrecht.

Goldman, A. (1986). *Epistemology and Cognition*. Harvard University Press, Cambridge, Mass.

Hardegree, G. (1982). An approach to the logic of natural kinds. *Pacific Phil. Quarterly*, **63**, 122–132.

Hartonis, C., and J. M. Dunn (1993). Duality theorems for partial orders, semilattics, galois connections and lattices. Technical report, #IULG-93-26. Preprint Indiana University Logic Group. Bloomington, IN.

Hayes, P. (1985). Naive physics, i, Ontology for liquids. In *Formal Theories of the Commonsense World*, R. Hobbs and R. Moore, eds., pp. 71–108. Ablex Press, Norwood, New Jersey.

Kochen, S., and E. Specker (1967). The problem of hidden variables in quantum mechanics. *Journal of Mathematics and Mechanics*, **17**, 59–87.

Koons, R. (1996). Information, representation, and the possibility of error. In *Logic, Language and Computation*. Number 58, CSLI Lecture Notes, J. Seligman and D. Westerståhl, eds., pp. 333–346. CSLI Publications, Stanford, Calif.

Lewis, D. (1973). *Counterfactuals*. Harvard University Press, Cambridge, Mass.

Nozick, R. (1981). *Philosophical Explanations*. Harvard University Press, Cambridge, Mass.

Rabin, M. (1974). Decidable theories. In *Handbook of Mathematical Logic*. J. Barwise, ed. North Holland, Amsterdam.

Seligman, J. (1990). Perspectives in situation theory. In *Situation Theory and Its Applications, I*, Number 22, CSLI Lecture Notes. R. Cooper, K. Mukai, and J. Perry, eds., pp. 147–191. CSLI Publications. Stanford, Calif.

Seligman, J. (1991a). *Perspectives: A Relativistic Approach to the Theory of Information*. Ph.D. thesis, University of Edinburgh.

Seligman, J. (1991b). Physical situations and information flow. In *Situation Theory and Its Applications, II*, Number 26, CSLI Lecture Notes, J. Barwise et al., eds. pp. 257–292. CSLI Publications, Stanford, Calif.

Shannon, C. (1948). The mathematical theory of communication. *Bell System Technical Journal, July and October*, Volume 27, pp. 37–423; 623–656.

Shimojima, A. (1996). *On the Efficacy of Representation*. Ph.D. thesis, Indiana University, Bloomington, IN.

Shope, R. (1983). *The Analysis of Knowing*. Princeton University Press, Princeton, N.J.

Stalnaker, R. (1984). *Inquiry*. MIT Press, Cambridge, Mass.

Swain, M. (1981). *Reasons and Knowledge*. Cornell University Press, Ithaca, N.Y.

Glossary of Notation

AP(A): The *a priori* logic on the classification A.

Boole(A): The Boolean closure of the classification A.

Cha($\mathfrak{L}$): The binary channel representing the local logic $\mathfrak{L}$, a channel relating the classification cla($\mathfrak{L}$) with the idealization Idl($\mathfrak{L}$) of $\mathfrak{L}$.

cla($\mathcal{A}$): The classifications of the distributed system $\mathcal{A}$.

cla($\mathfrak{L}$): The classification of the local logic $\mathfrak{L}$.

Cla(T): The classification generated by the regular theory T.

Cla(f): The infomorphism associated with the theory interpretation f.

Cmp($\mathfrak{L}$): The completion of the local logic $\mathfrak{L}$.

core(C): The core classification of a channel C.

DLog$_C$($\mathfrak{L}$): The logic obtained by distributing the logic $\mathfrak{L}$ on the core of the channel C to its component classifications.

DLog($\mathcal{S}$): The logic obtained by distributing the logic on the core of the state space $\mathcal{S}$ to its projected state spaces.

Evt($\mathcal{S}$): The event classifications generated by the state space $\mathcal{S}$.

Evt(f): The infomorphism on event classifications corresponding to a projection f of the generating state spaces.

Idl($\mathfrak{L}$): The idealization classification of the local logic $\mathfrak{L}$.

inf($\mathcal{A}$): The infomorphisms of the distributed system $\mathcal{A}$.

lim $\mathcal{A}$: The limit channel of the distributed system $\mathcal{A}$.

Lind($\mathfrak{L}$): The Lindenbaum logic of $\mathfrak{L}$.

Log($\mathcal{L}$): The systemwide logic of an information system.

Log(A): The local logic generated by the classification A.

Log$_C$ (D): The local logic on the distal classification D generated by the binary channel C.

Log(f): The logic infomorphism naturally associated with an infomorphism, projection, or interpretation f.

Log($\mathcal{L}$): The systemwide logic of an information system $\mathcal{L}$.

Log(S): The local logic generated by the state space S.

Log(T): The local logic generated by the regular theory T.

SC($\mathfrak{L}$): The sound completion the local logic $\mathfrak{L}$.

Sep(A): The separated quotient of A, obtained by identifying indistinguishable tokens.

Snd($\mathfrak{L}$): The sound part of the local logic $\mathfrak{L}$.

Ssp(A): The free state space generated by a classification A.

Ssp(f): The state-space projection generated by the infomorphism f.

Ssp($\mathfrak{L}$): The state space generated by the logic $\mathfrak{L}$.

state$_S$ (a): The state of the object a in the state space S.

state$_A$ (a): The state description of a in the classification A.

Th(A): The theory of the classification A.

Th(f): The interpretation associated with an infomorphism f or a projection.

tok(A): The set of tokens of the classification A.

Triv(S): The trivial logic on a state space.

typ(A): The set of types of the classification A.

$\vDash_A$: The classification relation of A.

$f : A \rightleftarrows B$: f is a contravariant pair of functions, typically an infomorphism.

$f^{\wedge}$: The type part of an infomorphism or projection.

$f^{\vee}$: The token part of an infomorphism or projection.

1_A: The identity infomorphism of the classification A.

h_i^C: The ith infomorphism of the channel C.

$A^{\perp}$: The flip dual of the classification A, obtained by interchanging types and tokens.

$f^{\perp}$: The flip dual of the infomorphism f.

$A + B$: The sum of the classifications A and B.

σ_A: The infomorphism $\sigma_A : A \rightleftarrows A + B$ from the classification A into the sum $A + B$.

A/I: The quotient of A by the invariant I. The notation A/J is likewise used for the dual notion when J is a dual invariant.

$A \mid \Sigma$: The restriction of the classification A to the types in Σ.

τ_I: The canonical quotient infomorphism $\tau_I : A/I \rightleftarrows A$.

$\vee A$: The disjunctive power classification of the classification A.

$\wedge A$: The conjunctive power classification of the classification A.

η_A^d: The natural embedding infomorphism of A into its disjunctive power $\vee A$.

η_A^c: The natural embedding infomorphism of A into its conjunctive power $\wedge A$.

$\neg A$: The negation of the classification A.

$\vee f$: The lifting of $f : A \rightleftarrows B$ to $\vee f : \vee A \rightleftarrows \vee B$.

$\wedge f$: The lifting of $f : A \rightleftarrows B$ to $\wedge f : \wedge A \rightleftarrows \wedge B$.

$\neg f$: The lifting of $f : A \rightleftarrows B$ to $\neg f : \neg A \rightleftarrows \neg B$.

$f : S_1 \rightrightarrows S_2$: A covariant pair of functions f from one state space to another, usually a projection.

$S_1 \times S_2$: The product of state spaces S_1 and S_2.

π_{S_i}: The projection from a product state space onto its ith factor.

$T + T'$: The sum of theories T and T'.

$\sqsubseteq$: The inclusion ordering on theories.

$T \mid \Sigma$: The restriction of the theory T to the set Σ of types.

T/R: The quotient of the theory T by the relation R.

$f^{-1}[T]$: The inverse image of the theory T under the function f.

$f[T]$: The image of the theory T under the function f.

$\vee T$: The disjunctive power of the theory T.

$\wedge T$: The conjunctive power the theory T.

$\neg T$: The negation of the theory T.

$\vdash_{\mathfrak{L}}$: The consequence relation of the local logic $\mathfrak{L}$.

$N_{\mathfrak{L}}$: The set of normal tokens of the local logic $\mathfrak{L}$.

$\mathfrak{L} \mid \Theta$: The conditionalization of the local logic $\mathfrak{L}$ on the set Θ of types.

$\mathfrak{L}_1 + \mathfrak{L}_2$: The sum of local logics.

$\mathfrak{L}/I$: The quotient of the local logic $\mathfrak{L}$ by the invariant or dual invariant I

$\mathfrak{L}_1 \sqsubseteq \mathfrak{L}_2$: The information ordering on local logics.

$\mathfrak{L}_1 \sqcup \mathfrak{L}_2$: The join of local logics.

$\mathfrak{L}_1 \sqcap \mathfrak{L}_2$: The meet of local logics.

$f[\mathfrak{L}]$: An image of a local logic.

$f^{-1}[\mathfrak{L}]$: An inverse image of a local logic.

$S_{\mathfrak{L}}$: The subspace of the state space S determined by the $\mathfrak{L}$.

Index of Definitions

channel: 4.14
  core of: 4.14
classification: 4.1
  Boolean closure of: 7.9
  conjunctive power: 7.1
  disjunctive power: 7.1
  dual of a: 4.18
  event: 8.15
  flip of a: 4.18
connection: 4.14
consequence relation: 9.1
constraint:
  exception to: 12.1
  of a theory: 9.1
  of a logic: 12.1
core of a channel: 4.14
counterexample to a sequent: 9.4

distributed system: 6.1
  limit of: 6.9
  minimal cover of: 6.4
  distributed logic of: 15.2
dual of a classification: 4.18

event classification: 8.15
exception to a constraint: 12.1

Finite Cut rule: 9.8

Global Cut rule: 9.5

idealization of a local logic 14.5
Identity rule: 9.5
image of a
  local logic: 13.1
  theory: 10.14
indistinguishability relation: 5.11
information ordering: 12.24
information system: 6.1

invariant: 5.7
infomorphism: 4.8
  channel infomorphism: 14.10
  logic infomorphism: 12.16
  quotient: 5.15
  refinement: 4.15
  token identical: 5.19
  token surjective: p. 77
  type identical: 5.19
  type surjective: p. 77
interpretation, regular theory: 9.28
inverse image of a
  local logic: 13.2
  theory: 10.12

local logic: 12.1
  a priori: 12.27
  complete: 12.2
  natural: 12.3
  normal token of: 12.1
  of a classification: 12.3
  of a state space: 12.4
  postmodern: 12.27
  sound: 12.2
local logics: 12.1
  join of: 12.25
  meet of: 12.25

negation
  of a classification: 7.3
  of a theory: 11.5
normal tokens: 12.1

partition: 7.8
  Partition rule: 9.8
  realized: 9.16
  spurious: 9.16
projection: 8.7

quotient
    of a classification: 5.9
    of a local logic: 12.31
    of a theory: 10.8
    separated: 5.12

refinement: 4.15

sequent: p. 117
    consistent: 9.10
    constraint: 9.4
    counterexample to: 9.4
state description: 7.8
state space: 8.1
    complete: 8.1
    of a classification: 8.19
    subspace of: 16.3
state spaces: 8.1
    product of: 8.11

sum
    of classifications: 5.1
    of local logics: 12.21
    of theories: 10.1

theory: 9.1
    compact: 9.20
    conjunctive power: 11.5
    disjunctive power: 11.5
    consistent: 9.10
    interpretation: 9.28
    negation of: 11.5
    of classification: 9.4
    of state space: 9.27
    regular closure of: 9.7
    regular: 9.6

Weakening rule: 9.5

Index of Names

Allwein, G. xvii
Auster, P. vii, xvi, 286
Austin, J. L. 203–210, 268

Barr, M. 33, 92
Barwise, J. xvi, 203, 205, 213, 234, 242, 268
Bimbo, K. xvii
Birkhoff, G. 28, 268

Casti, J. 223, 225, 268
Chapman-Leyland, A. xvi
Chemero, A. xvii
Chu, M. 28, 33, 92
Cohen, D. W. 243, 244, 250, 252, 269
Cohen, P. 234
Cooper, R. xvi
Crick, F. 105
Crowley, D. xvii
Crowley, S. xvii

Davey, B. 28, 269
Devlin, K. xvi, xvii, 269
Dickson, M. xvi, 252
Dretske, F. 4, 10, 13–18, 21, 24–27, 33, 35, 36, 43, 89, 269
Dunn, M. 28, 119, 130, 269

Etchemendy, 242

Fodor, J. 235

Gabbay, D. xvi, 268
Gentzen, G. 23, 117
Gettier, E. 10, 11, 269

Godel, K. 31, 39
Goldman, A. 11, 268

Hardegree, G. 28, 119, 130, 269
Hartonis, C. xvi, 28, 268, 269
Hayes, P. 234, 269

Kochen, S. 252, 269
Koons, R. 16, 269
Kunen, K. xvi, 252

Lewis, D. 18, 24, 269

Murakami, Y. xvi

Nozick, R. 11, 18, 269

Perry, J. xvi, 203, 205, 234, 268
Pratt, V. 28, 33
Priestley, H. 28, 269

Rabin, M. 234, 269

Seligman, J. xvi, 213, 268
Shannon, C. 14, 268
Shimojima, A. 235, 238–242, 268
Shope, R. 10, 268
Specker, E. 252, 269
Stalnaker, R. 18, 20, 24, 268
Swain, M. 11, 268

Tarski, A. 234

Watson, J. 105
Wilcox, M. J. xvi